MOYI-BE-DRI-LATA: A HISTORY OF THE MA'DI IN SOUTH SUDAN

1860 to 1984

Victor Keri Wani

A Note from the Publisher

The publisher wishes to acknowledge and thank Dr Douglas H. Johnson for his invaluable help and support for Africa World Books and its mission of preserving and promoting African cultural and literary traditions and history. Dr Johnson and fellow historians have been instrumental in ensuring that African people remain connected to their past and their identity. Africa World Books is proud to carry on this mission.

© *Victor Keri Wani*, 2021

Paperback ISBN: 978-0-6453633-0-2
Hardcover ISBN: 978-0-6452105-0-7

All rights reserved.

No part of this publication may be reproduced, stored in a retrieval system, or transmitted, in any form, or by any means, electronic, mechanical, photocopying, recording or otherwise, without the prior permission of the publishers.

This book is sold subject to the conditions that it shall not, by way of trade or otherwise, be lent, re-sold, hired out or otherwise circulated without the publisher's prior consent in any form of binding or cover other than in which it is published and without a similar condition including the condition being imposed on the subsequent purchaser.

Cover design, typesetting and layout : Africa World Books

Contents

Chapter One
  1.1 Introduction
  1.2 Objectives of the Study
  1.3 Research Methodology
  1.4 Constraints and Limitations
  1.5 Layout of the Book

Chapter Two: Background of the Ma'di People in South Sudan
  2.1 Their Origins, Migrations, Geography and Distribution
  2.1.1 The Ma'di People
  2.1.2 The Origin of the Central Sudanic Peoples
  2.2 The Meaning of the Name 'Sudanic'
  2.2.1 Their Migrations
  2.3 The Central Sudanic People
  2.3.1 The Distribution of the Ma'di People
  2.4 The Clans of the Ma'di in South Sudan
  2.4.1 Structure of a Clan
  2.4.2 How Many Are the Ma'di Clans in South Sudan?
  2.5 The Geography of Ma'diland

2.5.1 Seasons according to the Ma'di
2.6 Trade and Commerce
2.7 Ma'diland before Foreign Intrusion
2.8 Ma'di Resistance to Colonial Penetration of their Land The Case of Chief Nyori
2.8.1 Mugi Counteract Turco-Egyptian Exploitation of their Resources

Chapter Three: The Ma'di Chieftainships in South Sudan

3.1 Introduction
3.2 The Ma'di Chieftainships, their Influences
3.3 The Roles of Ma'di Chiefs
3.4 Conditions for becoming a Chief in Ma'di Society
3.5 The Roles of Ma'di Rainmaker
3.5.1 Early Survey on Ma'di Rainmaking
3.5.2 Can anybody become a Rainmaker?
3.6 Other Objects in keeping Rain Stones
3.7 Drought can lead to an Environmental Disaster, Famine
3.8 Causes of Drought in Ma'di Perspective
3.9 The Ordeal of a Rainmaker in Nyongwa
3.9.1 Ala, Father of Uliya the Rainmaker, his Songs
3.10 Government Intervention in Rainmaking Abuses
3.10.1 Ma'di Belief that Nature can also act against Malicious Rainmakers
3.11 Where the Land Priest Fits in to Ma'di Traditional Leaderships
3.12 Summary of the Roles and Functions of Ma'di Chiefs during the pre-Colonial Era

Chapter Four: Eastern Sector Chieftainships of Bori-Opari

4.1 Its Borders with other Sectors

4.1.1 Geographical location of the Sector
4.1.2 Historical Background of Bori Chieftainships
4.1.3 The Chiefs of Bori
4.2 The Logopi Chieftainship
4.3 The Pandikeri Chieftainship
4.4 Chief Akeri Milla, His Life and Times
4.5 How the Logopi Chieftainship Shifted to the Pandikeri Clan
4.6 Brief Histories of Other Clans in Bori
4.6.1 The Ngaya (Paibonga) Clan of Bori
4.6.2 Leadership lineages of Ngaya (Pibonga), Pambili Clans
4.7 The Dongu Clan
4.8 Ayipa
4.9 The Loss of Refugees' Animal Wealth in Ayaci, Parajok
Akeri Milla back to Bori
4.10 How Male became a Centre for Blacksmiths
4.11 Villages of Bori-Opari, past and present
4.12 The List of Pandikeri Chiefs from Ker to Dari Kanyara Isra
4.13 Constitutional Post Holders from Bori-Opari Chieftainships (Eastern Sector)
4.14 The clans of Bori-Opari listed alphabetically

Chapter Five: Northern Sector Chieftainships of Moli
5.1 Borders of the Area
5.2 The Moli Chieftainships
5.3 Logili Leadership in Moli
5.3.1 Chief Urube
5.3.2 Chief Geri Ipele Acts on Suspected Poisoners
5.3.3 Chief Akeri Geri Ipele
Intertribal Marriages

5.4 The Mugi Clan Chieftainship in Moli
5.4.1 Kejikiri
5.4.2 Yongo Alimas Dumo
5.5 Logili-Mugi Rivalry
5.6 Ma'di people of Iyii and their Clans
5.7 Mejopadrani (Borokodongo)
5.8 The Clans in Moli
Population of Moli Chieftainships

Chapter Six: The Southern Sector Chieftainships of Lokai (Mugali), Nimule, Loa

6.1 The Extent of the Chieftainships
6.2 The Odupkwe Chieftainships in Lokai
Sub-Chief Ruben Surur Iforo of Odupkwe Clan
6.2.1 Ruben leads the attack on a lioness named Foni
6.3 The Clans in Mugali
6.4 A Brief History of Nimule Chieftainships
The Koyi Chieftainship of Nimule
6.4.1 Nimule, the Village, the District Town
6.5 The Nubi Community of Nimule
6.6 The Clans found in Nimule
6.7 The Chieftainships in Loa
6.7.1 The Clans in Loa

Chapter Seven: Central Sector Chieftainships of Arapi, Pageri, Nyongwa

7.1 The Extent of the Sector
7.2 Arapi Chieftainship of Palungwa
7.3 The Pageri Chieftainship
Ito Kafiri of Pageri Clan
7.4 Nyongwa Chieftainship
Ala, Father of Uliya the Rainmaker
7.4.1 The Ordeal of a Rainmaker in Nyongwa
7.5 The Clans of the Central Chieftainships of Arapi, Pageri and

Nyongwa

Chapter Eight: The Western Sector Chieftainships of Erepi (Kerepi)
8.1 The Extent of the Sector
8.2 The Erepi Chieftainships
8.3 The Tedire Clan Leadership
8.4 Economic Situation of the Sector
8.5 The Clans in Erepi (Kerepi)

Chapter Nine: Ma'di Chiefs and their Wars
9.1 The Inter-Tribal Wars and their Historical Causes
9.2 Lokoya-Langabu and Moli War
9.2.1 The death toll and the austerity measures
9.2.2 Moli mobilization
9.2.3 The Moli Reprisal Attack on Lokoya-Langabu
9.2.4 The Devastating End of the Attack
9.2.5 Lokoya Sends SOS Message to Lokoro (Pari)
9.2.6 The Lokoya-Langabu version of their war with the Moli
9.3 Who are the Lokoya-Langabu people?
9.4 Lokoro (Pari), Acholi-Agoro raids on the Moli Abductees trace their roots to Moli
9.4.1 Impacts of Lokoro-Acholi Agoro raids on the Moli
9.5 Arapi Palungwa and Acholi Panyikwara feud over Iwire Hill
9.5.1 The Cause of the Conflict
9.5.2 The Arapi-Palungwa response
9.6 How Ma'di Chiefs make peace among themselves
9.7 Marriage, another means of ending Tribal War
9.8 The Ma'di Conflict Resolution Mechanisms

Chapter Ten: Ma'di Chiefs and their Songs
10.1 Introduction
10.2 Songs of the Lokai Chieftainship of Odupkwee
10.2.1 A Song about Chief Cirino Odego

10.3 A Song from the Patibi Clan
10.4 A Song of the Tedire Clan of Erepi
10.5 Ma'di Headchief Sabazio Okumu abolishes War Songs
10.6 Effects of Abolition of War Songs
10.7 Social Songs of the Ma'di
Star Songs from Bori-Opari
10.8 A Social Song in praise of Sayed Siricio Iro

Chapter Eleven: Ma'di Chieftainships during Turco-Egyptian and British Colonial Eras

11.1 Turco-Egyptian Administration of Ma'diland (1860- 1889)

11.2 Ma'di under British Colonial Administration (1899- 1956)

11.3 The Colonial Education Policy and Ma'di Native Administration

11.4 Ma'di Chiefs suspicious of the Colonial Education Policy

Chapter Twelve: The End of Ma'di Traditional Powers

12.1 Election of Sabazio Okumu Abdalla as Headchief of Ma'di

12.2 Sabazio replaces traditional Chiefs with ordinary men

12.3 Abolition of Ma'di Native Administration and Introduction of the Local Government System

12.4 The abolition of Moli Chieftainship led to border problems

12.5 Loa Local Government Centre No. 1

12.6 Opari District Administration (1914-1935)

12.7 Nimule District Administration (1893-1913)

Chapter Thirteen: The History of Iyii (Kit)

13.1 Beginnings of the Border Contests, the Ma'di

Case
13.2 Iyii, its History and Inhabitants in Brief
13.2.1 The Ma'di of Iyii
13.2.2 The Bari in Kit
13.2.3 The Acholi in Iyii
Crossing two borders to Iyii
13.3 The Moli border with Acholi of Omeyo across River Ame
13.4 The Lulubo across Nyolo River
13.5 The beginnings of a Ma'di-Bari border contest
13.6 The 1952 minor clash over the River Nyolo border
13.6.1 Chief Lolik Lado on a peace mission to Moli
13.6.2 The 1982-83 Ma'di-Bari border Contest
13.7 Chief Akeri's testimony in Juba on the Ma'di-Bari border
13.8 Mejopadrani (Borokodongo)
13.9 The Dongu of Mejopadrani (Borokodongo)

Chapter Fourteen: Supernatural Men among the Ma'di

14.1 The Land of Supernatural Men
14.2 Construction of the Mongalla-Rejaf-Opari Pathway (1915-1919)
14.3 Geri Akudi
14.4 The Fall of the Muyu Tree
14.5 The Story of Tombe Bworo, his life and times
14.6 Tombe Bworo thrown into prison
14.7 Tombe Bworo's twenty-five Wives
14.7.1 Tombe Bworo's Wives from Bari and other Tribes
14.8 Wani Muganda - Son of Tombe Bworo
14.9 Wani Muganda and Kujur Okidi
14.10 'Siriba' - the Secret of it all

Chapter Fifteen: Findings, Observations, Conclusions and Recommendations
   15.1 Findings on Study of Ma'di Life
   15.2 Findings on Border Contests
   15.3 Observations
   15.4 Conclusions
   15.5 Recommendations

List Of Informants

Annex One: Ma'di Constitutional Post Holders In The Past And Present Years
Annex Two: Biographical Notes on Selected Distinguished Personalities Among the Ma'di

About The Author

Bibliography

Glossary

Chapter One

1.1 Introduction

This is an outline of the stories of the Ma'di traditional chieftainships and rainmakers in South Sudan covering part of the era long before the opening of the Ma'di region to outside influences including the periods of the administration of Southern Sudan by different colonial systems of government viz. the Turco-Egyptian (1820-1885)[1], the Mahdiyya (1885-1898)[2] and the Anglo-Egyptian (1898-1956)[3] rules. The reader should note that this is not the complete account about this important historical topic, but it is an attempt to answer a question which has been bothering many people including the Ma'di themselves, especially students, teachers, historians and researchers about the past of the Ma'di people and their system of traditional leadership including rainmakers, land priests and priestesses, their migration and settlements. One important question is: before they were brought under the control of the first colonizers, the Turco-Egyptians in 1860[4], were the Ma'di in any way organized in effective tribal organizations with strong leaderships? To give a positive answer to such an important question without substantiation and illustrations cannot persuade any researcher that it is realistic and convincing. Therefore, this research has been undertaken to examine the topic critically and analyse it before reaching a conclusion.

In fact, long before the arrival of foreigners in the Ma'di territory in the southern Nile valley, its inhabitants were already organized in small but effective and democratic nuclei consisting of clan chiefdoms in which the bigger clans had full control over the smaller ones which needed their protection in various areas of Ma'diland. These could be considered mini village-states. The past structures of these chieftainships can only be recovered and reconstructed for easy comprehension through ardent investigation based on actual realities. These can be found in the existing rare books whose authors have just touched on the historical facts about Ma'di people, their life and land and written about them. The writers included administrators, travelers like Gaetano Casati in his book *Ten Years in Equatoria, 1910*[5], Catholic missionaries who were based in Loa in Central Ma'diland from 1921, and the Protestant missionaries who were stationed at Opari in the eastern part of the Ma'diland from 1914. The colonial administrators of Equatoria province of the Turco-Egyptian era of 1820-1885 and later Mongalla and Equatoria Province officials of the Anglo-Egyptian Condominium era 1899-1956 and Opari and later Torit districts where the Ma'di people live have conducted research as colonial government policy and produced monographs on the people of South Sudan including the Ma'di. There are also literary works by other researchers like C. G. Seligman and Brenda Z. Seligman who had been assigned by the colonial government of the

Sudan to conduct social anthropological research on the Southern Sudanese among them the Ma'di and these were published in a book titled *Pagan Tribes of the Nilotic Sudan, 1937*[6], a government journal, the Sudan Notes and Records and several books. The works of these writers covered the period 1860-1956. Other reliable information about the Ma'di can also be obtained from official records left behind by the administrators of Opari and Torit Districts during the Anglo-Egyptian era (1898-1956) especially from the archive of the Sudan Notes and Records (SNR) Office in Khartoum on Gamhouria Street. At this juncture, the work on the Ma'di people by J. V. Rowley titled *Notes on the Ma'di of Equatoria Province*, is worth mentioning. He was the District Commissioner of Opari in the period 1931 to 1934 and of Torit from 1935 to 1938. The Ma'di people after the transfer of the Opari district headquarters and its subsequent amalgamation with Torit in 1935 were administered from there.

During the Turco-Egyptian administration of Equatoria, from 1840 to 1889, much has been written about the Ma'di as an important human component of the province and such works have been left behind by Governors Samuel White Baker, Colonel Charles Gordon and Emin Pasha. The writings by the first two governors were in English, their native language, while Emin Pasha, a German, wrote most of his literature about the Ma'di in the German language. Despite a large volume of written material about the Ma'di by these officials and others like Dr. G. Schweinfurth, who visited the province during their administrations, the most reliable source of information for the history of the Ma'di is through the oral medium. By listening to legendary stories, old songs and interviewing the few surviving elderly people who had listened to the oral histories of their clans from elders before them, a significant insight into Ma'di life can be gained. But the oral sources, due to the deaths of many elderly people among the Ma'di in the past and recent years, and lack of initiative by the educated members of the present generation to investigate their history critically including the leadership structures, have made the subject more complex and difficult to explore at the present time for conservation and the benefit of future generations. What I have therefore put down here are some basic facts which I have carefully obtained from available records (library research) and others I have collected casually through the sampling research technique which I conducted in the past in the Ma'di countryside and in recent periods in Juba, Khartoum and Torit.

Some of my oral sources are the living relatives and acquaintances of the past chiefs of the Ma'di, and people I have carefully selected as having some special knowledge and rare information about them and some of the living chiefs themselves. Among my oral sources are: Celestino Vuga Ruben son of Ruben Surur Iforo, an ex-chief from the royal lineage of Oddo Vollo, father of Kenyi Badaa of the Odupkwe clan of Lokai; Cuofo Oddu, eldest daughter of Chief Geri Ipele who was a grandson of Chief Urube of Moli from the Logili clan and Chief Odoriko Loku Diego of the Tedire royal clan from Bori-Opari. I was very fortunate also to have Chief Akeri Geri Ipele, one of the important chiefs of the Ma'di people, whose roles I had discussed with him in a long interview in 1982 when he was spending some time with the family of his nephew Joseph Ladro Clement in Juba.

This work is therefore a collection of facts from various sources and accumulated over a long period, and it is anticipated to give the reader an opportunity to gain an understanding of Ma'di traditional leadership structure in the past and its impact on Ma'di life.

Notwithstanding the shortcomings of this work, the author hopes that the reader will, after going through these pages, appreciate the effort involved, especially of those who have willingly contributed by giving the writer the required information for compiling this book.

1.2 Objectives of the Study

This survey was necessitated by an absence of books on Ma'di traditional chieftainships or history of the tribe in Southern Sudan. The scant information about this subject makes it imperative to undertake this study so that the data about it that exists in rudiments and in different oral accounts are collected and put together to constitute a base from which future research can be launched by other interested scholars in the same field for its better understanding. Besides creation of a document from available data, another main objective of this study is to highlight the stages through which the Ma'di chieftainships have evolved since their advent for better understanding of the subject. It is anticipated by the author that this effort may inspire other members of the Ma'di community and interested scholars to include the subject of this research in their future studies, the roles of Ma'di chiefs in shaping the future of traditional leadership not only in Ma'diland but in South Sudan and how their experiences might have influenced others or vice versa through a long period of interaction.

1.3 Research Methodology

As no books have been written solely about the history of the Ma'di tribe, let alone of its chieftainships in South Sudan, except the citations made by writers like C. G. Seligman and Brenda Z. Seligman in their book *Pagan Tribes of the Nilotic Sudan*, 1937,

Chauncy Hugh Stigand in his book *Equatoria, The Lado Enclave, 1957*[7] and some writings by Professor Merrick Posnansky and J. P. Crazzolara and others, library research, an important mode of data collection for this survey, was limited in scope. Most books on traditional leaderships in South Sudan do not contain much information about the roles of the tribal chiefs in the period reviewed. Most of the information about the chiefs can be obtained from the periodical *Sudan Notes and Records* (SNR) published by the colonial information office in Khartoum and the articles were studies conducted by the colonial administrators and researchers engaged by the government of the time according to policy in Southern Sudan.

Other materials are found in provincial handbooks compiled by respective province headquarters, for example, the *Equatoria Province Handbook*[8] published by the office of the Governor, Leonard C. Nalder, in Juba in 1936. Very few books, mostly those written by colonial administrators of the Anglo-Egyptian era and the Christian missionaries during the same period, can be found to have discussed to a limited extent the roles played by some prominent Southern Sudanese chiefs like Pitya Lugor of the Bari, James Tombura of the Azande and Lolik Lado of Lokoya in Lirya, Equatoria province, besides those of the Ma'di Chiefs Akeri Milla, Akeri Geri and Kenyi Badaa.

Many facts for this book about the Ma'di Chieftainships were collected through interview research or sampling technique conducted by the writer with several members of the Ma'di tribe and members of some South Sudanese tribes whose communities are neighbours of the Ma'di. The informants were either people who had witnessed the reigns of the chiefs included in this survey or are members of the families of the chiefs or in rare cases the chiefs themselves. Among those chiefs interviewed orally for this work are Chiefs Akeri Geri Ipele of Logili clan of Moli, Odoriko Loku Diego of Tedire clan of Bori-Opari and Saulo Obalkare Lotikaro of Paibonga-Ngaya clan of Bori-Opari. I also interviewed Chief Mamur Abdul Faraj of Acholi Panyikwara in El Haj Yousif, Takamul, Khartoum to obtain information on how the Ma'di and the Acholi interacted when they were put together under the administration of Opari district in 1914 when the district was created in that year following the border adjustments between Sudan and Uganda in 1913.

1.4 Constraints and Limitations

Undertaking a research work of this magnitude as a self-financing project without any outside funding or support of any kind has caused a delay of several years before accomplishment of the work. Despite this difficulty, due to the importance of the work and its significance to Ma'di studies, I persevered and continued with the effort of producing this book till I reached this stage. I limited the area of the study to fourteen chapters, though the scope could have been wider than this had there been some outside support. Another serious obstacle that hindered proper presentation of this work has been lack of documents for references because there are hardly any history books written solely on the Ma'di people. Existing works are those general history books covering the tribes in the region in which the Ma'di live and facts about them mentioned in those books are incomplete and in most cases in isolated monographs and do not meet the needs of the quest for the required information for this book.

1.5 Layout of the Book

This study is basically divided into fifteen chapters. Chapter One is an introduction to the work outlining the methods applied in conducting the research, its objectives and the constraints met in the process of the survey. Chapter Two gives the reader a brief historical background of the Ma'di people, their migrations, settlements and distribution. It also outlines the brief history of the tribe before the intrusion of the colonialists in their land and their resistance to it and the geography of Ma'diland. Chapter Three focuses on the Ma'di traditional chieftainships, their powers, extents and influences. It also describes the roles of the Ma'di rainmakers, and the parts played by the land priests, and in very rare cases of the land priestesses, in purifying the land so that it can be free of epidemics, drought and bird, grasshopper and locust invasions. Chapter Four highlights the eastern sector of Bori-Opari chieftainships, its borders with the Acholiland and with other sectors of Ma'diland and it also gives an insight into the three powerful clans of Pandikeri, Logopi, Patibi and their leaderships and the clans whose home is Bori-Opari. Chapter Five brings the northern sector of Moli chieftainships into the limelight and gives the clans, whose home is Moli, which includes Iyii and Mejopadrani, the original name which is today Borokodongo. Chapter Six discusses the southern sector chieftainships of Lokai (Mugali), Nimule, Loa, the extent of the chieftainships, the Odupkwe, Koyi leaderships and other clans of the sector. Chapter Seven covers the central chieftainships of the Arapi, Pageri and Nyongwa villages and the clans which inhabit them. Chapter Eight outlines the western sector chieftainships of Erepi (Kerepi) and gives the names of the clans who live there.

Ma'di chiefs in the past led their fighters in tribal wars as commanders-in-chief to defend their people and land against hostile attacks such as those launched intermittently by Lokoya-Langabu on the people of Moli in northern Ma'diland in the period estimated to be 1895-1911 and other raids mounted by the Pari and Acholi-Agoro clan of Koyo and Kicari on Moli villages up to 1927 when these raids ended. Chapter Nine discusses these feuds, examines their dimensions and impacts on socio-economic development and human relations in the region in general and on Ma'di people of Moli in particular. How the Ma'di chiefs make peace among themselves is another important human phenomenon that is worth understanding and this is also reviewed in this chapter. Chapter Ten looks at the impact of British colonization on Ma'di traditional leaderships, the objectives of the colonial educational policy towards native administration and its influences, abolition of the native administration, the introduction of a local government system in 1950s and the effects of these actions on Ma'di life especially their traditional leaderships.

From 1953, there has been a significant overhauling of the old structure of Ma'di traditional administrations following the election and installation of Sabazio Okumu Abdalla as Headchief in 1952 and the impacts of this new situation. Chapter Eleven examines the dimensions of the changes imposed by the British colonial administration on Ma'di traditional leaderships and their impacts on Ma'di life.

Supernatural men are found in human societies at all times, and their deeds exert much influence on the lives of their immediate communities and neighbouring ones. Chapter Twelve highlights the deeds of Tombe Bworo, a prominent member of the Ma'di community, from the Patibi clan, his son Wani Muganda and another man called Geri Akudi. These three members of the Ma'di tribe exerted much influence on the Ma'di people in the first half of the twentieth century. Tombe Bworo and Wani Muganda, because of the legacy of being known as turning from their human bodies to leopards, were greatly feared by the Ma'di people not only in Moli and Bori-Opari where they had lived at different periods but also by the communities neighbouring the Ma'di tribe. The Bari, Acholi, Kuku, Lulubo have been in the past touched by the influence exerted by Tombe Bworo in the southern Nile valley. Writer Taban lo Liyong from the Kuku tribe discusses him in his book *the Eating Chiefs* thus introducing him to the people of East Africa especially Uganda bordering Southern Sudan.

In the past, there were no tribal border contests in their present dimensions among the four tribes, namely: Ma'di, Bari, Lulubo and Acholi, who have been attracted to one focal point, which is the area between Iyii (Kit) and the Nyolo River bridges and the surrounding region by the Juba-Nimule Road, after its completion in 1932. As the twenty-first century surges forward, it seems new ideas are emerging among tribal communities about lands, their economic uses and future. These have given rise to what are experienced now as border contests among these four tribes who live in Iyii, which is variably called Iyii by the Ma'di, Ayii by the Achili, and Kit by the Bari. Chapter Thirteen discusses the significance and critical nature of these crises and their implications for these communities.

Chapter Fourteen sheds light on the contributions made by individual Ma'di, brought up in the different chieftainships, to national work in the Sudan. These men went to schools under the colonial policy announced in 1918 by the Opari District Commissioner, Captain E.T.N. Groves, that the sons of chiefs and notables in the district must go to school so that on completion of the primary level of education the chiefs' sons could replace their illiterate fathers and administer their chieftainships in a civilized way.[9] Distinguished personalities like Sayed Siricio Iro Wani from the Mugi clan, who was born in Opari and grew up there, was once a member of the Supreme State Council in Khartoum which ruled the Sudan from 1956 to 1958 when the government was overthrown by the army General Ibrahim Abboud. Catholic Bishop Paride Taban Kenyi from the Logopi clan, Bishop Andrea Vuni Wale from Beka clan of the Africa Inland Church (AIC), a Protestant group and Melichoir Lagu Damian of Mugi clan who is a former Member of Parliament in Eastern Equatoria State in Torit are all inhabitants of Opari, born and brought up there. Redento Ondzi who became Deputy Speaker in the Constituent Assembly elected in 1954 hailed from Erepi chieftainship and Melikiore Ingi Lumanyi who became a senator in the higher house of parliament established soon after independence of the Sudan in January 1956 hailed from Loa in the Southern sector chieftainships. This chapter, in addition, uncovers the historical facts about Ma'di administration during the colonial period, Opari and Nimule as district administrative headquarters before Torit in Latuho country became important in 1935. The last chapter is Chapter Fifteen which gives the findings from the survey, the conclusion and recommendations offered by the author.

Chapter One Notes and References

1 See Richard Gray. *A History of Southern Sudan 1838–1889*, London, 1961 for Turco-Egyptian (1820–1885) Administration.

2 Read Byron Farwell. *Prisoners of the Mahdi*, London, Longmans Green, 1967 for The Mahdiyya (1885–1898) Rule.

3 See Sir Harold MacMichael. *The Anglo-Egyptian Sudan*, London Faber and Faber, 1934 for The Anglo-Egyptian Sudan (1898–1956) Administration.

4 Op. Cit. Gray.

5 See Casati, Gaetano. *Ten Years in Equatoria*, 1910, London.

6 Seligman, C. G. and Brenda Z. Seligman. *Pagan Tribes of the Nilotic Sudan*, 1957, London, London University Press.

7 See Stigand, Chauncey, G. *Equatoria, The Lado Enclave*, 1957, London University Press.

8 In Nalder, Leonard C. *Equatoria Province Handbook*, 1940, Juba.

9 See Sanderson, L. M. Passmore and G. Neville Sanderson. *Education, Politics and Religion in Southern Sudan 1898–1972*, London, 1979.

Chapter Two

Background of the Ma'di People in South Sudan

2.1 Their Origins, Migrations, Geography and Distribution
2.1.1 The Ma'di People

The Ma'di are included among the Central Sudanic people who are an important division of the negro race in the vast area which covers parts of South Sudan, Uganda and the Democratic Republic of Congo, the former Zaire. Like the Lwoo and the Bantu peoples, the central Sudanic people too have made history by their long migrations from their supposed cradle land to other parts of the African continent. Due to linguistic considerations, they are variably classified into small units by different scholars like Arnold Norman Tucker who studied their languages as:

1. Moru-Ma'di group
2. Bongo - Baka - Bagirmi group
3. The Zande – Ndogosere speaking group
4. And others who include Lendu, Logo, Lugbari, Lulubo, Avukaya, and Keliko.[1]
5. The Moru is a large group which according to Professor G. P. Murdock, consists of the following sub-tribes: Miza, Andri, Kediro, Lakamadi, Kodo, Wira[2] and other researchers add to this group the Agyi and Bwaliba groups.

There is no specific literary work solely dedicated to a comprehensive study of each of these groups of the Central Sudanic people but numerous articles and academic papers have been written and presented in seminars and workshops about them. The Azande particularly have been lucky in the group for Evans Pritchard had written, at least two books about them. One of the books: *Witchcraft, Oracles and Magic among the Azande* is considered a masterpiece in addition to other works produced by researchers like Giorgetti F. and A. N. Tucker. Researchers and writers of Belgian and French origin have also written a number of books about the Azande in the Democratic Republic of Congo (DRC) for a big part of the tribe live in that French speaking country and the Central Africa Republic (CAR) where the lingua franca is also French. Facts about the rest of the central Sudanic peoples were cited or quoted in various general and history books written by scholars like Richard Gray, Merrick Posnansky, C. G. Seligman, Brenda Z. Seligman, L. M. Passmore Sanderson, G. Neville Sanderson, J. P. Crazzolara, Diedrich Westermann, Elias Toniolo, Richard Hill, and Sudanese writers like Mohammed Omer Beshir and Dunstan Wai Mogga.

2.1.2 The Origin of the Central Sudanic Peoples

Anthropologists, ethnologists, ethnographers and historians are in unanimity to a certain degree in classifying the Ma'di people with the central Sudanic group. This is one of the four major ethnic divisions of the heterogeneous tribal communities living in Southern Sudan. In 1931, Professor Seligman divided these tribes into four great sub-racial units, and these are:[3]

1. The Dolichocephals (long heads): in whom there are hamitic elements and consist of:

   a) The Nilotes.

   b) The Nilo-Hamites.

2. The Mesaticephals (broad heads) who are made up of:

   a) The Funj – Nuba peoples (of Central Sudan and Blue Nile region).

   b) The south-western group consists of the Azande and tribes of the ironstone plateau, Bongo-Mittu and kindred groups. They are in complete contrast to the two groups of Nilotes and Nilo-Hamites in physical appearance, temperament and culture, being medium headed, of medium stature and copper-coloured. They are essentially agricultural and have no cattle, but are keen hunters.[4] The Ma'di belong to this group.

The people in southern Sudan anthropologically belong to the Negro race. The Negroes are said to have come to Africa from Central Asia third in succession after the Negrillos or Pygmies, who followed the Bushmen, who came first.[5] The Negroes, according to historical theory belong to an ancient race which was once more widely dispersed than it is today, and occupied tropical Africa and other parts of the world such as southern Arabia, India, and even Australia.

2.2 The Meaning of the Name 'Sudanic'

In Southern Sudan, anthropologists often refer to the south-western group who after further studies were grouped as central Sudanic people. The adjective 'Sudanic' applied to this ethnic group is a derivative from the name *Sudan*. In fact, Bilad al Sudan or *land of the Blacks* was the term used by Arab geographers in the past to describe the lands lying south of the Sahara (Sahel).[6] The people who live in this belt are referred to as 'Sudanic' people. Besides their features, they can easily be identified from the similarities in their languages, just like the Bantu people who live mainly in the Equatorial belt and southern Africa are identified by their language similarities in which the term 'Abantu' which means *a person* and 'Bantu' the plural means *people*, is used. Hence the name 'Bantu' for the group.

Among the central Sudanic peoples, the Moru-Ma'di group uses the term 'Ma'di' in multiple ways in their similar languages. As well as being an important identifier of the Ma'di tribe, the term is also used to mean *a person* in the Ma'di language. Professor Seligman, aware of this compound usage of the noun 'Ma'di' once wrote, "The Ma'di not to be confused with the AMa'di, a tribe in the Congo (former Zaire) to the south of the Welle River, nor with AMa'di, a district in the Moru country, inhabit both banks of the Nile south of the Bari and extend westwards beyond the Congo frontier, their territory including the high, well watered almost mountainous country along the Nyiri (Nyeri) range where are found rich supplies of iron ore used by them and the Kuku."[7] There are other names like Laka-Ma'di, a sub-tribe of the Moru and Fi-Ma'di, a clan of the Mbeme sub-tribe of the Balanda-Viri tribe. [8] Keliko-Ma'di, a group who live in Yei district in Southern Sudan and north-eastern Congo consider themselves closer to Ma'di than any other related people and these can throw some light on the wider application of the term 'Ma'di' and its derivatives outside the Ma'di tribe and language. The Loggo-Ma'di is another group which strongly believe in their closeness to the Ma'di. This helps to explain the linguistic relation of the Ma'di with other central Sudanic people and it also points to the roots and the people of common origin with them.

There are also indications that the Moru-Ma'di group is linguistically related to some tribes in north-eastern Nigeria. This can be seen from the following discoveries and accounts by several members of the Moru-Ma'di group. Rt. Rev. Archbishop Elinana Ngalamu who was a Moru encountered a Moru related language speaking Nigerian diplomat in Addis Ababa, Ethiopia in 1975. Hilary Kanga, who is a Ma'di, then a student studying agriculture in Alexandria University in Egypt met a Nigerian student during the celebration of the Nigerian students' union occasion in Alexandria University campus, Egypt in 1976. He cited the word 'oko' in a Nigerian language which means a *woman* while in Ma'di the same word means *women*. Adelino Wani who went as a fellowship student delegate from Khartoum Islamic Centre to Kano, Nigeria met a young man who told him that his name was Awabiebi, which translated in both the language of the man and Ma'di means *fresh leaves of the shea butter tree*. The Nigerian academic, A. L. Ibrahim writing in a Nigerian journal said 'ori' in a Nigerian language means *spirit that lives in a river or under a huge tree*[9] and this is exactly what it also means in Ma'di. Another discovery of a Ma'di related language in Nigeria was made by Professor Pasi, a Ma'di from Uganda who went to teach in a Nigerian university in 1970's. These discoveries confirm the extent of Central Sudanic people in the continent of Africa just as the

Bantu groups of people are widely located in the Equatorial region and southern part of the continent. They are widely spread and as can be seen reach the southern Nile valley.

2.2.1 Their Migrations

Migration is one of the most important natural characteristics of humans in all ages. For example, in the African continent, there have been marked movements of peoples from one region to another in past centuries. The Bantu peoples who today occupy the territory of continental Africa approximately between latitude 2° N and beyond the Tropic of Capricorn 23° 30's are thought to have moved from the area south of Lake Chad long before the year 500AD.[10] Taking a southward route through the territory now part of Cameroon and passing through the northern Democratic Republic of Congo to avoid the dense forest, on reaching the Equator latitude 0°, they spread widely reaching Kenya in East Africa and as far as South Africa. The cradle land of the Bantu peoples is located somewhere in the present Cameroon from where they are believed to have moved south and south-east in the period 1–500AD.[11] The Nilo Saharans too emigrated from the north to the south following the Nile valley, while others moved to the south-west, and some headed to settle in the Sahel region. We need to consider migration in general terms in relation to Africa as a continent.

If the theory about the migratory route of the Negro race can be proved correct, that they emigrated to Africa from Central Asia third in succession to the Negrillos or Pygmies who followed the bushmen who came first,[12] then it is likely that every division of the original human stock in Sudan has experienced migration from one location to another. In Southern Sudan, we have learned about the Lwoo migration from the great lakes of East Africa to Southern Sudan according to Diedrich Westermann[13] whose theory was later disputed by J. P. Crazzolara who after meticulous investigation of his own into the same subject, concluded that the Lwoo trek began around Rumbek area in the former Bahr El Ghazal Province in Southern Sudan and headed towards East Africa where it ended.[14] The Azande people, another important group according to Evans Pritchard had moved from River Mbomu region eastward to Equatoria Province where they are found today.[15]

2.3 The Central Sudanic People

The Central Sudanic people who are another important division of the Negro race in the vast area which covers parts of Southern Sudan, Uganda and the Democratic Republic of Congo, formerly Zaire, like the Lwoo and the Bantu peoples have made history by their long migrations. These people due to linguistic considerations are variably classified into small units by different scholars who have studied their lives. Tracing the migration routes of the central Sudanic peoples, history professor, Richard Gray who had lectured in Khartoum University in the 1960's advances the theory that the cradle of these people is probably the land along River Shari south of Lake Chad which covers the southern part of modern Chad, the north-eastern area of modern Nigeria and eastern part of present Cameroon.[16]

In the period 1–500AD, this same area was said to have been occupied by the Bantu people before their movement through the present Republic of Cameroon to their current locations in continental Africa.[17] This theory suggests that the area south of Lake Chad must have been an important passage for the Negroes and other African peoples to the other parts of the continent. Professor Gray puts forward the theory that waves of Sudanic speaking people driven from the area south of Lake Chad and the River Shari region had entered the Wele (Uelle) basin. There, finding that the dense belt of equatorial forest, now part of the modern Democratic Republic of the Congo, presented an impenetrable barrier to the South, they had been deflected north-eastwards and forced into the south-western area of Southern Sudan by the continued pressure of fresh migratory waves.[18]

Although Professor Gray has not specified the origin of the invading waves or the causes for their action, an attempt to clear this anomaly in the theory has been made by another scholar, Professor Merrick Posnansky. He writes: "The only cogent reasons one can suggest are that these movements are political and environmental. From the thirteenth century onwards the Christian kingdoms of Nubia were declining in power and by the mid-thirteenth century there are indications of movements of Tibbu and other peoples into the Dar Fur and Lake Chad regions, whilst Kanem (state) was becoming more expansionist."[19] "There is also evidence of a decline of the Nile at this time. Whether the decline was the result of climatic deterioration is unknown, but it is possible that population had built up in the Bahr al Ghazal region by that time and the instability to the north and the expansion of the Muslim states of the western Sudan and of peoples from the desert, led to a breakdown of the political equilibrium at the time of a possible minor period of climatic deterioration," adds Professor Posnansky.[20] In Chad, at this period, as has been noted, there is evidence of movements of peoples, and in Ethiopia the Galla movements would appear to have begun to affect the medieval state in the fifteenth century. Once the progress of movement began, it set off a chain reaction of movements into which the Ma'di, Lwoo and that of various eastern and southerly Nilotes must be fitted.[21] Professor Richard Gray applying linguistic similarities to trace the relationship of the central Sudanic peoples, said that it is the linguistic considerations which suggest an ancient common origin of the Bongo-Baka and Moru-Ma'di groups whom he considered as being the first Sudanic speaking people to infiltrate the area of the River Welle long before the sixteenth century.[22]

In the succeeding centuries, they were forced north-eastwards until they stretched from northern Uganda through the Moru, Bongo and many smaller groups on the ironstone slopes of the south-western Sudan to the Kreish in the Dar Fertit area south of Darfur.[23] Some of the important tribes which belong to the Moru-Ma'di group besides being found in southern Sudan are also found in Uganda and the Congo. In Congo are the Loggo, part of Avukaya, and a section of the Lugbari tribe located in the north-eastern part of that country, and in Uganda, a larger section of the Lugbari are found in the north-western part where a section of the Ma'di, about two thirds, also live. Only about one third of Ma'di are found in South Sudan, and a very small number live in the Congo.[24] The Keliko and the Avukaya are found in both Sudan and the Congo. The Moru group which is made up of several sub-tribes: Miza, Andri, Kediro, Lakamadi, Morukodo, Wira, Bwaliba, and Agyi[25] are found only in Southern Sudan.

The Lulubo (Olu'bo) live close to the Ma'di and their nearest village Nyolo is about four miles away from the most northerly Ma'di village of Iyii (Kit). The Lulubo speak a Ma'di related-language and they are more akin to the central Sudanic stock than to the Nilo-Hamitic people although some anthropologists and historians tend to ascribe their origin to be an admixture of the

Nilotic, Nilo-Hamitic and Sudanic groups.[26] But Lulubo scholar, Professor Eluzai Mogga Ladu does not concur with the theory presented by other writers about their origin. He believes that the Lulubo, whose true name is Olu'bo are of central Sudanic stock linguistically, belonging to the ethnic group of Ma'di, Lugbara, Moru, Keliko and Loggo of the Congo.[27] The word *Olu'bo* in their language means *to exist forever*. It has the same meaning in the Ma'di language.

2.3.1 The Distribution of the Ma'di People

The Ma'di people are found in three modern countries, namely: Sudan, Uganda and the Democratic Republic of Congo, DRC.[28] After the independence of South Sudan in 2011, they are located in the southern Nile valley from where they are believed to have spread out southward, many settling in the north-western corner of Uganda forming the majority part of the tribe and a branch reaching the Congo and as already stated in this document, these were discovered in 1910 by C. H. Stigand, a British colonial administrator in Sudan to be living between the Rivers Ossa and Alla which are the tributaries of the Albert Nile neigbouring the Lugbari people[29] to their north and to the south their neighbours are the Alur, a Lwoo people. C. G. Seligman also sighted the presence of the Ma'di in the Congo.[30]

Furthermore, Leonard C. Nalder in his writing mentioned the presence of the Ma'di in the Congo.[31] This is their present status. Otherwise in late antiquity according to Professor Merrick Posnansky after their arrival from north-west Africa particularly from the areas along River Shari south of Lake Chad in late antiquity they had originally occupied a large area of northern Uganda where the Lwoo live today. This suggests that the Ma'di are the first people to have occupied the southern Nile valley. Posnansky gives place names in this area as indicators of this occupation before they were overlapped by the Lwoo.[32] Ma'di-Opei in northern Uganda, north of Kitgum district town is a typical example of the areas which might have been once occupied by the Ma'di people. In mid 1972, the author worked as a cooperative officer in Ma'di Opei and tried to find out the source of the name from the Acholi elders of the place and they said they had no idea but local stories indicated to them that the early occupants of the place were believed to be Ma'di who had left after fighting intermittently with the people from the east suggesting that these could be the Karamojong people who were said to have lived in Orom area before moving further east due to the Ma'di threat. Ma'di Opei could be a Lwoo corruption of Ma'di Ope which is a royal group who have been given that name by other Ma'di groups because of their gentleness that resembles the behavior of the guinea folk which are called *ope* by the Ma'di and these beautiful birds always move in a group of about a dozen or more. Ma'di Opei could also be a Lwoo corruption of Ma'di Opi, meaning Ma'di chiefs. In Palabek also in the Acholi area of northern Uganda, there is a place called Ma'di Kiloc and another area or village in the same region is called Ma'di Opoke. Okot P'Bitek, a member of the Lwoo community who had been a critic of J. P. Crazzolara, the Italian anthropologist, for suggesting that Ma'di were widespread in northern Uganda long before the Lwoo could occupy the area but have been ethnographically swallowed up by the Lwoo and Lango-Omiru at a certain point, contradicted himself by agreeing with the same hypothesis when he said most of Attiak and Palabek Acholi in northern Uganda are considered by central Lwoo people to be originally Ma'di.[33]

Just like their history which has not been comprehensively researched and documented, the numbers of the Ma'di people in the three countries are also sketchy due to irregular censuses and their results. Some sources put the Ma'di population in Uganda as 174,000 according to the population census of 1991[34] and those in South Sudan as 97,000 from the results of the census of 1983.[35] But the Ma'di convention staged in Nimule in 2007 put the population in South Sudan as 174,720[36] and in the Congo a few tens of thousands are found. From these figures the Ma'di population in the three African countries can be put as slightly over 400,000. However, Professor John Mairi Blackings, Ma'di academic from South Sudan puts the overall number of the Ma'di people in South Sudan and Uganda as over 390,000.[37] That estimate plus those in the Congo brings the overall population of the Ma'di in Africa to about 500,000.

2.4 The Clans of the Ma'di in South Sudan

The Ma'di tribe is made up of many exogamous and totemic clans. About 65 years ago, Professor C. G. Seligman who conducted a study among them documented his findings in the following account: "They are divided into exogamous clans with male descent and are probably totemic, for one of our informants (mission lads at Bor) recognized that he had a close relationship with a bird 'kuloloro' (kiloloro) as had his father, while his mother recognized another animal, perhaps a dog."[38] Kiloloro is the clan of the author and some of the clan members have spilled into the neighbouring tribe of Kuku. Another man told Seligman that if he speared a bush buck he would hand his spear to a comrade and never use it again and if one were caught in his hunting net he could not use the net until it had been washed, and he would probably get rid of it, while although he might kill his animal he would not eat it, lest his hair and nails should drop off, another man recognized relationship to the squirrel. Although Professor Seligman did not mention the names of his Ma'di informants in Bor, in the mid 1920's the following Ma'di youth were in the Church Missionary Society (CMS) elementary school at Malek under the administration of Archdeacon Shaw: Eberu Drani, Icaka Opi, Ruben Surur, Wani Muku, and Yakobo Yanga Lagu.[39] The account about the birds called by Seligman 'kuloloro' (kiloloro) used as totem by a Ma'di clan was certainly given by Yakobo Yanga Lagu who was a member of that clan whose totem are these birds. Yakobo was in the mission as a church worker under Archdeacon Shaw. Later he got married and became the father of General Joseph Lagu Yanga who was the leader of the Anya-Nya liberation army in Southern Sudan. The story about the bush buck was given to Seligman by Eberu Drani who was from the Tedire clan of Erepi for the bush buck (leba) is the totem of his clan. As for the account about the squirrel (kolonya), it must have been given by Wani Muku of the Mugi clan which treats that small animal as its totem. Although Icaka Opi's totem was not quoted by Seligman, the Moje clan to which he belonged has the kite (okoliro) as its totem.[40]

The many clans of the Ma'di who form the tribal community can be broadly divided into three main groups: the noble or royal clans (opii), the clans of the common people 'bonyi', and the blacksmiths or ironsmiths 'eremu' who do not have clearly cut clans for they are just referred to as 'eremu'.[41] However, the Gunyia and Mijale clans of Moli and Male in Bori respectively are 'eremu' clans. The 'opii' clans are made up of rainmakers (eyi opii) and land priests or priestesses (vu uvuba ko sa oyaya di ba) who are often mistakenly assumed by some people to be the owners of the land (vu-atakaba kosa vu ataba). Emmanuel Kitchere Gray defines this category of leaders among the Ma'di as landowners (vu atakaba/vu ata)⁽⁴²⁾ but actually they are not the owners of the land as such because the land belongs to all the Ma'di clans. What is special about them is that they are recognized as spiritual leaders whose main duties are to ensure that the land is not abused by any member of the community of the areas in which they live, to perform the rituals that are believed to be effective enough to prevent any outbreak of epidemic disease, and birds', locusts' or grasshoppers' invasions of the crop fields. They are believed to have spiritual powers over the land and are allowed by other clans to purify the land. One special observation about them is that their ancestors appointed themselves for this public service and have been recognized by other clans and they have convinced the people from the rest of the clans that they can perform this priestly work for the benefit of all. Otherwise, had people been unconvinced of their roles they would not have been given any approval to perform land purification rites. If the intention of the priests or priestesses of the land is to exploit the people and instead of bringing happiness to them they cause misery, then the result would be retaliation similar to what is done to rainmakers some of whom deliberately cause suffering to the people by imposing drought thus leading to crop failure and lack of drinking water for human beings as well as their domestic animals such as cattle, goats and sheep.

Mob punishment is culturally inflicted on harmful rainmakers in Ma'di society. For example, Urube of the Logili clan was hunted by male members of all the clans in Moli and killed on the bank of River Liro for imposing drought in the land leading to the death of most of the people's cattle in the late nineteenth century.⁽⁴³⁾ In

1977, Aride the rainmaker, who was suspected by the people of Nyongwa Opii of imposing a prolonged drought, was punished by tying his hands and legs and then laying him in a spot encircled with burning wood till he dried up and died. The Ma'di rainmakers are responsible for the rainfall in the respective parts of Ma'diland where they live. The 'eremu' clans are responsible for the ironworks and they produce the large quantities of knives, spears, arrow heads, hoes, bracelets, earrings, and rings for the lower parts of the leg (ingwee) used by the Ma'di people.

2.4.1 Structure of a Clan

Each Ma'di clan is composed of several families who are grouped together under a number of shrines (kaci).[44] Each shrine is headed by a man who must be from a senior family in the particular group of people whose ancestor must be known as a leader of that shrine. Members of a clan who belong to the same shrine are believed to be united by ties of consanguinity. It is due to this relationship that members of the same clan cannot conduct marriages among themselves for they consider themselves brothers and sisters. Any marriage between their members will automatically be considered as incest. Before any marriage can be arranged between two youth who have attained maturity, the clans of the young man and that of the girl must be first identified and if any relationship even the slightest can be traced between them then their proposed marriage will automatically be disqualified.

The existence of the Ma'di people in the form of exogamous clans from time immemorial and the marriages conducted among them have united them firmly. The main factor in their unity is the strict practice of marriages among different clans which are not united by ties of consanguinity, and which has brought the diverse segments of the tribes closer together. The shrine leaders form the respected leadership of the clan which is headed by the man among them whose ancestor had a reputation for some recognizable contribution to the tribe or part of it such as an exemplary performance in a tribal war or killing of a wild animal like a leopard or a lion. If such contribution is not available, the ability by an ancestor to settle disputes among families or members of the clan can qualify a man to be selected to be their head and spokesman in inter-clan conflicts. He can be their permanent representative in meetings with other clan leaders.

Some of the clans like the Patibi, Padombe and Logili are very large, and their members are found in most parts of Ma'diland. Where the members of any of the above-mentioned clans happen to occupy a part of the Ma'diland, they prefer to build their homes in the same location for easy communication and for tackling issues common to their clan. In time of disasters like drought followed by failure of the crops in the fields and famine, the clans usually share the little food in stock together and often migrate to other lands where they hope to find good fortune together. In the past in time of war with another tribe or clan, the men of the same clan joined members of other clans in the same locality (logo) to go to war to defend their families and property against attacks. During the rainy season, the men and women of the same clan often work the land together in a practice called 'oyaa'.

2.4.2 How Many Are the Ma'di Clans in South Sudan?

The Ma'di clans in South Sudan were more numerous in the past than they are today. Due to lack of written records about the history of the tribe, many of its clans which existed a long time ago and became extinct due to epidemics, famine and other factors cannot be called to mind. Some of the clans which make up the Ma'di tribe are hereby listed below alphabetically:[45]

1- Accopele (found in Nimule, Jeleyi in southern Ma'diland)

2- Adiba (in Moli, Malandu and Cukole, northern Ma'diland, are related to the Kuku tribe)

3- Afodo (in Erepi, Muruli and Moli, northern Ma'diland, Bori-Logopi)

4- Akunye (in Moli, Malandu, Mejopadrani (Borokodongo))

5- Ale (in Loa, southern Ma'diland)

6- Alu (in Nimule and Mugali in southern Ma'diland)

7- Alli (in Loa-Iriya where an elder called Icoko lived)

8- Angunga (in Mugali in southern Ma'diland)

9- Bari (in Bilinya-Mugali, southern Ma'diland)

10- Beka (in Bori-Opari, Malandu, Muruli, Ikwa-Erepi; also found among the Bari as Bekat)[46]

11- Cera (in Loa and Mugali; also, they exist among the Kuku tribe)

12- Dedi (in Iyii in northern Ma'diland, Moli, Malandu)

13- Degi (in Malandu, Moli, Erepi; also found among the Kuku and Kakwa of Gulumbi on Yei-Kaya Road)

14- Dugo (in Erepi, Malandu, Muruli-Cukole; also found among the Kuku)

15- Dungo (an emigrant clan from southern Bari; found in Moli, Mejopadrani (Borokodongo), Iyii, Bori-Opari and Winyalonga)[47]

16- Edre (found in Nimule, southern Ma'diland)

17- Eremu (blacksmiths' and ironsmiths' clan; found throughout the Ma'diland; not considered a pure clan because they were formed by members of other clans who as individuals were interested in the trade)

18- Eremu-Weli (found in Opari-Male, eastern Ma'diland)

19- Gimeri (in Nimule.)

20- Gonyapi (in Nyongwa-Gwere, Bori, Musura, Erepi-Lungayo, Moli, Iyii)

21- Gunyia (blacksmiths' clan found in Bori-Opari, Male, Moli, Mejopadrani (Borokodongo))

22- Ijupi (in Erepi, Malandu, Moli, Bori-Opari, Iyii; also found among the Kuku)

23- Itopele (in Nimule)

24- Jeru (in Bori-Opari, Arapi, Loa, Mugali, Malandu, Nyongwa Opii, Pageri)

25- Kamia (in Arapi, Loa, Nimule, Mugali; also found among the Kuku)

26- Kande (in Malandu, Erepi)

27- Kiloloro (in Moli, Malandu, Erepi, Lungayo, Pageri, Male, Bori-Opari, Arapi, Nimule, Mugali, Patibi, Winyalonga; also found among the Kuku)

28- Koyi (in Nimule, in southern Ma'diland)

29- Lamude (in Bori–Opari)

30- Lira (found in Bori-Opari)

30- Logili (in Moli, Iyii, Mejopadrani (Borokodongo), Malandu, Bori-Opari, Loa, Mugali; also found in the Uganda part of Ma'di)

31- Logopi (a Ma'di clan but believed to have some Bari blood through interaction because the latter were their immediate neighbours for a long period;[48] they are found mainly in Logopi, Nyongwa-Gwere, Bori-Opari, Borimvuku, Pageri, Mugali, Erepi, Nimule)

32- Lomura (in Bori and Male, eastern Ma'diland)

33- Lubule (in Muruli, Malandu, Bori-Opari; also found

among Kuku)

34- Lulubo (in Moli, Bori-Opari, Patibi, Pakworo, Liokwe)

35- Metu (in Mugali, Bori-Opari, Moli-Deretu)

36- Mijale (in Bori, Male and Cukole)

37- Moje (in Malandu, Muruli, Deretu, Loa; also found among Kuku and Bari tribes)[49]

38- Monocu (akin to the Nyongwa clan; found in Moli, Malandu, Iyii; believe their ancestor was set afloat on the Nile from the upper river)

39- Moyo (in Bori-Opari, Male)

40- Mugi (in Moli, Malandu, Erepi, Bori-Opari, Winyalonga, Liokwe, Iyii; the Bari section of the clan lives in southern Bari; also found among the Kuku especially in Nyefo)

41- Mujopele (in Nimule, in southern Ma'diland)

42- Murupele (in Nimule, in southern Ma'diland)

43- Ndogo (in Bori-Opari, Male)

44- Ngaya (found in Mulunge north of Opari trading centre; originally from Bari and known as Paibonga but some of its members today consider themselves Acholi)

45- Nyai (in Moli, Malandu, Iyii, Erepi, Bori-Opari, Muruli; some of its elders say the clan originated from the Bari but it is yet to be proved whether the Bari area called Nyaing is related to them)

46- Nyamudi (in Bori-Opari, Musura and neighbour to Ngaya)

47- Nyongwa (in Nyongwa-Opii, Nyongwa-Gwere, Nyongwa-Aringa, Bori–Opari)

48- Nyori (in Bori-Opari, Male)

49- Odupkwee (found mainly in Mugali, Loa, Nimule and some elements found in Erepi and Bori; also a section of it is found among the Aru, a sub-tribe of the Lulubo tribe where it enjoys an important position after Daba the royal clan of the Lulubo-Aru; among the Ma'di they supply chiefs for the Lokai area)[50]

50- Ogoropi (in Erepi-Ikwa, Agaduma)

51- Ogowa (in Nimule)

52- Oloro (found in Iyii, Bori-Opari, Winyalonga on the Ma'di-Acholi border, members of this clan who live among the Ma'di trace their origin to the Ukeyi clan of Moli, Malandu and Erepi; they were originally members of Ifogo's family living in Korokodia, Muruli; the section which is more of Acholi than Ma'di are found in Omeyo and Palabek-Panyikwara and have been totally integrated into that tribe)

53- Omunya (in Malandu, Erepi, Muruli)

54- Orobe (in Loa-Orobe, Bori-Opari, Male, Pakworo)

55- Owoyyo (in Nyongwa-Opii)

56- Oyapele (in Nimule)

57- Pa-Adi (in Ludiri-Muruli, Cukole)

58- Pa-Akori (in Loa, Arapi)

59- Pa-Amulu (in Loa, Nimule, Mugali)

60- Pacara (in Mugali, Nimule; also, a contingent is found among the Ugandan section of the Ma'di)

61- Pacunaki (in Mugali, Nimule; a contingent lives among the Ugandan section of the Ma'di)

62- Padiga (in Mugali, Loa)

63- Padombe (in Pageri, Agaduma, Loa, Arapi, Patibi, Nimule, Bori-Opari, Pakworo; also, a contingent is found among the Kuku)

64- Padriga (in Mugali, Loa; also, a contingent exists among the Ugandan section of the Ma'di)

65- Pafoki (in Mugali, Nimule)

66- Pageri (in Pageri-Langauro, Arapi, Loa, Bori-Opari, Nimule, Mugali. (J. P. Crazzolara, the Italian anthropologist thought they previously lived west of Lipul Mountain of Lafon in Pariland)[51]

67- Pajali (in Loa)

68- Pajawu (in Bori-Opari, Pakworo, Winyalonga, Borimvuku; the Sudan section of the clan is believed to have emigrated from Uganda where the bigger contingent today lives in Pakile, in Adjumani district; on arrival in Sudan they first settled in Moli as neighbours to the Paloi, Metu and Moje clans in Lerwa near Deretu, before they emigrated to Bori-Opari in about 1935, and some joined those who remained behind after seeking refuge among the Acholi during the reign of Chief Akeri Milla of the Pandikeri clan; today those in Bori claim to be Acholi because they speak the language)

69- Pakala (in Loa and Bori-Mulungeng; it is yet to be proved whether the Pakala clan of Acholi-Panyikwara is a section of this Ma'di clan whose main part is found in the Jaipi division in Adjumani district, Uganda)

70- Pakoli (in Moli a land-purifying clan, Malandu, Bori-Opari)

71- Pakurukwe (in Nimule)

72- Palaa (in Bori-Opari; also found among the Acholi who call them Paliec and among the Lulubo who call them Pabala)

73- Palinyi (in Arapi)

74- Paloi (in Moli, Deretu, Malandu, Loa, Bori-Opari, Mugali)

75- Palore (in Nimule and Erepi)

76- Palorinya (in Mugali; a contingent is also found among the Ugandan section of the Ma'di; in Erepi it is the name of a village)

77- Paluda (in Malandu, Muruli, Erepi, Bori-Opari)

78- Palungwa (in Mugali, Arapi; they are believed to have emigrated from Bari in ancient times and its womenfolk bear the honorific title 'Nya Bari' meaning daughter of Bari)

79- Paluru (in Loa, Mugali)

80- Pamajwa (in Nimule)

81- Pambili (found in Liokwe, Male and is a land-purifying clan of Bori)

82- Pameri (in Nimule, Loa and across the international border in the Ugandan section of Ma'di)

83- Pamoto (in Nimule, Loa-Melekwe; a section of the clan emigrated in the first half of the twentieth century to Bibia in Uganda)

84- Pamulu (in Mugali and Pacilo in Uganda)

85- Pamuru (in Mugali)

86- Pandikeri (in Bori-Opari, Erepi; a small section emigrated to Abalakodi in Uganda during famine known by Ma'di as Maacika-Joloro of the 1930's; originally, they came from Olwal, Loringa Parabongo north of present Gulu but claim to be originally Ma'di who went to Parabongo in antiquity as refugees hence the Acholi name *loringa* which means *those who ran from danger*)

87- Panyorojo (in Loa)

88- Paratiki (in Bori-Opari; a branch of the Pakala clan and claim that their ancestor fell from heaven)

89- Paridi (in Arapi)

90- Parombi (Loa-Iluma)

91- Paselo (in Patibi, Mugali, Loa)

92- Patibi (numerically the largest clan in the South Sudanese section of Ma'di; found practically in all parts of Ma'diland especially in Patibi, Bori-Opari, Erepi, Deretu, Malandu, Pageri, Arapi, Loa, Nimule, Mugali; a large section crossed into Uganda during the great famine called Maacika Joloro of the 1930's and today they are found in Bibia, Patibi, Abalokodi, Pacilo and Attiak; a small section is also found among the Kuku; their folk history points to an origin near the Two-Headed Mountain north-west of Torit which the Otuho speakers call Chubul or Ondiro; some are found among the Latuko[52] in Katire and Imotong)

93- Pavunde (in Bori-Opari and Patibi near Mount Remo; most of its members have emigrated to Paracele in Uganda where they live today)

94- Pavura (in Loa, Nimule, Bori-Opari and across the international border on the Ugandan side)

95- Pavuri (in Loa, in southern Ma'diland)

96- Payoko (in Winyalonga, Pakworo, Bori-Opari, Indzi near Atapi; they prefer to speak Acholi because they live close to them, and some have more pride in being called *Acholi* than *Ma'di* although originally, they belonged to the latter tribe)

97- Puceri (in Mugali-Kureru, Loa, Nimule)

98- Tedire (in Erepi, Bori-Opari, Male)

99- Udupi (in Erepi, Cukole)

100- Ukeyi (in Ndaka-Moli, Malandu, Erepi, Bori-Opari, Liokwe)

101- Urugu (in Erepi, Loa, Nimule; a section of the clan is found across the international border in Uganda)

102 - Utuno (in Erepi, Bori-Opari)

103 –Vuri (in Erepi, Mugali)

This study establishes that the names of the clans in the southern part of Ma'diland carry or bear the prefix 'pa' for example in Pa-Tibi which means descendants of Tibi or Pa-Akori which means the descendants of Akori. That means that 'pa' applied in this sense means belonging to a particular ancestor, hence 'pa' may also mean grouping around a certain ancestor and having the same totem. In contrast to this practice, the clans who live in the northern part of Ma'diland are called with different forms of names eg. Logili, Mugi, Tedire and Ukeyi. 'Pa' in the Ma'di language means to carve a figure out of wood or to make a circle around a figure hence the ancestor makes a circle around his offspring delineating them as belonging to him. Also 'pa' in Ma'di is the *foot* hence the descendants of a man spread out like the toes 'pa- borondzi' on a foot. Besides 'pa' the Ma'di use the prefixes 'nya' for *daughter of* somebody, 'ori' *son of,* 'oti' *children or descendants of* somebody.(53)

Similarly Okot P'Bitek defines 'pa' in Acholi to mean *belonging to* somebody or something hence Pa-Anywar clan has Anywar as their ancestor.(54) Some of these clans as pointed out by Professor C. G. Seligman are totemic and observe animals, birds and plants etc. as their totems. For examples the Tedire in Erepi and Bori treat the bushbuck as their totem while the Kilioloro clan in Moli, Bori and Erepi take small, long tailed birds which move in a group of over twenty, and the Puceri clan in Mugali treats a huge tropical tree called 'luceri' as its totem.

2.5 The Geography of Ma'diland

The Ma'di people of Southern Sudan occupy a land on both banks of the Albert Nile which in the Sudan is known as River of the Mountain (Bahr el Jebel) starting from latitude 30 N to latitude 4°30 N and from longitude 33° E to longitude 31°30 E. Their land is mainly mountainous. The southern hills dot the length of River Acca and descend along it towards the Nile where it ends with an escarpment north of Nimule and whose highest point is called Gordon, a name given by the Ma'di in memory of Colonel Charles George Gordon, Governor of Equatoria in the third quarter of the nineteenth century. The original name of this hill is Iboje. From Gordon Hill, the land descends northward towards Loa situated in the only area which lies in a plain. Across the River of the Mountain (Bahr el Jebel) lie the Nyeri Mountain ranges which extend from the Ugandan side of the border and run parallel to the Nile in its journey towards Juba in the North. A narrow strip of land divides the Nile and the Nyeri Mountains, and some Ma'di fishermen have established fishing posts across the river, using the land as a source of firewood for drying their fish. Residents of Loa used to cross the Nile to hunt on the slopes of the Nyeri Mountains which teemed with game. The eastern part of Ma'diland is also occupied by several hills, the prominent ones being Mount Adala facing Opari the former district administrative headquarters, Ako and Remo hills. In the North is Mount Foki which is the highest peak near Malandu and the Mijiki hills which lean southward.[55]

The rivers which water Ma'diland follow the pattern of the landscape. River Acca is the largest of the streams in the area and its tributary, River Atapi flows from the east joining it in its journey to the Nile in the west, a few metres from the bridge over it linking Juba to Nimule.[56] River Anyama, called by the Ma'di, River Ame which forms part of the international border between Sudan and Uganda near Nimule, also flows from the east into the Nile. In the north, River Eyibi and Vukade its tributary flow southward to join River Atapi a few hundred metres from its confluence with River Acca north of Nimule. There are several streams which flow seasonally into the perennial rivers. In the south are rivers Ulekwe, southeast of Nimule, rivers Choyi and Tolu in the Loa area. The northern drainage is carried out by a number of streams, the main ones of which are River Liro and its tributary Jumiya, Rivers Uratapkwe and Umo which flows northward for several kilometers before it turns west to form part of the border between the Ma'di and Bari tribes. Rivers Afoyi begins in the Mijiki highlands and flows northward while River Eyibi which begins on the opposite side of the peak flows southward. River Afoyi joins River Iyii near the Ma'di village of Iyii. River Iyii itself flows westward as if it is going directly to pour into the River Nile, but changes course and flows parallel to the River Nile for most of the distance to Juba only joining the mother river at Kit near Rejaf village. The only prominent valley is that which runs from the north bank of River Acca parallel to the River Nile to Malandu in the north. It is here that most of the Ma'di people have settled and built their villages in clusters, and it is where they cultivate their seasonal crops because in the valley lies the rich soil of the Savannah.

The Ma'di people are bounded in the east and north-east by the Acholi people. In the north, they share a border with the Lulubo (Olu'bo) who speak a language related to their own.[57] The Ma'di people who live in Erepi, Moli, Malandu, Bori (Opari) and Iyii speak a variant of Ma'di language called Burulo, and this is closely related to the Lulubo language especially its variant spoken in Aru, the southern part of that tribe. Father Giuseppe Baj of the Loa Catholic Mission who conducted a survey of Ma'di languages divided them into two: Lokai and Bori variants. To the northwest, the Ma'di have the Bari tribe as their neighbour. To their west separated by the mighty Nile River and Nyeri Mountains live the Kuku people. Despite this geographical barrier, the Ma'di intermarry more intermittently with the Kuku than with their Bari, Acholi and Lulubo neighbours.

2.5.1 Seasons according to the Ma'di

The Ma'di divide the year into two main seasons: wet and dry seasons. The wet season starts in March and ends in August, and the dry season covers the period from September to February. They have names for summer (ayi), winter (meli), autumn (keifo) and spring (kitcere).[58] In each of these seasons, they do particular work especially in their fields. For food crops, during the rainy season, they grow various cereals namely: *godo, deri, maacika, mereke, eji, dukwi, kureja, lope* and for pulses they grow a variety of beans, the common ones being *garawa, lobwidi, burukucu* and *coongo*. They also grow root crops, the most common being cassava (*bwanda*) and its varieties, sweet potato (*kiata*) and yams (*endre* and *mugu*). There are no permanent cash crops. In 1925, the department of agriculture in Mongalla, the provincial headquarters introduced cotton on an experimental basis in the Moli area and when it proved to grow well, villagers were encouraged to plant it on larger scale.[59] In 1927, a ginnery was established at Cukole on the east bank of the Nile for the cotton grown in the Moli area and that brought across the Nile from the Kajokeji side of Opari district. But the ginnery closed in 1931 when a decline in production was experienced following a drop in the cotton price. Cotton ginning was however resumed in 1933, and functioned till 1934 when it ceased to operate and finally it was dismantled and transferred to Maridi in western Equatoria where cotton growing has proved more viable than in Opari district. However, before the independence of Sudan in 1956, the growing of cotton was reintroduced by the Sudan Government in the district. But in the late 1950's, the crop was no longer viable and ceased to be grown by the Ma'di people.

In the early 1960's, in some areas, mainly those lying along the Juba-Nimule trunk road, the growth of tobacco was introduced and encouraged at a commercial level. Erepi, Nyongwa, Arapi and Loa were centres established by the Blue Nile Cigarette Company (BNCC) for collection of fresh tobacco leaves from private growers to be dried and transported to the company factory in Juba, where they were used to make cigarettes. Later, dried tobacco leaves were purchased with cash from private growers, who were encouraged to construct tobacco barns, grow tobacco, pick the leaves, cure and dry them locally and these barns were found at Moli, Aduro-Muruli, Erepi, Patibi and other places in Ma'diland.

Fishing is also practiced by some Ma'di people especially men who catch a variety of fish in the River Nile north of Nimule for food, and others for commercial purposes using nylon and coarse nets, hooks, harpoons, and other equipment. Fishing camps are numerous between Nimule and Loa, the main ones being Zelekoroa, Apala, Isumo, Aribo, Acca Issu and Tolu,[60] but become fewer as one goes northward apparently because the distance of the Nile from villages gets farther. The Ma'di have several fishing camps along the west bank of the Nile, and they include Palangwe and Ayu. The Ma'di smoke dry their fish before selling them, and the most popular meat is that of the Nile perch which is variously called 'erepe' or 'erele' by the fishermen. Some fish is also caught and sold fresh in the markets of Nimule, Loa, Pageri and other villages near the Nile.

Ma'diland is endowed with flora and fauna, and hunting using coarse nets is commonly practiced, to trap small animals such as bush buck and antelope for their meat. In the past they burnt bushes to trap and kill larger animals such as buffalo and even elephants for their meat for food and ivory for sale, but since the colonial period this kind of hunting has been prohibited by law for the protection of wildlife. Some Ma'di families rear goats and sheep for prestige, and these are slaughtered only on special occasions and not for meat to sell. Most of these animals are additionally used in customary marriages as bride price. In the past, large herds of cattle were kept but the presence of tsetse flies, which carry the parasites that cause sleeping sickness in humans and cattle, caused the death of large numbers of Ma'di cattle, and discouraged people from cattle rearing. Now only a few head are kept in the Nimule area, the only place in Ma'diland which seems to be safe from the tsetse flies.

2.6 Trade and Commerce

Commercial activities, especially the operation of small retailers' shops, are common in the trading centres of Nimule, Loa, Pageri, Erepi and Opari. There are also petty mobile traders who transport their goods by bicycle carriers to sell on market days in Mugali, Nimule, Loa, Pageri, Erepi, Aduro-Malandu, Opari and Mejopadrani (Borokodongo). Some of the markets have names such as Langauro of Pageri, Atidira of Loa and Jingolo of Mejopadrani.

The Juba-Nimule Road is the main artery of Ma'diland from Iyii in the far north to Nimule in the far south. There are feeder roads which connect to this road, and these are the Cukole-Erepi (Dereto), Pageri-Opari-Torit, Nimule-Mugali and Juba-Karpeto-Moli Tokuro Roads. These roads make transportation for commercial and private purposes easy and cheap. In 1980, a road was constructed by the United Nations High Commission for Refugees (UNHCR) and the Project Management of Refugees Affairs (PMRA) from Juba-Nimule Road to Pageri-Torit Road to connect the Uganda refugees camp located at Ame, northwest of Opari. This road was nicknamed Konga Road after the good-hearted lady who used to serve the labourers working on this road, free local beer made from sorghum. Konga is a Bari from the Dongu clan whose members settled at Mejopadrani (Borokodongo) in about 1939. Other social infrastructure in Ma'diland includes a secondary school in Loa, a teacher training institute for basic school masters at Arapi near Pageri and nine basic schools in Mugali, Nimule, Loa, Pageri, Erepi, Patibi, Moli, Moliandru (Malandu) and Opari.

In the field of health, there is a rural hospital built in Acca village in 1981 by the Islamic African Relief Agency (IARA) and dispensaries exist at Nimule, Loa, Opari, and there are several dressing stations. Although most of this health and socio-economic infrastructure was destroyed during the last civil war, since peace has been achieved, it is now imperative that cognisant plans be drawn up to rebuild it, to serve the people who are returning from internal displacement in Juba and from the North, and as refugees from the neighbouring countries.

2.7 Ma'diland before Foreign Intrusion

Prior to the mid-nineteenth century, nothing was written about the Ma'di people and the area which they occupy in the present-day southern region of South Sudan, north-western Uganda and a small spot in the eastern Democratic Republic of Congo. However, some historical accounts and references to the roles they played in the past in shaping the political, social and economic infrastructure of the larger sector of the southern part of the Nile valley, a part they inhabit today, can be found in the works of J. P. Crazzolara, the Italian researcher on the Lwoo people and investigations conducted by other scholars such as C. G. Seligman and Brenda Z. Seligman, Merrick Posnansky, Richard Gray, Sanderson Passmore and Neville S. Passmore, Mohammed Omer Beshir, Dunstan Wai de Mogga and other historians and researchers on the historical developments in the region. Volume Three of Father Crazzolara's book on the Lwoo published in the first half of the twentieth century in Verona gives an elaborate account of the substantial contributions which the Ma'di, a Central Sudanic people, had made in human, social, cultural, economic and organizational developments in the upper Nile Valley long before the region attracted outsiders who eventually colonized it in the first half of the nineteenth century.[61]

Merrick Posnansky said it has been suggested that the Lwoo movements were preceded by those of the Ma'di, a central Sudanic people who on the evidence of their traditions and existing place names, diffused over a wide area of northern Uganda.[62] He said they were later overlapped by the Lwoo and now survive in a more restricted area of Uganda and the southern Sudan. Posnansky further suggests that the territory occupied by the Ma'di in the past might have extended from the Nile valley to as far as River Semliki which is east of Masindi town in Bunyoro district of modern Uganda. He said the kingdom of the Bacwezi, who are believed to be the Hima-Tutsi people of Uganda and Rwanda and who owe their ultimate origin to the arrival of small groups of pastoralists from the north, existed during the period of the Bigo culture around 1350-1500AD[63] and that the Ma'di were the first people to come in contact with the Bacwezi. He said it was possibly the threat that the south-bound Ma'di movements posed which forced the Bahima groups of Uganda to form their loosely-knit kingdom with Bigo at its center, and its prestige-inspired oversized ditches and bank systems and its Bacwezi dynasty.[64] That the Ma'di have some links with the Bigo culture can be shown by their adoption of the name *Bigo* which they confer on some of their male children a few days after birth.

The view held by Posnansky was also entertained by J. P. Crazzolara who said there is evidence that the Ma'di Indri, an aristocratic group among their community, supplied the leaders for the Lwoo groups.[65]

The Ma'di Indri is a name given to a group of Ma'di clans which tend to behave like goats for *indri* in Ma'di are goats. They must have been a group of people who behave like goats which are tame, mild-mannered animals, not easily provoked. In other words, they are tolerant and friendly. From this account, it is clear that the Ma'di have contributed to the historical developments in the Nile valley significantly. Another group, the Ma'di Opei has also contributed significantly to Lwoo formation of leadership groups and given their name Ma'di Opei to an Acholi village north of Kitgum district town. However, what is completely unknown is their participation in affecting changes in their original settlements along the Shari River, south of Lake Chad in antiquity.

2.8 Ma'di Resistance to Colonial Penetration of their Land
The Case of Chief Nyori

On March 16, 1860 an expedition force of one hundred men from Alfred Del Bono's garrison at Gondokoro left their base for the south where the unknown Ma'diland lay.[66] Reports which the garrison might have gathered about the Ma'di from their agents who were sent on advance missions over a long period, confirmed earlier reports by explorer Father Angelo Vinco of the Catholic Church that the Ma'di, like every other African community, were hostile to strangers who seemed intent on moving into their area. [67] Professor Richard Gray of the History Department, University of Khartoum wrote that the contingent of Del Bono's force of one hundred men was commanded by Wad Al Mak, a rascal from the Fazugli area of eastern Sudan whose expedition encountered resistance from a Ma'di chief and his people, and that the chief and many of his tribesmen and women were killed, and some three hundred head of cattle confiscated.[68] Although the historian did not mention the name of the Ma'di chief who resisted the intruders, local stories in Moli said it was Chief Nyori of the Paluda clan of Muruli, Iti Arro Village who with his people fought the white people who used guns ('munduku') in the fighting.[69]

It is said that the Paluda clan was previously a big group among the people of Moli and they lived in several villages, the largest of which was called Iti Arro in Muruli, near the Nile. Their chief, Nyori is said to have received the news of the invading Turks from a Bari man from Gondokoro who was sent ahead of the expedition. It is said that had he welcomed the agent at home warmly as a guest, he and his followers would have escaped the onslaught because the man would have broken to them the bad news of the impending danger. The man sent ahead was hungry and asked for some food to eat first before he could tell his hosts about his mission, but Nyori sent a word that such a person could be a spy against his people and that he might be exploring his land for an enemy attack and should not be entertained. He even half heartedly suggested that the man should be led away and killed in the bush but fell short of directing that action. So, the man went to the next village which belonged to Kuyu, the chief of the Ukeyi clan who were the neighbors of the Paluda clan and asked for some food to eat. Kuyu was a generous man and directed one of his wives to give the man some food and when he had eaten, the man offered to say why he was in Ma'di country. Kuyu was very eager to hear his message and the man told him that there were some white men carrying guns who were coming behind him to attack the Ma'di villages along the Nile, and that since their villages would be the first reached, he had better evacuate his people and their animal wealth so that they were not harmed. Kuyu took the message seriously and went to Nyori the chief of the Paluda clan to advise him to evacuate his people and their cattle as he would be doing.

But Nyori ignored the warning saying that such a man might have been sent by his Bari tribesmen to make them leave their well fortified villages so that they could easily attack and kill them and drive their cattle away while they were in unprotected settlements. But despite Nyori's reluctance to take the report from the Bari man seriously, Kuyu evacuated his people and their animals from their large, fortified village and headed eastward to avoid the area near the River Nile where the intruders would trek. Indeed, it took a few days from the day the Bari man appeared in Muruli that Nyori's large village came under intense attack from the Turks. The whole village, Muruli Iti-Arro was burnt to ashes. Nyori was killed alongside many of his people and three hundred head of their cattle confiscated and driven to Gondokoro. Today, because of the decimation of the members of the Paluda clan, those who escaped the onslaught of the Turks by fleeing eastward constitute a very small proportion of the clan. They are found in a place called Nyori, east of Malandu, a name apparently given to the place as a tribute to their chief who died defending his people. Others are found in Aduro, Muruli and Jombokokwe in eastern Erepi. Some members of Paluda clan are found in Bori-Opari and others have crossed over into northern Uganda where they are found today in Muruli, Pacilo and Abalolkodi north of Attiak.

Although the expedition managed to penetrate the unexplored Ma'diland, it was confined to the area along the White Nile River only and could not get inland because of Ma'di hostility.(70)

2.8.1 Mugi Counteract Turco-Egyptian Exploitation of their Resources

When General Charles George Gordon was appointed the governor of Equatoria Province in 1874, the staff who accompanied him on his maiden journey to Gondokoro, capital of his province, were Romolo Gessi, an Italian who was a former interpreter with Garibaldi in Crimea during the civil war there, three Englishmen, a Frenchman as an interpreter, a volunteer German botanist, two young German naturalists and two American officers already on the Khedive's payroll.(71) After transferring the capital from Gondokoro to Lado, Governor Gordon set off on a tour of the southern part of his province with his staff, a large number of soldiers and porters brought from Makaraka country to carry the parts of the steamers that had to be assembled for sailing along the Nile to the upper stations. The entourage came to Kirri which lay north of Muggi station and here Gordon encountered the southernmost sections of the Bari whom he described as shy and unknown tribesmen.(72) On the east bank opposite, stretched the lands of the Moggie (Mugi) section of the Bari.(73) In fact, the Mugi clan is a group of people the larger section of whom is today found among the Ma'di where they constitute a chieftainship of their own in Moli. The Mugi are also found in Bori-Opari, Erepi, Mejopadrani (Borokodongo) and Iyii. Those among the Ma'di are known as Cokorokwa and Koluwa, and the ones among the Bari are called Palumari. But most Mugi say they are Ma'di by origin and those who call themselves Bari have simply naturalized themselves through living on the border with the Bari people for a long period.

Gordon did not find the hospitality he expected from the tribes around Labore (Moli), Kirri and Muggi stations. He reflected on his unfavourable reaction to the hostile attitudes of these tribes in a letter he wrote and sent to his sister Augusta in September 1875 from Labore. He told her, "Here is a stretch of conscience: When we got here, the natives who were friendly could not sell or would not sell us dhorra (sorghum). There was a rather hostile (not very hostile) shiekh (chief) near us and so I sent and took the dhorra from him. This is fearful work for me, but what can I do. I must either throw up the whole matter and come down (to England) or else do this."[74] This looting was probably carried out among the Mugi section of the Ma'di who lived on the east bank of the Nile opposite Labore post. It was after the fierce fight between Gordon's soldiers and the Moogie (Mugi) section of the Bari. In this fight, Gordon lost thiry-six men of the detachment commanded by Linant de Bellefonds, the son of a distinguished French engineer and explorer. Linant himself died in this fight.[75]

The raid to seize corn, dhorra (sorghum), cattle and even slaves at the time of Baker and Gordon was known as 'razzia' a Turkish term.[76] Gordon finally came to regard Labore and Kirri as main stations since they possessed passages across the river and enabled raids to be made on the east bank where a vast extent of country existed belonging to the un-subdued Moogie (Mugi)[77] of both Ma'di and Bari sections.

Gordon blamed the hostility he encountered from the Ma'di and Bari tribes around the military stations on his predecessor, Samuel White Baker. His bitter feeling was reflected in another letter to his sister Augusta to whom he wrote that his greatest task would be to gain the people's confidence for they had been seriously mistreated during the administration of Baker. "It is extraordinary the intense hatred there is of Baker," Gordon wrote. [78] He noted that the soldiers could not go out in safety half a mile from the stations, all because they had been fighting the poor natives and taking their cattle.[79] It took Gordon some time to develop familiarity with the Ma'di and Bari, the people around his stations; Kirri, Muggi, Labore and Ayu. After winning their confidence, he became popular, and this facilitated his continued positive dealing with them.

During his tour of the tribal lands, the natives and their chiefs honoured Gordon by installing him as their honorary rainmaker, (for their chiefs were not only leaders but rainmakers) and gave him exotic gifts of much traditional importance. These gifts included leopard skins, royal headwear made of dura straw, a seat made of wood and thatched with dura straw, wooden tripod seats such as those carried by rainmakers or chiefs, fly whisks made of giraffe tails, skin shields, spears, bows and arrows stowed in their shafts or quivers. These gifts are today kept in a British museum at Brompton, Chatham as articles of General George Gordon of Sudan to remember him. The Ma'di have done two things to remember General Gordon for his friendliness and good deeds in his later years with them. Their men, even these days, shave the hair on their heads round and trim the hair short and call this 'gordon' because as a military officer, Colonel Gordon had always cut his hair short to look smart. They renamed the hill originally called Liboje located about three miles north of Nimule, 'Gordon' to honour their governor who protected them against the slave traders and exploitative merchants of Turkish, Egyptian, Arab and European origins.

Notes and References

1 Gray, Richard. *A History of Southern Sudan 1838–1889*, London, Oxford University Press, 1961, p.14.

2 G. P. Murdock. *Africa, Its People and their Culture History*, New York, 1959, p.226.

3 Seligman, C. G. and Brenda Z. Seligman. *Pagan Tribes of the Nilotic Sudan*, London, Routledge and Kegan Paul, 1965, pp.490-2.

4 Ibid. pp.490-1.

5 Tibble, Ann. *With Gordon in the Sudan*, London, Frederick Muller, 1960, p.22.

6 Beshir, Mohammed Omer. *The Southern Sudan Background to Conflict*, London, C. Hurst, 1969, p.6.

7 Op. Cit. Seligman, p.489.

8 Santandrea, Father Stefano. *The Little Unknown Tribes of Southern Sudan*, 1940, pp. 90-1. See also J. P. Crazzolara. *The Lwoo Emigrations Part I*. Verona, 1951, p.115.

9 See *The Guinness Encyclopedia of World History*, London, Guinness Publishing Ltd. 1992, p.66.

10 Ibid.

11 Op. Cit. Tribble.

12 Westernmann.

13 Op. Cit. Crazzalora.

14 Evans Pritchard. *Witchcraft, Oracles and Magic among the Azande*, Oxford, Claredon Press, 1972, pp.__

15 Op. Cit. Gray.

16 Op. Cit. The Guinness Encyclopedia.

17 Op. Cit. Gray.

18 Posnansky, Merrick. *East Africa and the Nile Valley in Early Times* quoted in Sudan in Africa ed. Yusuf Fadl Hasan, Khartoum, Khartoum University Press, 1969, p.57.

19 Ibid. p.58.

20 Ibid.

21 Op. Cit. Gray.

22 Ibid.

23 Op. Cit. Seligman pp. 490-1. See also C. H. Stigand. *Equatoria, The Lado Enclave,* London, Frank Cass, 1968, p. 115, and L. F. Nalder, *Equatoria Province Handbook,* 1936, Mongalla, p.18.

24 Dunstan Wai Mogga. *The Southern Sudan, The Problem of National Integration* ed., London, Frank Cass, 1974, p.10.

25 Ladu, Eluzai Mogga. *The Ceremonial Dance of the Lulubo, Kajuwaya,* Juba, New Day Publishers and Printers, w.d. p.3.

26 Op. Cit. Stigand. pp.92, 103, 115.

27 Op. Cit. Seligman, p.490.

28 Op. Cit. Nalder, Seligman and Stigand.

29 Op. Cit. Posnansky, p. 57-8.

30 P'Bitek, Okot. *The Religion of Central Luo,* East African Literature Bureau, Nairobi, Kampala, Dar es Salaam, 1969, p.30-1.

31 Website

32 Ministry of Finance and Economic Planning, Southern Region, *Juba Census Results of 1982.*

33 *Resolutions of the Second Ma'di National Convention* in Nimule 11th -16th September 2007, p.7.

34 John Mairi Blackings. Ed. *Narrating Our Future, Customs,*

Rituals and Practices of Ma'di of South Sudan and Uganda, CASAS, 2011, Cape Town.

35 Op. Cit. Seligman, p.490.

36 Informant of this fact to the author was Ruben Koka Yanga, eldest son of Yakobo Yanga Api in El Haj Yousif, Rudumiya, Khartoum North in September 1991.

37 See lists of totems and clans of Ma'di in Victor Keri Wani. *An Outline of Ma'di History, Culture, Traditions and Customs in Sudan,* Juba, 1992, unpublished.

38 Ibid. See also Emmanuel Kitchere Gray. *The Catholic Church in Loa,* Khartoum, 1994, p.19.

39 Ibid. Gray.

40 Interview of author with his paternal uncle Koka Lou Mbwele a.k.a. Iseni in Moli Tokuro on 21-1-1981.

41 Op. Cit. Wani, unpublished book.

42 See Keri Wani in *Narrating Our Future, Customs, Rituals and Practices of the Ma'di in South Sudan and Uganda* ed. Mairi, Blackings, CASAS Cape Town, 2011.

43 Op. Cit. Gray, pp.21-23. Wani Unpublished book. See also Sestilio Andruga Juma. *Notes on Ma'di Clans,* Juba, 1991, unpublished. See further Sudan Notes and Records Volume XIX, 1936 for Bari clans for comparison with those of Ma'di which are also found in the former.

44 Ibid. Sudan Notes and Records.

45 See Father Angelo Vinco's account in Elias Toniolo and Richard Hill. *The Opening of Nile Basin,* London, C. Hurst, 1974, p. 97. Also see J. V. Rowley. *Notes on the Ma'di of Equatoria Province,* Sudan Notes and Records Vol. XXIII 1940, p.292.

46 Op. Cit. Gray, Emmanuel, p.19. Also, in Wani, unpublished book.

47 Ibid. Wani in unpublished book.

48 Op. Cit. Crazzolara

49 Op. Cit. Rowley, p.292.

50 Op. Cit. Gray, Emmanuel. Also, Wani, unpublished book

51 Op. Cit. Okot P'Bitek. p.2.

52 Op. Cit. Gray Emmanuel, p.25

53 Ibid.

54 Op. Cit. Ladu, also Wani, unpublished book.

55 Op. Cit. Gray, Emmanuel, p.29, also Wani, unpublished book.

56 Op. Cit. Nalder, p.114.

57 Op. Cit. Gray, Emmanuel, p.55.

58 See J. P. Crazzolara. Lwoo Part III, Verona, 1951.

59 Op. Cit. Posnansky, p.57.

60 Ibid. pp.56, 57.

61 Ibid. p.57.

62 Op. Cit. Okot, p.6.

63 Op. Cit. Gray, p.38.

64 Op. Cit. Toniolo, and Hill.

65 Op. Cit. Gray, p.38.

69 Informant of this situation was Rita Keji Bilal whose mother was from Paluda clan. She related the story to author in El Haj Yousif, Khartoum North on 19-7-2001.

70 Op. Cit. Gray, p.58.

71 Lord Elton. *General Gordon,* London, Collins, 1954, p.159.

72 Op. Cit. Gray, Richard, p.110.

73 Ibid.

74 Ibid. p.111.

75 Ibid.

76 Ibid. p. 112. See also Samuel White Baker. *The Source of the*

Nile Basin, the White Nile, pp.275-301.
   77 Op, Cit. Gray, p.112.
   78 Op. Cit. Elton, p.171.
   79 Ibid. p.170.

Chapter Three

The Ma'di Chieftainships in South Sudan

3.1 Introduction

The Ma'di traditional chieftainships in South Sudan can be broadly divided into five main sectors: southern, central, eastern, western and northern chieftainships.[1]

The southern sector chieftainships are found in the area called Lokai which borders Uganda in the south and in the west where the line runs across the Albert Nile. The Eastern sector of Bori is to its north-east while the central sector chieftainships of Pageri, Arapi and Nyongwa lie to its north. This sector can be further divided into three parts — Mugali, Nimule and Loa. The dominant clan which led the population in this sector in the past is called Odupkwe, but there are other influential clans such as the

Puceri, Paselo, Paluru, Palungwa in Mugali, and other clans, for example, the Koyi (which is also known as Pamanini or Pa-Anini), Pamotto, Patibi and Accopele, who live in Nimule, and others like the Padombe, Logili, Orobe and Urugu who live in Loa.

The central sector chieftainships of Arapi, Pageri and Nyongwa consist of the main clans of Palungwa found in Arapi, Pageri who are in the place with the same name, and Nyongwa found in Nyongwa Opii. Compared with the other four sectors, the total number of clans who inhabit the central chieftainships are fewer, and the area under their control is correspondingly smaller than any other sectors. The central sector chieftainships are sandwiched between the southern sector chieftainships to the south, and Uganda in the west across the Albert Nile, and by the eastern sector chieftainships of Bori-Opari to the east, and the western sector chieftainships of Erepi to the north.

The eastern sector chieftainships occupy an area known as Bori or Opari which are two typical Ma'di names. Bori means *we are actually two!* 'Bo' stands for *actually* and 'ri' is the Burulo number *two*.[2] Opari on the other hand means 'encircled.' 'Opa' in Ma'di means *to encircle* and its affix 'ri' means *completely* hence 'opa-ri' — *completely encircled*. Indeed, when a person sees the physical geography of Opari trading centre, which was also the district headquarters from 1914-35, he will realize that it is almost completely encircled by hills. Adala Mount ranges stand to the east, Opari hill, itself as round as a circle on paper, stands at the southern gate of the town, then there is Avulogi hill in the south-west, next to it stands Motoyo Hill followed by Nyakaningwa Hill. Nyakiti mountain ranges close the western side encircling the village completely. The sector borders Acholiland in the east and the north.

The western sector chieftainships of Erepi lie west of it, and also the central sector chieftainships of Arapi, Pageri and Nyongwa bound it in the west and part of its western border is marked by River Eyibi. The most influential clan, although not so big, is Pandikeri and there are other influential and large clans like Logopi and Patibi found in Bori-Opari. The Logopi provided the first chieftainship of Bori but this was taken from them when their chief got stuck in a quagmire and was saved by some Pandikeri hunters, whose leader thought to be Ker, later demanded his rain-stones as compensation for saving his life.[3] The Patibi are numerically the largest clan in the whole of Ma'di and found in many chieftainships, contrary to what J. V. Rowley had documented,[4] and Bori was their first port of call when some of its main segments emigrated from the Two-headed Mountain (Peeping Tom) west of Torit and north-east of Magwi several centuries ago[5] following an outbreak of child disappearances. These disappearances coincided with the emergence of a section called Patibi Moyiba, whose members were suspected of having supernatural powers, in particular the ability to make relationships with leopards and other related animals to attack and kill people who were against them. Some people even believed that some members of one family from the Patibi Moyiba could turn into leopards from their human bodies. Tombe Bworo who inherited this power from his ancestor was famous and feared throughout the region. The Acholi, Lulubo, Bari and Kuku who live in this region need not be reminded about the influence of Tombe Bworo who died in 1935 at Opari and his son Wani Muganda who died in 1965 in Bibia, Uganda while a refugee during the first civil war in Southern Sudan fought by the Anya-Nya against the army of the central government in Khartoum.

The western sector on its eastern side is bounded by the eastern sector chieftainships of Bori, and west of it lies the mighty River Nile and Nyeri Mount ranges which separate it from the Kuku people of Kajokeji. In Erepi, the leading clan is the Tedire but there are other influential clans like the Patibi, Gonyapi, Afodo, Ijupi and Ogoropi who also live there. The northern sector chieftainships of Moli formerly had Logili and Mugi clan chieftainships, which were large entities in their own rights. The western sector of Erepi chieftainships lies south of this sector and north-east of it is found the Acholi chieftainship of Panyikwara. Its northern border is with the Lulubo (Olu'bo) tribe on the south bank of River Nyolo and Bariland which also bounds it in the north-west. Although the Lulubo writer, Eluzai Mogga Ladu, states in his book that the border between his people and the Ma'di is over Kit River bridge,[6] which statement was concurred with by MP Paul Yugusuk the representative of the Lulubo during the Kit Meeting of 6th September 2008 on the border dispute, the available maps of the area clearly indicate that the actual Lulubo-Ma'di border is on the south bank of River Nyolo and not over the bridge of Kit River.

But one important fact stated in the Lulubo document issued on 10th November 2008, which defines their position on the contested border in the lane between Rivers Kit and Nyolo and the statement which their representatives gave during the Kit meeting of 6th September, 2008, is that the Lulubo have a border with the Ma'di. Another important factor that might have led the Lulubo to think that the border is under Kit River bridge is that since the Juba-Nimule Road was opened in 1932, the Ma'di have not built a village in the two-mile space between Rivers Kit and Nyolo, and the first Ma'di village was Melia of Awira Rabo of Logili clan, built on the south bank of River Iyii (Kit) about five hundred meters from the river. It was this absence of Ma'di villages on the north bank of River Iyii that the Bari have exploited by building their homes in the space making them the immediate neigbours of the Lulubo. But legally the border is between the Lulubo and the Ma'di, and it has been drawn along the natural line between the two tribes.

To the west, the northern sector of Ma'di chieftainships borders the Nyeri Mountain across the Nile and beyond the Mountain lies the Kuku land. The northermost village of the sector is Iyii where nine Ma'di clans namely: Logili, Gonyapi, Nyai, Ijupi, Dedi, Monocu-Nyongwa, Mugi, Orolo Ma'di section, Kiloloro and Dongu, originally from Bari, live. Moli is the most northern area of the Ma'di land and in it there are several clans, but the most influential ones are the Logili and Mugi, which are organized as strong chieftainships. Because of a slight numerical advantage in population over the Mugi, the Logili is more influential and wields political and administrative power in Moli. But there are other prominent clans like the Ukeyi, Lulubo, Paluda, Pakoli, Kiloloro and Nyai which are also found in Moli.

The five sectors of Ma'di chieftainships constitute what is called Ma'di of Equatoria Province.[7]

3.2 The Ma'di Chieftainships, their Influences

A chieftainship has been described as a tribal entity headed by a leader. The community can have more than one chief and will still operate in a decentralized system of administration acceptable to all the minor chiefs, who can act as councillors or advisors, and the inhabitants of the area as a whole. The chief, who must be a rainmaker — the almost universal qualification to be a chief in

Ma'di society in the past — can exercise authority over several minor chiefs who live in the same area. Although naturally there can be rivalry between chiefs, as in the case of Urube the chief of Moli from the Logili clan and Kejikiri another chief from the Mugi clan, who lived with their followers in the same area, this can subside, and life can go on normally.

Ma'di chieftainships exist in plurality and an influential chieftainship accommodates almost all the other powers with which it cooperates in running the affairs of the subjects. In very rare instances a chief can originate from a non-rainmaking family. For example, Yongo Alimas Dumo was chosen by the Mugi royal family of Muku, which had declined to lead Moli after the Lokoya-Langabu feud when the incumbent chief Akeri Geri Ipele was in trouble with the colonial authorities. The first time was when he was too young to replace his father Chief Geri Ipele in about 1932 when the latter was sent to prison in Juba after being charged with torturing women of his chieftainship for allegedly poisoning people, one of whom, a man called Abudumoi who was the head of his orderlies (askari), died. The second time was when Chief Akeri Geri was accused of mismanagement of relief food items in the form of grain sent to the people of Moli by the district administrative authorities following crop failure after a prolonged drought. This was in early 1940's. Since the paramount chief of a particular Ma'di area such as Cirino Odego of Lokai in southern Ma'diland adjudicated in civil cases in collaboration with the minor chiefs, advisors and notables of the area, the subjects respected him highly. They knew that if any one of them were to seek justice in a case it would be granted to him because the chief was a man of justice. So, it can be said that the Ma'di were happy under their chiefs compared with being without chiefs.

Outside observers of Ma'di traditional leaderships like writer J. V. Rowley however considered them far less democratic. He said a Ma'di chief, provided he is in the right line of succession, is essentially aristocrat.[8] But Rowley agreed that a Ma'di chief will not adjudicate in a case alone as a dictator does, but with the minor chiefs and other notables as advisors to him. He writes, "With the Ma'di, the populace has little say in the decision which is made by the chief alone. They have a kind of public examiner who interrogates witnesses. The headmen interject remarks but do not appear to even suggest a decision because the chief will have his fingers on their pulse."[9]

Certainly, a chief like Akeri Geri Ipele of Moli, who treated the colonial administrators as sons of ordinary people and not like himself who was from a royal Ma'di family of the Logili clan, made the wrong impression on colonial administrators like Rowley, who thought all the Ma'di chiefs were aristocratic and dictatorial in behaviour. It has been reported that when Akeri Geri was the chief of Moli he would emerge from his house built on a small hill called Garamu and come down to join the District Commissioner, who was already seated ready to chair the court session under a shea butter tree ('awa pa ga') near his residence. His action, contrary to the rule followed by other chiefs who reported to their courts before the arrival of the DC to receive him as a VIP, was thought to be due to a superiority complex inspired by his royal background. Although there is no story of the DC ever cautioning him about this behaviour or misbehaviour, it counted against his future continuation as chief. Of the many other Ma'di traditional chiefs, Akeri was suspended twice by the DC, the first time for mismanaging relief grain sent to his chieftainship for the people who were facing famine due to prolonged drought and crop failure in the mid 1930's. The second suspension occurred when he was accused before the DC by the father of the author for using a banned trap for killing animals. He and his immediate relatives were engaged in digging large holes and covering them with twigs and earth so that buffalos and other large animals would fall into them and later be killed for their meat.[10]

3.3 The Roles of Ma'di Chiefs

Long before the advent of colonial rule and the introduction of a modern legal system, the Ma'di traditional chiefs had already in place their own laws to administer their subjects. These unwritten laws empowered the chiefs to arbitrate in land disputes, to handle such difficult and intricate matters as murders or accidental deaths, listen to cases of debt presented by their subjects and finding solutions for them, addressing the issue of wife eloping. The latter is a serious problem in the Ma'di community, which when not addressed, may lead to a deadly confrontation between the husband's relatives and those of the eloper. The chief is expected to ensure the return of the wife to her husband and to levy heavy fines on the offender for adultery and damages to the dignity of the husband. Usually, the fine is paid in the form of goats or rams or cattle in areas of Ma'di such as Nimule and Loa where there are some cattle. The fine is given to the victim of the offence and in the case of adultery to the husband of the woman involved. In the case of murder, the chief must ensure that the murderer's immediate relatives procure a girl to be given to the dead person's parents as compensation. The girl can be married to a brother of the deceased to bear and raise children for the family, and if there is no brother the girl can be married out of the family and the dowry is received by the late man's parents. This is done to prevent any revenge killing by the relatives of the family which has lost a member. There is no hanging in Ma'di murder cases.

In land disputes for hunting, cultivation or fishing spots along the main rivers including the River Nile, the chief must involve the neighbours and people who have knowledge of the boundaries of the disputed lands as witnesses before giving a final judgment on the matter. Sometimes a rainmaker attributes drought in the country to another rainmaker who lives in the same area. The chief is required to listen to statements from both and to involve elders of the area who are acquainted with the matter before reaching a conclusion as to who has caused the drought over the land and impose on him the appropriate punishment.

The Ma'di traditional chief is also the commander-in-chief of the army which is composed of the heads of families and mobilizes them only when there is an emergency. The tribe does not have standing battalions like those of the neighbouring tribes of Lokoya and Lulubo who have what are called *monyomiji* who have been trained to be standing foot soldiers of these tribes. The reason for this may be because they raid neighbouring tribes. The Lokoya-Langabu raided the Ma'di in Moli at the end of the nineteeth century and first quarter of the twentieth century. These tribes also expect similar attacks from other tribes with similar characteristics. But as for the Ma'di, they do not need to have standing armies because as the oldest community in this part of the southern Nile valley they have become peaceful and expect those people who have joined them such as their neighbours the Bari to be peaceful people. However, the Ma'di able-bodied men are always ready and at short notice they can mobilize for counter action should there be a threat of attack from any direction. A Ma'di man is trained in the use of traditional war weapons, bow and arrow, from the age of about ten years, and when he becomes an adult, he is already capable of defending himself or the community in the event of an enemy attack.

It is the responsibility of the chief to control his subjects to make sure they do not abuse the law of the land. For example, when the food crops are ripe, the owner is not allowed to harvest and begin eating them before supplying the first lots to the land priest to perform the rituals related to the arrival of the new crops. The land priest on receiving the first harvests of the food crops makes sacrifice to the land, the ancestors, the mountains, the rivers, the forests, and other sacred sites where rituals are performed, such as "koro" in Liro River in the Moli area of Ma'diland. In the Moli area, Jomboloko the tortoise is revered by mentioning it and throwing seeds of the new crops in its direction. Another sacred site included in the sacrifice is the small stream called Ongolubajwako in which invisible drums in the past were beaten and people could hear the sound but could not see the drums and their beaters. Traditional chiefs in other parts of Ma'diland must ensure harmony prevails in the other areas under their control. In Nimule, the chiefs ensure that there are no disputes over fishing rights along the banks of the River Nile where a string of fishing camps are found and nets are set for catching fish.

Traditional chiefs are also expected to ensure that their subjects do not set fire to the bush, because such action can result in burning of the habitats of fruit trees such as shea-butter commonly known as 'lulu' and/or grass needed by the villagers for thatching their roofs. Ma'di traditional chiefs have been studied by colonial officials sent to set up modern administration among them as reflected in the writings of former Opari District Commissioner, Mr. J. V. Rowley who writes: "A Ma'di chief, provided he is in the right line of succession, is almost essentially an autocrat. He is feared and respected by his people. With the Ma'di, the populace have little say in the decision which is made by the chief alone (during a judgment of a case.) They have a kind of public examiner who interrogates witnesses. The Headmen interject remarks but do not appear to even suggest a decision although the Chief no doubt has his fingers on their pulse. This may be the reason why joint meetings of the several courts, again in marked contrast with other tribes in the district, have not been a success. The chiefs are often at loggerheads over a case, private interests and quarrels are apt to creep in and fantastic decisions and sentences are sometimes arrived at."[11]

Another important duty of Ma'di chiefs is their pertinent attempts to eradicate poison (*enya-nya*) in society, especially among women some of whom are accused of concocting it or of having it in their possession. But the issue of poison comes and goes periodically without any resolution. This is because those accused always deny having it in their possession. Furthermore, the chiefs' failure to openly seize the potion, coupled with the dismissal of poison scares by the British officials in the district headquarters as typical African myth, which cannot be proved practically by obtaining the substance and scientifically proving it as dangerous, means that the cases are left unresolved. This is one of the prevalent problems which the colonial administration has inherited from the traditional system.

3.4 Conditions for becoming a Chief in Ma'di Society

The interesting point to note when talking about Ma'di chiefs is — how does a man become a chief in Ma'di society? In the first place, he must inherit the position from his father who must be a chief, having himself inherited it from his father who must be a rainmaker. Actually, the families of rainmakers supply the tribe with chiefs who then assume the powers to handle all cases concerning their subjects not only making rain to fall so that the people can cultivate food crops but also to see to it that the society is free of problems. The man must be sane and able-bodied.

3.5 The Roles of Ma'di Rainmaker

Rain making is one of the oldest traditional practices of the Ma'di people which is still being respected by most members of the tribe. Apparently, it was the ability to make rain fall or to control it that had earned the families of the rainmakers (*eyi-opii*) the prestige and positions of respect and chieftainships which they enjoyed in their community during different epochs of Ma'di societal development. In fact, rainmakers belong to the upper class of the Ma'di social structure. Some rainmakers besides their rainmaking profession doubled as priests for performance of the purification rites for the land. An example is Koribe Lubai, the rainmaker of the Pakoli clan in Moli, who was also the priest for a large swathe of land called Makede, used as a hunting ground by the people of Moli. [11] Being influential in their society as a result of the recognition given to them for being rainmakers, the first colonial administration in Equatoria Province, to win the tribesmen over for easy control, relied heavily on the leaderships of the rainmakers they found existing all over Ma'diland. The fact that rainmakers were found in both small and large clans of the Ma'di tribe makes it rather difficult to conclude that the size of a clan predetermined their selection as rainmakers. The Ma'di people believed that rainmakers were ordained by their creator Rubanga, to be their leaders.

3.5.1 Early Survey on Ma'di Rainmaking

The Ma'di rainmaking tradition had always attracted the interest of scholars, especially from abroad. At the beginning of the twentieth century, F. H. Rogers, a European conducted a full-scale survey of the rainmaking practices of the tribe. He made a list of over twenty places in Ma'di country where rain stones were kept.[12] His account gave details of the treatment of the stones used in rainmaking. Rogers was of the opinion that the system of chieftainships of the Ma'di was essentially similar to that of the Bari among whom he had also carried out a similar study, and that the stones used in rainmaking by members of the two tribes were practically identical.[13] He established that a highly prized set of four stones used in the Metu District of Ma'di in Uganda was brought there ten generations ago from the Bari country in the Sudan by the ancestor of the present rainmaker.

Over seventy years later nothing seems to have changed in the similarities of rainmaking among the Ma'di and Bari peoples. My uncle Koka Lou Mbwele a.k.a Iseni told me that most of the powerful rainmakers in Moli, northern Ma'di gave Bari names or names that sounded like Bari names to their rains for each rain has a name.[14] In Moli, there are several clans which have rainmakers. It is a competitive situation. The Logili clan has two or three rain shrines headed by different heads of families but the most powerful of them, which is also considered superior in the whole area, belongs to the family of Chief Geri Ipele. It is called 'Moken na adara.' This is a name believed by the owner of the rain stones to be in Bari language and which literally translated means — it will rain for such a long time that even a mother-in-law ('moken') who is on a visit and about to leave for home will get very tired ('na adara') of waiting for it to stop. If the rain organized at the shrine of 'moken na adara' begins to fall (which usually occurs at night) it will continue till next day. It is strong and the ground will be very wet.

The Mugi, the second largest clan in Moli call their rain 'Kabungo.' It rains with strong wind and breaks trees. The tree under which these rain stones are kept is also called 'Kabungo' and it is where any ceremony related to rainmaking by the Mugi clan is conducted. The small Pakoli clan under the leadership of Koribe Lubai call their rain 'Duma lubwada' a name also borrowed from the Bari language to emphasize its meaning which literally translated may mean 'who again is that giant who thinks he can bewitch me?' This is not a perfect translation for a person who speaks Bari fluently told me that it is made deliberately to sound like Bari probably to give the impression that it is so, and powerful. Kuyu of Ukeyi clan of Muruli called his rain 'Joloko'. When he died, Ingani his son inherited the rain and became in-charge of it. If Joloko begins to pour one gets tired of waiting for its stopping because it will not stop as soon as one would wish. Other rains with little significance include that of Kute Vulufura of Logili clan and it is called 'Afirindende.' It is light, sporadic and lasts for a short time.

As established by F. H. Rogers, some of the Ma'di rain stones have been bought from Bari rainmakers, such as those of the rainmaker he encountered in Metu district. He writes: "Four cows and a bull were paid for a set of six stones (three of either sex) at Laropi (Loropi) near Dufile (Odrupele), a further set was acquired from the Bari Chief Leju of Shindiru while others are stones that have been picked up from time to time and are venerated on account of their shape and smoothness."[15]

3.5.2 Can anybody become a Rainmaker?

Nobody can collect rain stones and declare himself a rainmaker. It can spell disaster for such a person who has not been a rainmaker before. In the early days, ordinary men who collected stones and declared themselves rainmakers suffered a sickness which caused swelling of the stomach and they died.[16] This had sounded the warning to would-be impostors. This confirms to the Ma'di that the ancestors of their rainmakers were indeed selected and ordained by Rubanga their creator as priests for this profession. In the past, men who found rain stones in the rivers or elsewhere would collect them and take them to their chiefs who were rainmakers. Rogers established that there are more rainmaking centres among the Ma'di than among the Bari. What is common however to the rainmakers of the two tribes are their identical rain stones. At Metu he saw two sets of stones, the first and most highly prized consisting of four conical pieces of quartz — one male and three females. "They are much feared and contact with them is avoided so far as possible, they may only be safely handled by boys or old men that is to say persons of maturity would be adversely affected in their relations with women so that although the stones are nominally in charge of the reigning chief, in effect he deputes someone else to guard them and to carry out the rain making ceremony," writes Rogers.[17] "At Metu, the stones are looked after by the chief's mother, and his son, a lad of about fourteen is being instructed in their use. They are kept in a pot in a small hut set aside for the purpose (though children may occasionally be allowed to sleep there)."[18]

Rain stones are also bought with girls. For example, Oguwa the rainmaker of the Pamotto clan in Olikwi, Nimule bought his rain pebbles from another rainmaker in Paracele, east of Nimule with a girl. He named his rain Nya-Robo[19] which means 'daughter of Robo.' Ala the rainmaker of Nyongwa village which lies between Pageri and Erepi (Kereppi) also bought some of his rain stones from an Acholi rainmaker in Paracele in Uganda with a girl. He named his rain Nya-Bira.[20]

The rainmakers in other parts of Ma'diland unlike those in Moli in the northern part who mostly gave Bari names to their rains or at least names which they thought sounded like Bari names so that the people would take them seriously, gave female names to their rains. Nya-Robo, the rain of Oguwa in Nimule mentioned above means *daughter of Robo* while Nya-Bira the rain of Ala of Nyongwa clan means *daughter of Bira*. The rains were so powerful that songs were even composed about some of them. The Nyongwa clan members composed a popular song about how Nya-Bira fell over their territory only and excluded the adjoining area of Pageri south of it and Lungayo area in the north.[21] Although the rain stones were feared by non-rainmakers because of the danger associated with them, sometimes children of rainmakers bore the risk in handling the stones because, being the offspring of rainmakers, they believed they were immune to such danger.

Others transferred the rain stones of their fathers without their knowledge. A typical example is an incident known throughout Ma'diland which involved the transfer of some of the rain stones of Akeri Milla, the great rainmaker of the Pandikeri in Opari by his daughter to her husband Surur, another rainmaker of the Koyi clan in Nimule.[22] The woman believed that the rain stones of her father were more powerful than those of her husband and therefore her inclusion of these new pebbles into his collection would replenish their power. The discovery of the disappearance of the stones from her father's collection caused considerable consternation to the owner who demanded their immediate return to Opari. This was effected with a ceremony involving the slaughter of a he-goat and entertainment augmented with some locally brewed beer served by Surur.

3.6 Other Objects in keeping Rain Stones

Besides the acquisition of chieftainship, another reason for keeping rain stones is to make rain fall because the people depend on rain for their survival. They need rain for their food crops to grow so that they can have enough food to eat. They need rain to water the vegetation which their cattle, goats, sheep and other domestic animals can feed on. They need rain to fill their rivers and pits from which they and their animals can get their drinking water. So, any man who has the power to control rain and make it fall must be an important man in his community. Rainmaking is the main characteristic of all the great men of the Ma'di tribe called chiefs or '*opii*'. Without this important qualification, nobody could become chief and enjoy the great honour and respect accorded to him by his people from his small clan to the bigger community which is the tribe.

The ancestor of the great Odupkwe clan in Lokai made a great name for himself because of the power he wielded to make rain fall so that all the people in his chieftainship could cultivate and have plenty of food to eat. Muamme Kara, the rainmaker of the Koyi clan in Nimule was respected because the people in his area trusted him in his rainmaking profession. However, rainmaking also has its difficulties. It sometimes causes a serious problem between rainmakers and the ordinary members of their societies. Such a problem arises when there is drought, and the people are heading towards an environmental disaster and famine.

3.7 Drought can lead to an Environmental Disaster, Famine

Quite often drought is believed to be the evil work of a malicious rainmaker when he is in a dispute with a member or several members of his community. A typical example of a dispute between a rainmaker and the ordinary beneficiaries of rain occurred in Moli some time in the nineteenth century. A bitter quarrel erupted between Urube, the greatest rainmaker of the Logili clan and the inhabitants of the whole area. The quarrel was over the refusal by members of other clans to contribute foodstuff for making an offering to the ancestors at the Logili rain shrine before the rainy season. Although the leaders of Mugi, Ukeyi, Pakoli and other smaller clans were in possession of rain stones, because the Logili rain stones were more powerful than theirs, it happened that Urube was the only rainmaker who could make rain fall in time of total failure by other rainmakers.

When the people refused to contribute the small quantity of foodstuff demanded by Urube from each family, on advice of Kejikiri the rainmaker of the Mugi clan, he stopped the rain from falling. Drought ensued leading to an environmental disaster. Although at first the people thought they would survive this disaster by feeding on milk produced by their cattle (for in those days the Moli people had a lot of cattle) when a cattle epidemic broke out and killed most of the cattle, it was believed that this was also the evil work of Urube. The anger of the people of Moli towards the chief increased. Despite the great suffering that the people were experiencing, Urube was never moved by their plight and the lack of rain continued. So, the people became very angry, went wild and decided to kill the rainmaker.

Urube alerted by Chief Kejikiri of the Mugi clan of the impending danger to him, fled and hid in a thicket near the junction of Liro and Jumiya Rivers. The people went to look for him in the forest. Oddly, on finding him hiding in a tree trunk, several men who saw him went by him pretending not to have seen him. It is the belief of the Ma'di people, particularly those of the Moli in the northern part of the tribe, that whoever sheds the blood of a rainmaker will pay for it for the rest of his life, which is a costly undertaking. Moreover, he who kills a chief must recompense for his noble blood with a girl who is presented to the bereaved clan who assign her a husband. It is only a person who is not of any significant status in the tribe, such as a servant or 'opigo,' who can kill a person of such an outstanding position as the chief and be least affected. When the servant of Kajamindi, a senior member of the Mugi clan came upon the hiding chief he shouted, "People of Moli, the man is here. Is it not Urube you are looking for? Why do you walk past him?" (*Anyi Molii! Ta egori ni di. Anya ndule rii Urube iko? Anya laga dri na si adosi?*)

The man threw his spear at the chief, and it struck him in the side of the abdomen. The chief cried out to the people that he should be brought down from the 'lugo' tree where he had been hiding, so that he could speak his last words before his death. They did as he asked and at once he said that after his death his son, Dupari Kolo, should inherit his rain stones and the first thing he should do for the people of Moli was to make rain fall. Then Urube died and he was buried at the site where he was slain, for tradition did not allow a rainmaker killed for imposing drought to be carried home for burial.[23]

3.8 Causes of Drought in Ma'di Perspective

F.H. Rogers pointed out that when the rainmaker wants to regulate rainfall so that it is not excessive, he empties the water in the container of the rain stones, leaving the stones dry.[24] It is believed that drought is also caused by a malicious rainmaker by draining out the water in the container of the rain stones, leaving them dry. Other malicious rainmakers when they want to cause drought, open the beak of a dead red feathered bird called 'nana'. An ordinary man who intends to complicate matters for rainmakers can also get a dead 'nana', opens its beak and place it looking eastward, where all rain clouds are believed to form. This practice can also cause a serious lack of rain.

Other people, excluding rainmakers, can further make things worse by emptying the gauge for filtering water salt ('aiso') causing clouds in the sky to disperse thus stopping rain from falling. Also, the rainbow is believed by the Ma'di to cause the dispersal of clouds in the sky resulting in lack of rain. Quite often when rainmakers are convinced that the cause of drought has not originated from them, after all the steps have been taken by them to redress the situation, the men of the area are mobilized as a last resort to go and check treetops for 'nana' beaks or anthills on which the contents of 'aiso' might have been emptied by a malicious person, who could have been a woman.[25] Other rainmakers cause drought by placing male and female rain stones near the fireplace or 'ati'. Upon their bodies becoming warm, they prevent rain from falling. This may explain the finding of Rogers who in his documenting states that each set of rain stones is kept in a pot containing water which is poured out in the dry season and replenished when indications of the new rains appear.[26] The water so used must come from running water. The water is emptied out in the case of excessive rain as an indication to the controlling power that there has been enough. It further explains the reason why rain stones must not be exposed to the sun. Should occasion arise for them to go a distance, they must be wrapped up and guarded against exposure; such occasions would be when changing ownership or to help some other country, but they can only be lent thus as a great favour and after much urging.[27] In a situation of failure of rain, usually a meeting is held at the local 'rudu' or sacred grove and if the matter is considered serious, the guardian of the stones is asked to perform the rainmaking ceremony.[28]

The method varies slightly in different parts of Ma'di country, but the general procedure is the same. The stones are washed, smeared with kidney fat and sometimes the stomach contents of a black sheep, then replaced in their pot while prayers are offered to the dead fathers, the former chiefs. Sesame (simsim) oil, oil from serpent and goat fat besides the leaves of a tree called 'avurukwe' found on riverbanks and the leaves of a type of plant called 'ayila' are also used to smear the rain stones when inviting rain to fall.[29]

3.9 The Ordeal of a Rainmaker in Nyongwa

In July 1977, Aride, who was also called Gulli, was the famous rainmaker of Nyongwa-Opii. He was hacked to death by an angry crowd who accused him of imposing a prolonged drought that caused the failure of food crops and consequently brought them to a state of starvation. The people surrounded Aride's body with some firewood by the roadside as was the Ma'di custom with a slain rainmaker. The body was left by the side of the road and surrounded with firewood as a warning to other rainmakers who might be contemplating similar harm to the people. On the day Gulli was killed, a heavy rainstorm drenched the area and coincidentally a motorcade of the former President of Sudan, Jaafar Mohamed Nimeri who was accompanied by his former Deputy, Abel Alier in a trip from Nimule to Juba, passed by. When the

President and his entourage became aware of the corpse, Nimeiri stopped the motorcade and enquired why the man was killed. An elderly man, who did not bother to hide away from the heavily armed army and policemen escorting the President, explained that the man was killed because he stopped the rain from falling for a long time, causing harm to the people of the land. He added that it was an old practice for dealing with harmful rainmakers. On learning this, Nimeiri ordered the motorcade to resume the journey, entrusting the case to the police and the head chief of the area to handle later.

3.9.1 Ala, Father of Uliya the Rainmaker, his Songs

Ala was the father of Uliya. Both him and his son who succeeded him were powerful rainmakers in Nyongwa-Opii and therefore were respected chiefs in their times. The first rain pebbles which went from Ala to his son are believed to have fallen from the sky during a heavy rainfall. Their bodies, smooth to the touch, are said to have been rubbed in the clouds from which they fell to earth, due to the strong action of hailstones. Other rain pebbles are said to have been found in the clenched fingers of the rainmaker's newborn baby. Ala, in order to replenish the power of his collection, acquired more rain stones by buying them from an Acholi rainmaker in exchange for a girl in Paracele. Each rainmaker is known by the song he composes about his rain and its powers. Ala of Nyongwa-Opii composed the following song about his rain stones:

> *Ebe Nya Bira kodi etcisi*
> *Jogo ori Uliya nyemu mingwire*
> *Mata amavu juru ga ko*
> *Sai amuzu juruga ko.*

The literal translation of the song probably sung by a supporter of Ala runs as follows:

> *Nya Bira daughter of Bira is left falling within its boundaries*
> *Jogo the son of Uliya come to take me back*
> *My father, we shall not go to foreign land*
> *Sai we shall not murmur in foreign land.*

This song implies that because their rainmaker was powerful and can always make rain fall successfully, there will always be plenty of food and therefore the Nyongwa people will not go searching for food in foreign lands.

The rain stones of Ala inherited by his son Uliya were called Nya-Bira. It is said that they were bought with a girl from another rainmaker in Acholiland.[30]

3.10 Government Intervention in Rainmaking Abuses

When the traditional practice of taking the law into their own hands and collectively deciding on the slaying of a rainmaker was replaced with civil law, the government administrators also found it necessary to side with the mass of people and impose some punishment on stubborn rainmakers. As recently as 1974, Arawa Alimu, a rainmaker of the Orobe clan in Loa, was held responsible by the inhabitants of Loa area for an extensive drought that had caused irreparable crop failure. They were about to apply the traditional punishment of getting hold of him, tying his arms and legs and placing him in the middle of a circle of burning wood until he dried up and died, when the head chief of Ma'di, Sabazio Okumu Abdallah, whose seat was at Loa, intervened by arresting the rainmaker before the angry villagers could lay their hands on him and apply mob justice. The head chief demanded from the rainmaker why there was no rain. Surprisingly, Arawa Alimu rebuffed the chief by retorting, "Do I live in the sky to know why there is no rain?" Angered by this retort, the head chief ordered the lashing of Arawa with fifteen strokes followed by his imprisonment for one month.[31]

Another civil action against four Ma'di rainmakers took place at Jaipi, in the Uganda section of the Ma'di in May 1955. It was recounted to the author by Philip Izama Gobi whose maternal grandfather, Abdrahaman Jaden, was one of the four rainmakers.[32] A dispute as usual broke out following a drought in the middle of a rainy season which the villagers suspected the four rainmakers to have caused. The people complained bitterly against them to the government authorities. To prevent the people taking the law into their hands and causing bodily harm or even death to the rainmakers, the authorities collected the four men for questioning. When their answers were not satisfactory, the latter decided to torture them. They were made to dig an active anthill and forced to sit in it half-naked so that the ants could bite them. This was meant to force them to accept responsibility for the drought and to make declaration that they would cause rain to fall.

After a long period of torture, the four rainmakers were made to go to their respective homes to make rain fall or else they would face a more serious punishment. On the fourth day after their release from custody, Abdrahaman Jaden summoned his immediate elderly male relatives. He gave them a goat to slaughter, and a ceremony was performed in his homestead. After eating, the elders were allowed to enter the rainmaker's special hut where he performed the magic for the rain to fall. He had some glittering pebbles which he kept by his bedside. The bed on which he used to sleep was of raised mud. The rain stones were kept in a large horn. Abdrahaman Jaden poured the stones into his hands and began uttering some magical incantations and singing a strange song. Then suddenly he dropped the pebbles on the floor. Immediately outside the hut a sudden strong wind with thunder broke. This continued for about half an hour and some clouds appeared overhead. Then heavy rain began to fall, and it fell for six or seven hours. When the rain started, clouds spread all over the area affected by the drought. During the downpour, the rain stones flew inside the room like fireflies without hitting anybody. People got scared and some of them wanted to leave the room, but the chief (for by his status as rainmaker he was a chief) advised them to keep calm because they were safe. This powerful rainmaker died in 1961. According to tradition his eldest son Rumbi Paskazio was to have inherited his chieftainship and gotten hold of the rain stones, but he declined and so nobody after the rainmaker's death took responsibility for the rain stones which remain unattended to this day.

In many similar instances, rain stones went unclaimed after the deaths of their owners thus leading to a decline in the number of rainmakers in the Ma'di tribe in general. The fear of leaving rain stones exposed and subject to handling by children, prompted the elder sons of rainmakers, having disavowed this tradition after their father's deaths, to take the stones secretly and hide them in deep holes or 'ogo' in trees. In 1974, children in Eyibi Ado east of Pageri discovered four rain stones hidden in a hole in a tree on the bank of River Eyibi. They used to touch them whenever they came home after swimming in the river. They did not realize that it was their touching of these stones which used to cause rain to fall on these same days.

People were prepared to travel long distances to buy rain stones. Akim, a rainmaker of the Palungwa clan in Arapi in the Sudan section of Ma'di bought his rain stones from Abdrahaman Jaden of Jaipi in Uganda. A man in Metu went as far as Shindiru in Bari country in Southern Sudan and another man in Nyongwa, southern Sudan walked to faraway Paracele in northern Uganda to buy rain stones. This practice confirms the importance of rainmaking among the Ma'di people. Furthermore, the fact that sometimes girls, cattle, goats and sheep were used in transactions to buy rain stones placed the practice of rainmaking at the apex of the cultural behaviours or norms of Ma'di life.

3.10.1 Ma'di Belief that Nature can also act against Malicious Rainmakers

Besides the joint action by the villagers against a rainmaker for causing drought and government intervention to punish him, Nature too is believed to act against malicious rainmakers. This is when the intentionally caused drought leads to the massive death of frogs. In such cases, the rainmaker can suffer a serious sickness and swelling of his stomach, suffering for a considerable period before he dies. Sometimes Nature extends its punishment to the rainmaker's wife or even his child or children.[33]

3.11 Where the Land Priest Fits in to Ma'di Traditional Leaderships

Within the Ma'di chieftainship there exists the practice of land purification to prevent epidemics, and bird, grasshopper or locust invasion of the fields, so that the people are not affected by hunger or disease. The members of society who carry out this spiritual work are known as priests or priestesses. They are not the owners of the land as assumed by some of them and other people who do not seem to understand their roles but rather spiritual characters whose purpose is to keep the land free of these calamities. The powers of these priests or priestesses are moderate and restricted according to their abilities to perform their spiritual actions in given areas. These areas are allocated in the form of hunting grounds like Makede in Moli, northern Ma'diland, or as shrines in rivers like the 'koro' sacrifice shrine in Liro River owned by the Pajawu clan elder who emigrated from Jaipi in Adjumani district of Uganda to live near his son-in-law from the Mugi clan of Moli and settled at Lerwa near Deretu beside the Paloi, Metu, Moje and Ukeyi clans. Makede forest includes Jomboloko Hill where the sacred tortoise with the same name once lived and most of the eastern part of River Liro. The priest who performs the purification rite comes from the Pakoli clan. In the twentieth century, the priest was Komure Lubai, the father of Adonia Wani whose wife Sopeta Goliba was at a certain time permitted to perform the rite on his behalf when he died. West of Makede is Mount Foki which was the shrine of a Logili family of Nyadiya, father of Swapere Katika who later emigrated to Iyii the ancestral land of the Logili clan. The small Ongolubajwako stream which is famous for generating the sound of invisible drums, is venerated by the Mugi clan elders because it is located in their backyard.

In the Moli area there are as many priests or priestesses as the numerous family shrines require them for staging the spiritual functions. For example, just a few kilometers from 'koro' river shrine, the land beyond the river is purified by another clan and family, and not by the Pajawu whose shrine was limited only to the patch in the Liro River, outside of which they are not in-charge. As an emigrant family they were allowed to sacrifice in this spot because the Ma'di by their nature prefer a person who is sacrifice-concious and observant of traditional belief to a person who is not because the latter can be a wizard who does not have a room in the hearts of the Ma'di people. In 1937, when the Pajawu, Paloi and Metu women in Leruwa were accused by Chief Akeri Geri of Moli of poisoning his sister-in law, Enderi Adiri, who was the wife of Jentilio Mukaru of Akunye clan, he massively arrested and transported them to Torit for trial. The rest of the villagers abandoned Lerwa en masse and Pajuwa clan members emigrated to Mede north of Opari, the former district headquarters. It was here that an earlier group of the Pajawu clan had settled after the return of the Ma'di people from Ayipa in about 1893 following the end of their refuge from the Mahdist intrusion of Ma'diland in 1888. Just a few kilometers north-east of the 'koro' river shrine lies the Adrwi area whose purification rite was performed by the cousin of Tombe Urutwe of Logili clan.

In Lokai, land purification rites are performed by several clans and there are several rain-making shrines in the region. The fishing camps along the Nile are typical examples of purification sites where different priests perform the spiritual rites close to each other. In Loa, the Alli clan is responsible for Appala, the biggest fishing camp on the eastern coast of River Nile near Fulla Rapids north of Nimule. Elder Icoko was responsible for performing the purification rite at this camp. In the same area along the White Nile, there exist a number of other fishing stations. The purification rite for Palenge fishing station was performed by Ida of Koyi clan of Nimule, while that of Zelekoroa fishing station was performed by Musoro of the Pamotto clan of Olikwi, Nimule. Muamme Kara of Koyi used to be responsible for the purification rite at the Isumo fishing camp.[34] Purification rites are performed at fishing camps so that the fishermen are protected from crocodile, hippo, snake and even fish attacks during their fishing activities. Performance of this rite even protects the fisherman from getting drowned in the river during his setting of the nets and hooks, or when using wooden canoes for setting nets or for crossing the river to reach the other bank.

In Mugali of southern Ma'diland, there are several priests who perform the land purification rite. Among the Puceri clan, Musurani, the father of Faladio Abdalla Abiri used to perform the rite around the Kureru area.[35] In Bori-Opari, the area has been divided into several parts and each part has its priest for performing the land purification rite. From Molugeng to Male, the priest is from the family of Jala Bakhiet from the Pambili clan. Towards the south-west beginning from Mount Njukudu and extending to Mount Remo, the land purification rite was previously performed by an elder of the Pavunde clan which has since then emigrated to Paracele and today some of its members are found in Owinykibul.[36] The land purification in the land west of Mount Ako up to Juba-Nimule Road in Erepi, was performed by Lemin of the Ijupi clan of Jombokokwe east of Erepi. Here Chief Akeri Milla once built his village called Bwolo before he returned to Nyakaningwa, Opari where he died in about 1910 and was buried near where the market is located today. This piece of land belongs to the Pandikeri clan, and it was Dari Kanyara Isra, the grandson of Milla who gave it to Lemin whose mother was a Pandikeri. In 1940's, Musa from the Pandikeri clan wanted to take over the land from Lemin who promptly informed Kanyara who sent a representative to inform Musa that this land was given by him to Lemin of Ijupi because the mother of the latter was a Pandikeri woman. Since that time the land ritual at this place has been performed by descendants of Lemin.[37]

In Pageri, the land purification rite around Pageri village up to River Eyibi is performed by a family head from the Logopi clan whose chief had once lived several meters north of the present Pageri market called Langauro. In Melekwe, the family of Konide Lomeda of Pamotto is responsible for performing the land purification rite at a cave across the Nile from Tolu. Here was a natural bridge across the Nile strong enough to support a bevy of elephants. The bridge was regarded as the most sacred site on the Nile by the Ma'di people who live in the area. It was first written about in Uganda Journal No. I by E. J. Wayland in 1934 and he located it seven miles downstream of the Fulla Rapids. The bridge occupies the whole width of the Nile, some 370 feet and is about 1200 feet wide. The surface consists of soft soil with a high percentage of vegetable matter but no papyrus. The bridge usually lasts for three or four years and then breaks up to form again a year or two later.[38] Ma'di elder Erodionne Murulu Jiribi in 1995 told the author that he, in the company of other Ma'di hunters including Chief Cirino Odego, crossed this natural bridge to get to the slope of Nyeri Mountain in the dry season of 1936 to hunt elephants and other animals. The bridge went through its disintegration phase in that same year and a few weeks later it was reported gone. That year was also a bad one for Chief Odego who was charged by the District Commissioner of Torit who appeared in Robijo, the chief's residence unexpectedly, as the latter and other hunters arrived from their hunting expedition. The chief and his subjects had broken the law regarding conservation of animals in his chieftainship and all the elephant tusks that they brought from the hunt were confiscated by the DC that day and taken to Torit as exhibits in their trial. Chief Cirino Odego was suspended from his position and sent with the rest of the men caught with elephant tusks to dig the Magwi-Parajok-Ayaci road as a group punishment.⁽³⁹⁾ Erodionne said he escaped this punishment because he told the DC that he was a student of Torit Artisan Technical School and had come for holidays. It was at that time that Alimu Dengu took over as chief of Lokai, only to be accused of collaborating with Abyssinian poachers, dismissed and imprisoned in Kajokeji for several months before being released as a commoner finding that his half brother Odego was reinstated.

3.12 Summary of the Roles and Functions of Ma'di Chiefs during the pre-Colonial Era

A proper understanding of the roles and functions of Ma'di traditional chiefs cannot be achieved without first exploring their roles and functions in the period long before their chieftainships were invaded by outsiders and colonized The Ma'di chiefs experienced the administrations of the three different colonial powers in the Sudan, namely, the Turco-Egyptian (1821–1885), Mahdiyya (1885–1898) and Anglo-Egyptian (1899–1956) administrations. Each administration had different system to which it subjected the Ma'di traditional chiefs.

During the Anglo-Egyptian administration, the chiefs were made the suppliers of foodstuffs for the personnel of the colonial administration encamped within their vicinities. These were the chiefs whose areas lay a short distance from the Nile because the administrators, civil and army, used the great footpath which ran along the Nile from Gondokoro in the North to Dufile (Odrupele) in the South. The foodstuff which the chiefs and their subjects produced was only sufficient for their own consumption, and it proved onerous to share this with outsiders; therefore, at certain times there was resistance from the chiefs and their subjects to these demands by the authorities resulting in the use of force by the latter. Governor Charles George Gordon of Equatoria province reported that he had to use force to take some food items from a tribal chief near Labore station who refused to supply his personnel with some grain. He blamed this on his predecessor, Samuel White Baker whom he said had used excessive force instead of diplomacy in taking food from the natives. [40] The chain of stations along the western bank of the River Nile, after Gondokoro the main base, included Bedden, Kirri, Moggie (Muggi), Labore (Moli), Ayu, and Dufile (Odrupele).

The several Ma'di chieftainships varied in size. In Burulo-speaking areas of Moli, Bori-Opari and the larger part of Erepi (Kerepi) in the northern part of Ma'diland, the dominant chieftainships were those of Logili, Mugi in Moli, Tedire in Erepi (Kerepi) and Pandikeri in Bori-Opari clans. There were other smaller clans like the Ukeyi which were organized into chieftainships, but they were later amalgamated into larger chieftainships in the same areas. That these chieftainships were quite robust, and their authority effective can be seen from the case of the Paluda clan in Muruli. Their chief, Nyori, was the first Ma'di traditional leader to resist the Turkish and Arab forces who attacked his large village in Muruli Iti-Arro. Although he and many of his subjects were killed during the attack, this encounter sent a strong message to the garrison commander, Alfred Del Bono in Gondokoro, that only a friendly approach to the Ma'di chiefs would ensure peaceful relations, otherwise it would be disastrous for them on the one hand and the Ma'di people on the other, for the former to force their way into the Ma'di areas.

After the destruction of the Paluda chieftainship by the Turco-Egyptian forces in 1860, the remnants who had survived the enemy attack did not reconstitute, and no Ma'di group effectively resisted the Turco-Egyptian forces on their southward penetration on directives of Khedive Ismail Pasha to claim the southern territories for the Condominium.

The duties of a Ma'di traditional chief can be gleaned from his daily activities, as follows:

As a rainmaker he makes sure rain falls at the right season of the year so that his subjects can till the soil, plant food crops and have a good harvest, thus ensuring there is plenty of food for their consumption.

He adjudicates in cases presented to him by his subjects, individually or in groups, in such matters as disputes about the borders of crop fields, hunting areas and fishing sites along the big rivers which teem with fish. The Ma'di chief makes sure that there is no scrambling and rivalries among his subjects over lands, hunting fields and fishing points.

He acts as a judge to make sure there are no quarrels among his subjects. For example, he will make sure that the man who elopes with the wife of another man or commits adultery with her, is punished by having to pay compensation to the husband of the woman, in the form of cattle, goats or sheep.

He acts as commander-in-chief of his tribal army, which is constituted of the able-bodied men of his chieftainship and leads them to war when the tribe or a section of it, is attacked by other tribal groups. For example, in the last half of the 19th century, Chiefs Muku of Mugi clan and Mele of Logili clan became allies and jointly led the armed men of their chieftainships in reprisal attacks on the Lokoya-Langabu in the three large villages of Okire, Ofiri and Omangara, whose *monyomiji* (armed youth of that generation particularly) had for a long time been raiding Moli villages at Palutu and Pamidi. The reprisal attack was so effective and devastating that it decisively put an end to the attacks of Lokoya-Langabu on Moli villages henceforth.

The chief acts as an agent of public order and tidiness, by making sure that paths which join the villages of his subjects to rivers where the people fetch their drinking water, and to his village which is their assembly place for meetings including emergency ones, are kept open and clean by clearing the grass and other plants which can grow in them and block them. In Moli, Chief Akeri Geri used to organize path clearance campaigns in which every head of family took part, and anyone without an acceptable excuse who failed to turn up was fined and he would have to pay a ram as punishment to the leadership.

The chief encourages maintenance of the culture of his people, and he physically participates in all forms of dance, especially those dances which require the presence of men for there are some dances which are exclusively for females, such as the '*kejuwa*'. All the Ma'di chiefs included in this survey were found to be good performers of the royal dance '*mure*', '*nyakiro*', '*birabira*' and '*dra*' the funeral dance performed to mourn the elderly members of the tribe who have passed on. War songs composed in Moli after their attack and defeat of the Lokoya-Langabu warriors were composed by Chief Muku of Mugi clan and Chief Mele of Logili clan in the last half of the nineteenth century or at the start of the 20th century. Ma'di chiefs during their tenures of leadership were good performers of *mure* dance and examples are Chiefs Dari Kanyara of Bori-Opari, Cirino Odego of Lokayi, Akeri Geri of Moli and Odoriko Loku.

The chiefs lead campaigns to confront threats against their people. In the mid 1930's, when a lion nicknamed Rafaile and a lioness called Foni moved from the direction of Juba along the newly constructed Juba-Nimule Road towards Ma'diland and terrorized the people in the Mua area, Chief Ruben Surur Iforo led the hunt to track down Foni who had killed a woman and a child in the area and had her killed at Ibbi River. In Moli, Chief Akeri Geri mobilized the men in his area to trap the lion Rafaile, but he broke free from the net several times and avoided being killed. Akeri also once led a campaign to chase away a herd of elephants which had invaded the Moli area and destroyed cassava, sweet potato and grain crops. The villagers blew trumpets (*turulu*) and other wind instruments such as 'ture' producing a frightening cacophony which drove the elephants away from the field crops.

The Chiefs control indiscriminate cutting of natural vegetation such as trees and bamboo for construction of huts, granaries and other structures in their villages. They make sure that bushfires are not started and take hold because fire can destroy the grass needed for thatching the roofs of huts and granaries and destroys vegetation. Violators of this control measure are fined one goat or ram so that other people know that the trees, bamboo and grass are for all people and indiscriminate use of them, and their destruction cannot be tolerated. The chief normally coordinates information on this matter with the land priests who are directly concerned with such issues.

The Ma'di chiefs act as judges and impose heavy penalties on people in their chieftainships who kill other people intentionally or accidentally. The decreed punishment is by way of compensation paid with a girl from the family of the killer to the family of the victim. A murderer is not sentenced to death in Ma'di traditional law but is made to compensate the person he has killed with a girl. A boy is not chosen because the people presume that he will return to his family or clan on coming of age. A girl on the other hand will be given to a young man within the family of the victim to give birth to children who will increase the size of the family, or she can be married off to a young man of another clan as a wife and her marriage will bring some wealth in the form of bride price to the family being compensated. Giving a boy as compensation will instead cause the family of the victim to lose twice by having to spend their wealth on the marriage of the boy. In a rare case, a boy was given as compensation in the killing of Chief Urube of Logili clan in Moli by the family of a notable called Kajamindi of Mugi clan whose servant (*opigo*) killed the chief. The family of the slain chief accepted compensation in the form of the boy with great reluctance when the killer's side could not produce a girl. Indeed, the boy on growing up was sent away by the late Chief's son who inherited the seat of his slain father because he feared that the boy could easily inherit his seat and by default become a chief. The original clan refused to accept the youth back into their family and sent him away and he founded the Mugi-Kolowa clan. The story behind the origin of this name is that when the boy was presented as compensation for killing the chief, the latter's elders asked the compensating family, "Since this is not a girl but a boy, will he stay?" And the compensating family replied, "Yes, he will." But this never proved to be the case. He never stayed and was sent away to establish his own clan called Mugi-Kolowa. Ma'di do not kill the murderer in revenge as practised in other cultures in the country. They let him go but retain his daughter or sister as a compensation for the dead.

When the Ma'di chiefdoms came under the sway of Turco-Egyptian rulers, the Ma'di system of government and to some extent their social fabric was destroyed, but the chiefs worked out a way of managing the affairs of their subjects by compromising with the new system of administration. The Turco-Egyptian era lasted in Ma'diland for about thirty years ie. 1860–1889. The Mahdists in 1885 defeated the Turco-Egyptian rulers in the Sudan and established in some parts of southern Sudan a system of government which the Ma'di called Jediyya (Jihadiyya) which was notorious for enslaving young people and for its harsh discipline. If a slave escaped and was recaptured and returned to his or her master, a limb of the slave was cut off. The Mahdists did not pay much attention to the chiefs whose influence among their subjects they ignored except for the purpose of supplying porters (*swalini*) to carry booty, and foodstuff such as cattle, goats, sheep, durra, sesame and honey; food items which were available in the Ma'di area at the time. The capture of slaves by Mahdists among the Ma'di was rampant.[41] One of the victims was my great paternal grandmother, Tete Nya Anyira, who was caught in the Palutu area in the northern part of Moli. My grandfather Lou Mbwele, her son, followed the captors of his mother and used an arrow, one with a head having sharpened spikes on the sides called *nyi mavu yira* meaning *you will stop following me when you shoot one of the captors dead*. The Mahdists caused much suffering in the central Nile valley. To escape capture Ma'di in Moli and Erepi (Kerepi) were forced to flee in hundreds of thousands to Bori-Opari to seek the protection of Chief Akeri Milla.[42] The Mahdists' role in destabilizing the region was also reported by European historians who investigated the impacts of this predation. Sanderson reports that the Mahdiyya destruction in areas along the Nile had nullified any semblance of traditional authority forcing the tribal chiefs to strengthen control in their jurisdictions to protect the people from attacks by other neighbouring tribes.

It was during the administration of the Sudan under the Anglo-Egyptian Condominium system that attention was focused on the role of Ma'di chiefs. The British introduced them to the colonial administrative system, their traditional roles were compromised, and they became part of the colonial government machinery. They were used as government agents to effect changes in their chieftainships which were in contradiction to their own system and co-opted in the process of its abolition.

Notes and References

1 Wani, Victor Keri. *An Outline of Ma'di History, Culture, Traditions and Customs in Sudan,* Juba, 1992, unpublished.

2 Blackings, John Mairi. *Ma'di English-English Ma'di Dictionary,* Muenchen, Lincom Europa, 2000, p.86.

3 Interviews of author with Lazaro Nyago Dumo in Al Amarat, Khartoum on 12-6-2001 and with Chief Odoriko Loku Diego of Bori in Torit on 15-5-2005. Also see J. V. Rowley. *Notes on the Ma'di of Equatoria Province,* Sudan Notes and Records, No. XXIII, 1940, pp.288-291.

4 Ibid. Rowley. p.290.

5 Ibid.

6 Ladu, Eluzai Mogga. *The Cultural Ceremonial Dance of the Lulubo, Kajuwaya,* Juba, New Day Publishers and Printers, w.d. p.3.

7 Op. Cit. Rowley, pp.279-294.

8 Ibid. p.280.

9 Ibid. p.281.

10 Koka Lou Mbwele a.k.a Iseni, my paternal uncle, narrated to me these facts in Juba in 1974.

11 Op. Cit. Rowley, pp.280-281.

12 Seligman, C. G. and Brenda N. Seligman. *The Pagan Tribes of the Nilotic Sudan*, London, Routledge and Kegan, 1965, p.491.

13 Ibid.

14 Op. Cit. Lou narration.

15 Op. Cit. Seligman.

16 Op. Cit. Lou.

17 Op. Cit. Seligman.

18 Ibid.

19 Interview of author with Paulo Dralile Lodu Bigo in Al Diknat, Khartoum on 4-2-1995.

20 Ibid.

21 Interview of author with Azaria Gilo Emilio in El Haj Yousif, Dar Es Salaam, Khartoum North on 16-8-1998.

22 Interview of author with Philip Izama Gobi in Juba on 28-11-1994.

23 Op. Cit. Lou.

24. Op. Cit. Seligman, p.491.

25 Op. Cit. Emilio Interview.

26 Op. Cit. Seligman.

27 Ibid.

28 Ibid. p.490.

29 Op. Cit. Lou interview.

30 Op. Cit. Dralile Interview.

31 Op. Cit. Emilio.

32 Op. Cit. Izama interview.

33 Op. Cit. Nyago and Lou interviews.

34 Op. Cit. Bigo interview. See also Emmanuel Kitchere Gray. *The Catholic Church in Loa*, Khartoum, 1994, p.55.

35 Faladio Abiri of Puceri clan Mugali related this fact to the author in 1983 in Juba.

36 Interview of author with Chief Odoriko Loku Diego of Bori-Opari in Juba on 20-6-2006.

37 Interview of author with John Baru Loku Kuruju in Juba on 13-9-2008.

38 Nalder, F. Leonard. *Equatoria Province Handbook Vol. 1*, Mongalla, 1936, p.8.

39 Interview of author with Erodionne Murulu Jiribi in El Haj Yousif, Khartoum North on 18-4-1995.

40 Elton, Lord. *General Gordon*, London, Collins, 1954, p.159.

41 Op. Cit. Rowley, p.294.

42 Boki, Severino Fuli. *Shaping a Free Southern Sudan, Memoirs of Our Struggle 1934 –1985,* Limuru, 2002, p.28.

Chapter Four

Eastern Sector Chieftainships of Bori-Opari

4.1 Its Borders with other Sectors

The Eastern Sector of the Ma'di Chieftainships of Bori-Opari, lies in the eastern part of Ma'di territory. The whole area is called *Bori* which has two meanings in the Ma'di language. It can mean, 'they are actually two.' *Bo* in Ma'di in this case can mean 'actually so' and *ri* means 'two.' *Bori* can also mean 'forever two' where *bo* is used to denote 'forever' while *ri* stands for 'two' as in the first definition. *Bori* is also the name of a Ma'di clan in the Ugandan part of the tribe[1] and since the Metu clan is found in Bori in Sudan[2] as well as in Moyo on the Ugandan side, one could argue that the name has found its way to this part of Ma'diland through emigrants whose descendants might not be there today. Whatever the case, the name Bo...ri is a typical Ma'di name. The name *Bori* is also used of a section of the Moru group, another Moru-Ma'di speaking people in the Mundri area.

The Opari area of Eastern Sector Chieftainships is surrounded by hills; Mount Adala in the east and Opari hill in the south, and Avulogi in the south-west. Where the Motoyo and Nyakaningwa hills join the Nyatiki ranges in the West the land is called *Opari* which means 'it is completely surrounded' for *opa* in the Ma'di language means 'surrounded' and *ri* means 'completely round.' The hill called Opari itself is so round in shape that the meaning of the name can even apply to it directly because it looks like something encircled. To shed more light on the meaning of names, *Nyakaningwa* in Ma'di means 'a young beast' for *nyaka* is 'a beast,' *ni* means 'of' and *ngwa* means 'a small or young one.' Hence Nyakaningwa stands for 'a small or young beast.' Some people who are unfamiliar with the name Nyakaningwa call it Lakaningwa which is a corruption of the real name. *Avulogi* means 'we have separated the large calabash' for *logi* means 'a large calabash.'[3] The calabash is used for keeping water or beer, the white stuff known as *kpwete*, and *avu* means 'we have separated.' In this instance there could have been several containers of fluids for consumption, perhaps the small calabash known as *kerije*, (a gourd is called in Ma'di *kere*), and the larger calabash, *logi*, containing fluid or if empty might have been separated from other containers. The act of separating the large calabash might have taken place near this hill, which was then named *Avulogi*, that is, 'we have separated the large calabash.'

4.1.1 Geographical location of the Sector

The eastern chieftainships sector is bound in the south by the southern sector chieftainships of Lokai and their border lies north of Mua the old settlement of the Lokai people before their emigration to Ndindi near their present settlement of Mugali. To the south-west of the sector lie the central sector chieftainships of Arapi, Pageri and Nyongwa. Its boundary with the central chieftainships is partly marked by River Eyibi which flows from the north to the south. The western chieftainships of Erepi and the northern sector chieftainships of Moli border it in the west and north-west respectively. The nearest village in the Northern Chieftainships to the Eastern Chieftainships is Mejopadrani (Borokodongo) which lies north-west of Liokwe village. Mejopadrani was renamed Borokodongo in 1932 by Andrea Farajalla of Bari tribe from Juba who was then the senior foreman of Juba-Nimule Road when it was under construction from Juba to Nimule in the period 1928-32.[4] He is said to have been allowed by the Greek road engineer called by the locals 'Mujaranga' to give names to the camps of the road gangs, separated by a distance of seven miles for easy identification. Andrea had given Bari names to thirteen of these camps and in Lulubo areas beginning from Juba up to Mejopadrani. But in Moli he met opposition from Chief Geri Ipele who said the camp could not be given a Bari name which would be foreign since his people were Ma'di. Since that time, the Bari emigrant road maintainers called Work Gang Camp No. 13 'Borokodongo', which name had superseded the original Ma'di name, 'Mejopadrani' which means "I stretch my legs for death." Borokodongo itself, according to some people who know the Bari language, means 'watch behind your head' since you might be attacked from behind. The camp lies in a place where some attackers from the neighbourhood who were hostile, could kill the newcomers from Juba.

To the east and north of the Bori Chieftainship lies Acholiland. The Acholi chieftainship to the north is the land of the Panyikwara, once headed by Chief Paito and in the years after the Addis Ababa Agreement between the Sudan Government (SG) and Southern Sudan Liberation Movement (SSLM), the Anya-Nya, Ambrozio Lado became chief, and he was based in Palabek.[5] To the north-east lies the Obbo Chieftainship of Acholi and in the south-east, it is bound by the Acholi Chieftainship of Parajok. The nearest Acholi village to the Bori Chieftainship in the east is Katire-Ayom where once the American missionaries of the Africa Interior Mission (AIM) had their evangelization centre.

Nyangorac, the local leader of the Dongu clan who moved with some of the members of his clan from Mede near Liokwe to a new site which he named Winyalonga north of the Ma'di village of Pakworo spoke better Acholi than their own language, the Bari.[6] This was because of a long stay among the Acholi Panyikwara people after their flight from Bariland in 1889 to escape from Mahdist attacks following the fall of Emin Pasha's Equatoria to the Mahdist forces commanded first by Omar Salih and later by Emir Arabi Daffallah. Nyangorac and his followers first settled in Mede after their return from Ayipa where they, the Ma'di, the Acholi of Panyikwara and Lulubo had hidden from the Mahdists. In Mede, near Liokwe and Mulungeng villages, the lands had become infertile after prolonged cultivation by a large number of people, and this had forced some members of the Dongu clan to move and settle in a new place north-east of Pakworo, a Ma'di village of Mugi, Lulubo, Patibi and Orobe clans where they could cultivate food crops.[7] In that area of Bori chieftainship (which Nyangorac named *Winyalonga* in Acholi, meaning 'the bird called me' for *winya* in that language is a certain bird and *longa* means 'it calls me') the Dongu clan lived with the clans of Payoko and Pajawu.[8]

4.1.2 Historical Background of Bori Chieftainships

The Eastern Chieftainships were first led by the Logopi clan, one of the first groups to settle in the area. Giving an account of these people in 1851, Father Angelo Vinco, a Catholic priest who explored the area described them as a community who were Ma'di but also spoke Bari because they lived in the Ma'di border area with the Bari.[9] In 1851, Vinco reported that the Logopi chief was Gwandako who refused him his men to accompany him to the Ma'di village of Muruli because the Ma'di were hostile to strangers at that time.[10] It was several years later that the leading chieftainship reverted from the Logopi to Pandikeri when an ancestor of Akeri Milla saved the Logopi chief from impending death in the mud in which he got stuck.[11] Akeri Milla, (some people call him Milla Akeri) had been the most powerful chief among the men of his clan.

The ancestor of the Pandikeri leaders had emigrated from Loringa Parabongo, Olwal south of Attiak in the present Uganda. Although Olwal is in Acholi land in Uganda and lies south-west of Pabbo near Gulu, the Pandikeri leaders emphatically state that they are Ma'di, and their ancestors had emigrated from Opari areas to Olwal as refugees in time immemorial as denoted by their name *loringa* which means 'the people who escaped from somewhere to another place.' They say they escaped from the Ma'di area to the Olwal Parabongo area in Uganda from where they had decided to return home. They say the clan related to them, as recorded in popular songs, are the Padieri who have long since ceased to live in the Opari area.[12] People who knew the history of the Pandikeri clan say they moved to Olwal when the place was close to the

Ma'di of Paloro west of Pabbo before its Ma'di population adopted the Acholi language and culture. When the Catholic missionaries first came to the southern Nile valley, they settled in Paloro among the Ma'di according to their writings and when the explorers John Henning Speke and James Augustus Grant in 1863 came to Paloro they documented that they found its Ma'di inhabitants and tribal leaders well organized.[13] The Ma'di people of Paloro during many years of interaction with the Acholi of Pabbo and other places close to them, adopted the Acholi language and culture and today they are Acholi in all human characteristics. The Ma'di language could be spoken in the neighbourbood of Indriani near Paloro.

The Logopi chief saved from death by Akeri Milla's ancestor who took over from him the rainstones which were the seal of chieftainship was not known, but before him such men as Gwandako, Loro and Awa are believed to have been chiefs of the Logopi clan at different times.[14]

4.1.3 The Chiefs of Bori

From local accounts, the active history of the Pandikeri (Pandiker) chieftainship began with Alimu Chori although the founding father of the clan who got his chieftainship from the Logopi clan of Ma'di is believed to have been Ker (Keri)[15] in whose honour the clan was named. Akeri Milla who became the thirteenth chief in succession after Ker and third after Alimu Chori[16] was regarded as the most powerful of them all. He succeeded his father Andruga[17] the son of Wani. When Alimu Chori was chief, he exerted much influence in the region not only on other Ma'di chieftainships of the southern, central, western and northern sectors but on the neighbouring chieftainships of the Acholi tribe as well.

Alimu Chori befriended Alimo the Acholi chief of Obbo.[18]

The story goes that the two chiefs exchanged visits several times culminating in closer ties between their two peoples as seen in the intermarriages that occurred amongst them and the tranquility that existed between the two communities. Because of the proximity of the Pandikeri chieftainship with the northern sector, chieftainships of Erepi and Moli through which the road from Gondokoro in the north passed to the southern fringes of the Turco-Egyptian Sudan, government influence on the chieftainship was significant. Alimu Chori traded with the agents of the colonial government and acquired rare items such as guns and gun powder in exchange for ivory and animal skins, for instance those of leopards and giraffes. Trade often took him outside his chieftainship, and he sometimes acquired some of the items needed by the Gondokoro traders through his friend Alimo of Obbo, to whom he had supplied a rifle. Alimo was said to have introduced Alimu Chori to the people of Irye in Leruwa for trade purposes.

One day, the two chiefs were said to have taken a gun and some gun powder and cartridges to a notable in the village of Iyire. Upon arrival they were invited into a house and the door of the hut was closed supposedly as a precaution to keep them safe from other men in the village who were always ready to spear to death any stranger who might set foot in their village. Meanwhile the notable told the rest of the villagers to leave the village because they were preparing to kill the visitors and the villagers moved away. By and by Alimu Chori and his friend got killed in Irye leading to reprisal attacks by the Pandikeri people of Ma'di supported by the people of Obbo.[19] This history is preserved in this Pandikeri song.

Mamu ayia aga
Galaka soma mbiri tro
Ori Chori
Amadi Irye iyo

The following is a translation of this short song:

I have gone into the bush
Half burned grass injures me
Son of Chori
We have killed the people of Iyre

4.2 The Logopi Chieftainship

The Logopi clan is one of the oldest groups of Ma'di who have lived in what is called Bori-Opari today for many decades. The large size of the clan has ensured that it has remained separate and safe from assimilation into larger groups, a process which would have resulted in the loss of identity or origin and even language. An example of a stronger and larger group assimilating smaller groups has been cited by Professor Richard Gray of the History Department, University of Khartoum where he states that more than half a dozen smaller groups such as the Pambia, Barambo and others were assimilated by the more powerful, influential and bigger Avongura group of Zande in western Equatoria in the past and it was groups like the Ma'di which resisted assimilation and have survived up to today.[20] Another example is the overlapping of the Ma'di by the Lwoo in parts of northern Uganda when they arrived in the region in a human wave from the north finding the Ma'di were already there. Professor Merrick Posnansky who reports this assimilation of Ma'di by Lwoo, supports his hypothesis with the presence of Ma'di names in areas today occupied entirely by the Lwoo especially the Acholi of Northern Uganda.[21] Names like Ma'di Opei, Ma'di Kiloc and Ma'di Oboke in the Kitgum District of Uganda and others occupied by the Acholi people are typical examples of these areas previously occupied by the Ma'di.

The members of the Logopi clan survived assimilation by the Bari who were their neighbours to the north and north-west. According to the Catholic missionary, Father Angelo Vinco who visited them in 1851[22] after visiting Lafon, (Liful) the land of the Pari (Lokoro) he found the Logopi speaking their original language, Ma'di but they could also speak Bari as a second language. The Logopi land was overlooking Muruli, the largest Ma'di village at the time by far. Muruli was west of the Logopi land. This shows that the villages in which Father Vinco found them were located somewhere near the confluence of the Ame, Afoyi and Iyii (Kit) rivers because if one looks east from Muruli, the area to the east is near the confluence of the three rivers. It is at this point that when one looks west to spot Muruli village which lay south of the Foki Mountain one can visualize the location of the Logopi villages in this area. Over the years, the people have slowly moved southward and built their homes around Opari. From here they have spread out to different parts of Ma'diland reaching up to the present Pageri where their land priest once built his home some meters away from where the present Langauro Market is located while many members of the clan continued to move southward reaching as far away as Mugali where many of them are found today. The majority of the Logopi have remained in the Opari area naming two of the large villages which they have constructed there as Logopi and Logopi Downstream (Logopi Vurule).

Father Angelo Vinco in 1851 found the Logopi people under a

chief called Gwandako.[23] The people and their chief welcomed the priest who later asked the chief to allow some of his young men to accompany him to Muruli, a Ma'di village about which very little was known at the time but the chief refused citing Ma'di hostilities.[24] Because the Logopi chiefs of the past were rainmakers, they rendered rainmaking service to the clans in the areas in which they were settled because not all the Ma'di clans have rainmakers.

In the past, the Logopi people were among the Ma'di who had powerful chieftainships and their chiefs who ruled in succession were based in the precincts of Opari. In their history one of the chiefs who was thought to be Awa, but some people thought was Chief Loro, (their records were poorly kept and orally) lost his chieftainship in a very peculiar way. He got submerged in a quagmire and three hunters from the small Pandikeri clan happened to pass by the edge of the swamp and when they saw the chief, they pulled him out of the mud on condition that he would give him the price that they would demand from him. Since it was a matter of life or death, the Logopi chief conceded to give any price if they would save his life. It was then that the three men pulled the chief out of the mud and demanded his chieftainship which he gave to the most senior member of the trio.

Due to a lack of written records, the genealogy of the Logopi chiefs cannot be credibly presented like most clans of the Ma'di in South Sudan but they had powerful chiefs and a huge population whose contributions to the welfare of the Ma'di people in Opari have made the area an important segment of Ma'diland. The known chiefs of the past were Gwandako, Awa and Loro. The shift of the powerful leadership of Logopi to a smaller Pandikeri clan, although it took place several decades ago, still haunts the Logopi people and impacts negatively on the present generation.

When I was discussing the important aspects of Ma'di history with some educated members of the tribe while preparing for the Kit meeting of September 4, 2008, to discuss border contests in Kit among the four tribes: Acholi, Bari, Ma'di and Lulubo, an elderly man from Logopi clan drew my attention to a song which was sung about the transfer of leadership to the Pandikeri by their chief. This is the one who was submerged in a quagmire and when he was rescued by three Pandikeri hunters, he had to surrender his goatskin bag in which the rainstones were kept and carried along whenever the chief was on the move, to the leader of the Pandikeri hunters who saved his life as compensation.

Part of this song of regret is as follows:

> *Anyindre juru karunyo ama eyi*
> *Awa ama ciri ree*
> *Oto oteko*
> *Ayi bazi karunyo ama eyi si*
> *Loro ama vulega ree*
> *Oto oteko*

Translation of this song goes like this:

> *Look foreigners are proud because of our rains*
> *Awa we the young people*
> *Will not be submerged in quagmire*
> *Watch others are being proud of our rain*
> *Loro we who are behind here*
> *Will not be swallowed by mud*

4.3 The Pandikeri Chieftainship

Akeri Milla whom other people call Milla Akeri distinguished himself as the strongest Ma'di chief of his time. The counting of the lineage of chiefs of Bori (Opari) from the Pandikeri clan began from Ker, believed to have been the first chief, to Dari Kanyara Isara, the fifteenth chief in succession.[25] That they emigrated from Loringa Parabongo of Acholi located south-west of Pabbo trading centre in Northern Uganda, is contained in the Bori legendary stories. The reasons for Ker and his group's flight from Loringa Parabongo are unknown. Many elders of Pandikeri and other clans believe that they were an offshoot of the Ma'di group who trekked south-westward in long antiquity. They might have even fled, for Loringa, the name they gave to the place which they inhabited in Uganda indicates that they were refugees in the area, for *loringa* translated from the Acholi language could mean "the ones who run away"[26] or "those who fled." Some people further say that this group was from the Ma'di tribe who ran from what is today Southern Sudan towards the south-west and settled in what is today northern Uganda. When they thought the factors which caused their ancestors to flee from Ma'diland were no longer present, they decided to return, tracking the route which they had previously taken back to the Bori-Opari area.

In his study of the Ma'di, J.V. Rowley, the British colonial administrator advanced the theory that Ker might have been lured by Pitya Lugor of Bari to be his ally in a fight against another group, but they later disagreed forcing Ker to seek the protection of the Ma'di people.[27] On their return, some settled on the way in a place called Abolkodi north of Attiak and their descendants are found there today. When the group that proceeded north-eastward reached the Acca banks near the present Mugali they continued their journey and came to Bori-Opari where they joined the Padieri clan of the Ma'di. Before arrival in Bori-Opari, the Pandikeri elders, who are conversant with their local history, say their ancestors had briefly settled around the hot springs east of the Atapi-Acca confluence. Here although they brought along their rainstones, they did not influence other peoples with their power of rainmaking because these were insignificant. In fact, Ker joined the Padieri and other clans as a commoner,[28] but he was a good hunter and used to go hunting with the men of the clan. At the time, the leadership in Bori was said to be firmly in the hands of the Logopi, a Ma'di clan. That the Logopi had their own chieftainship was first documented by Father Angelo Vinco of the Catholic Church after his tour of the land adjoining southern Bari in 1851.[29] At the time, Logopi was a large Ma'di group who spoke both Ma'di and Bari. That they forgot to speak Bari completely may be because in the years that followed 1851, when Father Angelo Vinco discovered them, they had completely integrated into their tribe and today they are found deep within the Ma'diland stretching from Bori-Opari to Mugali. At the time of Father Vinco's visit, the Logopi as reported by him were led by a chief called Gwandako and were in very close proximity to the Bari.[30]

In his account, Father Vinco said that when he asked Chief Gwandako to give him some strong men to accompany him to Muruli in the neighbouring land of the Ma'di, the chief refused to do so saying that his subjects would not be safe because the Ma'di were a hostile people.[31] Father Vinco wanted to go to Muruli which was then a Ma'di centre of great influence untouched by colonial administration which dominated the neighbouring tribes to the north. That the Logopi clan in the past might have been in close contact with the Bari can be ascertained from the common honorific title 'Nya Bari' that their women utter in the event of a sudden occurrence such as the fall of a pot accidentally from the head of a woman, making a sharp noise or after the noise of dry firewood when it is broken into two or more pieces.

The chieftainship in Bori-Opari changed hands between the clans of Logopi and that of Pandikeri, shifting from the former to the latter. The actual Bori clan that welcomed and integrated the Ma'di returnees from the Loringa Parabongo, Olwal north-west of Gulu in Uganda was Padieri, which on assumption of the chieftainship from the Logopi clan was renamed Pandikeri in honour of Ker who assumed the Logopi chieftainship.

4.4 Chief Akeri Milla, His Life and Times

Akeri Milla was the son of Andruga of the Pandikeri clan from his Acholi (Panyikwara) wife called Nyajele Joloko from Pajomo clan.[32] He was probably born in the first quarter of the nineteenth century in a village under Mount Adala which lies east of the present Opari trading centre. Some people call him Milla Akeri. But my paternal grandmother, Idreangwa Nya'agwele told me that her cousin brother was called Akeri Milla. Agwele the father of Idreangwa was the son of Koka who and Akeri Milla were the sons of Andruga. The Pandikeri leaders became protectors of the Ma'di people and land as demonstrated by Chief Akeri Milla when he led them away from the attacks of the Mahdists to safety in Acholiland of Parajok in the east.[33] From Ker to Opira who was the ninth chief in succession, their names were of Acholi ie Opira, Opoka and other names such as Jumon sounded like a name of Alur, another Lwoo group to their west when they were still in Loringa Parabongo, Olwal south-west of Pabbo in the present

Uganda. But beginning with Alimu through Wani, Andruga, Akeri Milla, Mene and going down to Jibi, Kanyara, Vumudri they were all called Ma'di names.[34]

As stated above, Rowley suggested in his writing that Ker was an Acholi chief from Parabongo, Olwal in the present Uganda brought to the Ma'di area in the present South Sudan by a Bari chief called Lugeir, possibly Lugor, as an ally to fight the neighbouring tribes.[35] But a quarrel broke out between the two men leading to their separation while Ker decided to remain in the new place. But considering their spread across a large area stretching from Abolokodi in Northern Uganda to Bori-Opari, the Pandikeri elders argue that they were originally Ma'di who had escaped to the Acholi area, hence their name *Loringa Parabongo*. They fled to save themselves from dangers which threatened their ancestors and because of this they had trekked back to the Ma'di area of Bori which is their original home after the return of calm. *Loringa* in the Acholi language means 'someone who is a refugee.' Ex-police sergeant Ezekiel Longa, a grandson of Andruga, Chief Akeri Milla's father said the history of his people that he had learned from his father is that they are Ma'di by origin and had run to the Acholi area in Uganda for safety hence *Loringa* Parabongo, Olwal. An educated member of the Pandikeri clan, Samuel Okomi, the son of Jibi, also known as Lakilonyi, who was a cousin of Akeri Milla, used to address people at the families' occasions of the Pandikeri and people related to them through marriages, that they are pure Ma'di and the Acholi language which their forefathers brought along to Bori from Loringa Parabongo, Olwal was the language of refuge which they learned in Uganda. It is said that when Ker and his followers joined the Padieri clan of Ma'di, they were not discriminated against because it is the tradition of the Ma'di people to welcome people who have come to join them in a peaceful way. The Pandikeri clan was one of the subject clans and the chieftainship of the area at the time was with the Logopi clan.

Ker was said to have assumed the chieftainship of the Logopi chief after saving him from death because he got stuck in a bog. Since that time the group had brought chieftainship to the Pandikeri clan and renamed *Lobode*, the Logopi powerful rain shrine *Jurubende*. *Juru* in Ma'di means 'foreign'[36] and *bende* means 'deep' hence *Jurubende* refers to the entrance of another clan from far deep into the chieftainship of another clan. However, the Pandikeri insist that they are Ma'di and that in antiquity their ancestors fled due to external threats to Olwal Parabongo, the previous land which they occupied somewhere south-west of the present Opari hence their name *loringa* which in Acholi language means 'refugees' and that they returned home because the situation was calm. My paternal grandmother Sarah Idreangwa Nya'Agwele, the daughter of Agwele, who was the grandson of Androga, Akeri Milla's father from his son Koka, explained to me in 1974 that her people, the Pandikeri are Ma'di by origin and had been forced out of the Bori-Opari area by external forces and sought refuge in Olwal, Parabongo in Uganda. On their return to the Bori-Opari area, being newcomers, their leadership was not fully recognized at first after the chieftainship shifted to them from the Logopi clan until they proved to be real protectors of their subjects who are the Ma'di people. Because the transfer of leadership from Logopi to Pandikeri was done in isolation without the knowledge of the many other clans in Bori-Opari, it took some time before the new leadership becomes popular. Eventually the Pandikeri leadership became popular.

Major Chauncy Hugh Stigand, former Governor of Mongalla

Province during his tour of the Lado Enclave following its restoration to Sudan by the Belgian monarchy in 1910 (after the death of King Leopold II of Belgium in 1909) discovered that most of the tribes in the region had community leaders or chiefs who had emigrated from neighbouring clans or other tribes.[37] This is one of the characteristics of civilizations. Even the Acholi of Padibe in northern Uganda believe that, if not their chief Ogwaki perhaps his father, was from the Ma'di clan called Pamotto who today live in Nimule and Loa, Melekwe in South Sudan. That is why his son Lasuto Obol used to come to the Pamotto people in Nimule and Loa, Melekwe to consult them about some rituals connected with childbirth and naming, because in Padibe many of their offspring used to die shortly after birth. It was thought that the rituals they performed might not be what their traditions required.[38] After Obol received the advice of Konide Lomeda, the notable of the Pamotto in Melekwe, concerning the performance of birth rites as required of a Pamotto family, the children in Padibe survived.[39]

Akeri Milla became a prominent chief in Bori during the administration of the Turco-Egyptians from 1821 to 1885. Oral history of the Ma'di people asserts that he was a chief to be reckoned with. Slavery was not widespread in his domain, and he did not allow many porters (swalini) to be drawn from his chieftainship to carry the plunder of the Turks to Gondokoro and other posts.[40] Akeri Milla also resisted the misbehavior of the Mahdists and lost their trust. They went to open war with him forcing him to leave his headquarters in Bori in about 1889 and to seek refuge with his subjects and with those who sought his protection in Acholiland. He died in 1910 when Bori, the land of his chieftainship was still under the administration of the Uganda Protectorate.[41]

4.5 How the Logopi Chieftainship Shifted to the Pandikeri Clan

The transfer of the chieftainship in Bori from the Logopi clan of Ma'di to Pandikeri was reported to have occurred in this way:[42] One day, the Logopi chief led the men of his village to a swamp to recover his biggest cow that supplied him with a lot of milk and gave birth to several calves, which had become stuck in a bog at the edge of a small lake. This stagnant pool has been formed in the south-east of Opari by River Atapi which had not yet broken the banks of the lake and poured into River Acca. The lake was just a few miles from the present confluence of River Atapi with River Acca near Nimule before it joins the latter. When the chief's followers declined to get into the mud to pull the cow out for fear of becoming stuck themselves, the chief himself risked doing so and he too got submerged in the mud. His people tried to rescue him by pulling him out using the coarse rope of a hunting net (*voi ni ongoli*) thrown to him to hold onto, but they failed to pull him out and then just gathered around him not knowing what to do next. Another version said after their failure to pull the chief out of the mud, they got tired and decided to leave for home despite a plea to them from their chief not to leave him in the wilderness to die alone.

After the men had gone home there came three hunters from the Pandikeri area. The most senior among these men was thought to be Ker, an ancestor of Akeri Milla. When they saw the Logopi chief in the mud, the senior of them asked him, "Chief, what are you doing over there in the mud?" The chief replied, "As you can see, I am stuck. I was trying to rescue my cow which you also see is stuck in the mud, but I failed and got stuck in the mud myself." He added that his people were nearby, and they tried to get him out but failed and had gone home leaving him behind in the bush to die alone. The man thought for awhile and then asked, "What will you give me if my two companions and I get you out of the mud?" "If you will get me out of this danger, I have my beautiful daughter whom I shall give to you as a wife," said the chief. "Your beautiful girl as a wife!" exclaimed Ker. "Why should we waste our time just for a beautiful girl while there are so many beautiful girls in the country?" the man replied to the chief. "Why, I can open for you my kraal so that you can drive out as many or all the cattle in it as you like," promised the chief. "Cattle! We have plenty in our kraal at home. We cannot waste our time for mere animals," said the leader of the group. "I promise to you that I shall give you whatever you will ask from me if you get me out of this danger," the chief pleaded. Immediately Akeri Milla's ancestor and his two companions set out to get the Logopi chief out of danger. They walked to a nearby thicket and cut a fleshy plant called *uno* in Ma'di and brought it to where they could see the chief clearly. They tied the plant's end in the shape of a large circle and threw it to the chief instructing him to push it down to his armpits and to hold it tightly with his hands while they would pull him. The chief did as he was instructed, and the three men pulled and pulled till the chief was out of the sticky mud thus saving him from death. The men after getting the chief out threw the fleshy plant at the cow's neck below the horns, struggled with the animal and finally pulled it out too. Then they accompanied the chief to his home to get their prize for saving his life.

In the large village of the chief his subjects who had failed to save him had come and were having a good time with their families. When they saw their chief in the company of the three strangers, they streamed out from their houses to greet them. Then the chief asked the head of the men who saved him to declare his prize for saving his life so that he could give it with honour before his subjects. "You offered me your most beautiful daughter as a wife, but I turned the offer down. Then you wanted to give me half or all the cattle in your kraal and I turned that offer down. Then you promised to give me whatever I shall ask from you, and you will honour my demand. Now it is my turn to present that demand," said the man with everybody around listening and the Logopi people were wondering what this prize would be. "Declare your demand and I shall honour it as I promised to you before my subjects to witness," said the chief when the man hesitated a little. "I want the goatskin bag which you are constantly carrying along so that I can become powerful like you are," declared the man. The chief without any hesitation handed his bag full of rainstones to the man who saved his life thus ending his chieftainship which was based on rainmaking. He told his astonished fellow Logopi people that their chieftainship from that day had come to an end because it was given to the Pandikeri clan due to their failure to save his life. Their rainstones called *Lobode* meaning 'full of a large clay pot' would no longer be theirs but belong to the Pandikeri clan. Power in Bori will no longer be of the Logopi people but of the Pandikeri clan. Since then, the Logopi have had no chieftainship because a chief must be a man who is able to make rain fall. The Logopi people became the subjects of the Pandikeri chief till this day.

The Pandikeri renamed the rain pebbles which they have received from the Logopi chief *Jurubende*. *Juru* in Ma'di means 'foreign' and *bende* in the same language means 'big' or 'great' or 'very deep'. The Logopi had called their rainstones *Lobode* meaning in Ma'di 'full of a big baking clay pot'. The Pandikeri who had acquired a new power had changed the name of the clan to Pandikeri after their chief 'Ker' who must have been the man who took over the Logopi chieftainship. When he and a small party of followers came to Bori from the lands in the south, they were warmly welcomed by the members of the Padieri clan of the Ma'di who lived there. It is the custom of the Ma'di people to receive and accord newcomers sanctuary who are seeking solace or freedom.

This custom is even recognized by foreigners. For example, J. P. Crazzolara, the Italian researcher who once observed that during the Lwoo migrations, a straggling group came from Wipari and joined the Pugari (Pageri) people at Liful and there they were well received, and they settled alongside the Pugari.[43] These Pugari people are thought by Crazzolara to be a group of Ma'di who are called Pageri and that the Pari called them *minde athum* meaning 'people who are carrying bows and arrows as weapons' unlike the traditional weapons, the spears, of the Pari.[44]

In the late 1960's during the Anya-Nya war, some Logopi elders asked the council of chiefs led by Odoriko Loku Diego Mude to make the Pandikeri hand back their chieftainship, but the council rejected this request on the ground that the shift of traditional leadership from Logopi to Pandikeri was by mutual agreement between the two clans and they alone should solve it. Upon failing to resolve the issue themselves, they could then involve leaders of other clans in Bori to help.[45] Writer J. V Rowley who was the District Commissioner first of Opari and later of Torit, under whose administration Loa local government No. 1 in which Opari fell gave a string of names of Chief Akeri Milla's ancestors from Ker to Dari Kanyara Isara who was in power in 1937, the year he conducted his research. But he did not state among these men who had assumed the leadership for the Pandikeri clan in Bori from the Logopi clan. At the time of his research, Dari was the chief in the lineage of the Pandikeri clan and this was in 1937.[46]

Fig. 1: Chief Odoriko Loku Diego of Bori - Opari Chieftainship in 2008 (with his courtesy)

4.6 Brief Histories of Other Clans in Bori
4.6.1 The Ngaya (Paibonga) Clan of Bori

The man all members of Paibonga clan know as their leader, who brought them into contact with the Ma'di clan of Pambili under the leadership of Bire, was Sokiri Yuggu, the father of Lotikaro in Kugi forest north-west of Bori-Opari. According to Chief Saulo Obaloker Yugu, their ancestor had led them into Ma'diland from Bari. He said his father Lotikaro was the first to be appointed by Mene, the chief of the Pandikeri in Bori to be a sub-chief, or *mukungu* for the Ngaya people.[47] When Lotikaro was too old to continue as sub-chief, he handed the sub-chieftainship to his son Iyiali, otherwise known as Kenyi, who in turn gave it to another member of the clan called Logulu who served barely six months and returned the leadership to Iyiali who in turn gave it to a female member of the clan called Foni Nya Lei (Foni daughter of Lei) who became a *mukungu* the first woman ever to do so in Opari district. As a woman, Foni did not get the respect she needed as sub-chief from the men folk who discriminated against her and so she decided to give power to Yugu whom she brought from Palabek in Uganda for the purpose. Foni introduced Yugu to Mene the chief of Bori from the Pandikeri clan who assigned him the duty of *mukungu*. Yugu did not spend a long time as a sub-chief and gave power to Jameson Amune who gave it to Yugu Iyiali who in turn handed it over to Arunye Adok. From him Jameson Amune assumed it again before Adok took it over during the Anya-Nya movement. When the author asked why the members of Ngaya clan were not stable in sub-chieftainship as clearly indicated by their not holding the seat for longer periods, Saulo Obaloker Yugu said he thought the position of sub-chief might not have been attractive to them. He himself assumed power as *mukungu* in 1986 and later he was elected chief in the 'B' Court building in Torit.

4.6.2 Leadership lineages of Ngaya (Pibonga), Pambili Clans

Saulo Obaloker, a member of the section of Paibonga clan which broke off from the main body in Bari, said the group later called itself Ngaya which in Acholi means 'bitter grain to swallow', the grain being a kind of sorghum called *igi* and that the group believes it cannot be defeated in battles.[48] They say they were not beaten in fighting by the Acholi Ayom when they joined the

Pambili people of Ma'di in their war with the Acholi Ayom.⁽⁴⁹⁾

The lineage of the Pambili family from the time the members of the two clans came into contact in Kugi plain in northern Bori can be counted from: Mbili to Bire then Longa Itoke to Vuga (Loreng), from Kajacu to Jala Bakhiet and Sabuni Bari to Ajjugo son of Jala to Philipo Olaa Okire to Onesimo Vuni Longa, who is alive and performs *oyaya*, the land ritual. Today the Pambili clan is mainly found in Male in south-west Bori where they have moved from Kugi plain. Their village was Liokwe north of Opari trading centre.

Saulo says the Pambili did not use to eat cattle meat because they feared that they would die when they did so. They had some cattle and when one of these died, they would bury it. They began to taste the meat of a bull when one day an animal of a Paibonga man died and he and his relatives cut the meat into large pieces and boiled it. When the meat was still in the boiling pot on the fire, Mbili was said to have come with members of his family around to know why the meat was being cooked. They were told that it was food and on hearing this they were alarmed because they had always believed that cattle meat was poison. When Ibonga and members of his family ate the meat, the next morning Mbili and his relatives came to check whether they were still alive. On seeing them, Ibonga told them that he was fine and did not even have bad dreams. So Mbili and his relatives became convinced that cattle meat was after all not harmful and so they participated in eating the portion that was left by the Ibonga family for the next day. Thereafter the Pambili people ate cattle meat just like any other people.

In the meantime, the Paibonga, Pabala and Pambili clans joined together to have a sizeable group in northern Bori that the other clans joined. The language they speak is Ma'di because even those who came from Bari learned to speak it from the Pambili clan members.[50] As for the Ngaya people who joined them according to Saulo Obaloker, the distant ancestor was Ibonga who brought his followers to Pambili area in the present Kugi forest north-west of Bori. The group was from Bari. The great grandfather of the present Ngaya of Ma'di tribe he said was Iyiali. The name itself means 'deep water' in Ma'di language for *iyi* is 'water' and *ali* is 'deep'. His son was Lotikaro. When they arrived in the Pambili area with Lojobi as their leader, they were constantly attacked by Acholi of Ayom clan and Koyo of Agoro who used spears. The Pambili used *lobwote* (mud balls) for counter attacking, and as a result they were heavily depopulated.[51]

"Today there are very few members of the Pambili clan because most of them have been killed by Acholi Ayom and Agoro warriors before our ancestors joined them many years ago," lamented Saulo. "Members of the Paibonga clan came and helped them fight the enemies using bows and arrows thus making the enemies to run away. The Acholi Ayom were chased by the Ngaya up to Mount Mugo and they continued running up to Mount Banda. This is the history of our people." Saulo said the dances of the Ngaya were *kore* and *gayi*, the same dances that the Ma'di dance. That the Ngaya once lived in the northern part of Kugi plain which lies between Moli Tokuro and Bori-Opari was revealed to the author by Lazaro Yugu Lotikaro who was a senior staff clerk in the Ministry of Culture and Information in Juba in 1976. The author was then a broadcaster at Radio Juba.

4.7 The Dongu Clan

The Ma'di call them Dongu while in Bari they are known as Dong. This is the largest of the Bari clans who left their original homes in Southern Bari in places called Nyokir and Gumosi seeking the protection of Chief Akeri Milla of the Pandikeri clan of Bori from the Mahdists who had occupied the northern part of Equatoria Province selecting Rejaf as their headquarters in 1888. From the dispersion at Ayipa, the Dongu on their way back home in Nyokir and Gumosi passed through what is now called Winyalonga. This place is within Ma'di territory but falls somewhere near the border of the Ma'di with the Acholi of Katire Ayom.[(52)] A Ma'di who speaks the Acholi language told the author that the name means 'the bird calls me' for in that language, *winya* is a kind of bird and *longa* means 'calls me'. Winyalonga was founded by Nyangorac, an elderly man from the Dongu clan who first settled in Mede and left to establish Winyalonga because it lies in fertile land good for cultivation. His fellow Dongu settled down beside him for some years with the intention of continuing their journey to Bariland later. But due to conditions conducive to living and several other social issues such as marriages to Ma'di and Acholi wives, and their own daughters married to members of the two tribes, many of these Bari decided to remain there and in other parts of Opari Chieftainships till today. Those who settled closer to the Acholi speak better Acholi and the few who built their homes near the Ma'di speak better Ma'di than any other language. But most have forgotten their Bari language and they can only be referred to as Bari because of their origin. Some of the Dongu people who left their kinsmen and women behind and set off for Nyokir never reached their destination and settled on the way. It is said that very few who felt homesick reached their original land. Some of them settled in Liokwe where they found some Ma'di clans. Drongwa Musukani, a Dongu elder who became a headman for his people built his home in Nyajogi near Ogwariregege the original place where the Bari group of Paibonga found the Pambili, the Ma'di clan and became Ngaya. Another group of Dongu which went ahead reached a Ma'di village called Mejopadrani where they found members of Logili, Mugi Kolowa, Gunyia and Dedi clans of the Ma'di and decided to settle there short of reaching their homeland which was not far away from there. There was also a gang of road repairers of the Public Works Department (PWD) who lived in camp No.13, and they were mainly from Logopi and Ngaya clans and some Bari men brought from Juba.[53] This camp was named Borokodongo by Andrea Farajalla, the road foreman who accompanied the Greek road engineer who was nicknamed Mujaranga in 1928-32 from Juba. The original name of this Ma'di village is Mejopadrani. The Dongu families who settled near the PWD Camp No.13 were those of Kaconi Paulo, Jakalia Lodu, Titifano Tombe, Yokano and Ben Lado and others. From here these Dongu elders used to pay visits to their relatives in Southern Bari and return to their new homes in Borokodongo. The relatives too used to visit them and went back to Nyokir.

During their five-year stay among the Ma'di and Acholi people, the Dongu interacted socially with members of these communities through marriages. For example, Leju the son of Mori Jote a prominent member of the Dongu clan went to Ayipa as a young man. He married Moria Nya Bande of Pajawu clan of Ma'di while in Ayipa. Their son Lodu Bilal, the maternal grandfather of the author married Ossa Eriani of Paluda clan of the Ma'di in Aduro-Muruli part of Moli. Their daughter was Rita Keji the mother of the author. Also, Geri Ipele, the Ma'di chief from Logili clan of Moli married Juru Nya Leju of Dongu clan and their son Akeri Geri later succeeded his father as chief in about 1933.[54] Akeri died in 1986 in his Garamu home in Moli Tokuro. Many other Dongu men married from Acholi while men from other clans married from their womenfolk making them more attached to these communities than to their own kinsfolk back home in Nyokir, Southern Bari. That made their return home not a priority.

4.8 Ayipa

When the Ma'di people of several clans led by Chief Akeri Milla of the Pandikeri clan fled Bori, their first place of refuge from the Mahdist forces who were based in Rejaf, was the land of the Acholi Parajok.[55] The chief of Parajok was Ochieng Anyodo, who having known Akeri Milla a long time, decided to show him an area near the Parajok villages of Ayaci for settlement of the refugees whom Milla led. Among the many Ma'di clans who accompanied Chief Akeri Milla from Bori to Parajok those from Moli included the Mugi, Logili, Ukeyi, Nyai, Pakoli, Kiloloro, Gonyapi, Lulubo and Ijupi. Those from Erepi included Tedire, Afodo, Patibi, Mugi, Ukeyi, Paluda and Gonyapi and the clans from Arapi included Palungwa, Palinyi, Adavu, Cera, Pa-Akori, Urugu, Kamia. The clans from Bori itself included the Pandikeri, Logopi, Gonyapi, Patibi, Payoko, Nyongwa, Beka, Mugi, Ukeyi, Tedire, Logili, Lulubo, Jeru, Metu, Ndogo, Pambili etc. Besides the Ma'di clans, more than one clan of the Bari, the main one being the Dongu also fled their homeland in Nyokir in southern Bariland due to the Mahdist threat and joined the great trek led by Chief Akeri Milla to Parajok.[56]

Acholi of Panyikwara from which Nyajele Joloko, the mother of Akeri Milla hailed and some clans of the Lulubo-Aru tribe also joined Milla's people in their trek to safety from the Mahdist threat. The refugees had many goats, sheep and some cattle and drove them along the way to Parajok. One of the reasons why the

Mahdist forces raided the tribal areas was for their animals which they needed for food. They also wanted to capture as slaves the young men and women. While the Parajok chief Ochieng Anyodo had shown hospitality to Chief Akeri Milla and the refugees, the ordinary Parajok people were apprehensive of the presence of a large population of strangers in their midst. They feared that these refugees though still exhausted by their flight first from their original abodes to Bori and then from there to Parajok would eventually recover from their long journey and present a great threat to their existence. The Parajok people were also envious of the animal wealth the refugees possessed. So, they met secretly and decided to attack and kill the refugees. But before they could put their plan into action, they sent representatives to their chief to tell him of their planned attack. The chief was very alarmed to learn of this appalling plan and he asked his subjects through their representatives not to carry out the attack until he had consulted with Chief Akeri Milla so that he could immediately take his followers back to Bori from whence they had come. Indeed, the Acholi chief was very serious and went to meet Chief Akeri Milla and told him of the decision of his people.[57]

4.9 The Loss of Refugees' Animal Wealth in Ayaci, Parajok

Milla said it was very unfortunate that the residents of Parajok had planned to do such a dreadful deed, and as for his involvement, he could only hope that they did not carry out their plan for he had no power to stop them and left the entire matter in the hands of the Parajok chief Ochieng Anyodo. However, he entreated the Acholi chief to tell his people not to kill the settlers who were ready to move away from their settlements near Ayaci and go westward towards Bori. The latter said he would try to persuade his subjects to drop their plan. When Chief Ochieng Anyodo met with his anxious people who were ready to attack and kill the refugees, he told them that he had come to a compromise with Chief Akeri Milla and that was to let the refugees leave the vicinity of Parajok and move further away to an uninhabited area which lay north-west of Parajok and settle there. This was Ayipa. When the people heard this, they softened their position but told their chief that since they had sharpened their spears for their planned attack, they should be allowed to use their weapons to kill the numerous goats, sheep and cattle of the refugees. Furthermore, if they were to abandon their murderous scheme, they insisted that on the day of slaughtering the animals no settler should be outside his dwelling, otherwise he or she would be speared together with the animals.[58]

The Parajok chief thought this was a better proposition than killing the people and he consented to it but said he would take the message to Chief Milla first so that the refugees did not react violently in defence of their animal wealth. When the Parajok chief told Akeri Milla of the new demands of his people, Milla felt distressed but there was nothing he could do and warned the settlers against trying to protect their animals lest they be killed. He told the Parajok chief that he would instruct the refugees through their community leaders to remain indoors when the Acholi spearmen came to slay their goats, sheep and cattle en masse. And indeed, the following day, the Acholi warriors with their spears slaughtered almost all the sheep, goats and the few cattle of the refugees. The refugees were overcome by sadness and awe following the loss of their animal wealth. The men among them could have reacted unfavourably by taking up their spears, bows and arrows and facing the Parajok warriors but they feared that such action could escalate and lead to mass killing of their vulnerable womenfolk, the elderly people and children who were within easy reach of the Parajok. The refugees said the jediya (jihaddiya) were to blame for all this loss for they had chased them and placed them in this bleak situation.

Severino Fuli's account of the event has it that the Acholi Parajok people had marked out the Arapi clans for slaying and not all the Ma'di clans who had sought refuge in their land.[59] He also says it was the domestic animals of the same people which were killed by the Acholi Parajok, and this followed the spell of a witch doctor.

But other narrators of the history of this event, among them Rev. Archbishop Nikalao Oling Andrea, son of Bishop Andrea Vuni Wale said all the refugees were targeted because after the killing of their animals, all the refugees left Ayaci and followed Chief Akeri Milla to their new settlement in Ayipa en masse.[60]

After the Parajok people killed the animals of the settlers, Milla told the refugees that they had been offered Ayipa as a settlement destination by the Parajok Chief Ochieng. So Akeri Milla hurriedly led the settlers to Ayipa, west of Parajok and south of Obbo, for safety. *Ayipa* in Ma'di language means 'a large swathe of grassland' for *ayi* means 'grass' and *pa* means 'large or spread out'. Some people think that *Ayipa* stands for the hill that rises in this grassland, others the vast plain of extensive grass itself. The plain in which the small hill called Ayipa stands, lies between Rivers Ayii and Atapi and is a stretch of fertile land.

When the settlers built their homes round this hill, they dug deep ditches round their homes to prevent nightly and daylight attacks by some Parajok and Obbo intruders. Some of these ditches are still there as historical monuments.[61] It was in Ayipa that Akeri Milla got news of the defeat of the Mahdists by the joint British and forces of the Free Congo State and their total withdrawal from Bor where they had entrenched themselves under the command of Emir Arabi Daffallah close to Equatoria. The unified force which fought the dervishes of the Mahdists in their last stronghold of Bor was commanded by Lt. Col Martyr, a British officer from the Uganda Protectorate.[62]

Following this turn of events Milla gathered the community leaders of the settlers together at his home in Ayipa and told them that they should return to their original homes because the danger that had forced them to flee no longer existed. It is not known how many years the refugees had spent in Ayipa. But some elderly men and women recalling what their parents had told them, are of the opinion that the people settled here for about three summers, *ayi na* meaning 'three cultivation seasons,' which is three years. The sites where they built their huts were surrounded by ditches dug as defensive measures to prevent enemy attacks during the hours of darkness. At nightfall the wood which served as foot bridges during the day was drawn back and only put down again in the morning when the refugees went out to fetch essential items such as firewood and water from the surrounding forest and nearby streams. Ditches were employed instead of building a stockade (known in Ma'di as *kiri*) because the latter involved cutting and collection of a special kind of wood called *poyi*. Another reason for resorting to ditches was that they were quick and easy to dig, the settlement in Ayipa being temporary.

When it was determined for certain that the threat that forced the people from their original homes no longer existed, Chief Akeri Milla gathered together all the heads of families and famously said: "You the people of Moli, you the people of Erepi, you the people of Nyongwa, you the people of Arapi, you the Bari people, you the Lulubo people, you the Acholi of Panyikwara, and you my people of Bori. I have gathered reliable information that the Jihadiyya who were the cause of our flight from our homes have left Rejaf and there is no longer any threat to our lives and the few properties in your possession. We can now leave Ayipa and go to our original homes through Bori my home where you first got me."[63] This was in about 1898. Each head of community thanked Milla for his leadership and courage in keeping them safe despite the dangers to which they were subjected in Acholiland and wished him long life. After this all the people returned to their original home areas.

Akeri Milla back to Bori
Chief Akeri Milla and his family left Ayipa and built a temporary home in Borimvuku on the southern foot of Mount Adala. Before he could move his headquarters back to the present Opari, he sent his aide, Wale of Beka clan and father of Bishop Andrea Vuni on reconnaissance to Bori instructing him to take a he-goat along and tie it to a pole in the bush at Nyakaningwa hill where he intended to build his permanent home.[64] *Nyakaningwa* is a Ma'di name which means 'a small one of a wild cat'; *nyaka* means 'a wild cat' and *ni* means 'of', while *ngwa* means 'a young one'. Wale did as he was instructed by Milla and tied the animal to a small tree and left it there for the night. He went to a small hill which lies west of the spot where the Opari district headquarters was later built and spent the night on the slope of the hill. In the morning, he went to check the goat he had tied to a tree and found that it had not been killed by a beast although the place was infested with leopards and hyenas. He reported the favourable outcome to Chief Akeri Milla

who immediately gave orders to his subjects to transfer his home and the rain pebbles called *Jurubende*, the tokens of his power, to Nyakaningwa. About 1900, most Ma'di clans who were in transit left their temporary homes in Bori (Opari) and headed towards their original homes in Moli, Erepi, Nyongwa, Pageri, Patibi and Arapi leaving those clans who were originally in Bori settling in their ancestral home areas.

Milla and the refugees settled in Ayipa in about 1892, three years after their flight from Bori. They constructed huts and dug trenches round them to keep off night attackers from the neighbouring Acholi of Obbo and even Acholi of Parajok some of whom still used to come to kill people unexpectedly.[65] Today the trenches dug by the Ma'di and other refugees to ward off night or unexpected daytime attacks exist as the historic monument of the flight to Parajok during the Mahdiyya era. In fact, the new settlement in Ayipa attracted the attention of the Acholi of Obbo who like the Parajok people became unfriendly. There were reports of mysterious disappearances of people regularly, especially the individuals who went out of the settlement to fetch building materials such as wood, grass, shrubs and fibres as string for tying during the construction of their structures. Others, especially women went out to fetch water for drinking from the rivers and firewood for cooking food.

The great grandfather of the author, Leju Jote from the Dongu clan of Bari tribe was abandoned by his clansmen who feared that they could be subjected to a violent attack by Acholi wayfarers because of the large herd of goats and sheep he was driving from Ayipa to Opari. He was ambushed by some Acholi men and killed, and his large herd of goats and sheep driven away by the attackers.
[66]

4.10 How Male became a Centre for Blacksmiths

Before the construction of Male village there were no blacksmiths (*eremu*) in the Opari area.[67] Today, Male is a prominent centre for the crafting of hand tools and traditional weapons of all kinds. According to local legends, iron working was brought to the village by a certain man called Wani Kireacu and another man called Tuja who were both from Nyori clan and came from Moli.[68] Amono and Ginawi were from Gunyia clan, and they also went to Male from Moli to join the other blacksmiths in their trade. They were followed by Lino Wani and his brother Zozimo Koce from the same clan. There was also Manjamali of Eremu-Weli clan and Cukole the father of Yamba of Mijale clan who were blacksmiths, and they too went there from Moli.[69] These were the men who made Male a famous centre for the production of large quantities of knives, spears, arrows, cutlery and weapon heads.

Among the Ma'di people, blacksmiths were treated with reserve because of the nature of their trade, social interaction with them was restricted and marriages with them were unthinkable. Against this background the song *Anya Ta Ili Ili Ili Ka Ado Idre Bani* (Your knives, knives. What can knives do for people?) became very popular. It was sung by a girl called Acopi from Lokai, Mua who eloped with Obadia son of Ginawi of Gunyia clan. However, he never married her.[70] It was this song that made the Ma'di people change their attitude towards blacksmiths. The words of the song illustrate this point:

> *Anya ta ili ili ili ka ado ide?*
> *Mani oluka Male*
> *Obadia dri lori aa*
> *Anya ta ajju ajju ajju ka ado ide ba ni?*

Male oluka Male
Ori Jala dri mali aa

A literal translation of the song reads as follows:

Your talks about knives, knives, knives
What can knives do for people?
I want to live in Male
Obadia has a lorry
Your talks about spears, spears, spears
What can spears do for people?
After all the son of Jala has wealth

The singer challenges the people who harbour adverse attitudes towards blacksmiths, to think about the role of knives and spears in the community. And despite the taboo that ordinary members of the Ma'di community should not marry daughters of these tradesmen or get married to their sons, she as an ordinary member of the tribe is determined to live in Male with a husband from within the blacksmithing community. Moreover, her suitor Obadia has acquired a lorry from the profit of his trade.

4.11 Villages of Bori-Opari, past and present

There are several villages in Bori-Opari and the main ones are the following:

1- Borimvuku

This is a village in which members of Pandikeri clan live. It was where Chief Akeri Milla's home was built after his return from refuge in Ayaci (Parajok) and then Ayipa.

2- Pakworo
Pakworo village is where the members of Lulubo, Mugi, Patibi, Orobe clans live.

3- Nyakaningwa
This village accommodates the Christian mission, first the Church Missionary Society (CMS) whose pastor was Rev. Davies who came from Uganda in about 1918, then the mission was run from Malek mission by Archdeacon Shaw, became the evangelization centre for the Churchmen Missionary Society, then it was taken over by the African Inland Mission (AIM) and lastly it became the centre for Africa Inland Church (AIC) of which Rev. Andrea Vuni became its first indigenous bishop. This is also a village for several families including those of Jibi Lakilonyi, father of Samuel Okomi the school headmaster from the Pandikeri clan. Some families of Beka clan are also found here.

4- Ogwangmeda
Ogwang is 'a wildcat' in the Acholi language and someone who built his home here felt lonely and named it Ogwangmeda meaning 'he has been joined by the wildcat'. But according to sources the man who founded the village was from Pandikeri clan who was joined later by some members of his clan, others from Logopi and other clans and they lived together. This village has been given an Acholi name by that man from Pandikeri clan because he spoke Acholi, besides Ma'di his original language, and indeed many Ma'di people sometimes take pleasure in using the Acholi language for communication and entertainment because they are bilingual. General Joseph Lagu from the Ma'di community is bilingual which disposed him to give Owinykibul its name in a Ma'di territory.

5- Adura village

This is where members of Pandikeri, the family of Duku Logoria from Tedire clan and Beka clan of Wale, father of Bishop Andrea Vuni live.

6- Panyarada village is where members of the Pandikeri clan live.

7- Mede village

This village is where the family of Jangara Modi of Dongu clan, the family of Acamu of Payoko clan, members of Orolo and Palabek clans live. The last two clans left for Acholi Panyikwara in about 1947. The Palabek are believed to have come from the Mundari of Terekeka.[71] Those who are in Panyikwara today are said to have remained behind to collect termites while the bigger group left for Palabek in northern Uganda where today they speak Acholi.[72] Pakala also left for Acholi from Mede in the same year as Palabek but a man called Agwaya whose son was Ipere says he and his family will remain among the Ma'di because his father came there for protection during Chief Akeri Milla's era. Ipere lives in Owinykibul.[73]

8- Molungeng

This is the village where the family of Yugu Lotikaro, a descendant of Iyiali of Paibonga (Ngaya) clan lives. The residents of this village moved from Labormor, an old village located at the northern edge of Kugi forest.

9- Liokwe

This village belongs to the Pambili clan of Jala Bakhiet and members of Paibonga (Ngaya) clan. Also, the families of Ugiri of Lulubo, Bandasi of Ukeyi and Aturusi of Mugi clan live here. The name Liokwe in Ma'di language refers to a tropical tree whose fibre is used for spiralling ropes for making nets for catching animals or as sinew for bows.

10- Kenya

Kenya is the name of a village located between Nyakaningwa and Liokwe where some Paibonga (Ngaya) people live.

11- Nyongwa Gwere

This is where the larger group of Nyongwa clan live. It is named after a Nyongwa chief called Mitte who burned the villages of his people because they refused to emigrate to Poiya near the Juba-Nimule road by order of the District Commissioner of Opari.

12- Logopi village

This is the abode of the larger group of Logopi clan.

13- Logopi-Vurule

As the name suggests in Ma'di, this is Logopi village which is downstream. There are several elders from different clans who lived in this cluster of villages joined by part of the Pageri-Torit Road, and they included Vuraga Mulu of Patibi, Ikoli and Erkolano Jote of Lulubo, Adala Sibirit of Ijupi, Emilio of Paselo, Furutasio of Kiloloro, Sua Mairi and Ibigo of Jeru clans. These clans are in addition to that of Logopi.

14- Winyalonga village

This village was founded by Nyagorac, an elder from Dongu clan who moved from Mede to open fields for cultivation because the land in the former village was old and crops no longer could grow well in it.

15- Rarengo village

This was the village founded by elder Nyama of Logili clan who was the father of Awira Rabo, Jojo and Primo Ayira. Besides them several other members of the Aruju section of Logili clan lived here. Nyama later moved to Adrwi in Moli from where his sons Awira, Jojo, Primo and others moved to Iyii in about 1934.

16- Nyajogi village

This was the village of the Dongu clan of Bari, and their most elderly man was Drongwa Musukani. Part of the group led by Titifano Tombe latter moved to Mejopadrani (Borokodongo) on their way to Nyokir in southern Bari in about 1939.

17- Male village

This is one of the largest villages of Bori and was inhabited by the families of Diego Mude Muhamme, father of Chief Odoriko Loku Diego of Tedire clan. There were also other inhabitants who included Salvatore Modi of Logopi, Okondo of Gonyapi, Abala of Ndogo, Kakamoi Modi of Nyori, Kireatcu Wani and Tuja of Logili, Pirimo Ajjugo of Lomura, Kongoro of Paibonga (Ngaya), Jala Bokit and his half brother Ajju of Pambili who moved here from Liokwe to join Jala's maternal uncle Muhamme, father of Odoriko and Ajju, Modi Yamba of Mijale clans. Before the creation of Male village within Opari area there were no blacksmiths (eremu) found in it. But today this village is a famous centre throughout Madiland for the bountiful production of all sorts of hand tools and traditional weapons. These include knives, matchetes, spears, arrow heads and other cutlery. According to local legends, iron craft was brought to the village by a certain man called Wani Kireacu and another man called Tuja who were both from Nyori clan and went from Moli.[74] Amono and Ginawi were from Gunyia clan.

18- Musura

This village lies between Male and Patibi primary school and is inhabited by Liama and his brother Melebi of Gonyapi,

Tikwasi of Kiloloro, Arkangelo Oku of Padombe, Samuele Idira of Pageri, Kafaire father of Martino Amadra of Ukeyi, Rubangati Undzi of Nyongwa and Nereo of Logopi clans.

19- Owinykibul

This village was established after the Addis Ababa Agreement of March 1972 between the Sudan Government (SG) and Southern Sudan Liberation Movement (SSLM) by several Ma'di clans mostly from Bori-Opari within Ma'di territory. It is located close to the border between Ma'di and Acholi people. The village came into existence in the middle of the forest after it was selected and built as a hidden headquarters of the Anya-Nya liberation army by its Commander-in-Chief, General Joseph Lagu who named it Owinykibul in the Acholi language which he speaks, writes and reads very well being bilingual in Acholi and Ma'di his mother tongue. The name *Owinykibul* means 'heard by the drum' and because of its military strategic location and importance it was attacked by a combined force from Sudan and Egypt on January 25, 1971, who took and occupied it. The camp was abandoned when these troops withdrew following the signing of the peace agreement which ended the civil war. Owinykibul was an empty spot in the middle of the forest on the Ma'di side of the common border with their Acholi neighbour of Parajok when General Lagu selected it to be his headquarters. More than a dozen clans from Bori-Opari rebuilt it and they included Pandikeri, Logopi, Mugi, Tedire, Jeru, Kiloloro, Padombe, Beka, Pambili, etc. Later some members of the Acholi community joined the Ma'di in the village and were administered by a Ma'di chief, Odoriko Loku Diego Mude for more than ten years from 1972 to 1984. The Norwegian Church Aid Equatoria

Programme (NCA/EP) opened a motorable road from Obbo to Owinykibul making the village a growing trading centre connected to neighbouring Uganda from where some of the mercantile goods came. When the Acholi saw this progress, they decided to take over the responsibility of administering the affluent village by raising an accusation to the Commissioner of Eastern Equatoria Province George Lomoro Muras that the Ma'di were illegally administering an Acholi village. When the case was examined because the name Owinykibul is in Acholi language and the village falls close to the border between the two tribes, Ma'di and Acholi, the case was adjudicated in favour of the Acholi thus the Ma'di administration of Owinykibul came to an end. But since the village falls inside Ma'di territory the Ma'di have not given up their ownership right of the village till today and hope one day the Acholi will recognize this right and hand over Owinykibul to them.[75]

20- Envoketu village

This was established by members of the Pandikeri clan from which most inhabitants are descended.

21- Nyongwa Arinya

This is a big village of Nyongwa clan who live in it with some members of the Jeru clan.

22- Patibi-Eyibiado

In this large village a number of clans live, the most numerous being the Patibi, then there are Gonyapi, Logopi, Mugi, Paselo, Padombe, Kiloloro and other clans. Patibi-Eyibiado includes the villages around the old school on Kadafoyo hill.

23- Idele village

This lies on the bank of River Atapi and is inhabited by members of Jeru clan.

24- Ayipa village

This was an important large village created to accommodate several hundred Ma'di families and other refugees who were returning from Ayaci in the Acholi Parajok area. Chief Milla Akeri had led them there to take refuge and to avoid being attacked, captured, and enslaved by the Mahdist forces who were based in Rejaf. Rejaf was close to Ma'di areas and to those people who sought Milla's protection.

25- Opari Township

Opari, before it adopted its urban characteristics, was a large village where the residence of the chief was located. It later grew into an administrative centre where the District Commissioner was based in 1918 and the first DC to assume his duties in Opari was Captain E. T. N. Groves, an Englishman. Between 1918 and 1932, Opari served as the district headquarters for Ma'di, Acholi and Kuku of Kajokeji. The Kajokeji sub-district was ceded to Yei River District in 1932 when Captain G. P. Cann was District Commissioner of Opari. The administrative centre grew into a trading centre and a health centre was also constructed to render medical services to the residents of the township and inhabitants from the surrounding area. Former member of the rotating presidency of Sudan, Sayed Siricio Iro Wani who was born in Opari in the early 1920's built his residence here. It was the most magnificent house ever constructed in the township by a citizen from the area. Besides the staff of the district headquarters, Opari as an urban centre attracted members from several clans of Bori who came to settle here, the Pandikeri, Padombe, Pageri, Beka, Mugi, Ukeyi, Logopi, Paibonga (Ngaya), Pakoli, Patibi, Logili, Jeru, Tedire, Kiloloro, Nyongwa, etc. Being an urban centre some

Nubians, commonly known as Fallah, who were mostly petty traders, were also found in Opari. Some of these people moved from Nimule where they were numerous.

4.12 The List of Pandikeri Chiefs from Ker to Dari Kanyara Isra

Although Akeri Milla was the most prominent chief of the Pandikeri clan leadership of Bori-Opari, the active role of the chieftainship can best be understood from the contribution of each of them differently starting from Ker, the ancestor of the group.

The genealogy of the chieftainship constructed from the available data is as follows:

- Ker
- Asivo
- Kiribungo
- Kumo
- Lubango
- Jumon
- Olek Apoka
- Opira
- Alimu
- Wani
- Andruga
- Milla
- Mene
- Dari.[74]

After the death of Dari Kanyara Isara in 1952 immediately after his return from a visit to Loa where he accompanied Adrisi for a traditional funeral dance (*dra*) organized in memory of Ajju of Pageri clan at Loa, Melekwe, his son Sumai became chief. Ajju was the father-in-law of Adrisi of Bori-Opari.[76]

Rivalry among sons and grandsons of Chief Akeri Milla for the post of chieftainship:
- Ismail versus Jibi (a.k.a Lakilonyi, father of Ustaz Samuel Okomi, an elementary school headmaster)
- Clemente Vumudri (father of Radio Juba chief engineer Joseph Ladro) versus Furunato Modo

The chiefs of the Pandikeri chieftainship after Andruga, father of Akeri Milla and other children are:
- Akeri Milla Minnai
- Mene Isara
- Dari Kanyara Isara
- Sumai Kanyara
- Clement Vumudri Mamur
- Furunato Modo, nicknamed (Gedia ile) Manibaba
- Gulli Mukungu of Nyongwa rejected by the Pandikeri outright
- Ginawi Mondi of Palungwa Arapi chieftainship
- Mohamme Ismail, nicknamed Yamo
- Rafaile Abuni of Padombe clan who was appointed by Headchief Sabazio Okumu Abdalla in 1958.

Akeri Milla's stepbrothers were Minyori and Koka. The latter was the father of Agwele, the great paternal grandfather of the author. Another son of Koka was Keri Nyolima whose name was given to the author at birth by his paternal grandmother Idreangwa Nya-Agwele a.k.a. Asiali, the daughter of Agwele. Jibi the other stepbrother of Akeri Milla had a son called Samuel Liyo who became a government official. Another son, Samuel Okomi became the headmaster of an elementary school, and there was another son called Nehemiah.

4.13 Constitutional Post Holders from Bori-Opari Chieftainships (Eastern Sector)

Past and present Constitutional post holders, other prominent national figures who were born and brought up in Bori-Opari chieftainships, went to schools of the time and later contributed to national work in different capacities are as follows:

1- Siricio lro Wani (from Mugi clan) was MP in the first Constituent Assembly of 1954 in Khartoum then he was elected as Member of Supreme Council of State in 1956 and his term ended abruptly when General Ibrahim Abboud overthrew the government on November 17, 1958. In the 1960's Iro served as Member of Provincial Council in Juba.

2- Sabazio Okumu Abdalla (Gilo) (from Gonyapi clan) was elected Head Chief of Ma'di in 1952 by members of the Ma'di community from different chieftainships and representatives of Ma'di Council whose members were government officials in the urban centres of Juba and Torit. He was appointed Member of Provincial Council by the Governor of Equatoria Province and served in the early 1960's. Sabazio was head chief of Ma'di till 1984 when he passed on.

3- Severino Fuli Bwoki (from Ukeyi clan) was elected MP in the National Parliament in Khartoum twice in the 1970's and 1980's. He participated in the Anya-Nya movement in a civilian capacity in most of the 1960's up to 1972 when the Addis Ababa Agreement was signed between the Sudan Government and South Sudan Liberation Movement. He wrote his memoir which revealed a wealth of information previously unknown about the liberation struggle. The book titled: *Shaping a Free Southern Sudan, Memoirs of Our Struggle 1934–1985* was reviewed by one of the North Sudanese academics who sounded a warning to policy makers in Khartoum that if they did not act quickly the South would secede from the union and eight years later this came to pass.

4- Mary Siricio Iro (from Mugi clan) MP in the 1980's.

5- Abednego Kenyi Andrea (from Beka clan) became Commissioner of Imotong Province in 1985 and Advisor in the Southern Kordofan State Government in 2000.

6- Melichior Lagu Damiano (from Mugi clan) was MP in the 1990's and deputy speaker in the 2000's State Assembly in Torit.

7- Nicola Oboya Lazarus (from Ngaya-Paibonga clan) appointed province Commissioner in the 2000's and became MP in Torit in 2005-6.

8- Tereza Siricio Iro (from Mugi clan) was State Minister in the Government of National Unity, Khartoum 2006.

9- Bishop Andrea Vuni Wale (from Beka clan) of Africa Inland Church (AIC).

10- Bishop Paride Taban (from Logopi clan) of the Catholic Church. His autobiography titled: *Give Peace A Chance* edited by Eisman is a fascinating book that has earned the bishop worldwide acclaim. The book has opened a window for the world to see what has happened in Southern Sudan from the time Paride was a village boy, a pupil in a tribally mixed school at Katire, where his father was an employee of a forestry sawmill, his life as a seminarian and priest and the ups and downs of life as a bishop during the second civil war of 1983-2005 in Southern Sudan. The book also describes how the bishop became involved with mountain communities who had never known peace, development or education. He created for them a model village called Kuron in which to interact peacefully and get a taste of what was happening in other parts of the country as well as a fleeting impression of the wider world.

11- Archbishop Nikalao Oling Andrea (from Beka clan).

12- Colonel Ezekiel Ondu Aturusi served in the Anya-Nya liberation army and in 1972 was absorbed as a major into the Sudan army where he rose gradually to the post of Colonel in the signal corps.

13- Alexander Lodu Rueben was from the Paluda clan. He was the first from Opari to join the University of Khartoum in 1963/64 and eventually became a secondary school teacher and taught in schools in Sudan, Uganda and South Sudan.

14- Clement Otto Kullo, MP in the State Assembly in Torit. He replaced his cousin (Rtd.) Maj. Gen Nicola Oboya Lazarus.

15- Maj. Gen Nicola Oboya Lazarus who passed on in 2006.

4.14 The clans of Bori-Opari listed alphabetically

1- Afodo

2- Beka

3- Cera

4- Degi

5- Dongu – They emigrated from Nyokir and Gumosi in Southern Bari during the tumultuous era of the Mahdists at the end of the nineteenth century. They first settled among the Ma'di in Bori-Opari under the protection of Chief Akeri Milla who took them to Parajok, Ayaci for safety. On their return to Bori-Opari they camped briefly around Ayipa Hill. Due to their large population Opari could not accommodate them all and so many crossed into the Acholi area for settlement and naturally adopted much from Acholi culture including the language. Those who remain in Bori-Opari and Moli chieftainships have integrated into the Ma'di tribe and speak Ma'di. What is interesting is that they still maintain their customs and rituals in such practices as birth and death rites.

6- Eremu-Weli

7- Gonyapi

8- Gunyia

9- Ijupi

10- Jeru

11- Kacura

12- Kiloloro

13- Lamude

14- Lira

15- Lobule

16- Logili

17- Logopi

18- Lomura

19- Lulubo

20- Metu

21- Mijale

22- Moyo

23- Mugi

24- Ndogo

25- Nyai

26- Nyamundi

27- Nyongwa

28- Nyori

29- Oloro – They are originally believed to be a Ma'di group who came from Korokodia near Muruli of Chief Kuyu of Ukeyi clan and moved during the violent Turco-Egyptian era to Bori-Opari. The clan lived in Mede, north of Opari village before moving to Panyikwara area in the company of the Palabek and Pakala clans in 1947.

30- Orobe

31- Padombe

32- Pageri

33- Paibonga (Ngaya) – They are originally from Bari and today they live in Molungeng in the Bori-Opari border area with the Acholi of Panyikwara and have adopted Ma'di as well as Acholi customs and traditions. They speak both Ma'di of the Burulo variant and Acholi and some of them prefer now to be called Acholi. They campaign for the rest of the Ma'di clans of Bori-Opari who number forty-seven to join the Acholi community in Panyikwara which these clans say cannot happen because Ma'di are Ma'di, and Acholi are Acholi and neither of them can deny their origin because that is how God has created them.

34- Pakoli

35- Palaa – Some are found among the Acholi in Panyikwara who call them Paliec and among the Lulubo they are called Pabala.

36- Paloi

37- Paluda

38- Pambili

39- Pandikeri – They are also found in Erepi. A small section emigrated to Abalakodi in Uganda during famine known as *Maacika joloro* in the 1930's. The clan is believed to be originally from the Ma'di tribe but emigrated to Loringa Parabongo,

Olwal in Uganda during the Turkish invasion of Ma'diland where they were influenced by Lwo culture and adopted the Acholi language during their stay there as refugees. A small group of them led by Ker (Keri) came back when there was a measure of calm and joined the Ma'di clan called Padieri around the present Opari. One European writer, J. V. Rowley who was District Commissioner of Opari and later of Torit, quoting oral sources said Ker and his followers were brought by Bari Chief Lugor (Pitya).[77] When Ker took over the Logopi chieftainship as compensation for saving the life of the Logopi chief, the clan assumed the current name Pandikeri after his family name, for *pa* in Ma'di means 'family'.

40- Paratiki – a branch of Pakala clan and claim that their ancestor fell from heaven

41- Paselo

42- Patibi

43- Pavunde – They previously occupied an area in Patibi, near Mount Remo. Most of its members have moved to Owinykibul and some have emigrated to Paracele in Uganda where they live today.

44- Pavura – A part lives in Loa, Iriya and another section is found across the international boundary on the Ugandan side of Ma'diland.

45- Pawaro (Obute Kacura)

46- Payoko in Winyalonga, Pakworo, around Indzi hill near River Atapi. They prefer to speak Acholi because of proximity to them and some have more pride in being called Acholi than Ma'di, although originally, they belonged to the latter tribe.

47- Tanyanyina

48- Tedire

49- Udupi
50- Ukeyi
51- Utuno

Of the fifty-one clans in Bori-Opari, forty-seven are Ma'di. Three, the Oloro, Paibonga (Ngaya), and Payoko claim to be Acholi and the fourth, the Oloro clan left Bori-Opari for Panyikwara in 1947. The Dongu are originally from Bari but today most of them have been integrated into Acholi while a small number are found among the Ma'di.

Notes and references

1 Wani, Victor Keri. *An Outline of Ma'di History, Culture, Traditions and Customs in Sudan*, Juba, 1992, unpublished (MS). See also Mairi John Blackings ed. et al. *Narrating Our Future, Customs, Rituals and Practices of Ma'di of South Sudan and Uganda*, Centre for Advanced Studies of African Societies (CASAS), Cape Town, 2011.

2 Ibid. See also interview of author with Chief Odoriko Loku Diego in Torit on 12 May 2005.

3 Blackings, John Mairi. *English-Ma'di, Ma'di-English Dictionary*, Munchen, 2001.

4 Interview of author with Koka Lou Mbwele a.k.a Iseni, his paternal uncle in Juba in 1981. Koka was a road headman between Mejopadrani (Borokodongo) and Dereto, Moli during the construction of Juba-Nimule Road in 1931.

5 Op. Cit. Odoriko.

6 Ibid.

7 Jephson, A. J. Mounteney. *Emin Pasha and the Rebellion at the Equator*, 1899, London and L. F. Nalder. *Equatoria Province*

Handbook Vol. 1, Mongalla, 1940. p.291.

8 Op. Cit. Odoriko.

9 Toniolo, Elias and Richard Hill, eds. *The Opening of the Nile Basin*, C. Hurst, London, 1974, p.97.

10 Ibid.

11 Op. Cit. Odoriko.

12 Ibid. See also J. V. Rowley. *Notes on the Ma'di of Equatoria Province*, Sudan Notes and Records No. XXIII, 1940, p.291. See also L. F. Nalder. *Equatoria Province Handbook Vol. 1*, Mongalla, 1940 p.291. Also, information supplied to author by Sarah Idreangwa Nya Agwele his paternal grandmother in 1975; and the interview of author with Lazaro Nyago Dumo in Amarat, Khartoum in 1999.

13 Ibid. Dumo interview and Op. Cit.Toniolo.

14 Op. Cit. Rowley. p.291.

15 Ibid. Also Op. Cit. L. F. Nalder and information supplied to author by Sarah Idreangwa Nya Agwele his paternal grandmother; and in interviews of author with Chief Odoriko Loku Diego in Juba in 2011, Lazaro Nyago Dumo in Khartoum Amarat 1999.

16 Op. Cit. Rowley and Odoriko interview.

17 Ibid. Rowley.

18 Informant of this story was Savia Pita Siricio Iro in El Haj Yousif, Korton Kassala, Khartoum North, in 1995.

19 Op. Cit. Odoriko Interview.

20 Gray, Richard. *A History of Southern Sudan 1838 – 1889*, Oxford University Press, London, 1961, p.18

21 Posnansky, Merrick. *East Africa and the Nile Valley in Early Times* quoted in *Sudan in Africa* ed.Yusuf Fadl Hasan, Khartoum, Khartoum University Press, 1969, pp.55-8

22 Op. Cit. Toniolo and Hill, p.97 and Gray, p.18.

23 Ibid. Toniolo and Hill.

24 Op. Cit. Gray, p.8.

25 Op. Cit. Rowley.

26 Op. Cit. Dumo interview.

27 Op. Cit. Rowley.

28 Op. Cit. Dumo. Also, a remark made by Chief Dario Yona Modomun during Ma'di-Acholi border meeting in Torit in the period 17-19 April 2012.

29 Op. Cit. Toniolo.

30 Ibid.

31 Ibid.

32 Op.Cit. Dumo interview and Modomun remark.

33 Op. Cit. Wani book. See also Severino Fuli Boki. *Shaping a Free Southern Sudan, Memoirs of Our Struggle 1934-1985,* Loa Catholic Mission Council, Limuru, 2002.

34 Op. Cit. Rowley, p.291.

35 Ibid. p.292.

36 Op. Cit. Mairi dictionary.

37 Stigand, C. H. *Equatoria, The Lado Enclave,* London, Frank Cass, 1968.

38 Interview of author with Karamello Dagala Balabas Lomeda, in El Haj Yousif, Khartoum North, in 1995.

39 Ibid.

40 Op. Cit. Idreangwa.

41 Op. Cit. Odoriko and Dumo. Also interview of author with Erodionne Murulu Jiribi in El Haj Yousif, Khartoum North in 1995.

42 Ibid. Odoriko and Dumo.

43 Crazzolara, J. P. *The Lwoo* Verona, 1951, p.155.

44 Ibid.

45 Op. Cit. Odoriko. Also interview of author with William Alira Yanga in Al Haj Yousif, Khartoum North on 12 September 1995.

46 Op. Cit. Rowley, p.291.

47 Interview of author with Saulo Obaloker Yugu in Torit on 20 May 2005.

48 Ibid.

49 Ibid.

50 Ibid.

51 Op. Cit. Odoriko interview.

52 Interview of author with his mother Rita Keji Lodu in Juba, in Al Haj Yousif, Khartoum North on January 12, 1993.

53 Op. Cit. Odoriko interview and see Boki book.

54 Ibid. Odoriko.

55 Interview of author with Rev. Bishop Nikolao Oling Andrea in El Haj Yousif, Rudumiya, Khartoum North in July 1996.

56 Op. Cit. Odoriko interview and see Boki book.

57 Ibid. Boki.

58 Op. Cit. Rev.Oling Interview.

59 Op. Cit. Boki book.

61 Op. Cit. Rev. Oling.

62 Op. Cit. Nalder.

63 This was part of the last speech by Chief Akeri Milla to the people who sought his protection from the Mahdists and was often quoted by my paternal grandmother Sarah Idreangwa Nya'Agwele in the 1950's, 1960's and even Lazaro Nyago Dumo said his grandfather used to narrate it to him. See also Severino Fuli Boki's book.

64 Op. Cit. Rev. Oling. See also Boki's book.

65 Op. Cit. Dumo and Odoriko interviews.

66 Interview of author with his mother Rita Keji Lodu Bilal in Juba on 10 January 1992.

67 Op. Cit. Odoriko.

68 Ibid.

69 Ibid.

70 My mother Rita Keji Lodu resung this song for me.

71 Op. Cit. Odoriko Interview in Torit.

72 Ibid.

73 Ibid.

74 Ibid.

75 Ibid.

76 Interview of author with Joseph Ladro Clement son of Chief Clemente Mamur Vumudri of Pandikeri clan in Bori-Opari, in El Haj Yousif, Al Takamul, Khartoum North, 1996.

77 Op. Cit. Rowley.

Chapter Five

Northern Sector Chieftainships of Moli

5.1 Borders of the Area

The Northern Chieftainships of Moli are found in the area starting from three miles south of Deretu village part of which is the camp for workers' gang No. 15 on Juba-Nimule Road. This is its southern border with the area of the western chieftainships of Erepi at a place called Odruforo and runs northward ending on the southern bank of Nyolo River in the north forming the border between Ma'di and Lulubo-Aru people. The latter speak a language which is similar to the Ma'di variant called Burulo spoken in Moli, Erepi and Bori-Opari.[1] The distance between the two points is about 28 miles when measured from three miles south of Deretu to the southern bank of River Nyolo in the north. The border of the area of the chieftainships with the sector of the Eastern Chieftainships of Bori-Opari is marked by the western side of Nyakiti Mountain Ranges which forms its eastern limits. North of the Nyakiti ranges lies the Kugi plain which is used by the people of Moli Tokuro, Mejopadrani (Borokodongo) and those of northern Bori-Opari as a hunting ground. It teems with different species of game before the law restricting hunting of wild game was enacted. Part of the border between Moli and Bori chieftainships runs through Kugi plain northward.

The border of the Northern Ma'di chieftainships of Moli with the Bori-Opari chieftainships is marked by an imaginary line across River Afoyi. The geography of the two chiefainships in the north was greatly affected by the opening of Juba-Nile Road in 1932 which acted as a magnet for the Bari and Acholi communities who were not previously in the Rivers Afoyi-Kit-Nyolo region. The Bari moved eastward from Nyokir, Gumosi and Nyangiri in the Karpeto chieftainship of Southern Bari and settled in the narrow strip of land between Rivers Nyolo and Kit, and the Acholi moved westward across Rivers Ame and Afoyi from Palabek in Panyikwara Chieftainship across Bori-Opari chieftainship into Moli chieftainships area and settled along the eastern side of Juba-Nimule Road, south of the Ma'di villages of Iyii in about 1939.[2] The Acholi of Panyikwara crossed two administrative borders to come to where they are settled today. These borders are those of Bori-Opari with Acholi Chieftainship of Abara and the border between the sisterly Ma'di Chieftainships of Bori-Opari and Moli.

The Bari spontaneous settlement across River Kit closed the natural and official border between the Ma'di and Lulubo-Aru people just as the Acholi have closed the communication link between the Ma'di in Iyii and those living in Moli. Before and after their settlement, Chief Akeri Geri of Moli controlled an area up to the southern bank of River Nyolo and the sub-chief in Iyii was Kute Musa his cousin.[3] The distance between Rivers Iyii and Nyolo is about two miles. The Acholi came and built their villages south of the Ma'di villages severing the direct communication link of the Iyii people with their chieftainship headquarters, their kith and kin in Moli, some fourteen miles to the south. Indeed, if any Ma'di wants to visit his or her relatives in Moli or elsewhere in Ma'diland he or she must cross through the Acholi villages of Ombiyo which the Ma'di named Boriangwa ('small Bori') because they crossed Bori from Abara chieftainship to reach Iyii where they have settled today.

The short border of the northern Chieftainships of Moli with the Kajokeji in the west is partly marked by the Nyeri Mountain Range which forms a natural boundary. The place where the old track from the escarpment leads into the crossing point on the Nile opposite Cukole is part of Kajokeji territory. Running along the east coast of the Nile River for a considerable distance northward and extending beyond the confluence of River Umo with the Nile, the border encloses Mount Foki and Lafonia hill inside Ma'di territory to form its boundary with the Bari land. It then extends north-eastward for a short distance before it turns towards Juba-Nimule Road which it joins over two miles north of Monocu, a village of Moli-Tokuro, to the road junction of Karpeto and Juba-Nimule Road. It then runs along the western side of this main road from a varying distances of two hundred metres and two kilometers west of Mejopadrani till Kit.[4] From the road deep inside the eastern territory and across Afoyi and Ame Rivers is Ma'di territory under Bori-Opari chieftainship bounded by Acholi country further east. The territory north-west of the

Ma'di chieftainship of Moli is Karpeto, a village of southern Bari, whose famous chief Koce Gumbiri from the Bari clan of Kela used to visit Chief Akeri Geri of Logili clan in Moli in the 1940's and 1950's regularly. The nearest Bari village to their border with Moli is Nyarabanga while that of the Ma'di to the Bari is Gori not far from the foot of Foki Mountain. In the early 1950's, Orisoko used to be the nearest Ma'di village to the Bari village of Nyarabanga. *Orisoko* in Ma'di language means 'a coward cannot cultivate in the area' for the village was surrounded by crop fields, and lions and lionesses constantly attacked the farmers forcing them to abandon the village and move south-east to other Moli villages such as Malandu, Gori, Cecere, Nyori, Ambayo and Moli-Baribari to avoid being killed and eaten by the beasts.

Orisoko was named by Jangara of Degi clan. Traditionally the Ma'di consider River Lupaingwe which begins in the hills west of Mejopadrani (Borokodongo) and runs northward becoming a tributary of River Kit as their border with the Bari,[5] but since the drawing of the boundary between the two tribes by the colonialists along the western side of Juba-Nimule Road to the southern bank of River Nyolo near Kit, the Ma'di have not claimed their part of the land joined to Bari territory in its northern parts but nevertheless assert hunting and collecting rights over any natural resources found there without hindrance.

To the south of the northern chieftainships of Moli lies the chieftainships of Erepi in the western sector. In fact, the northern chieftainships make up one of the three sectors which are territorially large, the other two being the southern and eastern sectors of Lokai and Bori that occupy larger areas than the other two. Its length from south to north is an estimated 28 miles, its width from land across River Afoyi its eastern boundary with Bor-Opari chieftainships to a few meters across Juba-Nimule Road is the only narrow part of its territory and measures a few miles wide. Otherwise, its width from west of Nyakiti mount ranges across to the Nile is about fifteen miles.

5.2 The Moli Chieftainships

There are several chieftainships in Moli but the most important ones are those of the Logili, Mugi, Ukeyi and Pakoli clans. The Paluda clan was very populous and powerful but was destroyed by the Turco-Egyptian forces in March 1860.[6] These are chieftainships on account of being rain-making clans. But there are others like the Pakoli whose leaders are not only rainmakers but priests who perform the rituals related to the purification of tracts of Moli territory such as Makede to ensure that the people who live in these lands are free from all kinds of diseases, attacks by wild animals and food crops are protected from destruction by insects, birds, worms and plant diseases. The leaders of the early inhabitants of Moli have divided the lands into zones, so that there is no rivalry among the priests concerning land purification. This is contrary to the practices of the rainmaking clans which contend for dominance because their magic has no boundaries, and if one of them is able to influence the weather over the whole of Moli, this ability is greatly appreciated. Leadership rivalry is seen among Ma'di rainmakers and not among priests or prietesses who perform land purification rites. In this study, the author has established the existence of rivalry between the Odupkwe and Puceri clans in Lokai, between Logili and Mugi clans in Moli and between Odupkwe and Pandikeri clans along their common border.

5.3 Logili Leadership in Moli

The Logili clan chieftainship is the largest of the chieftainships in Moli. The clan next to it in size is that of the Mugi. This explains why there has always been rivalry between these two chieftainships. According to Moli legends, the chief who was said to have left a name in the Logili chieftainship was Ayu. He is remembered in war songs which refer to him as a powerful figure on whose nose no fly would dare to sit. One of the songs was sung after the Lokoya-Langabu raids on Moli villages and the reprisal raid carried out by the Moli warriors on the Lokoya-Langabu villages of Omangara, Okire and Ofiri.[7] This raid resulted in their defeat as witness the song sung by Logili fighters to recall to memory the greatness of Ayu.

The song runs as follows:

> *Odi Kire ra*
> *Kire onyo ama ajjukwe*
> *Ama Opi Ayu ni yo mindra osu ma lu*
> *Ago ori Manya ni owo yoo*
> *Adi Ori ra*
> *Ori onyo ama ajjukwe*
> *Bilinya Opi Ayu ni yoo mindra osu ma luu*
> *Ago ori Manya ni owo yo*

The literal translation of this *mure* song is as follows:

> *Kire were killed and they broke our spear sticks*
> *Our Chief Ayu is not there and so I am covered with tears*
> *This was the cry of son of Manya*
> *We killed Ori and they broke our spear sticks*

> *Bilinya, our Chief Ayu is not there and so I am covered with tears*
> *This was the cry of son of Manya*

Ayu was certainly a powerful Logili chief who lived before Urube another Moli chief from the same clan, but it is not known whether Ayu was the father of Urube or his grandfather or great grandfather. However he was related to Urube who inherited the leadership from him or from one of his descendants because his name is always linked to past Logili chiefs. The present Logili leadership has its origin from Urube, the father of Dupari Kollo who inherited the leadership from him. Dupari was the father of Mele who was nicknamed Mwamwara and Mele had several sons with several wives. With his first wife called Loria from Monocu-Nyongwa clan he had a son called Geri Ipele.[8] With another wife he had a son called Tombe Moli. It was Geri Ipele who succeeded his father as chief but that was not without some resistance from his half brother Tombe Moli. When Geri Ipele died in about 1935, his son Akeri Geri became chief in his place. It is believed by the Moli people that Akeri Geri followed the methods his father had applied in handling public issues. This was seen in his way of dealing with some women who were suspected of poisoning some persons during his rule in 1937 and in 1976. Cuofo Oddu, the eldest daughter of Chief Geri Ipele said before her father's death, that he told his son Akeri Geri to be tough with poisoners and that he should not forget that he had gone to prison because of them.[9]

In Moli, the names of the past chiefs can be remembered from old songs as already stated in the case of Ayu and from names of places on which the names were conferred. Labore was the previous name for Moli although Labore was also the name of a man. Moli like Ayu, was also the name of a great chief in Labore from the Logili clan. The small military post which lay west of the present Erepi established by Colonel Charles Gordon when he was the Governor of Equatoria province in 1874[10] was named after Ayu. Besides his name being given to a place where Chief Ayu lived in the last half of the nineteenth century, the name also appears in a Logili *mure* song sung after the last and successful reprisal raid by Moli clans on the Lokoya-Langabu villages whose inhabitants used to raid the northern part of Moli area intermittently in the first quarter of the twentieth century with impunity. The unknown composer of this song lamented that had their chief Ayu been alive, the Lokoya-Langabu would not have killed them. Ayu was known as a fearless chief who was ruthless in dealing with the enemies of his people. As for Moli, he must have been one of the descendants of Ayu because he was also from the Logili clan. Moli's name was given to a grandson of Ayu and by succession the name was given to a son of Chief Mele Mwamwara from the Logili leadership lineage who reigned probably towards the end of the nineteenth century. Moli's son Tombe known at the beginning of the twentieth century as Tombe Moli assumed the leadership, following the death of his paternal uncle pending the first son Geri Ipele coming of age briefly as a regent.[11]

It cannot be ascertained whether the son of Urube called Dupari Kolo was the direct ancestor of Tombe Moli or a cousin within the same royal family. Urube was stabbed in the stomach by the servant or *opigo* of Kajamindi, a notable from the Mugi clan, and before his death he stated in his will that his son Dupari Kollo was to assume the position of chief.[12] The Logili clan leadership passed from Ayu through Urube and Dupari Kollo, then to Mele and on to Geri Ipele, then to his son Akeri Geri, the last chief in the Logili lineage who died in July, 1985. Cuofo Oddu, the eldest daughter of Chief Geri Ipele told me in November, 1994 that one of her ancestors was Dupari and whether this was the son of Urube or another Dupari in the leadership succession she did not know.[13] The record of the Logili leadership from Urube to Mele is confused and difficult to follow. The colonial administrator, J. V. Rowley who compiled the lineages of the Ma'di chieftainships, particularly those of the Pandikeri in Bori, Odupkwe and Koyi in Lokai and that of Tedire in Erepi comprehensively in 1940 in his book: *'Notes on the Ma'di of Equatoria Province'* did not elaborate on the Moli chieftainships, especially that of the Logili then the ruling clan the way he did for Odupkwe in Loa, Pamanini in Nimule, Tedire in Erepi and Pandikeri in Opari-Bori.[14] Although Urube was succeeded by his son Dupari Kollo, it cannot be established with certainty who succeeded Dupari as chief. But from Mele, the leadership briefly went to Tombe Moli then on to Geri Ipele his half brother and then to Akeri the son of Geri.[15] I will now give an account of the reign of each Logili chief and the background to the period of their reign.

5.3.1 Chief Urube

Urube was considered by the Moli people to be less intelligent and less sympathetic than his predecessors. In the reign of Ayu the Moli people had been protected. Due to weakness of character, Chief Urube was easily misled by Kejikiri, the chief of the Mugi who vied for his position.[16] Urube may have lived in the second half of the nineteenth century. His home was in the Liro River valley in the present Malandu where the Moli clans lived in scattered villages. Urube's power was demonstrated by his ability to make rain fall or stop it, thus causing drought in the lands. He died at the hands of a Moli man because the people living in the area had reached a consensus that he must be killed for causing a devastating drought. It was thought that he imposed drought in Moli because of his rivalry with Kejikiri, the chief of Mugi clan. Kejikiri was the leader of the second biggest chieftainship in Moli and it was believed that he plotted to depose Urube by deceit, leading him to cause a drought. This action would lose Urube the respect of his subjects and eventually lead to his death, paving the way for Kejikiri to take over the leadership of the whole of Moli. But as things transpired, Kejikiri never became chief after the death of the reigning chief. The chief before his death and suffering from the wound inflicted upon him by his attacker, stipulated in his will that his own son take over as chief, reverse the situation that had brought about his downfall and cause rain to fall, thus accomplishing what his subjects expected of him. Urube was not buried in the special way rainmakers are interred. Tradition requires that their toe and fingernails are covered with special clay sourced from an anthill called *api* and other treatments.

5.3.2 Chief Geri Ipele Acts on Suspected Poisoners

Around 1932, Chief Geri Ipele of Moli in the Ma'di area and Kuku chief Kole Yengi of Kajokeji, Caregoro area were arrested on orders of the Opari District Commissioner for torturing several women following a witch-hunt in their respective chieftainships. At that time, Kajokeji was administered from the Opari District headquarters and all the Kuku chiefs including Buccu and Kole Yengi (Ingi) used to come for "C" court sessions in Opari. It was in 1934 that Kajokeji was ceded from Opari and reverted to Yei District, thus on 1st January, 1935 its administration from Opari on the east bank of the Nile officially ended.[17] The two chiefs were

Fig. 2. Chief Urube seen outside his hut. Beside him seated on the right is Kejikiri his rival. (Illustration by Samuel Jok with his courtesy)

tried in Opari and later transferred to Juba when they appealed against their sentences. In 1932, the District Commissioner of Opari was J. Winder[18] and it was he who tried the two chiefs. In Juba, the verdict was upheld; they were again found guilty of ordering the arrest and torture of many women in their chieftainships, having accused them of being in possession of poison (*enyanya*) and of killing some people using the lethal substance. Having not seized the poison, the two chiefs could not prove their case by displaying it in court, and so they were kept in Juba prison.

The Governor of Equatoria Province in Juba at the time was L. F. Nalder (1930–36)[19] who chaired the jury formed to try the two chiefs for the alleged crime of organizing the arrest and torture of several women of their chieftainships leading to the deaths of a number of them. Nalder issued orders that new chiefs should be appointed in their places by the DC of Opari. In Moli, Yongo Alimas Dumo from the Mugi clan was appointed as chief in the place of Geri Ipele. Akeri Geri the son of Ipele was too young to replace his father although the latter had asked the District Commissioner of Opari to let his son succeed him, a request that the DC promised to honour in future.[20] Some Logili elders who did not like their traditional leadership to go out of the clan suggested Sub-chief Tombe Urutwe from the Logili clan to take over the chieftainship temporarily but there was no immediate consensus.[21] Many Moli people lost confidence in Geri Ipele for the arrest, torture and even death of some of the women suspected of being poisoners, and in consideration of this the DC thought the appointment of Yongo Alimas Dumo was a good alternative, at least temporarily, until Akeri became of age.

5.3.3 Chief Akeri Geri Ipele

As Akeri Geri Ipele was considered too young to inherit his father's chieftainship in 1932 as noted in the trial of his father by the District Commissioner of Opari, Mr. John Winder, then he might have been born in about 1916. (His father had been tried for making women of his chieftainship undergo ritual to prove that they were not in possession of deadly poison – *enyanya*.) He became chief for the first time in 1933 and in 1934 he suggested to his fellows of the Logili clan to move and settle in Iyii because it was their ancestral land.[22] In 1934, the control of the Logili chieftainship was confined to Moli. Muruli up to Cukole near the Nile was under the leadership of Ingani Kuyu of the Ukeyi clan. In 1934, the DC of Opari, Mr. J. V Rowley came to Melikwe in Muruli to chair a meeting in which the Moli and Ludiri Muruli people had gathered to witness the amalgamation of the smaller chieftainship of the Ukeyi clan to the bigger one led by the Logili clan. In the meeting, the DC told Ingani Kuyu that since he had fewer families (about 50) under his chieftainship while Chief Akeri Geri had about 200 he was giving the overall chieftainship of Moli to Akeri Geri while appointing Ingani as a sub-chief (*mukungu*). [23] Adislao Loduma Mairi who was from Muruli said he witnessed the changeover. So Akeri Geri assumed the chieftainship of the whole of Moli including Muruli and he would come to conduct "A" court sessions in Melikwe.

During his chieftainship, Akeri is remembered for following in the footsteps of his father, that is, arresting women suspected of being poisoners. He did this at Lerwa Village in Deretu area in 1937 when he brought policemen from Torit to arrest all the suspected womenfolk in the village and take them to Torit for trial. What happened was that his sister-in-law called Enderi Adiri, who was the wife of Jentilio Mukaru a village medical dresser from Gunyia clan, died while giving birth. It was suspected that she was poisoned when Chief Akeri's wife Ile Jakaliya who was pregnant developed skin itchiness after touching the body of her sister before and after her death. Alarmed that his pregnant wife would also die, Chief Akeri Geri rushed to Torit and asked the District Commissioner to give him some policemen to go and arrest some notorious women he believed had poisoned his sister-in-law. His request was responded to positively by the DC. When Chief Akeri arrived in Moli with several policemen and his orderlies, he immediately ordered them to arrest and torture the suspected women in Lerwa village. Here lived members of Pajawu, Paloi, Metu and Gunyia clans. It was suspected that at least one of the women who had attended to her late sister-in-law as midwife during her labour or one of the attendants, was responsible for the crime of having poisoned her. But who this woman was among several of these village women was not known and this situation prompted Chief Akeri Geri to order the policemen to extract from the women information as to who among them was the poisoner. Despite torture, none of the women admitted to being the poisoner. One of the women suspected was Nya Mujo who had consistently declared her innocence even under torture. Despite this she was taken with the other women to Torit where she was detained indefinitely until she died while in prison. Before boarding the lorry for Torit, she composed and sang a funeral song (*owoloro*) about Chief Akeri Geri equating him to a lion. The song goes as follows:

> *Ori Ipele ni nani mondiri ko ebbi*
> *Nya Mujo koya Tori a ga di na*
> *Owo vulega keriru idre ko.*

The literal translation of the song goes like this:

> *That son of Ipele is not a governor but a lion*
> *Nya Mujo is hereby going to Torit*
> *Let weeping not be heard again behind here.*

This is a very sensible song sung by a woman who was suspected of poisoning Enderi Adiri, the sister-in-law of Chief Akeri Geri but she defended herself by saying that if she had been the cause of death in the village, now that she was being taken to Torit for imprisonment then let there be no further death after she was gone. Nearly fifty years later, in 1976, Chief Akeri Geri again ordered the arrest of some women in his village area of Moli, Erepi and as far as Pageri in another chieftainship, an action the Member of Parliament for the constituency, Dr. Gama Hassan opposed and described as damaging the good name of the tribe. He asked Headchief Sabazio Okumu Abdalla to caution Chief Akeri Geri of the legal implications of his action but apparently Sabazio avoiding a clash with Akeri did not deliver the message directly. But all the same, Akeri heard about it and became more arrogant saying that anyone trying to stop him from dealing ruthlessly with suspected poisoners was encouraging possession of the deadly substance and he would not obey their orders.

We know that in the world individuals in almost all communities have had access to poison at different times but the circumstances, reasons and methods of using it have varied from one society to another. Amongst the Ma'di it has been reported that some womenfolk possess poison and that they concoct it by killing snakes in the bush, where they are unobserved. But it is a thought too horrible to contemplate that a human being, especially one as weak as a woman, would be brave enough to kill and slash that part of the creature so feared by even the bravest man and extract the venon for use as poison. Several writers, among them J. V. Rowley, Cecil Eprile, Joseph Lagu and Severino Fuli Boki, have mentioned Ma'di poison in their books, but none ever recorded that they had seen a sample of confiscated poison from the chief's court or any from the natives themselves. The existence of poison amongst the Ma'di appears to be nothing more than a story and no evidence has ever been presented to convince the scientifically minded otherwise. If poison existed in the community it should have been seized by the law enforcement agents since they have had all the means at their disposal to do this. A chief like Akeri

Geri who managed to arrest several women in a large area beyond his chieftainship should have concentrated his efforts on seizing the substance so that people could see what poison looked like, its texture, colour and even smell. This would have justified his action against the women he had arrested and tortured. It is believed that the notorious Ma'di women who concoct the deadly poison secrete it securely, barring all access to it. Driven by the desire to eradicate what is believed to be a deadly potion from society and protect people from its danger, the poisoning issue persists. However to resolve the matter those who have been assigned the task of apprehending the alleged criminals must adopt stricter methods and seize the substance by surprise raids. It can then be used for public show, scientific analysis and court display.

Intertribal Marriages

The custom of intertribal marriage have been cited as one of the most important features affecting the lives of Ma'di, Bari, Acholi and Lulubo people in the lands where authority is the only element that is contested. Akeri married wives from all four tribes. His first wife was Ile Jakaliya from the Patibi clan of his Ma'di tribe. Then he married Aleka from the Lulubo-Aru tribe in the 1950's. This was followed by his two Bari wives, Cizarina and another woman, both from southern Bari. In the 1970's he married Maria of the Acholi tribe completing his socializaion circle and creating unity among the people of Iyii tribal society. Chief Akeri Geri was not the first prominent Ma'di man to marry wives from these neighbouring tribes. Tombe Bworo who lived alternately in Bori-Opari and Moli chieftainships was famous throughout the region during the first half of the twentieth century as he was believed to be able to change from his human form to that of a leopard to settle scores with his adversaries. He married a total of twenty-five wives from the Ma'di, his tribe, then from the Kuku, Acholi, Bari and Lulubo.[24]

The following is a list of Logili chiefs produced from oral information gathered from various sources, one of whom was the eldest daughter of Chief Ipele Geri Ipele, called Cuofo Oddu, whom I met twice while gathering information about her family.

1- Ayu
2- Urube
3- Dupari Kolo
4- Yanga Mele
5- Tombe Moli
6- Geri Ipele
7- Akeri Geri
8- Andrew Aloa Geri

The names of the predecessors of Chief Andrew Alao Geri, as suggested by him, does not conform exactly to the above list because this particular family of chiefs did not record the names of their ancestors accurately, a situation reported by writer J. V. Rowley who conducted a study of Ma'di chief genealogies. He declared that the Odupkwe in Mugali, Pandikeri in Bori-Opari, Tedire in Erepi were being properly kept while pointing out problems with other chieftainships and even families.

5.4 The Mugi Clan Chieftainship in Moli

Among the chiefs of the Mugi clan of Moli, Kejikiri is the man whose lineage can best be followed. This is because the Logili leadership had overshadowed the Mugi clan chieftainship. Being the second most powerful leadership after the Logili clan in Moli, the members of the Mugi royal family who assumed power were not keenly followed. After Kejikiri, men like Muku assumed the Mugi leadership and was popular only during the successful reprisal war against the Lokoya-Langabu towards the end of the nineteenth century. When he died, his son Lagu took over as chief and seemed to be weak. After Lagu, his son Wani became chief and from him, the chieftainship went to Keri. But in the Muku family, the only person who had featured in the annals of Ma'di history was the senior Muku because the first Lokoya-Langabu attack on Moli villages was during his chieftainship. It was his big he-goat called Kongiru, stolen by the Lokoya-Langabu warriors that sparked off the skirmishes which followed and which lasted for several years. Muku's power is reflected in the war song sung by an unknown Mugi man after the attack on the three Lokoya-Langabu villages of Okire, Omangara and Ofiri. The Lokoya historian asserted that four villages were destroyed naming the fourth as Omiling[25] notwithstanding the Moli historians' repeated claim that three villages were destroyed.[26] The singer tells Muku how they have attacked (O)kire and destroyed it. This is because their houses cannot burn partially. The Catholic missionary historians who documented this feud said it was the goat of Tombe Bworo which was stolen by the Lokoya that sparked off the fighting between them and the Moli people[27] but in reality, the goat belonged to Chief Muku.[28] Tombe Bworo's part in this war was that he acted very successfully as a reconnaissance agent or spy for the Moli by following a group of Lokoya-Langabu raiders from the Moli area up to their villages in the Langabu Mountains overlooking the Nile. It was his incisive report about the enemy position and behaviour after his return from the mission that helped the Moli attackers execute their war plans successfully on the three villages of Okire, Omangara and Ofiri although the smaller village of Omiling which was also destroyed according to the Lokoya historian is hardly mentioned in the Moli legends. Tombe Bworo took such steps because his own father Mori who lived in Nyori Kotopila village, the home of his maternal uncle of the Paluda clan, was killed secretly by Lokoya-Langabu raiders who hid the body and which until this day has not been found.[29]

5.4.1 Kejikiri

Kejikiri was the great rainmaker of the Mugi clan who probably lived in the last quarter of the nineteenth century. He was succeeded by his son Kadini whose power as a rainmaker in turn was inherited by his son Aleka who was also famous in Moli for being a great archer.[30] In Moli, it was usual to have more than one rain shrine in the same clan. Within the Mugi clan itself, there was another rain shrine owned by the ancestor of Muku. Muku's son Wani inherited it from him on his death. There had been a breakdown of leadership within the Logili clan, since Kejikiri did not take the place of the slain Logili chief who left a will that his son Dupari Kollo must be chief. Had any member of the Mugi clan become chief, the curse of Urube could have caused a calamity, a death in the family or other misfortune. So when Tombe Moli the son of Mele who became chief briefly for health reasons abandoned the chieftainship, Wani Muku succeeded him but he too for personal reasons could not continue as chief and the leadership went back to the Logili clan and was assumed by Geri Ipele.[31] He was succeeded by his son Akeri Geri. When Akeri was accused by the Moli people on the initiative of Wani Lou Morjan, the father of the author, for mismanaging grain brought by the local government authorities in Torit as relief food during a spell of starvation in Moli following drought circa 1939, he was briefly replaced by Yongo Alimas Dumo, a Mugi. The family of the new chief had no rain shrine but he assumed leadership on behalf of Wani Muku who had refused to be chief. Yongo Alimas Dumo having no rain shrine was reflected in a folksong composed by Mindraa Nya Amure of Beka clan.

5.4.2 Yongo Alimas Dumo

Yongo Alimas Dumo was the son of Amoni of the Mugi clan. In the early 1920's, he was one of the few sons of chiefs who benefitted from the colonial policy of offering education to the chiefs' sons in Opari elementary school run by the Church Missionary Society (CMS). Although he only attended the school for about a year, he was able to write his name and to do some arithmetic on his personal account. He first became chief briefly in 1932 when Geri Ipele was taken to prison in Juba and his son Akeri was too young to replace him. This occurred when the reigning chief was accused by some families in Moli of ordering a witch hunt and making a number of women undergo a ritual performed by a man called Lokudo brought from Ngaya in Bori-Opari because they were suspected of being in possession of poison which they had allegedly used to kill some persons. At least two of the women who underwent the ritual died. Yongo Alimas Dumo did not spend a long time as chief of Moli because in 1933 when drought hit the region and he was unable to make rain fall (his parents not being rainmakers) the people of Moli cried out for his resignation and subsequent assumption of power by Akeri Geri who was a rainmaker. A song titled Ndeke was composed by a woman called Mindraa Nya Amure of Beka clan to that effect.[32] It goes like this:

Ori Omena ba kodra pelere
Opi nyiba eyirii kodi bani
Yongo esu eyi ni ekwi ko
Ori Omena ba kodra nyini troa
Opi nyiba eyiri kodi ba ni
Yongo pidri eyi ni ekwi yoo

A literal translation of this song from Ma'di:

Son of Omena people will perish
Chief make rain to fall for the people
Yongo does not possess a rain pebble
Son of Omena people will all die for you
Chief make rain to fall for the people
Yongo does not possess a rain stone

It was during his chieftainship that Yongo Alimas ordered the abandonment of Adrwi and Moli Tokuro, and the move to Aduro near the present Malandu. Akeri Geri built his home at a place he named Yomokwe. Others call it Momokwe. Chief Yongo Alimas was implementing the order of the District Commissioner in Opari to allow the people of Moli to move to the old road which ran from Mongalla through Rejaf along the White Nile to Deretu. From Deretu, the road ran south-east passing near Jombokokwe and through Nyongwa Poiya to Male and then on to Opari, its final destination. But after a short time, the road was abandoned when Opari was transferred to Torit in 1935. Most of the Moli people returned to Tokuro where there were a number of natural resources such as bamboo and shea butter fruits, and they were serviced by the Juba-Nimule Road.

5.5 Logili-Mugi Rivalry

Urube, one of the most powerful chiefs of the Moli people from the Logili clan was challenged by Kejikiri the chief of the Mugi clan. Urube's popularity could be measured by the overwhelming support he received from the following clans: Gonyapi, Paloi, Ukeyi, Monocu-Nyongwa, Degi, Gunyia, Pakoli, Lulubo, Utuno, Omunya etc. But the real power of the Logili chiefs rested on their ability to make rain fall. The size of the clan was not considered as automatically giving rise to tribal leadership because if it were so, the Ukeyi clan which at certain times in Moli history was nearly as large as that of the Logili, could have claimed the leadership. Their leader Kuyu, the father of Ingani was a great chief and a rainmaker too. The legend about the rain stones of the Logili called *moken na adara* has it that the stones dropped from the sky during a rainstorm over the homestead of the current chief, whose ancestor who collected the rain pebbles was said to have been selected by the divine power that lives in the sky.[33] Another version of the story of the origin of the rain stones says that a son was born to a Logili chief with a rain stone clenched in his right hand.[34] Other rainmakers' clans have a similar story about the origin of their stones. The rivalry between Urube of the Logili clan and Kejikiri of the Mugi clan led to the death of Urube because he caused a prolonged state of drought after he was ill-advised by Kejikiri to do so. The drought eventually angered the people of Moli who took up their spears and went to hunt for him in the bush where he had hidden. After a wide ranging search, they found him and one of them who was a servant (*opigo*) of Kajamindi, a notable from the Mugi clan, stabbed him in the abdomen with a spear contrary to the practice of killing a rainmaker by tying his hands and feet and laying him in a circle of burning wood to dry him till he dies. As a result of this action the Logili demanded compensation from the family of Kajamindi in the form of a girl. As he did not have a girl he presented a boy, prompting Chief Dupari Kollo's reservation about whether he would stay once he had grown up and got married. Kajamindi replied, "Yes, he will stay" and the name *kolu wa*, meaning "he would stay" has remained the name of the branch of Mugi after the man who was sent away by the Logili clan elders. It was suspected that as a man he might assume their chieftainship should the chief die suddenly and there was no direct inheritor in his family to assume leadership.

5.6 Ma'di people of Iyii and their Clans

By about 1932, the new Juba-Nimule road had reached Nimule on the border between Anglo-Egyptian Condominium Sudan and the Uganda Protectorate.[35] A chain of twenty road camps seven miles apart was constructed from Juba to Nimule to accommodate eleven workers in each gang including their headman who were to maintain the road section allocated to each camp. Between Camp No. 11 at Nyolo and Mejopadrani Camp No. 13 (renamed *Borokodongo* by Andrea Farajalla, the Bari road foreman in 1932) the labourers were often attacked by lions due to a shortage of people. In about 1934, Chief Akeri Geri of Moli encouraged by the onset of stability, security and the presence of law enforcement agents decided to send an advanced team from his clan of Logili to set off and build a home along the road in Iyii which falls east of Barijokwe Hill and Lupaingwe River because this was the original homeland of the ancestors of the Logili clan and other Ma'di clans associated with it.[36] *Barijokwe* and *Lupaingwe* are two Ma'di names which translate as 'Bari people are as numerous as wood' (*jo-kwe* means 'wood') while *lupa* is a kind of rock or stone and *ingwe* is 'white' hence *lupaingwe* means 'white stone.'

The team to Iyii was headed by Awira Rabo, the son of Nyama of the Aruju section of the Logili clan. His brothers, Jojo and Pirimo Ayira, accompanied him to the new home. Jojo later became more influential in Iyii than his elder brother Awira. The families of Awira, Jojo and Pirimo moved to Iyii from Adrwi in Moli where they had settled in about 1932 following their emigration from Rarengo village near Opari where they had been living since their return from Ayipa. In Rarengo, they built their home near that of Yasoni of the Dungo clan of Bari.(37) Members of the Dongu clan had settled for many years among the Ma'di and Acholi tribes. Those among the former regard themselves as Ma'di while those in the latter who are numerous think they are Acholi because they have forgotten their original Bari language and speak either Acholi or Ma'di instead. Other members of the Logili clan from Moli who followed Awira and his brothers to Iyii included Mogga Sai, the son of Mondi, and his half brother, Sai Paco, both of the Aruju section of the Logili clan, and Kute Musa the son of Tombe Moli, a cousin of Geri Ipele of Logili Luworo, the royal section of the clan. Swapere Katika, Longa Gangiri, Thomas Droko Nyamucungu, his brother Andruga Lotwoni and Wani Lokili Boronji also belonged to the Logili clan and they joined the others in Iyii. Lodu Bilal of the Dongu clan and maternal uncle of Chief Akeri Geri who was also the maternal grandfather of the author was also encouraged by Akeri to emigrate to Iyii because it was Logili land and thither he went. Other families who emigrated to Iyii included Yanga Itiri of Ijupi clan, Mattia Mandu, Karlo Hindi, Aride father of Romeo Inyani, a senior government official in Eastern Equatoria State capital, Torit and Amisi of Nyai clan, Aciko the father of Pitya Ulu Cavu and Loguta, father of Rubano, a school teacher, both of

Oloro-Ukeyi clan. Lodro Guwala and his brother Milla Placido, both sons of Akure of the Mugi clan, Alimas Adibara of Gonyapi clan, Sumai Betcu of Monocu-Nyongwa clan and Parizio Betcu of Dedi also moved from Moli to Iyii. Wani Lou Morjan, father of the author from Kiloloro clan also built a home near to that of his father-in-law Lodu Bilal Leju Jote in Iyii where his family members used to go seasonally to cultivate various food crops.[38]

From the above account, the clans of Iyii can be listed as follows:

1- Dedi
2- Dongu (of Bari origin)
3- Gonyapi
4- Ijupi
5- Kiloloro
6- Logili (its Luworo and Aruju sections, the former is the royal group)
7- Monocu-Nyongwa
8- Mugi
9- Nyai
10- Oloro (the Ukeyi section from Ifoga of Korokodia near Muruli but today because they speak Acholi they regard themselves more as Acholi than Ma'di)

The emigration of members of the above Ma'di clans to Iyii in 1934 and their settlement on the west bank of River Iyii viewed from the east or from the south bank of the same river after it turns sharply north of the Ma'di villages and flows westward, encouraged members of the Acholi and Bari tribes a few years later to move to the same area. From the bridge built over the river in 1932, the position of the Ma'di villages of Iyii is to the south. The first Bari man who came after the Ma'di clans had settled there was one Babala.(39) He was followed by other Bari men who included Nyombe, Gore, Umba and Tombe Nyudu of the Gumosi clan from Cecere. He and his followers settled across Iyii River north of the Ma'di settlement in about 1936. Tombe Nyudu was joined a few years later by other Bari families.

Among the first Acholi elders who came to settle in the area in about 1939 was Lojukureng father of Latana Omiyati from *Oloro* clan as the Acholi know them while those among the Ma'di are called *Orolo*. Other heads of families who came to Iyii included Leji Atanga, Israel Olebe, Felice Kenya, Remijo Aremo, Timateo Alimu and Ochira. They built their villages in an area they named Ombiyo located south of the Ma'di villages and a visitor from Moli to come to the Ma'di villages of Iyii had to pass these homes to reach his destination. The fact is that the Ma'di people are there because they had settled in the ancestral land of the Logili and other Ma'di clans allied to them. They were displaced from the area by Lokoya-Langabu raids on their villages in the area at the end of the nineteenth century up to the first quarter of the twentieth century when the place of the Lokoya-Langabu was taken by Pari (Lokoro) and Acholi Agoro raiders. The last raid on Moli villages by these latter people took place in the villages of Palutu in 1927.(40)

5.7 Mejopadrani (Borokodongo)

The Ma'di clans who lived in Mejopadrani are:

1- Mugi-Koluwa of Lango Julu Rocu son of Nyainga and brother of Angoji Rocu, Odego Rocu, Silverio Fulli, Sumai Rocu, Toke Rocu, Avelino Rocu and Feliciano Yugu as its leader.

2- Logili with Ovu Manya as its leader.

3- Dedi with Ruba as its leader,

4- Gunyia with Kidi Aguluru father of Awolo Kute, Lino Wani, George Modi, Jali Kidi, and Zozimo Koce as its leader.
5- Kiloloro with Aganas father of John Oddu as its leader.
6- Ijupi with Kolima Avudumoi as its leader.
7- Nyongwa-Monocu with Lukamari Tibi Waya as its leader.

About 1939 these clans were joined by a group of Dongu clan led by Titifano Tombe assisted by Paulo Kaconi with memberships of other elders, namely Jakalia Loro, Yasoni, Yokana Lodu, Benjamino Lodu, Kudang Otim, Nikalao Yanga, Emaliano Mogga, Thomasi Loro, Aurelio Loro, Kulang Dunasiano, Wilson Mori, Tartisio Okumu, Ladu Agapito, Kresensio Lodu, Emilio Mori, Tombe Ogili, Emmanuel Opoka, Loro Lojutoboi, Vitale Loro, Raimondo Kenyi, Gabureel Jore, Oti Langwel, Kenyi Oti, Krispino Mori, Daniel Loku, Paulino Lodu, John Yugu, Selestino Ongole, Odiya Ladu, Stephano Oti, Jildo Tombe, Lodu Remijo, Joseph Langoya and their families who were on their way to southern Bari, their original homeland which they fled due to Mahdist attacks when they decided to settle in Mejopadrani (Borokodongo) for a while.

5.8 The Clans in Moli

There are over 30 clans whose abode is in the northern Ma'di chieftainships of Moli. The Logili, Mugi, Paluda, Ukeyi and Pakoli are the most influential clans because of their traditional role in making rain fall and in maintenance of the land, keeping it free of epidemic diseases, insect or bird invasions of crops or crop diseases through performance of land purification rites.

The following is the list of the clans found in Moli chieftainships.[41]

1- Adiba
2- Afodo
3- Akunye
4- Beka
5- Dedi
6- Degi
7- Dugo
8- Dungo (of Bari origin)
9- Eremu-Weli
10- Gonyapi
11- Gunyia (eremu)
12- Ijupi
13- Jeru
14- Kande
15- Kiloloro
16- Logili
17- Lubule
18- Lulubo
19- Metu
20- Mijale
21- Moje
22- Monocu-Nyongwa
23- Mugi
24- Nyai
25- Nyori
26- Omunya
27- Orolo (a section which broke away from Ifoga's leadership in Korokodia, near Muruli and went to Acholi and today they consider themselves from that tribe and are called Oloro)[42]
28- Pa-Adi

29- Pajawu (who left their large village called Lerwa in Deretu area in 1937 after Chief Akeri Geri arrested a number of their women whom he suspected of being poisoners and accused them of killing his sister-in-law Enderi Adiri, wife of medical dresser Jentilio Mukaru of Gunyia with poison shortly after giving birth in the same village)
30- Pakoli
31- Paloi
32- Paluda
33- Patibi
34- Tugo (also found among the Bari)
35- Ukeyi
36- Utuno

Population of Moli Chieftainships

These 36 clans make up the overall population of Moli chieftainships. Due to irregular censuses in the areas, low estimates of population are often given for Moli which in the past had been one of the most populous areas of Ma'diland with the large villages of Iyii, Monocu, Garamu, Mugi, Lolubo, Ndaka-Ukeyi, Deretu all along Juba-Nimule Road, Avatindi, Moli-Baribari, Mutala, Molonyi, Ambayo, which were a little farther away from the trunk road and Mojoro, Aduro, Muruli, Cukole along the Dereto (Erepi)-Cukole feeder road then Okwaaliyo, Malandu, Nyori, Gori, Cecere, located in the Liro River basin where the inhabitants live. The current population figure of 29,913 quoted from the Ma'di Development Plan – Obuni 2004 document was calculated using the factor 1.5579674166 to arrive at the population growth rate to produce the 2019 estimate. According to this calculation based on the population in 2004 given as 19,200 for

Moli (Tokuro and Moliandro – Malandu) in 2004, the current population is 29,913. But this may be inaccurate because in 2004, most of the Moli people were either in Uganda as refugees or in significant numbers in Juba and Khartoum as internally displaced persons (IDPs). Furthermore, if persons of Moli descent were hiding in the deep bush from the Sudan Government Army, reemerging after the Comprehensive Peace Agreement (CPA) of 2005, then the actual population figure could be larger than this. Indeed, there were a large number of people living in the Liro region under the leadership of Chief Lagu Akiro who told me in April, 2009 during the Ma'di Community Convention in Arapi that the population of Moliandro (Malandu) was estimated to be over 21,000.[43] As for Moli Tokuro, the Chief at the time, Andrew Alao Geri, told me in April, 2010 that during the population census of 2008, most inhabitants of Moli Tokuro were not counted because they were still being repatriated from refugees' camps in Uganda, a population movement which coincided with the National Census of 2008. He said in the 2010 general elections, during the enumeration of the eligible voters in which he was involved, the population could not be less than 15,000. [44] So if the estimates of 21,000 for Moliandro and 15,000 for Tokuro are added together, the population of Moli chieftainships becomes 35,000 in 2010 and not 29,200 in 2019 from the figures of the Ma'di Development Plan-Obuni. Moreover because of disagreement between the Government of South Sudan (GOSS) and the Government of National Unity in Khartoum over the 2008 census results for the South given as slightly over 8 million, the Government in Juba was not bold enough to publicize figures it considered incredible.

Notes and References

1 Gray, Emmanuel Kitchere. *The Catholic Church in Loa*, Khartoum, 1994, p.18. See also Victor Keri Wani, *An Outline of Ma'di History, Culture, Traditions and Customs in Sudan*, Juba, 1992, (unpublished). Father Giuseppe Baj, *Linguistic Guide on Ma'di Language: a) Opari dialect, b) Lokai dialect*, MS.

2 Interview of author with Chief Akeri Geri in Juba, August 1982.

3 Op. Cit. Wani.

4 Maps attached to Equatoria Province Handbook written in 1936 by Governor F. L. Nalder indicates this border. Another map from 1956 presented during the 6 September 2008 Kit Border Conference also clearly shows this.

5 Interview of author with Chief Akeri Geri of Moli in Juba in August 1982.

6 Gray, Richard. *A History of Southern Sudan 1838–1889*, London, Oxford University Press, 1961, p.38.

7 Interview of author with Alex Locor Nartisio, a Lokoya traditional historian in Torit in 27-5-2005.

8 Interview of Cuofo Oddu, daughter of Chief Geri Ipele in Hai Game, Juba on 24-11-1994.

9 Ibid.

10 Op. Cit. Gray, p.170.

11 Op. Cit. Oddu.

12 Informant Koka Iseni Lou in Juba in 1974.

13 Op. Cit. Oddu Interview.

14 Rowley, J. V. *Notes on the Ma'di of Equatoria Province*, Sudan Notes and Records No. XXIII, 1940, pp. 283, 286, 291.

15 Interview of author with his mother Rita Keji Lodu in Juba on 26-11-1994.

16 Interview of author with his paternal uncle Koka Lou Mbwele a.k.a. Iseni in Juba in 1981.

17 Nalder, L. F. *Equatoria Province Handbook, Vol. 1*, Mongalla, 1936, p. 50.

18 Ibid. p. 164.

19 Ibid.

20 Op. Cit. Oddu Interview.

21 Op. Cit. Lodu interview of 1992.

22 Op. Cit. Interview with Geri.

23 Interview of author with Adislao Loduma Mairi in Hai Buluk, Juba on 20-11-1994.

24 Op. Cit. Wani.

25 Op. Cit. Nartisio on 20-5-2005.

26 See '*Ofo Ma'di Ti Si*' (History in Ma'di Language), Loa, 1945, p.46.

27 Ibid. p. 44.

28 Op. Cit. Lou interview in 1974.

29 This information was given to author by his mother Rita Keji whose mother was from Paluda clan in Juba on 15-10-1974.

30 Informant is Koka Lou Mbwele a.k.a. Iseni in Juba in 1981.

31 Ibid.

32 Op. Cit. Lodu interview on 10-12-2004.

33 Op. Cit. Mairi interview.

34 Ibid.

35 Op. Cit. Nalder, p. 8.

36 Op. Cit. Geri interview.

37 Op. Cit. Lodu interview, 1992.

38 Op. Cit Geri interview.

39 Informant is Rita Keji Lodu mother of author who was brought to Iyii in 1935 by her father Lodu Jote Bilal of Dongu

clan. She gave the information in Juba on 20-11-1994.

40 Interview of Ukal Kawang Julu in El Haj Yousif, Takamul, Khartoum North on 14-4-1996.

41 Op. Cit. Wani. See also *Narrating Our Future, Customs, Rituals and Practices of the Ma'di of South Sudan and Uganda*, Centre of Advanced Studies of African Societies (CASAS), Cape Town, 2011.

42 This fact was stated to the author by Peter Oni Ibrahim of Moli in Juba on 13-9-2008.

43 Interview of author with Chief Lagu Akiro in Arapi, on April 6, 2009.

44 Interview of author with Chief Andrew Alao Geri in Moli Tokuro in April 2010.

Chapter Six

The Southern Sector Chieftainships of Lokai (Mugali), Nimule, Loa

6.1 The Extent of the Chieftainships

The area of the southern chieftainships of Lokai (Lokayi) borders Uganda in the south, the Nile and the Nyeri Mountain ranges to the west. The central sector of Arapi-Pageri-Nyongwa chieftainships lies to its north while the eastern chieftainships of Bori-Opari is located north-east of the chieftainships. The longest span of the area measures roughly 23 miles from River Anyama (called by the Ma'di, River Ame) in the south to Eyietcako, a village a mile away from Pajokwa-Loa, the last village of the sector in the north. The old historic settlements of Lokai people where the Odupkwe leadership resided are Ndindi and Mua, both east of Loa which is another base of the chief and then Mugali. Once the former chief of Lokai, Alimu Dengu built his home across River Eyibi in Loa territory.

6.2 The Odupkwe Chieftainships in Lokai
Sub-Chief Ruben Surur Iforo of Odupkwe Clan

Ruben Surur Iforo was the son of Surur Iforo, the brother of Alimu Dengu. Their father was Chief Kenyi Badaa of the Odupkwe clan from his second wife called Kaku. The first wife was Opio who begot Loku the father of Lubai, Odego, Debele and Bafura.[1] Ruben Surur Iforo was the first educated member of Odupkwe family to become sub-chief in Mugali. Although his elder brother Lubai was handed over to the Catholic missionaries by his father Loku and taken to Paloro for primary education, he came back home without completing the programme.[2] As for Cirino Odego, he barely tolerated practical carpentry lessons conducted by a Catholic brother in the Loa Mission in the late 1920's.[3] Ruben Surur Iforo, benefited from the colonial policy of education for chiefs' sons introduced in Opari by the District Inspector, Captain E. T. N. Grove in 1919.[4] Ruben was enrolled in the Church Missionary School (CMS) primary school at Opari, Nyakaningwa in around 1920 and he proceeded to Malek two years later where he received instruction in primary education from Archdeacon Shaw, a Britisher. Before his cousin Cirino Odego lost power as head chief of Ma'di at Loa in 1950, he appointed Ruben as chief for Mugali and Nimule areas. When Sabazio Okumu Abdalla was elected headchief of Ma'di in April 1952, in the reshuffle of traditional chiefs and their replacements with their court clerks, Ruben Surur Iforo was spared in his position of leadership but demoted to the junior post of a sub-chief (*mukungu*) of Mugali probably because he was semi-literate but subordinated to Chief Aniceto Amoli of Urugu, a non-royal clan, who was based in Nimule.

6.2.1 Ruben leads the attack on a lioness named Foni

One of the duties of a tribal chief among the Ma'di is to lead his people against anything threatening their lives. In Lokai, when Ruben Surur Iforo was chief, a lioness called Foni terrorized the Ma'di people from Moli in the north to Mua in the south. Erodionne Murulu Jiribi, who said he was a teenage boy at the time, witnessed the havoc and fear caused by the lioness.[5] It killed a number of people in Mua in the late 1930's when Juba-Nimule Road was newly opened to traffic. It is believed that the lioness Foni followed the newly opened road from the Bari country in the north through Moli where it terrorized people before coming southward. Erodionne said he followed elders led by Chief Ruben Surur Iforo in their mission to kill the lioness when an alarm was raised after the lioness killed a woman and her child. The mother killed was called Marli Alimo Lilia.[6] The beast was finally killed in Ibbi River, a tributary of River Eyibi on the way to Mua. It is said that the lioness Foni was found with a white ring on each of its ears. Another story going around about the lioness was that when it was killed in Lokai area and its stomach was opened, the ear and arm rings and anklets of the people it had killed and eaten over the years were discovered in its gut. The Ma'di people blamed the opening of the Juba-Nimule Road in 1932 for the appearance of Foni in their area.

An elder in Moli once said that Foni was searching for her husband called Rafaile who had become separated from her. She thought he had come towards Ma'di country and possibly had been killed and so she set off along the Juba-Nimule Road looking for him. The hungry lioness resorted to killing and eating people who came her way because she had become weak due to the extensive trip she had made from the north and was unable to kill her usual prey. Her great age also affected her ability to hunt. The elder said Foni approached the Ma'di area from Bariland in the north and several times broke the traps laid by people in Moli and escaped southward seriously imperilling the people of Lokai. It was thought that her husband Rafaile was the lion which asked the watchman Lokulu, in the crop fields of the Catholic mission at Choyi, to come out in the middle of the night, a demand which the watchman stoutly rejected. Musicians at the time converted Lokulu's supposed conversation with Rafaile into a famous song sung by players of the Ma'di harp or *lakambe* throughout Ma'diland. The song goes as follows:

> *Ebigo oce Lokulu nyi ingo,*
> *Alo mai makwi angwe ko.*
> *Kanya kotce Lokulu nyefu,*
> *Kwakwa mafu angwe ko*
>
> *Lion said Lokulu where are you?*
> *I am the only one I shall not come out.*
> *Great Lion demanded that Lokulu must come out.*
> *Never! Never! Shall I come out!*

Both Erodionne Murulu Jiribi of Arapi and Bernardo Mele Alimo of Mugali said that when the Ma'di people heard that hunters led by Chief Ruben Surur had trapped and killed the lioness Foni, there was general relief and jubilation everywhere.[7] Songs were composed to express this jubilation and one of them from a Lokai artist runs as follows:

Nyolo nyini ao Ruben odi Foni ni ra
Esu amadri ke-egwe
Occa eni na ko karindzi
Nyindre nyini Ruben odi Foni pkwo
Esu amadri karuki
Occa eni na ko karindzi [8]

Don't panic, Ruben has killed Foni
Otherwise we were getting lost
Don't pierce its skin it will get spoiled
See Ruben has killed Foni
Otherwise we were getting confused
Don't spoil its skin

In fact, when the Juba-Nimule Road was opened, it became a highway for a bevy of lions and lionesses. Most of them were aged and they wondered along the road from the north in Bariland to the south in Ma'diland and attacked anybody they came upon and killed them. Even the workers in the road camps built along the Juba-Nimule Road at seven miles intervals were often attacked by these beasts. The attacks on the occupants of the camps were frequent in areas where the population was thin, and the attacks were launched at night and sometimes even in broad daylight.

6.3 The Clans in Mugali: [9]
These are the names of the clans found in Lokai southern chieftainships in the villages of Mugali, Nimule and Loa.

1- Agunga
2- Alu
3- Bari

4- Cera
5- Jeru
6- Kamia
7- Kiloloro
8- Logili
9- Logopi
10- Metu
11- Odupkwe (royal clan)
12- Pa-Amulu
13- Pacara
14- Pacunaki
15- Padiga
16- Pafoki
17- Pageri
18- Paika
19- Paloi
20- Palungwa
21- Paluru
22- Pamulu
23- Pamuru
24- Paselo
25- Patibi
26- Puceri

6.4 A Brief History of Nimule Chieftainships
The Koyi Chieftainship of Nimule

The beginning of Nimule as an administrative centre can be traced back to the period when Lt. Col Martyr of the British forces in Uganda Protectorate with the support of the Congo Free State troops based in Rejaf drove away the Mahdist forces under the command of Emir Arabi Daffallah in 1893 from their last base at Bor towards the North.[10]

Before the amalgamation of Mugali and Nimule chieftainships into a single administrative unit known as Nimule 'A' court, in 1952 or thereabouts, Kara of Pa-manini clan was chief in Nimule and he held the requisite rain stones. He took over from his brother Eyitca. In 1913, following a border adjustment between Anglo-Egyptian Sudan and Uganda British Protectorate,[11] Nimule reverted from the latter to the former. This action was related to the return of the Lado Enclave to Sudan by the Belgian Congo. It had been agreed between the Belgian monarch and the British Crown in 1884 that King Leopold II of Belgium was to possess the Lado Enclave till his death, upon which the territory would be given back to the British administration. Hence when King Leopold died in 1909[12] in compliance with that agreement, the Belgians gave back Lado Enclave to the British in 1910. But Kara the chief was deposed because he did not know Arabic. Surur Lerikowo who was also known as Surur Abu Kara was an interpreter at Opari and he was installed in his place.[13] Before his appointment, Surur Abu Kara had made an abortive attempt to usurp the crown by entering a house in which the dead body of the chief lay, taking a coat and bracelet from the body and presenting them to the District Commissioner of Opari as the seal of office, claiming the throne. He reigned for a few days until the District Commissioner was told what had happened, gave him a thrashing and sent him about his business.[14] Surur Lerikowo remained chief of Nimule until 1936 when he resigned as he refused to be subordinated to Chief Cirino Odego in Loa.[15] Muhamme (Muhammed) Kara of the Pa-manini was unanimously elected sub-chief (*mukungu*) of Nimule to work under Cirino Odego. After him, Agala ruled as sub-chief of Nimule and he cooperated fully with Chief Cirino Odego his senior, and always identified himself with the latter. On one of the occasions in which the headchief and sub-chief of Lokai officiated at the Loa elementary school under the Catholic missionaries, the school children composed a song in which they praised the two personalities. The song runs as follows:

> *Cirino ama nyandzo yoo!*
> *Agala ama nyandzo!*
> *Opii amadri Ma'diga ree*
> *Cirino ama nyetcu yoo!*
> *Agala ama nyetcu!*
> *Opii amadri Ma'diga ree*
>
> *Cirino we thank you oh!*
> *Agala we thank you!*
> *Our Chiefs of Ma'di*
> *Cirino we praise you oh!*
> *Agala we praise you!*
> *Our Chiefs of Ma'di.*[16]

Agala was removed as sub-chief of Nimule in 1952 by Headchief Sabazio Okumu Abdalla during his overhaulling of the Ma'di traditional administration by replacing him with Chief Aniceto Amoli under whom Mugali (Lokai) chieftainship of Ruben Surur Iforo was subordinated. Ruben Surur was demoted by appointing him to the post of sub-chief (*mukungu*) and annexing Mugali to Nimule.[17] The situation was similar to what had happened in Moli chieftainship in the northern Ma'di sector where Chief Akeri Geri was dismissed and his influential chieftainship abolished and annexed to Erepi chieftainship and Jelindo Chaka Aperiya, who was the court clerk in Erepi court of Chief Eberu Drani, was appointed as the responsible chief. The difference between the Headchief's reaction to Ruben Surur Iforo and Chief Akeri Geri was that while Ruben considered himself chief and undermined the authority of Chief Aniceto Amoli, in Moli, Chief Akeri remained defiant despite his dismissal and considered himself chief without authority. He neither recognized Sabazio Okumu Abdalla as headchief nor Jelindo Chaka as chief of Erepi, Moli and Nyongwa. For reasons unknown, Headchief Sabazio Okumu Abdalla refrained from reprimanding former Chief Akeri Geri about his negative attitude towards him and Chief Jelindo Chaka also feared to communicate with his predecessor. Some people surmised that Akeri Geri's coming from Logili clan being the most influential royal clan in Moli ignored Okumu because he originated from Gonyapi clan which is an ordinary group. As for Chief Jelinda Chaka, although he was from the Mugi clan hailing from Muruli which is a smaller royal clan in Moli, he came from the Palumari section of the Mugi and hence Akeri regarded him as an ordinary countryman without sufficient royal blood to be his chief. Jelindo Chaka tried his best by befriending several notables in Moli so that they could distance themselves from Akeri Geri and support him. He kept both Okumu Alibei, the son of Kajamindi of Mugi clan as sub-chief (*mukungu*) and Vuni Tusu of Kiloloro clan as assistant-chief (*nyampara* in Moli). He also kept Akeri Geri's cousin Kute Musa in his position as sub-chief for Iyii. He later married Buta the daughter of Kute Musa to cement his closeness to the sub-chief.

6.4.1 Nimule, the Village, the District Town

The name *Nimule* is a foreign corruption of the Ma'di name *Nyimule*, meaning 'you are secretly targeting me or observing my movements'.[18] Likewise the Ma'di village *Odrupele* was called *Dufile* by foreigners under the sovereignty of Turco-Egyptian Sudan (1820-1885). Odrupele, because of its strategic location, was selected by Emin Pasha, Governor of Equatoria Province to serve as a capital in his last stand against the invading Mahdist forces commanded by Emir Karamallah who was later replaced by Omar Salih in 1889.[19] Omar Salih himself was replaced by Emir Arabi Daffallah.

In 1869 the old station of Nimule was used as a resting place by Samuel White Baker and his men, availing themselves of the shade provided by the great tamarind tree (*iti*). Baker was the first European Governor of Equatoria Province. Soon the station became a small town, its position lying west of Mugali and east of the River Nile. In the north, it was joined to Juba by a permanent murram road in 1932 and to Gulu in Uganda through Attiak by an all-season road. A motorway now joins it to Mugali, a cluster of Ma'di villages whose inhabitants are agriculturalists producing quantities of cereals and pulses, especially beans (*ossu*) the surplus of which they sell in Mugali and Nimule markets. In 1932, the colonial administration constructed an airstrip at Nimule in its eastern part. The semi-urban and rural areas of Nimule are inhabited by about two dozen Ma'di clans, but the most influential ones are the Pamotto, Pa-anini (Koyi), Accopele and Patibi. Pa-anini (also known as Koyi) are grouped together under a common name *Guru* and they had traditional chiefs. In the lineage of the Pamotto clan, Beshir Duku was the most influential chief of his time. It was he who tricked the armed group who were thought by some people to be the remnants of the forces of the Governor of Equatoria Province, Emin Pasha, who retreated from his capital at Dufile (Odrupele) southward from the Mahdist attacks. Other people say these were a group of Belgian soldiers known as Tukutuku who crossed over from New Dufile which they called Dufile Moke in Bangala[20] near Igwo on the west bank of the Nile. Other people thought they were a unit from the colonial forces of Uganda. Whoever these armed men were, they had been assembled by Beshir Duku to fight the Odupkwe clan. The Odupkwe clan had invited the Pamotto clan to fight with the Puceri clan, who had been accused of some wrongdoing.[21] However, Beshir Duku's mother was from the Puceri clan so he could not let danger come their way and used his knowledge and acquaintance with these people to divert the danger from the intended target to the very people who incited it, members of the Odupkwe clan. In the attack that ensued, several members of Odupkwe clan were killed and Alimu Dengu, the son of chief Loku escaped with his young sister Ruduwa to Gulu where she lived at Obokwe till the 1960's.[22]

6.5 The Nubi Community of Nimule

The Nubi people of Nimule are the descendants of the former soldiers of African descent in the Turco-Egyptian army from the garrisons in Equatoria Province commanded by Governor Emin Pasha. The origin of the word *Nubi* is difficult to establish. The eminent Sudanese historian at Makerere University, Professor Al Zein Al Saghairon who is an authority on the history of the Sudanese Muslim factor in Uganda and who followed the former soldiers in the 1960's to Uganda for research purposes, has had little success. By all accounts the name appeared in Uganda where the former soldiers were enlisted in Kavalli and taken and resettled in Buganda by Captain Lugard. The likely origin of the name is suggested by several stories. One version given by Mohammed El Haj of Malakia Juba says the second-in-command of the garrisons of the Turco-Egyptian army in Equatoria province was a man from the Nuba Mountains in central Sudan and his soldiers were named for his origin.[23] However the most senior officer who served under Emin Pasha was Selim Eddin Bey and whether he was from one of the Nuba tribes or from one of the African tribes of western Sudan, Darfur or Kordofan, who were numerous in the Turco-Egyptian army, is not recorded. The Nuba people of central Sudan as they are known in the modern era are made up of more than ninety tribes.[24] Another hypothesis says the womenfolk of the soldiers of Emin Pasha plaited their hair in many tiny plaits from the forehead backward. This popular hair style is called *nubi* and the name might have been applied to the former soldiers who had remained tightly bound together according to their units after the army in which they had served was disbanded in 1889. What is certain is that the name refers to a group of people who are descendants of the African soldiers who last served under Governor Emin Pasha of Equatoria Province excluding the Turkish, Egyptian and Arab elements who served in the same garrisons of the khedival army. The descendants of the soldiers chose to be brought to Nimule because the town is near Dufile (Odrupele) which was their last station before retreating to Wadelai in Alur country in the face of the advancing Mahdist forces under the command of the first Emir, Karamallah. Karamallah was later succeeded by Omar Salih in 1889, who was in turn replaced by Emir Arabi Daffallah. Dufile is a restricted mountainous area facing the Nile River whereas Nimule is situated in an open plain overlooked by the Gordon Hills to the north. To the south is open land belonging to Uganda. The Nile is west of Nimule and flows northwards.

The Nubi were brought to Nimule in two waves and to the other southern Sudanese towns of Juba, Kajokeji, Morobo, Kaya and Yei from East Africa. In East Africa they had been settled in towns like Bombo some twenty-one miles north of Kampala and in Kibuli a suburb of the same city. Some are found in Dar es Salaam, Tanganyika, Zanzibar and Kibira near Nairobi in Kenya. The first arrivals were resettled in these places in 1919 after some of them participated in the First World War (WWI) of 1914-1918 on behalf of the British and the second wave of arrivals were resettled in 1946 after their participation in the Second World War (WWII) of 1939-1945 serving with the King's African Rifle (KAR) of East Africa.[25] Those who chose Nimule believed that they were Ma'di by origin because many Ma'di were recruited in the Emin Pasha army in garrisons like Paloro, Dufile, Labore (Moli), Ayu and Muggi which were located within Ma'di territory.[26] When they arrived at Nimule after the First World War in about 1917, they found among the indigenous Ma'di people living in the border town and its adjoining areas, members of Pamanini, Pamotto, Accopele, Alu, Patibi and other clans.

Although the district headquarters in Nimule was transferred to Opari because the town was ceded to Sudan following a border adjustment between Uganda and Sudan in 1913,[27] Nimule, because of its strategic position and as a port of call for steamers sailing from the Ugandan port of Pakwach on the Nile and Butiaba on Lake Edward, remained a town of affluence and trade. The Nubi individuals came with some cash which they were probably given by the British administration in East Africa as gratuity for taking part as soldiers in WWI and WWII on the side of the British. Some of them established small shops and ran retail businesses thus contributing to the economy of the people of Nimule. Besides their name *Nubi*, the Ma'di called the new arrivals *Fala* and embraced them as their own. Some of the Nubi families went and settled in Opari where the district headquarters was moved to, in 1914. The name 'Fala' also has its origin in the Turco-Egyptian era during which those who tilled the land to produce the food required by the soldiers, especially army officers, were often referred to by the Egyptian officers and officials as 'fallah' which in their country means tillers of the land. Hence this name remained as an identification for those associated with the former system of the Turco-Egyptians. The Nubi were resettled in Nimule and Opari because they were a people familiar with town life and adept at petty trading and thus contributed to the economic development of Ma'diland. A few of them such as Romano built his home and petty shop in Pageri near the market called Langauro. Because the Ma'di are a social community, they intermingled with the Nubi easily and many of their girls were married to young Nubi men establishing a mixed society in the Nimule and Opari townships.

The Nubi are Muslims and introduced active Islamic life in Nimule and Opari where they constructed mosques for performing their prayers and for instructing their children in Islamic doctrine, especially in recitation of the Quran. They also speak a pidgin form of Arabic. In Nimule when the first returnees arrived, they found Ma'di leadership in place and were at first administered by Ma'di chiefs. At the time of their arrival, Kara of Pa-manini clan was chief and this chieftainship rotated among his descendants. Due to their interest in living under a strong and just system of administration, the Nubi were also eager to contribute to the welfare of the community and they decided to select a sub-chief to forge a link with the Ma'di leadership in Nimule. It was this that led to Keralla Wani the grandfather of Rajab Juma, the Nubi, becoming sub-chief in Nimule.[28]

6.6 The Clans found in Nimule:[29]

1- Accopele
2- Alu
3- Gimeri
4- Itopele
5- Kiloloro
6- Odupkwe
7- Ogowa
8- Oyapele
9- Pa-Anini (Koyi)
10- Pacara
11- Pacunaki
12- Padombe
13- Pafoki
14- Paika
15- Pakurukwe
16- Palore
17- Pamajwa
18- Pameri
19- Pamotto
20- Patibi
21- Pavura
22- Puceri
23- Mujopele
24- Murupele
25- Urugu

6.7 The Chieftainships in Loa

Loa has enjoyed the position of being the headquarters of Ma'di native administration since the 1930's when Chief Cirino Odego built his home at Robijo, about a mile north of his office. His father Lubai who was also chief, lived in Mua but since the construction of the Juba-Nimule Road in the period 1928-32[30] which connected Loa to other Ma'di villages from Iyii to Mugali, it became necessary to locate the main centre of Ma'di traditional leadership at Loa. Loa was regarded as the capital of Ma'diland. The village itself is near the Catholic mission, about four miles from the local government centre, where the elementary school for teaching the Ma'di children, especially the chiefs' sons and those of notables is located. The Protestant church at Nyakaningwa in Opari and the Catholic mission at Loa opened schools within their premises in 1920[31] and 1923[32] respectively. They were directed by the District Commissioner of Opari in 1920 to implement the government policy of making educational opportunities available to the sons of chiefs and notables of Ma'di so that a class of educated elites would be created in the chieftainships. The main aim of this was to prepare the sons of the chiefs for the eventual handover of authority from their uneducated fathers, thereby realizing the colonial policy of having literate traditional leaders. The educational proposal adopted by Mongalla Province Headquarters for the whole province was drawn up by E. T. N. Grove, the District Commissioner of Opari in 1919.[33] In Ma'diland after 1952, all the new chiefs appointed to take charge of the reorganized chieftainships had attained at least a basic level of education that enabled them to read in the Ma'di language and some English from the Catholic elementary school of Loa. They were Headchief Sabazio Okumu Abdalla, Chiefs Jelindo Chaka

Aperiya of Moli-Erepi-Nyongwa, Aniceto Amoli of Nimule-Mogali, Rafaile Abuni of Opari and Kerebino Drapaga of Loa.

In Loa itself there were no other influential clans which had traditional chiefs that could challenge the leadership of the Odupkwe clan. The Odupkwe clan was considered by all clans as the source of absolute authority in Lokai. There were however some influential clans whose leaders were customarily brought closer to the centre of power by Cirino Odego and chosen to play advisory roles in his court sessions, and they included Konide Lomeda of Pamotto clan in Melekwe, Akile of Logili clan in Ongoro, Icoko of Orobe clan and Olympio of Puceri clan in Iriya. Loa is also where the costumes for the Ma'di royal dance *mure* are produced. An industrious man called Ereyi Bassa used to produce headgear known as *ayomi* for this dance in his village of Pajokwa about two miles north of Loa local government headquarters. Since 1952, Loa has been named Opari-angwa by Headchief Sabazio Okumu Abdalla because after the transfer of the District Headquarters to Torit in 1935, the importance of Opari declined. It became the headquarters of Chief Dari Kanyara Isra of the Pandikeri clan in 1935. Opari-angwa means 'Little-Opari.'

6.7.1 The Clans in Loa[34]

1- Alli
2- Cera
3- Kamia
4- Kiloloro
5- Logili (Eyia section)
6- Metu
7- Moje
8- Odupkwe

9- Oloro (family of Tito Alimo at Pajokwa, Loa.)
11- Padombe
12- Pageri
13- Pajali
14- Pakala
15- Paloi
16- Paluru
17- Pameri
18- Pamotto
19- Paselo
20- Patibi
21- Pavura
22- Pavuri
23- Puceri
24- Urugu
25- Vura

Notes and References

1 Rowley, J. V. *Notes on the Ma'di of Equatoria Province*, Sudan Notes and Records, No. XXIII, 1940, p.283.

2 Dellagiacoma, V. *History of the Catholic Church in Southern Sudan 1900–1995*, Khartoum, 1996, p.33.

3 Interview of author with Karamello Dragala Balabas Lomeda in El Haj Yousif, Al Takamul, Khartoum North on 20-5-1995.

4 Passmore, Sanderson and Neville Passmore. *Politics, Education and Religion in Southern Sudan 1898–1964*, London, Ithaca Press, 1979, p.62.

5 Interview of author with Erodionne Murulu Jiribi in El Haj Yousif, Takamul, Khartoum North on 14-12-1996.

6 Interview of author with Bernardo Mele Alimo in Omdurman,

Ombada on 25-8-2008.

7 Ibid.

8 The song was resung to author by Erodionne Murulu Jiribi in El Haj Yousif, Takamul, Khartoum North in 1996 and repeated by Bernardo Mele Alimo in Omdurman, Umbada on 25-8-2008.

9 Gray, Emmanuel Kitchere. *The Catholic Church in Loa, Khartoum*, 1994, pp.21-23. See also Notes by Sestilio Andruga Juma on Ma'di clans in Sudan, Juba, 1991 and Victor Keri Wani, *An Outline of Ma'di History, Culture, Traditions and Customs in Sudan*, Juba, 1992, unpublished.

10 Nalder, L. F. *Equatoria Province Yearbook, Vol. I*, Mongalla, 1936, p.24.

11 Ibid. p.26.

12 Ibid.

13 Rowley, op. cit. p.287.

14 Ibid.

15 Ibid.

16 This song was sung to the author for research purposes in El Haj Yousif, Rudumiya, Khartoum North in 1994 by Sestilio Loku Silimani Vuni who was one of the pupils at Loa Elementary School in the 1940's.

17 Interview of author with William Alira Yanga in El Haj Yousif, Khartoum North, on 18-9-995.

18 See Jephson, A. J. Mounteney. *Emin Pasha and the Rebellion at the Equator*, London, Sampson Low, 1899.

19 Stigand, C. H. *Equatoria, The Lado Enclave*, London, Frank Cass, 1968, p.99.

20 Interview of author with Paul Dralile Lodu Bigo in Al Diknat, Khartoum on 14-8-1995.

21 Op. Cit. Yanga interview.

22 Ibid.

23 The speech he delivered during the Nubi-Malakiya Muslim Welfare Association (NUMA) second meeting on 3 October 2008, Khartoum International Fair ground.

24 Interview of Rev. Philip Abbas Gaboush with author in his Omdurman, Irsaliya home in January 1986.

25 Interview of author with Juma Magara Biluka, a descendant of a Nubi family of Nimule in El Haj Yousif, Khartoum North on 15-6-1996.

26 Op. Cit. Sanderson and Jephson.

27 Nalder, L. F. *Equatorial Province Handbook Vol. I,* Mongalla, 1936, p.26.

28 Interview of author with Rajab Juma in his home at Rudmiya, El Haj Yousif, Khartoum North on 21-4-1994.

29 Op. Cit. Gray, Juma and Wani. Some of the names of clans in Nimule were given by Chief Ben Maku Lukada from Koyi clan from the area in El Haj Yousif, Khartoum North on 21-11-2008.

30 Op. Cit. Nalder, p.105.

31 Op. Cit. Sanderson, p.62.

32 Op. Cit. Dellagiacoma.

33 Op. Cit. Sanderson, (education policy of E.N.T. Grove).

34 Op. Cit. Gray, Wani and Juma.

Chapter Seven

Central Sector Chieftainships of Arapi, Pageri, Nyongwa

7.1 The Extent of the Sector

This is the smallest of the five sectors of Ma'di chieftainships in the Sudan. In the south, it is bounded by the southern chieftainships of Lokai, in the west its border is marked by the River Nile and the northern part of Nyeri mountain ranges, in the north it shared a boundary with the western chieftainships of Erepi and to its east lies the larger eastern chieftainships of Bori-Opari. The longest span of the area of the chieftainships runs from River Eyibi, its eastern limit with Bori chieftainships and reaches across the Nile to the middle part of Mount Nyeri, measuring more than ten miles. From Eyietcako in the south to the Nyongwa-Lungayo border, its most northerly point, the distance is nearly five miles.

The main villages of the chieftainships are found in Arapi, Pageri and Nyongwa areas. They include; in the Arapi area, the villages of Eyietcako, Iloma, Adavu, Palinyi, Palungwa, Elema and Nyangiri, in the Pageri area, Pageri itself, Agaduma, and Mutuvu and in the Nyongwa area, Nyongwa Opii, Poiya, Matamaiza, Vuradoga, Jeru, Owoyyo etc.[1]

7.2 Arapi Chieftainship of Palungwa

During the period which preceded the era of colonial administration of Ma'diland, the Palungwa clan was in control in Arapi, and the Chief was Nyengwi Iro. After he was slain by the Acholi Panyikwara in Kadakada forest under Iwire Hill in about 1892,[2] his son Sai Mondi replaced him. Ginawi took over from Sai Mondi and he was among the sons of traditional chiefs who became leaders of areas other than in their own traditionally controlled regions. Ginawi was once appointed a chief in Opari when the leadership of Bori was in confusion caused by rivalry among the grandsons of Akeri Milla and his brothers who aspired to the same post but were not competent to run the affairs of the chieftainship efficiently as undertaken by Milla, Mene and Dari.

The Palungwa clan of Arapi believes that they descended from Bari in long antiquity[3] and that they are related to the Logopi clan whose ancestors had once lived close to the Bari before moving further south to integrate with the Ma'di to whom they are more akin than to Bari. The womenfolk of the two clans use the words *Nya Bari* as their honorific title *azaka*. 'Nya Bari' means daughter of Bari. Clan elders explain the meaning of this honorific title by suggesting that the men from these Ma'di clans married wives from the families of the neighbouring Bari and these women used to utter these honorific words as a way of identifying their origin or maintaining it, a custom which has been kept till this day by the womenfolk of these two clans.[4] The Ma'di are a patrilineal or patriachial society and not matrilineal so the origin of its clans cannot be traced through the female but through the lineage of the male.[5] The Palungwa clan became the focus of historical attention after the Acholi-Panyikwara killed their chief Nyengwi Iro in the hunting ground called Kadakada under Iwire Hill. According to Severino Fuli Boki, Chief Nyengwi was lured to his death by being invited as a friend by the Acholi chief and then murdered.[6] He was succeeded by his son Sai Mondi who in turn was succeeded by his son Jinawi Nyengwi. The Palungwa chief has several clans under his leadership in Arapi, the main ones being: Paridi, Palinyi, Pa-Akori, Kiloloro, Kamia, Jeru, Pageri, Patibi, Urugu and Padombe.[7]

The Arapi chieftainship is located between Loa, the headquarters of the Lokai chieftainship of Odupkwee in the south and to its north is the small Pageri chieftainship founded by Ito Kafiri whose father is said to not have been a rainmaker and therefore not a chief according to Ma'di traditional leadership rules.[8] To the east of the chieftainship is the Eyibi River and Remo Mountain under which the Pavunde clan, whose priest was responsible for performance of the land purification rite starting from the area and going towards Musura in the south-west, lived.[9]

The small hill called Amoria stands slightly off the Juba-Nimule Road which almost cuts the chieftainship into two equal parts. To the west of the chieftainship is the White Nile where its inhabitants regularly go to catch plenty of fish for food and sale in Langauro market of the Pageri. The most important economic infrastructure in the chieftainship is the tobacco curing plant constructed by the Blue Nile Cigarettes Company (BNCC) near Amoria Hill in about 1959. The men in Arapi were encouraged to grow tobacco and sell its leaves first in fresh form and later after air drying them, and in about 1961 barns were built locally by selected growers for drying the tobacco leaves before selling them to the company on a cash basis.

7.3 The Pageri Chieftainship
Ito Kafiri of Pageri Clan

According to the booklet '*Ofo Ma'di Ti Si – History in Ma'di Language*' Ito Kafiri made his fortune from his relationship with the Belgians of Lado Enclave. The Enclave bordered the southernmost part of Equatoria province which was administered by the Uganda Protectorate from Entebbe and was marked by the River Nile in the east.[10] The British district administration in Nimule was ineffectual here and this gave an opportunity to the Belgians, known locally by the Ma'di people as Tukutuku,[11] to cross the Nile and conduct business with the locals illegally. It was through such contact that Ito Kafiri came to be employed by the Belgians as a watchman 'kafir.' But J. V. Rowley the District Commissioner of Opari and later of Torit in the period 1934-38 in his booklet 'Notes on Ma'di of Equatoria Province' described Ito Kafiri as being at one time a sergeant in the Belgian army.[12] The Ma'di people say that he had no previous royal ties and his ascension to the throne of chief of Pageri was due to his influence with the Belgians who promoted him.[13] Rowley further wrote: 'Chief Ito Gaferi (Kafiri) has no hereditary claim to be a chief.'[14] But as fate would have it, he became a chief and a man of influence for many years. He died in Pageri in 1957 and was mourned by a great number of people who came from as far away as Ma'di

Metu of Uganda in December 1957 to perform the *mure* dance at his graveside. The dance coincided with Christmas eve because when the author was in the company of the youth of his village of Moli going to Loa to celebrate the feast, he saw the dancers in full *mure* costume performing around the grave of the dead chief in Pageri on the way to Loa. Ito Kafiri's son Silimani Ito inherited his chieftainship and entered the circle of Ma'di traditional leaderships. He was once appointed chief of Pageri, Nyongwa, Erepi and Moli by the colonial administration in Torit in the mid 1940's. But the suspended chiefs of Erepi and Moli opposed his jurisdiction over them. Chief Akeri Geri of Moli in particular, incited his people against Silimani Ito, saying that he was from an ordinary clan whose ancestors did not possess the rain influencing rainstones which were required to be chief of the people.[15] Even in Erepi, the royal Tedire clan did not recognize his chieftainship and privately did not talk favourably of him.[16]

7.4 Nyongwa Chieftainship
Ala, Father of Uliya the Rainmaker

Ala of Nyongwa clan was the father of Uliya. Both him and his son who succeeded him were powerful rainmakers in Nyongwa-Opii in their respective tenures and therefore were respected chiefs of their subjects. The rain pebbles which were handed down from Ala to his son are believed to have fallen from the sky during a heavy downpour. Their bodies, smooth to the touch, are said to have been polished in the clouds from which they fell to earth due to the strong action of hail. Other rain pebbles are said to have been found in the clenched fingers of the rainmaker's newborn baby. To make the rainstones even more powerful, some of the stones were bought with a girl from Acholiland.

Ala named his rain-making shrine Nya-Bira meaning 'the daughter of Bira.'[17] However, despite their reputation for being powerful rainmakers, Ala and his son Uliya did not influence the Ma'di general traditional leadership as other chiefs (namely Cirino Odego of Lokai, Dari Kanyara Isra of Bori, Geri Ipele of Moli and Loku Kitcere of Erepi) had done during their periods in power. It was only Gulli from the Nyongwa lineage who was singled out by the colonial administrators in Opari as a promising character and appointed chief to replace Clemente Mamur Vumudri, son of Mene who succeeded his cousin Furunato Modo who had failed to lead in the Pandikeri lineage. However, the Pandikeri and other people of Bori rejected Gulli and sent him back to Nyongwa. At the time Gulli was a sub-chief under the chief in Pandikeri.[18]

7.4.1 The Ordeal of a Rainmaker in Nyongwa

In July 1977, Aride the famous rainmaker of Nyongwa-Opii was hacked to death by an angry local crowd who accused him of imposing a prolonged drought that caused food crops to fail and brought starvation in its wake. The people encircled Aride's body with stubs of half burnt firewood as was the Ma'di custom with a slain rainmaker, and the body was left by the roadside as a warning to other rainmakers who might be contemplating similar harm to the people. On the day Aride was killed, there was a heavy downpour in the area and coincidentally a motorcade of the former President of Sudan, Jaafar Mohammed Nimeiri passed by. The President, accompanied by his former Deputy, Abel Alier, was returning to Juba from a trip to Nimule and were passing by when the President and his entourage came upon the corpse. Nimeiri stopped the motorcade and enquired why the man had been killed. An elderly man who did not trouble to hide himself away from the heavily armed army and policemen escorting the President explained that the man was killed because he had stopped the rain from falling for a long time, causing harm to the people of the land. He added that it was an old practice designed to deal with harmful rainmakers. On hearing this, Nimeiri ordered the motorcade to resume the journey to Juba meanwhile entrusting the case to the police and the head-chief of the area to handle later.

7.5 The Clans of the Central Chieftainships of Arapi, Pageri and Nyongwa:[19]

1- Jeru
2- Kamia
3- Kiloloro
4- Logopi
5- Nyongwa
6- Owoyyo
7- Pa-Akori
8- Padombe
9- Pageri
10- Palinyi
11- Palungwa
12- Paridi
13- Patibi
14- Urugu

Notes and References

1 Quoted from document prepared by Romeo Inyani Aride for the proposed Pageri Area Council in 1997. See also Victor Keri Wani. *An Outline of Ma'di History, Culture, Traditions and Customs in Sudan*, Juba, 1992, unpublished.

2 Interview of author with Eroddione Murulu Jiribi in El Haj Yousif, Al Takamul, Khartoum North on 18-4-1994. See also Severino Fuli Boki. *Shaping a Free Southern Sudan, Memoirs of Our Struggle 1934 – 1985*, Loa Catholic Mission Council, Limuru, 2002, p.26.

3 Rowley, J. V. *Notes on the Ma'di of Equatoria Province*, Sudan Notes and Records, Vol. XXIII, 1940, p.288.

4 Angelo Vinco's account quoted in Elias Toniolo and Richard Hill, *The Opening of the Nile Basin*, London, C. Hurst, 1974, p.97.

5 Op. Cit. Jiribi.

6 Op. Cit. Wani. See also Emmanuel Kitchere Gray. *The Catholic Church in Loa*, Khartoum, 1994, p.19. Also see Victor Keri Wani., Juba, 1992, unpublished.

7 Op. Cit. Boki.

8 Op. Cit. Gray, pp.21-23 and Wani.

9 Op. Cit. Rowley, p.291.

10 Interview of author with Chief Odoriko Loku Diego in Torit on
12-5-2005.

11 Stigand, C. H. Equatoria. *The Lado Enclave*, London, Frank Cass, 1968, p.1.

12 Ofo Ma'di Ti Si (History in Ma'di Language), Loa, 1945, p.61.

13 Op. Cit. Rowley, p.291.

14 Op. Cit. Ofo, p.62.

15 Op. Cit. Rowley.

16 Informant of this fact was Rita Keji Lodu Bilal mother of the author in Juba in 2005.

17 Op. Cit. Diego.

18 Interview of author with Paulo Dralile Lodu Bigo in Diknat,

Khartoum on 4-2-1995.

19 Op. Cit. Wani, Gray. Also See *Narrating Our Future, Customs, Rituals and Practices of the Ma'di of South Sudan and Uganda*, Centre for Advanced Studies of African Society (CASAS), Cape Town, 2011, p.220.

Chapter Eight

The Western Sector Chieftainships of Erepi (Kerepi)

8.1 The Extent of the Sector

To the north of the western sector chieftainships lies Moli with its chieftainships referred to in this survey as the northern sector. In fact, the western chieftainships occupy the second smallest area after the central sector of Arapi, Pageri and Nyongwa compared with the eastern, southern and northern sectors of the Ma'di chieftainships. It is bounded in the east by the sector of the eastern chieftainships of Bori-Opari and south of it lies the central sector of Arapi, Pageri and Nyongwa chieftainships. To its west lies the Nile River and beyond the river are the Nyeri mountain ranges which together with the river separate the chieftainships from the Kajokeji district of the Kuku people. Its estimated length from Lungayo in the south to the tamarind tree in a place called Odruforo, which is only a mile to the south-east of the tobacco curing plant at Dereto as its border with Moli chieftainships, measures about seven miles. Its greatest width from east to west is roughly fifteen miles and that is from west of Mount Ako to the River Nile.

There are over 30 clans who inhabit the western Ma'di chieftainships of Erepi.[1]

The clans of influence in the sector include the Tedire royal clan, Patibi, Ijupi, Ogoropi, Kiloloro, Degi and Afodo. Eberu Drani was the chief of Erepi when the area was annexed to the larger Moli chieftainship on order of the newly elected Headchief Sabazio Okumu Abdalla in late 1952 to create Moli-Erepi-Nyongwa 'A' Court. Jelindo Chaka Aperiya of Mugi clan and former court clerk of Eberu Drani was appointed by Sabazio as chief of this Erepi-Moli-Nyongwa combined chieftainship. From 1952, Jelindo Chaka was chief of Moli-Erepi-Nyongwa, a combination most Ma'di people considered absurd. Many people believe that Sabazio did this to punish Chief Akeri Geri Ipele of Moli who said he would not recognize Sabazio as headchief after the announcement of the election results in Loa chieftainship headquarters in April 1952 because he was from Gonyapi, a non-royal clan of the Ma'di. Loa, the headquarters of the five sectors after the election of Sabazio Okumu as headchief, he renamed Opari-angwa.

8.2 The Erepi Chieftainships

Erepi, considering all the Ma'di areas where strong chieftainships were instituted, had its share of leadership rivalry. Sovereignty in the area was held by the members of the royal family of the Tedire clan. The power behind the leadership machinery originated from the ancestors of Loku Kitcere, the father of Eberu Drani. After the death of Eberu, his cousin Ame Jiribi became a figurehead because by that time the chieftainship had reverted to Chief Jelindo Chaka Aperiya who was until his appointment the court clerk of Eberu Drani. There are several clans behind the Tedire, and these are: Ijupi, Afodo, Ukeyi, Ogoropi, Moje, Degi, Jeru, Paluda, Patibi, Kiloloro, Gonyapi, Udupi, Pandikeri, Dugo, Lubule etc.[2] According to historians of the district, there was rivalry between the Tedire and Gonyapi leaderships in the past which led to a brief period of intra-tribal fighting that ended with the defeat of the latter.[3] The Gonyapi were already living in Erepi area when the Tedire arrived from Fajulu country in the west. This was a long time ago, perhaps several centuries ago, and today the Tedire like many other clans who had emigrated from other tribal groups have been Ma'di-ised[4] if we can use the term coined by J. V. Rowley who conducted research on the Ma'di people in 1936 and 1937 and published his work in 1940. In the beginning the Gonyapi had the upper hand, as the legendary story goes, and they used to strangle the baby boys of the Tedire clan to death. However, in due course they were thwarted by a Tedire woman who gave birth to a son and pretended that it was a daughter. It was this boy who grew up to save his clan from treachery and assume the position of chief in the area.[5] There is more to be told than this legendary story in the history of the Tedire clan for besides their dispute with the Gonyapi, the Palungwa clan were also accommodated by the Tedire on their arrival from the north before their emigration to their present area of Arapi which lies between Pageri and Loa. Vexed by the strict control exercised by their host, they decided to move and ally with the Pandikeri (Pandiker) of Bori before they were incorporated into Loa chieftainship in 1936.[6]

The chiefs of the Nyongwa chieftainship, which lay south of Erepi, did not compete overly with the Tedire leadership. The Nyongwa people according to Fideli Jengwa Delefino from the area are former speakers of the Burulo variant of the Ma'di language like the people of Erepi. He said they used to sing *kore* and other songs in Burulo.[7] But recent contact with people who speak the variant of the Ma'di spoken in Lokai, the southern sector of Ma'di chieftainships, has eventually forced them to speak that variant of the language. The Vuri, a Ma'di clan whose members lived not far from the settlements of the Tedire got embroiled in a fight with them but were defeated. As punishment they were asked to present a beautiful maid to the Tedire chief as a wife or else they would be held as captives indefinitely.[8] The Vuri could not supply a girl because they did not have one. When the Odupkwe arrived from the Lulubo-Aru area, Jukeri their leader decided to provide a beautiful girl whom the Tedire accepted thus setting the Vuri free. The Vuri who were leaders for other clans such as Pamotto, Pa-Akori, Paloi, Paluru, Puceri and Bari clans decided to give this leadership to Jukeri of the Odupkwe who from that time have become leaders in Lokai.[9]

8.3 The Tedire Clan Leadership

Odoriko Loku Diego Mohamme said that when the Tedire clan arrived in the Erepi area in antiquity from the Fajulu country, they found members of the Gonyapi clan already living there.[10] The Tedire, he said, came with their leadership and the first chief was Muludiang who was the son of Bara. When the Tedire settled down, the Gonyapi were afraid they might multiply and take over their land, so they began to strangle their baby boys at birth, leaving only girls because they believed that girls would not grow strong enough to challenge them. When Muludiang was born the mother announced that her child was a girl and without checking the sex of the child the Gonyapi traditional midwives, who were entrusted by their menfolk to do the checking on behalf of the community, believed her. The woman nourished the baby and when Muludiang was big, he wore the feather of a long-tailed bird called *torono* on his head. His first action was to kill a Gonyapi man. The Gonyapi reacted by attacking the Tedire, and the latter responded with bows and arrows and the Gonyapi scattered. A few months after the fighting rains fell, termites were collected and many Gonyapi people who ate them died. Mulundiang was replaced by Bara who was succeeded by Nyungura from whom Loku Kitcere took over and from him, Eberu Drani assumed power as chief.[11] But according to J. V. Rowley who researched the leadership of the Tedire in 1937, their first leader was Moroki followed by Lado Kirripi (Kerepi). He omitted Loku Kitcere from the list, otherwise there would be twelve chiefs.[12] Eberu Drani who was born in about 1908[13] was one of the young men taken to the Opari Protestant run school and later admitted to higher classes in the same school system in Malek in southern Bor in Dinka land. But the education he acquired was not sufficient to enable him to rule his people like an enlightened man as anticipated by the colonial administrators of the time. The Tedire chieftainship then became weak during his reign and Ito Kafiri who was chief of the Pageri was assigned by the colonial administrators, who oversaw the traditional chiefs, to rule it for some time before his son Silimani Ito came up as chief. After Siliman Ito, Jelindo Chaka was appointed by Sabazio Okumu as chief. Jelindo was the court clerk of Chief Eberu Drani. Jelindo himself appointed Lendzio as his court clerk.

8.4 Economic Situation of the Sector

The inhabitants of the neighbouring central chieftainships of Arapi, Pageri and Nyongwa, being close to the Nile, are provided with a bountiful supply of fresh or smoked dry fish to augment their vegetable diet. However, the river is far from the western chieftainship of Erepi, and whenever these people want to eat fish, they must go and buy it in the market of Pageri-Langauro. Erepi has no big rivers besides the Eyibi which flows in the eastern part of the sector. This is a perennial river and the fish in it are too small to attract catchers during rainy seasons.

The sector was however fortunate in being selected as the site for an experimental forestry station in the 1950's although in 1976, Dr. Gama Hassan, the Minister of Agriculture, Forestry, Animal Production and Fisheries, criticized the selector of the site for being unwise because of the poor growth of the mainly acacia trees planted on a rocky piece of land in Dereto. However, the colonial administrators in Mongalla provincial headquarters were aware that this part of the province was not good for forestry development and recommended acacia scrub for plantation and not other seedlings which flourished in other parts.[14] Further experimental tree planting in an area east of Lungayo and Vukade in the 1960's, south-east of Auefuni, however has proved productive for forestry seedlings transplanted there.

In 1957, the British American Tobacco Company (BATCo) built a tobacco curing factory opposite the forestry station in Dereto and distributed seedlings grown along Liro River near Dulemi to selected growers in Erepi area who were guided by the company staff on how to treat the tobacco plant up to leaf harvest stage. The green leaves were bought from the growers on a cash basis. Around 1959, the tobacco business was taken over by the Blue Nile

Cigarette Company (BNCC) which embarked on construction of tobacco barns in Nyongwa, Arapi and Loa thus increasing the area of Ma'diland engaged in the tobacco business. BNCC was a Sudanese company while the British American Tobacco Company was Uganda-based. Its first British manager was called 'Aringa', a nickname he acquired while working in the same business in the Aringa area of West Nile Province of Uganda. More growers were recruited and guided in tobacco growth and treatment. At first the crop was harvested and sold fresh to the company which dried it in its own barns at Nyongwa, Arapi and Loa. But around 1961, the policy of BNCC changed and growers were compelled to construct local barns with grass thatched roofs for drying their own tobacco leaves before selling them to the company. Through this trade, many growers earned sufficient income to improve the lives of their families and some even bought bicycles which were rare in the area before the introduction of the tobacco crop. The tobacco business was disrupted by the civil war in South Sudan in the period 1955-72 which intensified in mid 1960's.

After the 1972 Addis Ababa Peace Agreement, the people of Erepi for the first time established a market not far from the primary school. Marketeers would come from as far away as Kajokeji across the Nile to sell their products, mainly food items like beans, grain and cassava flour and to buy what they needed.

8.5 The Clans in Erepi (Kerepi)
The following clans live in Erepi chieftainships:[15]
    1- Afodo
    2- Beka
    3- Degi
    4- Dugo

5- Gonyapi
6- Guno/Eremu
7- Ijupi
8- Kande
9- Kiloloro
10- Logili
11- Logopi
12- Lubule
13- Lulubo
14- Moje
15- Mugi
16- Nyai
17- Odupkwe
18- Ogoropi
19- Omunya
20- Pa-Adi
21- Padombe
22- Palore
23- Palorinya
24- Paluda
25- Pandikeri
25- Paselo
26- Patibi
27- Tedire (the royal clan believed to have come in antiquity from Fajulu country)
28- Udupi
29- Ukeyi (Ifogo who lived at Korokodia also claimed some sort of chieftainship like the other Ukeyi family of Ingani-Kuyu)
29- Urugu

30- Utuno

31- Vuri

Notes and References

1 Gray, Emmanuel Kitchere. *The Catholic Church in Loa*, Khartoum, 1994, pp.21-3. Also see Victor Keri Wani. *An Outline of Madi History, Culture, Traditions and Customs*, Juba, 1992, (unpublished). See also J.V. Rowley. *Notes on the Ma'di of Equatoria Province*, Sudan Notes and Records, Vol. XXIII, 1940, pp.289-290. See also the notes prepared by Isaac Vuni in 2005 on Erepi clans and villages.

2 Ibid.

3 Interview of author with Chief Odoriko Loku Diego in Torit on 12-5-2005.

4 Op. Cit. Rowley, p.293.

5 Op. Cit. Diego.

6 Op. Cit. Rowley, p.288.

7 Interview of author with Fideli Jengwa Delefino in El Haj Yousif, Al Takamul, Khartoum North, 12-10-1995.

8 Op. Cit. Rowley, p.283.

9 Ibid. p.264.

10 Op. Cit. Diego.

11 Ibid.

12 Op. Cit. Rowley.

13 Ibid.

14 Nalder, L. F. *The Equatoria Proovince Handbook Vol. I*, Mongalla 1936, p.137.

15 Op. Cit. Wani, Gray and Vuni. See also *Narrating Our Future, Customs, Rituals and Practices of Ma'di of South Sudan and Uganda* ed. Mairi Blackings (PhD), Cape Town, 2011.

Chapter Nine

Ma'di Chiefs and their Wars

9.1 The Inter-Tribal Wars and their Historical Causes
Over fifty years ago, the Catholic missionaries in Loa, who were the sole educators in Ma'diland, brought together from various parts of Ma'di country, some Ma'di elders and teachers they had trained, and gleaned from them some useful facts about Ma'di history. Their efforts bore fruit in the production of the booklet titled: '*Ofo Ma'di Ti Si*' meaning 'history in the Ma'di language.' The authors of the booklet translated it as *Notions of Ma'di History*. It was published by the Loa Catholic Mission in 1945. The headmaster of the Loa Elementary School, Mr. Kristino Dridulu Mona was in the habit of addressing the pupils of the school every month. This popular evening lesson, which was attended by all classes, was known as 'Moral Talk.' In 1960, during one

of his traditional addresses to the pupils, the headmaster hinted that the little account about Ma'di history was the work of several resident priests of Loa Mission, among them fathers Lombardi Angelo, who was a teacher and founder of the school in Ma'diland in the mid 1920's[1] and Caldora Ernesto, another educator who came to Loa in 1939 and worked for several years before he was transferred to Okaru Intermediate School. Another resident priest in Loa who contributed to the book was Giuseppe Baj, whom the Ma'di called Father Bai. Father Avelino Wani, the first Ma'di Catholic to be ordained a priest on December 21, 1946, at Lacor, Gulu in Uganda[2] while still in his probation year, was said to have contributed immensely to the production of the booklet. The priests obtained the information orally from a cross section of Ma'di chiefs, teachers, notables, and elders who were well versed in the history of the Ma'di people and their land. This history is preserved mostly in songs and oral legends.

In 1945, the year of the compilation of these impressions of Ma'di history, Cirino Odego, a Catholic from the Odupkwee clan was the chief of Lokai, Akeri Geri from the Logili clan was the chief of Moli, Eberu Drani from Tedire clan was the chief of Erepi and Dari Kanyara Isara of the Pandikeri clan was the chief of Bori (Opari). In 1991, Sestilio Andruga Juma told the author in Juba that among the Ma'di elders contacted by Catholic missionaries for information about some events witnessed by the Ma'di people in their immediate localities were Ifoga of Ukeyi clan in Muruli, Moli, Alimu Dengu of Odupkwee clan in Lokai, Ito Kafiri of Pageri clan, Dari Kanyara Isara of Bori and among the teachers were Ibolo Abiyo of Moli, Kristino Dridulu Mona of Bilinya, Lokai, he himself Sestilio Androga Juma from Mugali and several other selected elders throughout Ma'diland.[3] The book was published in the Ma'di language indicating a shift towards the introduction and development of the language as a medium of education and for printing primers, textbooks for schools in Ma'diland and the Bible by the priests.

The first studies of the Ma'di tribe were conducted by Father Luigi Molinaro and published in *La Nigrizia* magazine in 1927 in Verona. He also authored the first Ma'di grammar book in 1925 and a dictionary *Italiano-Ma'di, Ma'di-Italiano* (MS) from Loa Catholic Mission. He also left a good deal of unpublished material which could include what was published in 1945 because the most extensive research on Ma'di oral literature was conducted only by him at the time. Professor A.N. Tucker followed Father Molinari and in 1940 he published his research under the title 'The Eastern Sudanic Languages' which is a careful and detailed study of the Moru-Ma'di language. In '*Ofo Ma'di Ti Si*' only the tribal feud between the Moli people of northern Ma'diland and Lokoya, and the inter-tribal fighting between the Lokai and Paracele were cited.[4] Important details about the Pandikeri-Iyire skirmishes in Lerwa near Obbo, the slaying of the Arapi chief Nyengwi Iro by the Acholi-Panyikwara in the Kadakada hunting field over Iwire Hill north-east of Opari, which the Acholi people of Panyikwara regarded as sacred, and the intermittent killings though limited that followed the assassination of the chief, the Pari (Lokoro) and Acholi-Agoro raids on Moli villages in 1927 during the reign of the Lokoro youth leader called Alangure[5] with the group then known as Akim – all these events were not covered by the booklet.

There were other important intra-tribal skirmishes within the Ma'di such as the Pageri-Pacara and Pamotto-Pacara clashes in Jeleyi north of Nimule, after which the Ma'di chiefs introduced a procedure for making peace amongst themselves. This deserves mention but was left out of the small history booklet of 1945. These events and the general history of the lives of the inhabitants of the southern Nile valley, Ma'di among them, the present as well as future generations should prize for their historical value. It ought to be recognised that the histories of other peoples of the world, that we read about in books as students or as researchers, have been made in a way similar to the way the Ma'di and their neighbours have made their histories. Therefore, to not endeavour to uncover the truth and record these events would be tantamount to depriving the world of the opportunity to learn about the important and active past of these peoples. The process of writing history is not to judge its makers but rather to present an unbiased and fair recording of those events and their impacts on the peoples concerned. This qualifies it to be called history, and the descendants of those communities whose ancestors were actors in these events will surely value its preservation.

It must be understood that the circumstances under which the feuds referred to in this compilation were fought do not exist today, at least for the Ma'di people with their neighbours. The introduction of modern mechanisms to check such unnecessary depredations have lessened their occurrence. Law and order enforcement organs have been set up by the colonial government, bringing together tribes which used to exist as independent communities. These communities would, without warning or provocation, declare war on or raid neighbouring tribes for cattle or human booty. However, laws are often broken by those willing to risk the taste of their bitter consequences. The factors most regarded as pacifying the region are the introduction of education and most importantly Christianity and to some extent Islam. Christianity, particularly Catholicism and to some degree the

Protestant churches, have brought the inhabitants of the region including the Ma'di and their neighbours very close together. It is unthinkable for any community of the Christian faith to declare war on another community today because the holy Bible teaches people to be at peace and love their fellow human beings and opposes such acts of violence. It can be clearly seen that where the foundations of education and Christianity have not been securely laid among some communities of the southern Nile valley, tribal, intra and inter-tribal fighting is still rampant.

9.2 Lokoya-Langabu and Moli War

There are eight bush schools in the area namely, Moli, Erepi, Pageri, Patibi Lomura, Opari-Motoyo, Iriya, Porio-Nimule and Mugali, and the elementary school at Loa. For many Ma'di men and women who had attended one of these schools some 50 years ago, the following facts about Ma'di history can easily be recalled. *Ofo Ma'di a ru garee. Ojja aedri ezeree. Moli Lokoya tro. Lokoya ba cidro oni Moli ote. Adosi? Adosiko ojaki ra.* This, the opening passage of the textbook, can be translated into English as follows: History of the Ma'di. Their past wars. Moli and Lokoya. All the Lokoya people know the Moli. Why? Because they have fought.[6] Another caption in the same book runs in Ma'di: *Paracele pi Lokayi tro kolu alo pkwe. Adosi esu naninga ama abi nga ba ole asi ko. Kaki ja ditrii. Esu Lokayi ba kolu Bibia. Ae a laga ga Paracele kolu ni....* Translation: Paracele and Lokayi cannot live together. Because during the period of our ancestors, people hated each other, and they always fought among themselves. At that time, the Lokayi people were living in Bibia. Near them were the Paracele people. [7] These are the elements of Ma'di history documented more than half a century ago for the enlightenment of the people.

After the publication of that booklet, considered by the Ma'di people a masterpiece, no further investigation of the subject was undertaken by Catholic missionaries or any institution or individual Ma'di who had been taught in schools run by these missionaries. This work is a reminder to all history-conscious people, Ma'di and non-Ma'di alike, that the subject is too important to be shrouded in mystery and assigned to oblivion; it must be kept alive for further study and publication.

The history booklet: *Ofo Ma'di Ti Si* (History in Ma'di Language) published in 1945 had the following introductory note about the fighting between the two communities of Lokoya-Langabu and Moli (Lobure) in Ma'di language. *Ojja dii idoru indrigo si. Lokoya ogu Tombe Bworo a indrigo runa Kongiru e. Indrigo dii si ba ojja kareako. Ojja atiree si Moli eko Lokoya ni vu ayia, evu ojjaki laka. Ki ojja dii ga oza Lokoya ra adosi esu ae ni toro. Tia aru Lokoya ole Moli tcele aedri baru. Ki otceki koro adosi eri 'lutulutu' odro ae pi.* The above text when translated into English says: "This feud started because of a he-goat. The Lokoya stole Tombe Bworo's he-goat called Kongiru, meaning 'the one that walks majestically'. Because of this he-goat, people have fought a great deal. In the first fighting, the Moli followed the Lokoya in the bush. It was there that they fought. But in this fight, the Lokoya were defeated because they were few. Afterwards, the Lokoya wanted to encircle the Moli in their villages. But they did not do so because the great whirlwind known as 'lutulutu' chased them away."[8]

The intermittent attacks on Moli, the northern section of the Ma'di, by the Lokoya-Langabu people who lived in the Okaru mountain ranges some 40 miles north-east of Moli settlements occurred between 1895 and 1910. This was after the return of the Moli people from exile in Parajok-Ayaci and then Ayipa, their places of refuge when they fled from the attacks of the Mahdist forces from the North. Although the Catholic missionaries in Loa, who highlighted these events in the booklet produced in 1945, did not give the dates of the skirmishes, from oral Moli legends, the Moli-Lokoya clashes had intermittently taken place probably between 1895 and 1910. One of the Moli fighters who took part in the reprisal attack on the Lokoya-Langabu villages was Akeri Acaku who was also called Beshir Ongu of the Logili clan. He was 15 years old at the time and in 1957 he looked like a man of about 75 years. From this observation we conclude that he could have been born in 1882 and the fight might have taken place around 1897. Acaku died in Ukeyi, Moli in 1964. The fight took place one year before the last stronghold of the Mahdists under the command of Emir Arabi Dafallah, at Bor was attacked and taken by British forces from Uganda, commanded by Lt. Col. Martyr whose contingent was supported by Belgian soldiers of the Congo Free State in the Lado Enclave.[9]

Most British and other writers of Sudanese history point out that inter-tribal and tribal fighting was revived by the tribesmen and flared up throughout Southern Sudan during the Mahdist rule of 1885-1898 and during the period which followed their loss of power in the South, especially in Equatoria. According to Professor Richard Gray of the History Department, University of Khartoum, many regions of the South experienced, during the Mahdiyya (1885-1898), a period of chronic localized violence which seems to have been even more destructive and disruptive than the more spectacular depredations of Khartoumers and Turco-Egyptians.[10] In this violent struggle for existence, the weaker people suffered. Even Byron Farwell in his writing pointed out that when Emin Pasha left, Equatoria drifted into anarchy[11] and the Lokoya-Langabu and Moli feud should be viewed from this perspective.

As explained in the booklet *'Ofo Ma'di Ti Si'*, the Lokoya-Moli dispute erupted when a group of Lokoya warriors trekked the long distance of about 40 miles to the Moli neighbourhood at Palutu which lies south-east of Mount Foki. From Lokoyaland, Moli is to the south-west. The warriors stole several goats and sheep of the Moli while village boys were herding them and among the stolen animals was the he-goat of Chief Muku, who was also a rainmaker, from the Mugi clan. The goat was not, as reported in the booklet, the property of Tombe Bworo.[11] The animals were being looked after by the boys in the grazing field on the banks of River Belekendu. When the terrified shepherd boys ran home and broke the news of the theft to the chief and other elders, the chief immediately sounded the alarm by beating the drum. The local men (*logo*) on hearing the drum at this odd time suspected a serious situation and promptly responded to the summons to gather at the home of the chief. They brought with them their weapons – bows and arrows. Chief Muku immediately told them about the theft and the men without delay set off in pursuit of the thieves. They caught up with them far away from Palutu in the middle of the wilderness and a bloody confrontation ensued, the Lokoya were defeated, and the stolen animals retrieved. One account says that the Chief's he-goat Kongiru was not recovered because it was rushed ahead of the rest of the animals by the thieves.

The account of this event published in 1945 by the Catholic missionary historians, states that the Lokoya were defeated in the fight because they were fewer in number than the Moli pursuers. [12] But Wani, the eldest son of Chief Muku has been quoted as saying that the Lokoya were beaten because the bows and arrows of the Moli attackers were more effective than the Lokoya spears and shields. Although some of the Lokoya carried bows and arrows as weapons of war the Ma'di had proved to be superior to them in bush fighting. Several weeks after the confrontation, a larger force of Lokoya approached Moli villages at Pamidi and Palutu with the aim of surrounding them and slaying their inhabitants. But when they reached the banks of River Belekendu, a strong whirlwind, called *lutulutu* in Ma'di, broke out and blew across their formation. In the sudden tumult, many of the Lokoya warriors were killed, thrown against large nearby trees and rocks. Some of them died when they were pierced by their own spears in the confusion. When the whirlwind subsided the terrified survivors of the *lutulutu* attack fled back to their own country leaving behind their dead with their weapons on the banks of the river. Today the Moli people call that point of the river *Lodi-ama-ru si* meaning 'killing can be experienced by the body'. They believe that the whirlwind attack was direct intervention and punishment from the heavenly power upon a group of people who wanted to shed the blood of the innocent Moli people. Many people in Moli believe that even without the whirlwind their defenders could have beaten off the Lokoya-Langabu attack had it come, because while the Lokoya-Langabu would be attacking Pamidi and Palutu, support would have come from Ludiri-Muruli, Aduro and other villages to relieve the defenders of the two villages.

Despite the mysterious attack of the *lutulutu* whirlwind the Lokoya-Langabu did not learn a lesson and several months later they began to foray in smaller groups, especially during the summer months when people were harvesting their food crops such as groundnuts and beans. These were the months of July, August and

September. This was the season when the grass in the bush was tall and the leaves on trees had grown thick and green making it possible for the Lokoya-Langabu warriors to sneak in unnoticed. It was reported that some Lokoya-Langabu raiders used to hide in the heaps of dry grass and shrubs (*owu-owu*) dumped at the far edges of the fields. The raiders would wait until sunset when most cultivators have gone home and only a few were remaining behind to finish their work, then quickly emerge from their hiding places to spear them to death or to capture and make off with the younger people especially the girls. They were also reported to lie in wait for people, especially women, fetching water from the river or firewood from the forest, in order to spear them to death or to take the younger ones alive to their country. The Lokoya-Langabu would hide the corpses of the people they had killed along the bush path to prevent the birds of prey which fed on corpses from detecting them. They feared that the Moli people would see the movements of the birds in the sky from afar and hastening to find the cause, uncover their evil deeds. Reports of individuals getting lost were common and these losses caused much fear among the Moli people, especially as in most cases the bodies of the victims were not recovered, being hidden by their slayers.

9.2.1 The death toll and the austerity measures

Among the people killed by the Lokoya-Langabu warriors secretly and considered simply lost, was Mori the father of Tombe Bworo of the Patibi-Moyiba clan. He was living in Nyori, under Kotopila Hill. So, orders went out from the Moli chiefs, Muku the powerful leader of the Mugi clan and his Logili counterpart Tombe Moli, that all men sleep in the afternoon and at night leave their sleeeping quarters and keep watch. Women were instructed not to fetch water from the river or firewood from the bush by themselves and be accompanied by armed men to defend them in case of attacks.[13] But despite these strict measures, it was not immediately established that the clever Lokoya-Langabu killers were secretly taking the lives of many innocent people. Although the Lokoya-Langabu raiders were high on the list of suspects because of their previous attacks, other suspects were the warriors of Acholi-Agoro who were called by the Moli people, Koyo. The Moli people and their chiefs did not want to rely on speculation as a pretext for an attack on any of the suspected tribes. They wanted to catch the killers of their people red-handed so that the retaliatory attack that they planned to mete out against them would be justified and decisively effective.

The Lokoya-Langabu warriors continued to come to Moli secretly to kill people, but nobody caught them. It was said that they used to uproot the young bean plants from the Moli fields and take them home where they would transplant them. When these plants began to flower, it would indicate to them that the Moli women were engaged in picking the leaves for processing as vegetables, a sign to arm themselves and come to the Moli area to commit acts of savagery.

One day however, a group of Lokoya-Langabu raiders were spotted from afar by Tombe Bworo. As they came towards him, he hid himself to escape detection. Tombe was a man believed by the whole Ma'di tribe and the neighbouring communities of Kuku, Bari, Acholi, Lulubo and even Lokoya to have the supernatural power of being able to change his human form to that of a leopard and back again. He decided to follow the group up to the Lokoya villages in Langabu in the Okaru mountain ranges. On his return to Moli, he rested for five days before approaching Chief Muku and telling him about his discovery of the real enemies of the Moli people.⁽¹⁴⁾ Muku was very pleased to hear this and he at once summoned the people so that they could hear for themselves this message from Tombe Bworo. Muku beat the drum as usual to summon the people.

When the men and some elderly women assembled under a large tree near the chief's house, Tombe was asked by Chief Muku to narrate his story. He told them that he had at last found the killers of their family members and where these enemies lived. He offered to lead the brave and strong men among them to the homes of the killers who slew their beloved ones unhindered, while their own children and wives were not killed by the Moli people. The people were happy to hear that Tombe Bworo had discovered the whereabouts of the people who killed them unjustly and that he was ready to lead their fighters in a reprisal raid on Lokoya-Langabu villages. Many able-bodied men expressed their willingness and determination to go to war against their enemies. Chief Muku in collaboration with the chiefs of Logili, Ukeyi and elders of other large clans of the Moli instructed all heads of families and young men in the villages to craft bows and arrows, the main weapon of war of the Ma'di people. A small group of men with special abilities in using spears were assigned to make a cache of these for use in the war. Women were asked to fry beans and mix them with sesame (*simsim*) as *odo* to be taken along by each fighter in skin bags as food during the expedition to the Lokoya land. Boys were also encouraged to craft arrows and bows and to concentrate on training in archery so that they could join those elders who would be left behind to guard the villages and their inhabitants.

9.2.2 Moli mobilization

It is a tradition of the Ma'di people to train their boys to become good archers by requiring them to hit the pods of a tropical tree called *loduu*. A suitable field is marked out and the tips of two such fruits or pods are buried in the ground in one spot and another pair are fixed some 50 to 75 metres away. If there are four or five lads in the group, each is permitted to discharge one arrow at the target. After every arrow has been shot, the group moves to the other end of the field to remove their arrows from the pods or from the ground if any has missed its target. They then shoot at the pods at the other end of the field.

As part of the Moli mobilization for the reprisal attack on the Lokoya-Langabu, the boys were compelled to remain at home with the male elders to guard the other village folk comprising children, mothers, and the elderly people, both women and men during the absence of the larger group of men going to war. The Lokoya called the Moli people *Lobure* a corruption of *Labore* which was the military station built during the rule of Samuel Baker when he was the Governor of Equatoria Province, and which was used as a temporary capital by Governor Charles George Gordon.

9.2.3 The Moli Reprisal Attack on Lokoya-Langabu

The Moli chiefs agreed on the date for setting off for Lokoyaland and set aside ten days for preparation. During this time, all over Moli the sites where the blacksmiths (*eremu*) and ironsmiths (*vodo*) worked were filled with smoke from the iron smelting furnaces, as hundreds of arrow heads (*ee*), spears (*ajju*) and knives (*iligo*) of various shapes were crafted. Before the task force could leave for Lokoyaland all gathered at the home of Chief Muku. Chief Muku had previously visited a witch doctor whose incantation assured him that since the Lokoya people were the first to provoke the Moli tribe by killing their innocent members, they would inflict heavy casualties on the people of Langabu, and these people were the cause of the war. The chief then performed the rite which was always done before going to war. A black he-goat was stabbed with a spear at the edge of his range and the contents of his stomach were emptied on the path along which all the warriors were to step as they walked out of the village.[15] Everybody was told to pick a small piece of cud and rub it over his heart and on his face. The Moli warriors were led by Chief Muku himself who was guided by Tombe Bworo the only man who knew the way leading to the Lokoya-Langabu villages north-east of Moli, some 40 miles away.

The group walked the whole day and spent the night in the bush under Okaru Mountain.[16] The next day they walked and camped in the bush not far away from Langabu, the villages where the warriors whom Tombe Bworo had followed entered. Muku was said to have given a strict order to his fighters that only the villages of the Lokoya whose inhabitants had killed his people must be attacked. Before midnight, the order to climb the mountain through an old path was given by the chief. This was after Tombe Bworo and half a dozen brave men had gone on reconnaissance and come back to the main group to brief them about the nature of the territory and the kinds of villages they were about to attack. By midnight, the whole group was on the top of the mountain and had divided into three groups and each one of them surrounded a large village of the Lokoya-Langabu marked by Tombe Bworo during his first reconnaissance trip as sheltering the killers of the innocent Moli villagers. These villages were Okire, Ofiri and Omangara. There was a fourth village, Omiling, but it was not mentioned in Ma'di history. The fourth village according to the Lokoya historical account was also attacked.

9.2.4 The Devastating End of the Attack

The order to attack was signalled by Chief Muku and the Moli warriors went into action. It is said that the Lokoya people, who used spears and shields in war, were sleeping in camps outside their houses and had placed their weapons besides their wooden beds around the fireplaces. Some of them had placed their spears against wooden frameworks and large granaries not far from where they were sleeping. Apparently, they had no scouts to guard their villages at night against enemy attacks. This might be because they had not known enmity in their parts because the two tribes who are their neighbours, the Lulubo and Bari to their west and north respectively, were not raiders and the Pari (Lokoro) to their east were their allies. The Lokoya men put their spears near their sleeping places so that they could readily grab them in case of a surprise attack. The Moli warriors who were assigned the forward position quickly and silently removed the spears of the Lokoya men leaving only the skin shields which were nothing without spears and placed these weapons behind their lines. It is considered base by Moli fighters to kill their enemies while they are asleep, so the war cry was delivered to stir the sleeping men, and the attack was launched. Bows and arrows could not be used as the targets were too close, and in some cases the Moli attackers themselves were too close to each other. To avoid accidental injuries only spears were employed and most of these belonged to the sleeping Lokoya men. The Moli attackers had carried few spears, their usual weapons being bows and arrows. Despite the darkness, great care was taken to differentiate the girls and young women from the rest of the population, because according to Moli practice and the ethics of war it is improper to kill a woman especially a young girl. They are taken as war captives. Moreover, during the previous raids on Moli people the Lokoya had captured and abducted many girls and brought them to their homes as daughters or wives. The Moli carefulness in this attack was therefore principally to save the lives of their own daughters and young wives. If they could find any, they could take them back to Moli. And indeed, some of the Lokoya females captured by the Moli fighters were found to be their own Ma'di girls and young wives and they quickly whisked them away to safety.

Akeri Acaku, who was also called Beshir Ongu, was a lad of about fifteen years when he accompanied the expeditionary force to Langabu. During a confrontation with a huge woman, she cut the tip off his left ear. In 1957, the author saw this ugly reminder of the war which had indeed disfigured the outer part of his ear. The Moli fighters were given the signal to set the huts and the granaries of the three villages on fire and to retreat to leave only the archers in position. As soon as the huts and granaries were in flames, Lokoya men from villages east and south of Langabu rushed towards the site with the intention of putting out the fire. As the whole area was brightly lit, these rescuers could clearly be seen by the Moli fighters who shot at them with bows and arrows. In this way, the final destruction of the three villages was assured. The chief of Langabu, who was simply known by the Moli people as *Arinya* was not in any of the three villages attacked. (Some historians of which R.C. Rowley is an example, thought his name was Chulung[17]) His special hut was built on another nearby hill some distance from the villages of his subjects. When there was silence, a man's voice was heard saying that he was the chief of the villages attacked and he wanted to know whether the attackers were government soldiers. One Moli man shouted back that they were indeed government soldiers and that the chief must come out quickly to make a peace treaty with them or else the situation would deteriorate. This was a device to lure Arinya out into the open. When he emerged and drew nearer to the Moli fighters believing that they were government people, the same man shouted to him that the attackers of his villages were Lobure as the Lokoya called the Moli people, and this action was in retaliation for his unprovoked attacks on Moli. Chief Arinya turned to run away but he was quickly shot in the back with an arrow, and he fell down and died with the arrow still in his body. Although the history booklet '*Ofo Ma'di Ti Si*' of 1945 lacks this information, most Moli elders believe that Arinya was the name of the chief of the Lokoya-Langabu people and that he was killed during the attack on the villages of his people by the Moli warriors. Members of the Mugi clan of Chief Muku celebrated after their return from the retaliatory war on Lokoya-Langabu, and during their victory celebration one of the fighters composed and sang the following *jenyi* song:

> *Muku adi Kire ni alira*
> *Ayi dara lukuku*
> *Ama dzo kogwe ililiya*
>
> *Muku, we have speared Kire and made him fall,*
> *Oh, the great wasps*
> *Should our huts burn alone?*

The Logili clan whose members also took part in the reprisal fight on the Lokoya-Langabu composed a *mure* song to commemorate their victory and it goes as follows:

Adi Kire ra
Kire onyo ama ajjukwe
Ama Opi Ayu ni yoo
Mindra osu ma lu
Ago ori Manya ni owo yoo

Adi Ori ra
Ori onyo ama ajjukwe
Ama Opi Ayu ni yoo
Mindra osu ma lu
Ago ori Manya ni owo yoo

A literal translation of the *mure* song goes like this:

We have killed Kire
Kire broke the stick of our spear
Our Chief Ayu is not there
Tears have covered me completely
It is just like the cry of a man called Manya

We have killed Ori
Ori broke the stick of our spear
Our Chief Ayu is not there
Tears have covered me completely
It is just like the cry of a man called Manya

The Moli version of Okire is *Kire* and their *Ori* is for Lokoya-Langabu Ofiri. After the raid on the three villages of the Lokoya-Langabu, the Moli fighters hastily retreated towards the mountains and moved down towards the bush on their way back home. They were afraid that enemies who might come from other villages not attacked by them and who knew the geography of the land better, might close the mountain gap they used as a path, and trap them. They took with them the young Moli girls taken by the Lokoya-Langabu in previous raids and several young Lokoya-Langabu womenfolk and brought them to Moli. The Moli girls recovered from the Langabu villages were identified and handed over to their parents or guardians amid relief and happiness for the reunion. On the other hand, the Lokoya-Langabu girls seized by some Moli fighters during the battle for the Langabu villages and brought to Moli, were adopted as daughters by their captors. Today there are several families in Moli whose great grandmothers can be traced to Lokoya. But not all the Moli girls seized by Lokoya-Langabu warriors in earlier raids were recovered because they might have been given to men of other Lokoya villages as wives. The nearest Lokoya village to Langabu was Liria and today there are some Lokoya who say that their great grandmothers or grandfathers were Ma'di from Moli. Lodro Mure, a cousin of Tombe Urutwe of Logili clan was taken captive as a boy by Lokoya raiders and raised as a Lokoya. He was given a wife by the man who raised him up as his son and he produced a daughter. When she was a mature woman, she came to Juba in 1950 and contacted a Lulubo woman called Aleka who was the wife of Chief Akeri Geri enquiring after Tombe Urutwe or someone directly related to him so that she could introduce herself to him.

9.2.5 Lokoya Sends SOS Message to Lokoro (Pari)

After the reprisal raid by the Moli fighters on the Lokoya-Langabu villages, the Lokoya are believed to have sent an SOS (Save Our Souls) message to the Lokoro (Pari) of Lafon who were their allies.

Fig. No. 3 & 4
The below are traditional weapons of the Ma'di representing spears, bow and arrows. (Photos by author in 2000)

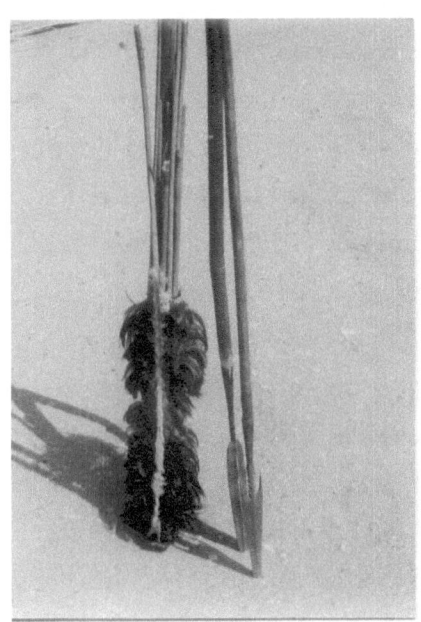

(18) The Lokoro leaders and their warriors according to the writers of Ma'di history of the war are said to have promptly come to Langabu. They asked the Lokoya leaders to tell them the reasons why they had sent for them. The Lokoya leaders said they called for them to come and increase their number in the pursuit of the *Lobure* meaning the Moli people who had killed their people[11] including their chief Arinyang.

The Moli burned to ashes the three villages of Omangara, Ofiri and Okire and carried off a number of their girls to their land. The Lokoro enquired further from the Lokoya as to how many from amongst the Lobure attackers they had killed. "None," the Lokoya spokesman replied. Indeed, the Lokoya had not injured any of the Moli attackers except a lad called Akeri Acaku, part of whose left ear was cut by a woman and a few men who sustained light injuries. Upon hearing this truthful revelation, the Lokoro (Pari) were seized with fear and refused to accompany the Lokoya in their planned pursuit of the Moli fighters. The Lokoro leader said that the fact that the Lokoya were beaten so decisively indicated that they were the first to shed the blood of the Moli people and therefore they would suffer great losses in any unjustified fighting that they would engage in. He said that if the Lokoya were serious, they could follow their Moli enemies but as for them, they could not get involved in a war in which the people they were asked to sacrifice their lives and blood for, were doomed to lose. So, the Lokoro decided to return to Lafon the same afternoon of their arrival and the Lokoya similarly decided to drop the idea of following the Moli people in order to attack them.[12]

That the Lokoya-Langabu sent for the Pari (Lokoro) to come to support them in their planned pursuit of the Moli attackers is contained in the Moli account of the war, but Lokoya historian, Alex Locor Nartisio has said that this addition to the story is fictional. If a message for support was sent at all, he said, it would have been to the people of Liria and not directly to the Pari (Lokoro) who had good relations with the Lokoya of Liria, but not of Langabu.[19] Pari (Lokoro) historian and researcher, Ukal Kawang Julu has also said that very little is known about this Langabu-Moli war by the general public of Pari (Lokoro) and only the leadership of the time might have been aware of it, and it was doubtful that the *monyomiji* (armed youth) would have been sent on such a mission.

After that decisive reprisal attack on the Lokoya-Langabu who had raided the Moli villages intermittently for a long time and killed many people, the former never came to attack the Moli people again. It was reported many years later that the descendants of the Lokoya-Langabu did not want to see any person from Moli on private or government business in their land. Cube Ajjusi and Milla Angube were road foremen from Moli who had worked at different periods in Lokoyaland, and they reported how the Langabu were apprehensive of their presence in their land but were afraid to harm them because of the government laws. The Lokoya paramount Chief Lolik Lado was said to be a serious law-abiding man who refused to tolerate the making of death threats by his people to non-Lokoya coming to Lokoyaland for government work. Moli students were among other Ma'di who attended Okaru Minor Seminary and the intermediate school on Lowoi Mountain near Lokoya-Langabu in the period 1938-1965, and none of them were ever threatened by the Langabu people. Apparently many Langabu after becoming Catholic Christians and receiving a good education, realized that their ertswhile pastime of killing their fellow human beings was not a worthy occupation, their new religion teaching against the practice in one of its ten commandments which says, "thou shalt not kill."[20]

9.2.6 The Lokoya-Langabu version of their war with the Moli

According to Alex Locor Nartisio of the Lokoya community of Lowoi, the Lokoya section called Langabu went to war against the Moli without a cause, confirming the Moli belief that there was nothing common that they shared with the Lokoya-Langabu that could have incited the latter to wage war against them.[21] Members of the four camps, namely Omangara, Okire, Ofiri and Omiling which composed the Langabu section of the Lokoya, according to Alex were simply egotistical and went to war against the Moli in order to appear brave members of the *monyomiji*, who could do good or bad and be reknowned as the courageous and powerful generation of their time. He said they were a group ready to fight, with or without a cause, because they were at a certain time a ruling generation. The Langabu age group of *monyomiji* who attacked Moli was called *Akim*,[22] for each age group was known by its chosen name. For the Lokoya-Langabu to execute a war plan, Alex said the preliminary steps they always take are to explore the target area by sending a small reconnaissance team whose assignment would be to find out where the domestic animals such as goats and sheep are reared, where fields are dug, the hunting grounds where people hunt animals for meat, rivers where people fetch their drinking water, and the forests where the women collect firewood or cut grass for thatching the roofs of the family huts. They would also study the routes leading outside or inside the villages, the types of huts built for accommodation and the types of weapons carried by the menfolk of the target tribe. When it is time for executing the war plans, a larger number of the *monyomiji*, the youthful fighters, go on the expedition carrying bows and arrows and spears. Many of them wear large bells tied to leather strings above their ankles and these bells are called *osongor*. They are stuffed with leaves when approaching enemy territory so that the enemy are not alerted by the noise the bells produce. The bells are released when the attack is in progress, the tumultuous noise they make striking fear in the enemy and causing them to flee. Alex's explanation is similar to that which the Moli elders narrate about the behaviour of their attackers.

9.3 Who are the Lokoya-Langabu people?

According to Alex Locor Nartisio, the historian of the Lokoya Lowoi community, *Langabu* in Lokoya language means 'people without a chief.' *La* means 'nothing' and *ngabu* is 'chief' hence 'without chief.'[23] This section of Lokoya consists of four villages whose different youth *monyomiji* camps are called Omangara, Okire, Ofiri and Omiling. These were the places where war programmes against other tribes were drawn up. The nearest section of the Lokoya to the Langabu are the Liria people who often go hunting with them, sometimes dance with them and when necessary, go to war against other tribes with them. Due to the lack of a proper chief during the colonial period, Lado a Nyambwara, a member of the Bari speaking tribe was brought to Langabu to be chief. Arinyakono was the father of Lolik, who was the father of Lado.

The Lokoya side of the story about the Langabu-Moli war was told through songs preserved till this day. The songs answer some of the questions asked by researchers about the causes of the war and how it was fought, whereas the account in the Ma'di history book tells only the Moli side of the story. In research parlance, this is considered to be one-sided. So, the contribution of Alex Locor Nartisio, a Lokoya, who is history conscious, clarifies many of the conundrums the account of the war as proffered by Ma'di historians, presents. Alex confirms the Moli story that when their fighters entered the Langabu *monyomiji* camps they found their spears resting against wooden frameworks ready for taking up in case of emergency. The frameworks according to Alex are the camp shrines made of ebony, built to last for several generations. He also confirms the Moli assertion that when they attacked the camps it looked like the Lokoya-Langabu were not expecting an enemy attack. Alex says the *monyomiji* of the four Langabu camps of Omangara, Okire, Ofiri and Omiling had until then enjoyed impunity from attacks as they were had never been attacked in reprisal by Moli or Acholi-Panyikwara people whom they used to raid in their home territory. There was no preparedness for defence when the Moli launched a reprisal offensive in their heartland. The camps had never been attacked on home soil before, so they were in the habit of relaxing after returning from attacking other people. The Langabu never expected anything of the kind of lightning attack launched by the Moli raiders. It was very devastating and left the camps in total ruin. The petrified survivors who escaped the onslaught, sent envoys to request assistance, first to the Liria people who were their closest neigbours, but sensing the magnitude of the disaster in the aftermath of the Moli attack, extended the call for assistance to the eight camps of the Lowoi namely: Ohira, Ohojofi, Ohwa, Oyata, Ohilo, Opura, Osok and Obuhi. Langairo and Loirika are the two factions of Lowoi whose people speak a mixture of Otuho and Lokoya but are connected to other Lowoi people through common interests. In addition to that division, Lowoi is divided into two main branches, and these are Omirai which is southern Lowoi and Otuho which is northern Lowoi. Despite being a homogenous community, the people often fight each other because of challenging or abusive songs sung during dances organized in the months of September, October and November when there is plenty of food following the harvest. Besides the pretext of songs, men fight and kill each other when wives or girls promised in marriage, are engaged to other men.[24]

Alex has stated that he does not know whether the Langabu people sent a message to the Lokoro people, who in the afternoon of the day of the attack, according to Moli historians, arrived in Langabu in response to their call. He has said moreover, that should there have been any such message sent to Lokoro people to come to the aid of the Langabu in their war with the Moli after the disastrous attacks on Omangara, Okire and Ofiri camps, it might have been sent to the Liria people who are closely associated with the Lokoro people through intermarriage and that the message could not have been directly sent by the Langabu, the western neighbour of the Liria people. So, the Liria-Lokoya who share many activities with the Langabu including dancing which they perform together, and hunting, might have sent for Lokoro warriors because of the serious defeat the Langabu had suffered at the hands of the Moli fighters and their inability to face such serious attackers. Liria itself has nine camps, the chief ones being: Ohwa, Ongole, Ofwara, and Ovotong. These camps have *monyomiji* who can go to war to assist the Langabu, Lowoi and any other allies. The Lokoya, like other African tribes, have internal disputes between different factions. This explains why instead of the Liria sending for Lowoi after the Moli devastating attack on the Langabu, they sent for Lokoro[25] if this has indeed taken place.

To understand the Lokoya version of their war with the *Moli*, which they commonly refer to as *Lobure* (for Labore), the following songs in Lokoya language sung by and translated into English by Alex Locor Nartisio, will suffice:

Song No. 1
Title: *Ewahai lo Lobure*
(War of Lobure)

> *Ewahai ofere lonya*
> *Ewahai ofere lohito lo Lobure*
> *Hobu layo-layo*
> *Lokitik loindu dohoi*

Efwo ohoi itaturio amiji Lobure

A literal translation of the song from Lokoya follows:

War was declared
A big war was declared against Lobure
The chief cried, cried
A strong hurricane came to us
We went and destroyed Lobure village

Song No. 2
Title: Opwak hati naferya di-mura
(Spears were abandoned in a deserted village)

Loudo inyahara miji
Ida inya hobu netiho
Efwo inya ohoi itaturio a Lobure

A literal translation of the song from Lokoya follows:

Loudo, you return home
The chief refused to stop
We went and destroyed Lobure

The first song confirms an item from the Moli version of events, the claim that a strong hurricane known in Ma'di as *eri lutulutu* blew across the formation of the Langabu warriors.

According to the Moli account, the hurricane devastated the Langabu force by impelling them to pierce themselves with their own spears and throwing them against trees and nearby rocks, and the survivors fled in panic. But the Lokoya say that despite the strong hurricane, they were able to continue their journey to Lobure which they destroyed.

The second song desribes how a chief called Loudo participated in the war against Moli. He refused to return home and the group continued on their journey to Lobure which they destroyed. Such is the Lokoya version of the war. This is important information because it helps solve some of the puzzles thrown up by the account of the war as related by the Ma'di historians. Other Lokoya-Langabu songs about the war which can give shed some light on the subject are the following:

Song No. 3
Title: Lani Ofere
(Which War)

> *Lani ofere lerum ohoi? x 2*
> *Ofere lerem ohoi da Achwa*
> *Eromio ohoi Amoli x 2*
> *Ewaha Loro, ewaha Loro ofere ijai*
> *Eromio ohoi Amoli x 2*

A literal translation of the above song follows:

> *Which war did we fight? x 2*
> *We fought the war at Achwa*
> *We fought the people of Moli x 2*
> *Loro declared, Loro declared war without reason*
> *We fought Moli x 2)*

This song confirms the Moli belief that the Lokoya-Langabu had fought them without cause. The statement that the war was fought at Achwa (Acca) cannot be true, because the Achwa River is about 30 miles south of Moli and about 65 miles from Lokoyaland. For the Lokoya to reach it for purposes of war, they would have had to walk through Ma'diland, which would not have been possible firstly, because of the distance and secondly, because of the density of the population through which they would have had to pass. In fact, the river on whose banks the Lokoya-Langabu warriors fought with the Moli was the northern part of Peku River, which is known as Belekendu, and not River Acca as such.

Another song in the Lokoya language runs as follows:

Song No. 4
Title: *Ida Longere*
(Longere refused)

> *Ida Longere Etairio x 2*
> *Ida Longere Etairio omerok horomio*
> *Da Ayii (Do Nyolo) x 2*
> *Erum ohoi lani ofere lerum ohoi x 2*
> *Kanyuma horomio do Onyolo-Da Ayii*
> *Afan atwari di Moli x 2*

A literal translation of the above song follows:

> *Longere refused to hear reason*
> *Longere refused to hear (reason) the enemy*
> *Is fighting at Ayii or Onyolo? x 2*
> *We marched, which war did we fight? x 2*

Kanyuma fought at Onyolo (Ayii)
The funeral reached up to Moli x 2

This is yet another song composed by one of the Lokoya-Langabu singers about the war and it confirms the stubbornness of one of the war leaders called Longere, who refused to listen to reason before going to war against the Moli people. The line "Longere refused to hear reason" repeated in the song is evidence that in the version of the story of the Lokoya-Langabu themselves, their participation in the war was without cause. It is stated that one of the Lokoya-Langabu fighters was Kanyuma, which is relevant for those who want to know the fighters on their side, and further that they fought in Iyii and also in Nyolo indicating clearly that the Moli followed the Lokoya-Langabu during their retreat after the engagement with them near their land.

Another song which sheds light on the history of the Lokoya-Langabu Moli feud is the following:

Song No. 5
Title: Ohoi Hillangi
(We the Hillangi)

Ara ohoi hillangi ho hobu
Ofanyarik Akim nalama ohoi hillangi ho hobu
Odwa inyong hobu ohoi Arinyang x 2
Odwa inyong hobu ohoi etur ohoi Amoli hoiriok

A literal translation of the above song follows:

We Hillangi of the Chief

> *Akim went very far, we Hillangi of the Chief*
> *Our powerful Chief Arinyang*
> *Our powerfuf Chief, we destroyed Moli in darkness.*

This song gives the name of the Lokoya-Langabu chief who reigned during their war with Moli as *Arinyang*, which is a very important historical reference. The song also gives the name of the ruling *monyomiji*, the age group at the time being *Akim* and the hours of darkness as the time of the fighting. This indicates that the Lokoya preferred to attack the Moli people at night.

(All of the above five songs in the Lokoya language were sung to the author by Mr. Alex Locor Nartisio, the Lokoya historian who also translated them into English.)

9.4 Lokoro (Pari), Acholi-Agoro raids on the Moli

At the beginning of the twentieth century, the *Lokoro* as the Moli people know them (not *Pari* as they wish to be called today) were so seized with fear of the Moli, a section of the Ma'di tribe, that they refused to accompany their Lokoya-Langabu ally to their area for a fight following the defeat of the latter by Moli warriors.[26] But at the end of the first quarter of the century there was a change of leadership of the Lokoro people and the new leaders prompted by the desire to abduct boys and girls changed their attitude towards the Moli people and began to carry out raids on their villages located on the northern periphery of Ma'diland. Of these villages, the important ones affected by these raids were Barijokwe, situated west of the present Moli villages of Iyii, on the original border between Ma'di and Bari, Mejopadrani, now called Borokodongo (after its renaming by Andrea Farajalla, a road foreman from the Bari tribe who accompanied the road engineer thought to be a

Greek and nicknamed Mujaranga by Bari labourers from Juba in about 1931), Vollo, a village west of Mejopadrani and Orisoko, a village south of Nyarabanga, a village of the Bari people who later came under Chief Koce Gumbiri.

Concerning the raids on the Moli villages, Lokoro researcher Ukal Kawang Julu told the author that his people were motivated by the desire to capture Moli children, especially boys to increase their insignificant population.[27] He said that among his people today can be found families whose members can vividly remember and trace their origin to Moli clans especially to the Logili, the largest clan in the area affected by the raids. Because of its large size, the Logili clan was widely distributed in Moli territory and some of its members lived at the periphery of the Moli area in the north where they were exposed to raids by the Lokoro and Acholi-Agoro, who were known as Koyo or Kicari or Bido warriors by the Moli people. Researcher Ukal said his people, the Lokoro live far distant from Moliland and did not know the lie of the land very well and would have been at a great disadvantage from a strategic point of view had it not been for the Acholi-Agoro people, especially the Koyo who acted as guides for them. The distance between Lafon and Moli is about 60 miles and therefore for the Lokoro to conduct a successful raid, they must have a good rest on the way, and this was provided by the Koyo people whose leader was Ukal Kawang, also known by the name of Olal Onak. The Agoro-Acholi people live to the north-east of Moli, the target area for the raids.

Alex Locor Nartisio of the Lokoya community describes the Koyo as a mixture of Lokoya, Lulubo and Acholi people.[28] The Lokoro whose real name is *Pari* are a segment of the Lwoo people who had settled in Lafon during the migration of the

Lwoo southwards. They consist of several exogamous clans who live in six separate villages clustered round Mount Lipul (Lafon). The villages are called Kor, Wiatoa, Bura, Pucwaa, Pugari and Angulumere.[29] According to Ukal, the Pari raids on Moli villages were carried out mostly in 1927 during the youth leadership rule of Angalure, who dismissed the fear of his predecessors that the Moli people were invincible based on the refusal of his people to follow them in support of the Lokoya-Langabu people who were defeated by Moli fighters in a reprisal attack earlier.

Abductees trace their roots to Moli

At the beginning of the twentieth century, the Moli villages around Barijokwe Hill and west of Mejopadrani were scenes of bloody fighting between Lokoya, Lokoro (Pari) and Acholi-Agoro raiders on one hand and Moli defenders on the other. For example, Akeri the son of Godo of Paluda clan of the Ugiko section, whose home was west of Mejopadrani, and his cousin, Ori-Nyori were forced to defend their families against such raids. Ori-Nyori used to blow a trumpet to summon the people of Mejopadrani or alert them to the presence of either Lokoya-Langabu, Lokoro (Pari) or even Acholi-Agoro raiders.[30] He constructed a high wooden framework (*loro*) surrounded by a strong fence made of dry mahogany wood (*poyi*) with sharpened tips, to support him against the attacks. He was reputed to have shot a number of the raiders with arrows from his wooden fortification from a distance and to have killed some of them. A man who was seriously wounded in the hip by one of the raiders before he could kill the raider to save himself, was Yugu Musura of Logili clan. As recently as the 1930's, he was alive and walking as a disabled person.

9.4.1 Impacts of Lokoro-Acholi Agoro raids on the Moli

The raids on Moli villages by joint Lokoro (Pari) and Acholi-Agoro bands of warriors occurred in the period 1926 – 1927 according to Ukal Kawang Julu, a Lokoro researcher. This was during the youth leadership of Alangure[31] when Rwot Kidi was ruling the Pari (Lokoro). The account of these raids from the point of view of the Moli people is that the most affected areas were the north and the north-eastern parts of their land.[26] In the north, the Moli villages of Palutu and Pamidi were frequently attacked, and in the north-east the villages of Mejopadrani and Vollo, west of it were the targets. It was from Mejopadrani, now called Borokodongo after its renaming by Andrea Farajalla, a Bari of Juba who was the road foreman who accompanied the Greek engineer from Juba in about 1931, that a number of Logili children were abducted by these raiders and today their Lokoro descendants can remember the histories of their origins vividly. In 1995, when Ukal Kawang Julu was accompanying me from his home in Hai Korton, renamed Hai Baraka, in Khartoum, North Sudan after my visit to him, we met a middle aged Lokoro man on the way. Ukal shook hands with him, and the man stretched his arm to me, and I too shook hands with him. After the greeting, Ukal introduced me to the man as his friend. After we parted from the man, Ukal said he was in fact one of those persons in his Lokoro community whose ancestors were abducted from Logili Moli villages during the raids of 1927.

Before the Logili and other Ma'di clans abandoned Mejopadrani due to constant and intensive raids by different groups of attackers and retreated southward where the bulk of other clans lived, they suffered a great deal. The different groups of attackers ranged from Lokoya-Langabu, Lokoro (Pari) people to the Koyo section of the Acholi-Agoro. Many members of the Ma'di communities fell victims to the raiders. The Lokoro and Acholi-Agoro raiders carried away many Moli children. Mule, a daughter of Tombe Jiribi, a sister to Akeri Acaku of the Logili clan was carried away by one of the groups of raiders. Lodro Mure, a cousin of Tombe Urutwe also of Logili clan was taken by Lokoya raiders. Members of the family of a man from the Logili clan, called Kagunyi, were also captured and taken away by raiders of the same origin. After the total suppression of tribal raids by the government and the prevalence of stability in the region, some Moli people found traces of their children in the lands of their captors. Moria, a daughter of Lodro Mure with a Lokoya wife identified herself to Tombe Urutwe in 1950 in Juba. Her father must have told her about his Logili origin, that he was captured and taken as a small boy and brought up as a Lokoya. The Lokoro people also gave information about the existence of families within their communities whose origins could be traced back to Moli. Ukal Kawang Julu, the Lokoro researcher, told the author of the existence of some families among his people whose origins can be traced to the Logili of Moli. As for the Acholi-Agoro, no information has ever been received about the captives from Moli they might have taken to their lands. Kawang said that because the distance from Lafon to Moli was far and it took several days to cover the distance to this part of Ma'diland, their warriors rested in the home of the Agoro leader before resuming the trip to Moli in company of the Acholi-Agoro warriors. On their way back home, they also used to rest there.

According to Father J. P. Crazzolara, the Italian researcher, the Agoro are made up of about ten clans. Among them there are the Wili-baari or Panyulu, the oldest and the original group which others joined, Ariimi, and Pathoko.[32] Moli elders often mention the Koyo as being the ones raiding the people as a group or in company with the Lokoro. Many people have wondered why the Moli, having some of the best archers such as Aleka and others in the region, did not consider protecting themselves against the Lokoro and Acholi-Agoro by taking the fight to *their* doorsteps. The Moli elders, in replying to such criticism, have said that their ancestors probably did not take the battle to the lands of the Lokoro for strategic reasons. Firstly, Lafon, the homeland of the Lokoro is very far from Moli, about 60 miles away, and to reach it the Moli fighters would have had to cross the hostile territory of the Lokoya people. Secondly, the counter measures taken by the Moli strategists against the raiders proved effective, and as a result their activities were minimized, and it was only during the dry seasons when the bush was burnt, and the area became too extensive for the defenders and trackers of the raiders, that in isolated situations they were able to kill or abduct a person here or there. With counter measures put in place, gradually the Lokoro and their Koyo allies ceased their raids on Moli people.

Despite this improvement in security, the Moli leaders at the time drew the attention of those who doubted their ability to defend themselves, to the big lesson their fathers had taught the Lokoya-Langabu people who had disturbed them for a couple of years before the devastating counterattack was launched, resulting in the complete destruction of their three camps of Okire, Ofiri and Omangara. The Moli people have always maintained that they reserve the right to retaliate against those who cause them physical harm, and that their slowness to act does not imply that they are not serious about their security.

9.5 Arapi Palungwa and Acholi Panyikwara feud over Iwire Hill

Today the Arapi clans do not share a border with the Acholi of Panyikwara. A large number of clans of Bori namely: Pandikeri, Logopi, Gonyapi, Nyongwa, Mugi, Beka, Tedire, Lulubo, Ukeyi, Jeru, Utuno, Pambili, Metu, Ndogo, Eremu-Weli, Pakoli, Lira, Mijale, Paluda, Paibonga (Ngaya), Kiloloro etc. and a number of clans in the Patibi area namely: Patibi, Kiloloro, Paselo, Lulubo, Gonyapi, Pavunde, Padrombe etc., live between the Arapi clans of Palungwa, Paridi, Jeru, Kiloloro, Pa-Akori, Cera, Kamia, Pageri, Patibi who are located south of Pageri village. The Arapi and Acholi have nothing in common today which could be the cause of rivalry or trigger bloody clashes after their confrontation near Iwire Hill, because they are far apart. The distance separating them is unimaginable. Yet a twist of fate had the two communities embroiled in serious clashes after the Acholi-Panyikwara assassination of the Arapi Palungwa chief, Nyengwi Iro in cold blood. This was not the result of a passionate struggle but a calculated act when the two communities were neighbours in Ayipa area after their return from Ayaci in the Parajok area. Severino Fuli Boki writes: "At Kadakada, the Panyikwara and the Logopi, their neighbours, organized a hunting party, which the Arapi who happened to be there also joined. When the hunt ended, the Panyikwara mischievously invited Chief Nyengwi of Arapi to rest in a cool place as their guest. Chief Nyengwi accepted the invitation, since he believed that they were one people, and sat with a few Arapi followers in a place pointed out to them. Suddenly the would-be hosts fell upon them and killed Chief Nyengwi instantly. Some other Arapi were wounded, and they escaped and ran off, carrying the news of their chief's murder to the Logopi and the Arapi."[33]

There were some men killed alongside Chief Nyengwi according to other reports and one of them was a man called Tobu from the Kiloloro clan.(34) The clashes which followed resulted in the deaths of other people from both sides of the Arapi-Palungwa and Acholi-Panyikwara clans. Oboya, a warlord of the Panyikwara side was one of those killed in the retaliatory action by the Arapi people. This is contained in a song composed and sung by one of the warriors from the Arapi side.(35) The Arapi and Panyikwara had come into contact in Ayipa in the period 1889 to 1892 when they were both under the protection of Chief Akeri Milla of the Pandikeri clan.

The Arapi and the Logopi people built their homes behind Ayipa, and the Acholi were near Iwire Hill at the eastern edge of Kadakada hunting forest. Ayipa Hill lies in an open grassland which appears to have given its name to the hill because *ayi* in Ma'di means 'grass' and *pa* means 'spread out like a veldt'. It was after the Acholi-Panyikwara, the Arapi and other people were displaced from their original homes in the southern Nile valley by the Mahdist raiders from Khartoum and had returned to Bori, settling east and north-east of Opari beyond Adala Mountain, that the two communities came into contact. The Acholi-Panyikwara had settled south of their present location near Iwire Hill and further south of them, which is not far away from River Atapi, lived the Arapi-Palungwa clan and besides them the Logopi people.

The two communities hunted in the same forest called Kadakada which lies north-east of Opari and west of the two communities. An Acholi informant told the author that he heard from an elder of his village that the Acholi-Panyikwara at the time of their war with the Arapi were led by Chief Dula, an ancestor of Chief Paito. Another Acholi informant disputes this name and the relationship with Paito who was chief in the 1930's and 1940's. Whatever the case, there was a man who posed as a local leader and lured Nyengwi Iro to a shady place supposedly to rest before he could go home. Then without warning the Ma'di chief, guarded by only a handful of men, was suddenly attacked by several spear and shield-bearing Acholi and killed. Among those killed with the chief was Tobu from Kiloloro clan.[36] Acholi accounts about the assassination of Chief Nyengwi Iro are conflicting. One informant said he was killed by a warrior from the Bura clan of the Acholi. Another said it was a man from Paliwa clan of the Panyikwara Acholi who killed him. Even the Acholi elder and chief Mamur Wod al-Faraj was not specific when he admitted that Ma'di Chief Nyengwi Iro was killed by an Acholi warrior. Whether the assassin was from Bura or Paliwa clan cannot be ascertained because the *otole* song about the killing did not name the killer, simply referring to anonymous Acholi assailants. Local accounts about the causes of the feud between the Arapi and Panyikwara communities all suggest that the Kadakada hunting ground was the cause of the conflict and particularly, Iwire, the small hill in the area, which is considered sacred by the Acholi people.

This large hunting ground teemed with various kinds of game. In the dry season, the two communities hunted in it, the Arapi and other clans such as the Logopi in the south and Panyikwara in the east. Even hunters from Magwi and Obbo used to cover the long distance to come and hunt in Kadakada forest by setting it on fire. They exploited the eastern part while the Panyikwara people hunted in its northern sector and the Ma'di people of Bori-Opari hunted in the south. The method employed is to light fires at the edge of the forest which progress towards the centre of the bush. The fires are lit from all directions, and the hunters who follow the fire from the part of the forest they have lit would often come face to face with those approaching from the opposite direction. It was this phenomenon that probably brought the Acholi-Panyikwara hunters face to face with their Arapi counterparts.

9.5.1 The Cause of the Conflict

The cause of the fight which took place over one hundred years ago is difficult to trace in the present day because all the actors in the fight and their immediate descendants have died and their grandchildren, who must be old men and women by now, cannot give vivid and credible accounts of it. The difficulty is aggravated by the absence of records of the event by historians of the era or the period immediately after it. However, oral sources, the songs from both the Acholi-Panyikwara and Arapi-Palungwa sides can provide the names of the main actors in the feud, and the cause or causes of it. The assassination of the Arapi chief, Nyengwi Iro occurred near or under Iwire Hill, between 1889 and 1892, however the acts that followed the incident cannot be fixed precisely or given in detail. I have listened to two songs from the Acholi expressing their reason for going to war against the Arapi-Palungwa, and three songs from the latter group saying why they, the Acholi-Panyikwara had attacked them. I have conducted interviews and listened to three Acholi respondents, one of whom, an elderly woman called Adelinda Aciro from Panyikwara knows a distant person, whose relative took part in the fight.[37] Another Acholi informant was former chief, Mamur Wod Abdel Faraj also from Panyikwara. I met both of them in El Haj Yousif, Takamul Khartoum in the 1990's. The third informant was from another part of Acholi and was an intellectual who works in the fields of mass media and research, and the fourth who knows very little about the fight and even the Arapi-Palungwa people of Ma'di, but said he knows about a song because it is sung during the *otole* dance. As a Ma'di, my access to information from the Arapi-Palungwa community members and people related to them was broad, giving me a wide scope to select the information I needed for research. In all, I drew up a short list of over ten persons for this particular topic.

The Acholi Panyikwara people justify their case against the Arapi-Palungwa by claiming that Iwire Hill is their sacred shrine. They say they warned Chief Nyengwi Iro against leading his people to hunt near it because they feared such action could anger the god of the shrine bringing natural disasters upon the Panyikwara people. In other words, by hunting there, they were desecrating their sacred hill. Their *otole* song which is a war song about the fight rests on the premise that they had warned Nyengwi, who did not take heed their warning and so they had to kill him.

To understand their claim, it is better to read the song in which they have expressed the warning itself. The song runs as follows:

>*Nyengwi yoo koo*
>*Yoo koo*
>*Morongole Got Iwire*
>*Maa ngaa itu Got Iwire*
>*Tong matero dano*
>*Kangolo mula*
>*Lwiri ma langeyo coon*
>*Ee! x 2*

A literal translation of the song:

Nyengwi does not listen
Does not listen.
He undermines sacred Mount Iwire
He who disrespects Mount Iwire
The small axe for cutting a person
Who wears copper ring
The small spear known long ago

The song was sung for the author by Adelinda Aciro, an Acholi from Panyikwara in Takamul, Khartoum North in 1995. Certainly, the Acholi people in their song try to tell the listener that they killed Chief Nyengwi because he did not listen to their warning that Mount Iwire was their sacred shrine and therefore hunting near it by Nyengwi's subjects was tantamount to desecration of it. Most of the words of the song according to someone familiar with the Acholi language are old words spoken in the last quarter of the nineteenth century.

The Ma'di songs composed and sung by the Arapi Palungwa also portray their position after the assassination of their chief.

9.5.2 The Arapi-Palungwa response

The Arapi-Palungwa dismissed the Acholi-Panyikwara excuse for slaying their chief and claimed that the act was predetermined and cowardly. The Acholi-Panyikwara did not formally declare war but killed their chief in cold blood. They maintained that if the Acholi had declared war, they would have responded appropriately, and their chief would not have been killed. They said he was entertained by the Panyikwara chief who pretended to be friendly, then suddenly he set his men upon him and killed him in cold blood. (38) The Palungwa argued that Iwire Hill was not a sacred shrine of the Acholi-Panyikwara, who like them were in transit to their original areas after seeking refuge from the Mahdist dervishes in 1888, first in Ayaci and later in Ayipa under the protection of Ma'di chief Akeri Milla, and that the killing of Nyengwi was a provocation. The reason that Arapi clans did not mobilize for a large-scale retaliatory assault on Panyikwara villages was due to pressure from Chief Akeri Milla of Bori under whose protection both they and the Panyikwara people were living.[39] Akeri's mother Nyajele Joloko was from the Acholi Panyikwara clan called Pajomo[40] and certainly he did not wish to see the problem between the two communities escalate. That is why the skirmishes between the parties were restricted to small groups in the depths of the forests. The Arapi Palungwa have several songs about their skirmishes with the Acholi and the following is one of them:

> *Arapi ama suru Logopi tro*
> *Ori Kimoni ama osu ayia*
> *Ojja Iwire ga rii ondza amani*
> *Mowu Suwa iyo*

This *mure* war song can be literally translated as follows:

> *Arapi, our clan is related to Logopi*
> *Son of Kimoni, our hero is in the bush*
> *The fighting in Iwire deceived me*
> *I am mourning Suwa*

This Arapi song was composed and sung immediately after the death of Chief Nyengwi Iro at the hands of the Acholi-Panyikwara warriors at the foot of Iwire Hill in Kadakada hunting ground north-east of Bori-Opari. The line which says '*ama osu ayia*' denotes that their hero was lost in the bush referring indirectly to Chief Nyengwi Iro. This is a mourning song.

A song that may be considered a song of victory by the Arapi people is the following:

> *Cuwa ka Oboya ni tee na*
> *Kiri ni wayigo rii asi na oga ko*
> *Ori Mule ka nya ganyi tu iniaga*

A literal translation of the song is as follows:

> *The weaver birds are feeding on Oboya over there*
> *Kiri, who is a shrewd man, will not worry*
> *The son of Mule will attack your home at night*

Another song of the Arapi Palungwa about the feud with the Acholi-Panyikwara goes as follows:

> *Ganyi Iwire ni ebe juru ni ko*
> *Wayigo oya sira sore logo dri*
> *Logopi tro ama endre alo*

A literal translation of this song goes as follows:

> *Area of Iwire will not be abandoned to foreigners*
> *Wayigo has gone to a high ground to yodel*
> *We and Logopi are brothers*

This song indicates that the Arapi also had a claim over Iwire Hill, hence their expression that the area of Iwire will not be left to foreigners.

The feud between the Panyikwara and the Arapi was so small in scale that it is not known whether all the clans of Panyikwara took part in it. Among the clans of Panyikwara are: Bura, the royal clan, known as *Jo-keer pa rwoot*, Paliwa, Ayiira, Goloba, Palabek, Pakala, Pamunda and Ayoom etc.[41] Among the Arapi hunters, the clans allied to Palungwa did not take part in the fighting because according to Arapi narrators of the event, quoting elders who were grownup children before Nyengwi was slain, the Acholi-Panyikwara did not declare open war against the Arapi. Their chief simply deceived Nyengwi Iro by pretending to be friendly at first and then seeing that only a few men were with him, set his fighters loose upon the chief thus killing him and some of his attendants. One of the men killed with Nyengwi was Tobu of the Kiloloro clan who lived with the Arapi people where they had settled after their return from Ayaci during the rule of Chief Akeri Milla. Tobu was the father of Bigo who eventually moved to Pamotto, Olikwi in Nimule leaving his relatives in Opari because his half brothers, afraid of getting involved in the fighting, did not accompany the armed Arapi men who went to bring the body of Nyengwi and those killed with him home for burial.[42]

9.6 How Ma'di Chiefs make peace among themselves

Conflict resolution among different communities varies a great deal. Among the Ma'di people, a typical example of peace-making is that achieved by the Lokai people led by the Odupkwee clan and the rival Pandikeri chiefs in the first half of the twentieth century in an area bordering their two chieftainships. In fact, the members of the two clans had gone into open war only once, but there had been intermittent killings of individuals in the bush separating their lands. The trouble started when a Vuri man went after his wife who had been stolen by a man from Bori-Opari, which was under the leadership of the Pandikeri clan, and was killed by the thief of his woman.[43] Eloping with another man's wife used to be one of the main causes of conflict between clans among the Ma'di people. In the case of the Vuri man killed by the man who stole his wife, the Lokai avenged the murder of the man because the Vuri clan were kin. In the skirmish the Pandikeri were defeated, and the mother of their chief was killed. The Pandikeri chief set out and brought some of the soldiers left at Dufile (Odrupele) by Governor Emin Pasha and arrested Chief Kenyi Badaa of the Lokai people and took him to Lebubu where they beheaded him. Before his death Kenyi sent a word to his people that they should make peace with the Pandikeri people. So it was on this basis that the Lokai elders approached the Pandikeri leaders. The elders of the two disturbed chieftainships gathered at their common border in the bush and after discussion of their grievances against each other, slaughtered a black goat and emptied its stomach contents in the place where they placed a flat stone called *gubo* as a sign to cover up the conflict between the two clans of Pandikeri and Odupkwee.[44]

After this ritual performance, anyone from either clan who kills a person from any of the two clans, is regarded as having unsealed the peace stone and must face the consequences of his actions in the form of serious illness befalling him or members of his family. Sometimes even death can seize a person or someone dear to him for violating the permanent solution agreed to between Lokai and Pandikeri clans. This area where they make peace is known as *Mvukaonzere*. Here one removes his shoes to cross on foot because the land is swampy. What had really prompted the peace-making ceremony was the frequent ambushing and killing of men who went to trap animals, by members of either clan. Revenge killings always followed suit. There was also an old path which connected the two chieftainships. Persons who traveled along this path were often killed by wayfarers from both sides. When it finally became inevitable, it was resolved that peace prevail to allow the free movement of members of the two chieftainships in the area dividing them, and a solution was found. This was the Mvukaonzere peace agreement concluded between Chief Dari Kanyara Isara of Pandikeri clan and Chief Iforo Loku of Odupkwee clan.[45] Moreover, the clans in Bori-Opari such as Logopi, Patibi, Jeru, Paselo, Padrombe, Orobe, Kiloloro, Logili and half a dozen others are of the same clans as found in Mugali, Lokai and therefore they also found that an isolated case of wife stealing by one man did not cause division.

Another important means of conflict resolution among the Ma'di is the placing of spears by leaders of the two warring clans across a pit dug by their subjects on their instructions, after a protracted peace dialogue between them. The recumbent spears, one from each warring side, is a sign that the gap that exists between them has been bridged and peace has been adopted by their people. Putting spears across a pit with the blade heads pointing in different directions symbolizes the end of hostilities because this shows the different directions the two clans can take after facing each other in war. In fighting, the blades of the spears from both sides face each other and fly towards each other. A black goat is killed as the final act of sealing the reasons for war. On the other hand, the licking of a spear head or blade is a sign of swearing to the truth. "If I did what I deny having done, let any calamity befall me after licking this spear," swears a person in making a testimony in a case before an elder or a chief. The spear is considered sacred because it is a weapon used for killing an animal for food. It is also used for killing an enemy who threatens the family and for chasing away the evil spirit believed to be inhabiting a human being as in the *ori* dance. When a whirlwind approaches, a spear is reached for and its head pointed at it to frighten the snake believed to be inside it, so that no harm comes to the people through whose home the whirlwind passes.

9.7 Marriage, another means of ending Tribal War

After many years of intra-tribal marriages, the Ma'di, who are made up of exogamous clans, have in one way or another become largely related to each other. This phenomenon has drastically curbed hostilities among them over the years. Another important aspect that has greatly contributed to the existence of peace and harmony within the Ma'di tribe is the homogeneity of the people and their common roots. Their assumed emigration from an area along River Shari south of Lake Chad nearly seven hundred years ago, to settle in the southern Nile valley, is another important factor that has acted as a neutralizing agent in any intra-tribal hostility amongst them. Nevertheless, the society being dynamic in nature and not static, cannot completely divorce itself from natural negative human characteristics seen in such conduct as the harbouring of intra-tribal feuds, if only at an insignificant scale. There are some tribal songs of the Ma'di which suggest that there has been intra-tribal fighting to a certain degree in some areas of the tribe's territory, after their settlement in the southern Nile valley. For example, the following song of the Ukeyi clan in Moli indicates clearly that there were intra-tribal killings before colonization, which has put an end to them.

The song runs as follows:[46]

> *Jurugo ka sire madri ei a ogo ogo*
> *Ori Luko kemu vura joree*
> *Kolo mundru kona maku Liro x 2*

Literally translated into English, the song is as follows:

> *The foreigner boasts ceaselessly in my home*
> *The son of Luko should come to arbitrate in the case*
> *If it were not for the government, I will pull this man into Liro River*

Clearly, the last line of the song is talking about pulling a dead body into River Liro after having attacked and killed the individual. This suggests that in the past some Ma'di people used the rivers to dispose of the bodies of the persons they had killed.

However, the intra-tribal feuds known to have occurred among the Ma'di clans were small scale and limited to a few clans. The causes of these fights varied from one location to another, but the commonest cause of a tribal fight was rivalry over area leadership or scramble for positions of regional influence or rarely the elopement and marrying of the wife of a man by another man from another clan.[47] Marrying someone else's wife is considered by the former husband's kinsmen to be the greatest challenge and they will readily go to war against the relatives of the man who marries their kinsman's wife.

9.8 The Ma'di Conflict Resolution Mechanisms

While social and cultural interactions are important means of removing conflicts among different communities in Africa, the following factors are considered as the actual ones that ended conflicts among the Ma'di clans, and between the Ma'di and other neighbouring tribes:

1- Inter- and intra-tribal marriages

The first factor to consider is that marriages have now taken place among many members of the Ma'di tribe and those of the neighbouring tribes. In the conflict-ridden days, such phenomena were unthinkable because the communities were suspicious of each other and regarded each other as enemies. But after the settling of marriages among their members, these tribes have come to realize that marriage between the communities has contributed to a reduction in conflict.

This phenomenon can be corroborated with the following example:

The members of the clans of Bori and Lokai Chieftainships waylaid and killed each other in the forest that divided their chieftainships near Mua after the crisis between the two chieftainships brought about by one man in Bori-Opari who stole the wife of a man from the Vuri clan whom he killed when the man followed his wife to take her back. The murdered man lived in Lokai and when the news of his death reached the leadership in Lokai they sent a group of men to go and kill the man who stole the woman and bring her back by force to her late husband's home. This resulted in the leaders in Bori-Opari responding with violence against the Lokai action. While this crisis was solved through a peace agreement, this step did not bode well with the ordinary people in the two chieftainships who continued to ambush one another in the bush which separated their territories. To end this conflict completely, Chief Akeri Milla gave one of his sisters as a wife to a Lokai chief. He was concerned that many clans in Bori-Opari like the Logopi, Patibi, Logili, and Jeru, were the same clans found in the Lokai chieftainship.

2- Christianity

The introduction of Christianity and conversion of many members of the Ma'di and other neighbouring tribes to Catholicism and Protestant denominations has made them, to some extent, abandon the practice of inter- and intra-tribal fighting. This is an indication that the teaching of the Holy Bible, which a true convert to Christianity abides by, and the Ten Commandments, especially the one which prohibits killing of a fellow human being, have been effective. The Commandment says, "You shall not murder."[48] This teaching has gained ground among most of these peoples.

3- Education

The opening of schools for the children in the region by the Christian missionaries has for the first time brought them together under the same roof. Boys from the tribes in the region came to Okaru Intermediate School in Lokoyaland, to Palotaka in Acholi and to Nyakaningwa in Opari, Ma'diland where they met for the first time in their tribal history. This coming together has forced them to learn about the tribal and cultural elements of each other. Also, by studying together, the boys automatically got to know each other, became acquainted and even became great friends. Furthermore, on their return home they influenced the attitudes of their people towards other tribes and persuaded them to be more genial in their relationships.

4- Rural and urban migration

Massive migration from the rural areas to the towns of the provinces or districts of southern Sudan, especially of the southern Nile valley, the area of this survey, has brought the members of various tribes together. They have learned a great deal about their different cultures, become friends, shared experiences, and some have married, thus dispelling any semblance of mistrust which their forefathers used to harbour about their neighbours.

5- Institution of the rule of law

The inception of an effective government in South Sudan in 1914, after the eastern bank of the Nile from Gondokoro to Nimule was ceded to Sudan by the Uganda British Protectorate Government in 1913, was followed by the establishment of the strong arm of the law. Severe punishment, which included punitive measures against the tribes that violated the law, prohibiting raids by tribes against neighbouring and other tribes to abduct children or to acquire cattle or other domestic animals, was effectively imposed. Frequent inspection of the tribal entities and very close supervision of the native administration machineries by district authorities have greatly reduced the independence of the tribesmen and prevented them from being able to behave as they liked. Thus, the practice of conducting raids against neighbours or other tribes was curbed.

In 1939, Wani Lou Mbwele, the father of the author, while working as head cook of the District Commissioner of Torit got married to Ojuwiny, a young Lokoro (Pari) woman who gave birth to twins, Opia and Muya who were followed by a daughter called Gune. The Lokoro had raided the Ma'di Moli villages in Mejopadrani (Borokodongo) especially in 1927 during the youth leadership of Angalure who killed many people and abducted many children of the Logili clan of Moli and carried them away to their land. If not for the institution of the rule of law by the government, it would have been unthinkable for Wani from Moli to marry such a woman and visit her home with the intertribal wars still raging.

6- Creation of social infrastructure

The opening up of the countryside by the construction of main and feeder roads has made it easier for local government authorities to reach the people with social services such as mobile courts, schools, health facilities, veterinary and security services. As these different units of social infrastructure are manned by personnel drawn from various tribes, the presence of these people discourages the members of the host tribes from acting unlawfully. Good roads that connect the main centres of the tribal lands with towns, facilitate the provision of bus services thus exposing the populations to law abiding life.

Notes and References

1 Gray, Emmanuel Kitchere. *The Catholic Church at Loa*, Khartoum, 1994, pp.134.

2 Dellagiacoma, Vittorino. *Sudanese Catholic Clergy and Major Seminarians*, VI Edition, Khartoum, 1992, p.52. See also Vittorino Dellagiacoma. *Sudanese Catholic Clergy*, Khartoum, 1997, p.68.

3 Interview of author with Sestilio Andruga Juma in Joborona, Omdurman West on 20-8-2000.

4 See *Ofo Ma'di Ti Si* (History in Ma'di Language), Loa, 1945,

pp.44, 47.

5 Interview of author with Ukal Kawang Julu, a Lokoro historian and researcher in El Haj Yousif, Takamul, Khartoum North on 10-8-1995.

6 Op. Cit. *Ofo Ma'di Ti Si* (History in Ma'di Language), p.44.

7 Ibid. p.47.

8 Ibid. p.44.

9 Gray, Richard. *A History of Southern Sudan 1838 – 1889*, London, Oxford University Press, 1961, p.12.

10 Farwell, Byron. *Prisoners of the Mahdi*, London, Longmans Green, 1967, p.288.

11 Interview of author with Koka Lou Mbwele a.k.a Iseni, his uncle in Juba in 1981.

12 Op. Cit. *Ofo Ma'di Ti Si* (History in Ma'di Language), p. 44.

13 Ibid. p. 45.

14 Ibid.

15 Informant of this fact to the author was his paternal uncle Koka Lou Mbwele a.k.a Iseni in Juba in 1974.

16 Op. Cit. '*Ofo Ma'di Ti Si*' (History in Ma'di Language), pp.45-6.

17 Ibid. p.46.

18 Ibid.

19 Ibid. p.45.

20 Interview of author with Alex Locor Nartisio in Torit on 19-5-2005.

21 Op. Cit. Julu interview.

22 Op. Cit. Nartisio. Interview.

23 Crazzolara, J. P. *The Lwoo Part I*, Verona, 1951, p.172. See also Ukal Kawang Julu. *The Pari in the Luo Community*, Khartoum, 2000, pp.10, 39.

24 This information was given to the author by Rita Keji Lodu Bilal, mother of the author, in Juba on 12-12-2005.

25 Op. Cit. Julu.

26 This information was given to the author by his paternal uncle, Koka Lou Mbwele a.k.a Iseni in 1981 in Juba.

27 Op. Cit. Crazzolara, p.172.

28 Nalder, L. F. *Equatoria Province Handbook Vol. I*, Mongalla, 1936, pp.58, 77.

29 Op. Cit. Crazzolara.

30 Boki, Severino Fulli. *Shaping a Free Southern Sudan, Memoirs of Our Struggle 1934 – 1985*, Loa Catholic Council, Limuru, 2002, p.24.

30 Ibid. p.26.

31 This information was given to the author by Moria Tali Koma, a sister-in-law of Tobu in El Haj Yousif, Takamul, Khartoum North on 15-8-1995.

32 Interview of author with Erodionne Murulu Jiribi from Arapi in El Haj Yousif, Takamul, Khartoum North on 14-10-1995.

33 Interview of author with Mrs. Adelinda Aciro in El Haj Yousiif, Takamul, Khartoum North, in 1995. She sung for me the song in Acholi on Chief Nyengwi, whom the Panyikwara killed under Iwire Hill.

34 Op. Cit. Murulu interview.

35 Ibid.

36 Op. Cit. Koma interview.

37 Rowley, J. V. *Notes on the Ma'di of Equatoria Province*, Sudan Notes and Records, Vol. XXIII, 1940, p.285.

38 Interview of author with Chief Odoriko Loku Diego in Torit on 25-5-2005.

39 Ibid. Op. Cit. Rowley.

40 Op. Cit. Koka interview, also Chief Dario Yona Modomun interview with author in Torit 14-4-2014.

41 Op. Cit. Crazzolara.

42 Op. Cit. Odoriko.

43 Ibid. Also, Rowley, J. V. *Notes on the Ma'di of Equatoria Province*, Sudan Notes and Records Vol. XXIII, 1940.

44 Op. Cit. Odoriko.

45 Ibid.

46 Op. Cit. Lodu.

47 Op. Cit. Diego interview.

48 See the Holy Bible, Exodus Chapter 20 Verse 13, New International Version (NIV), p.55, 1984.

Chapter Ten

Ma'di Chiefs and their Songs

10.1 Introduction

The work, power and popularity of the Ma'di chiefs were known by the songs composed about them or by them. Most of these songs are today sung in *mure*, the traditional dance of the Ma'di people. Through the oral medium of songs, the histories of the chieftainships were preserved and disseminated. These songs are found according to their origins and the families of the chiefs are their best keepers. An example of these important songs is the following of the Pandikeri chieftainship. It was sung in praise of Chief Kanyara Isara who ruled after his father Mene, the son of Chief Akeri Milla and his successor.[1]

Uliya, Isara ni ebbi
Ka ba nya vule ra
Opi ajjukwe nyidri rii oku da yaa
Bori ga Isara pi ebbi
Ka ba si vule ra
Opi ajjukwe nyidri di oku da yaa

Translation:

> *Uliya, Isara is a lion*
> *He will munch people one day*
> *Chief, your power is very famous*
> *In Bori, Kanyara Isara is a lion*
> *He will munch people one day*
> *Chief, this power of yours is very famous*

This song was composed by an unknown member of the Pandikeri clan in praise of Chief Kanyara Isara. In the song, the singer tells Chief Uliya of Attiak that Isara is a lion, and that he will one day kill people and so he should be wary of him. Chief Isara ruled at the time when Chief Uliya was Chief of Attiak with whom Ma'di chiefs in Bori-Opari and Lokai used to exchange visits.

In the 1920's and 1930's the influence and power of the Acholi Chief Uliya of Attiak was notorious among the Ma'di and Acholi people of Northern Uganda and Southern Sudan, and it is said such influence and power were only to be compared with that of Kanyara Isara in Bori. The song was therefore a message to Uliya that he should not think that he was the only powerful chief of that era in the region and that Dari Kanyara Isara was also a power to be reckoned with and therefore presented a real challenge to his fame and power.

10.2 Songs of the Lokai Chieftainship of Odupkwee

The Lokai people, under their chiefs from Odupkwee, are known for their artistic aptitude in composing songs for the traditional dance called *mure*. Of the past chiefs, Cirino Odego and Ruben Surur Iforo are often mentioned as great dancers, and song composers and singers for the *mure* royal dance. For example, the following song was sung for *birabira*, a dance performed as a prelude to *mure* dance. The song runs as follows:[2]

> *Iligo madri nyirobi dii ama tro ya*
> *Ma liya Dici (DC) a lijo rii ani*
> *Langaziri omba mundru ti ga*
> *Ta erire adite.*
> *Iligo madri nyirobi dii ama tro ya*
> *Ma liya Dici (DC) a lijo rii ani*
> *Langaziri oya mundru ti ga*
> *Ta ingwire adite*

A literal translation of the song might go like this:

> *The great knife is with me, can you compare yourself with us?*
> *I will judge as the DC (District Commissioner) does*
> *The great chief has gone to the colonial administrator to hear the message alone*

In the song the term 'great knife' means the power of the chief. The last part says that the great chief has gone to the colonial administrator to report issues alone.

Fig. No. 5: A Ma'di set of three drums for 'mure', the main dance (sketch drawn by author)

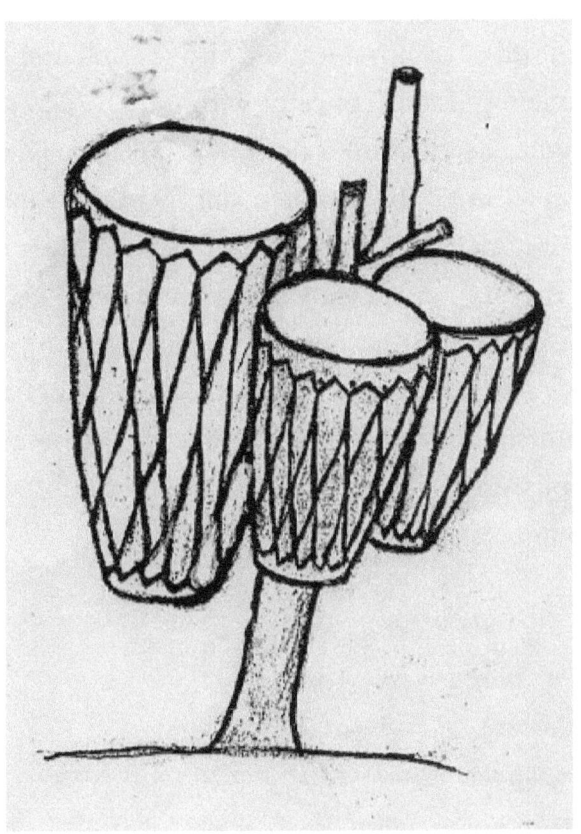

10.2.1 A Song about Chief Cirino Odego

The Ma'di people in the southern sector chieftainships of Lokai are skilled in composing songs about their leaders for *mure*, the popular, traditional and royal dance. When it became apparent that all the Ma'di chieftainships in the Sudan might be amalgamated under one headchief, it seemed likely that Dari Kanyara Isara of the eastern sector chieftainships of Bori would occupy that prestigious position because he was popular with the District Commissioner of Torit and spoke Arabic passably well. The relationship of the Lokai paramount Chief Cirino Odego with the District Commissioner of Opari was the reverse of that of Chief Dari at the time. Odego spoke very little or no Arabic, and Arabic was the medium of communication with the colonial administrators. This situation raised concerns with the DC and his assistant in Torit, and consternation among the Lokai people that their traditional chief might be demoted, and Dari the Pandikeri chief installed over him, a thing they could in nowise tolerate even for a single day. They responded with a song about their chief and it was even suggested that Cirino himself might have composed it. He was a good *mure* dance song composer. The song is about his own weakness but sounds a warning that despite this weakness, Dari would not be made welcome as a leader over him for as much as a day. The song goes as follows:[3]

> *Opi amadri Cirino ni oni ti ko*
> *Ta na mundru kodea ra*
> *Ori Loku, Dari le etca dia ko*
> *Opi amadri Lokai ga Cirino ngo oni ti ko*
> *Tana mundru kodea ni*
> *Ori Kenyi, Dari pi etca dia ko*

A translation of this song into English would run as follows:

> *Our chief Cirino does not speak the language*
> *The authority will stand with him*
> *Son of Loku, Dari will not reach here*
> *Our chief of Lokai Cirino does know to speak the language*
> *The authority will stand with him*
> *Son of Kenyi, Dari himself will not reach here*

Clearly the above song signals a protest against any attempt to make Chief Dari Kanyara Isra of Pandikeri in Bori the overall chief of the Ma'di including Lokai thus subordinating Cirino Odego, the Chief of Lokai.

10.3 A Song from the Patibi Clan

Another song for *mure* dance is the following composed by a member of Patibi clan. The Patibi are numerically the largest clan in Ma'di having three subsections. One of them is the Patibi Moyiba from whom Tombe Bworo came. (Tombe Bworo was regarded by all Ma'di as having the supernatural power of being able to turn from his human form into a leopard.) But the clan does not have a powerful system of leadership like the Pandikeri, Odupkwee, Logili and Mugi clans have. Despite this, this song of theirs is commonly sung in *mure* dance by members of the entire Ma'di community in many places because of the message it communicates to all. The song goes as follows:[4]

> *Elele kolu Patibi a*
> *Amaku Pawale*
> *Mata oluka jurua omba daya*

A literal translation of this song goes as follows:

> *Let provocation be among the Patibi*
> *We are known as descendants of Wale*
> *Father, living among foreigners is a difficult thing*

Fig. No. 6: Ma'di traditional musical instrument "Odi" the five-string harp played by chiefs and other ordinary people for entertainment. (Illustration by author in 2000)

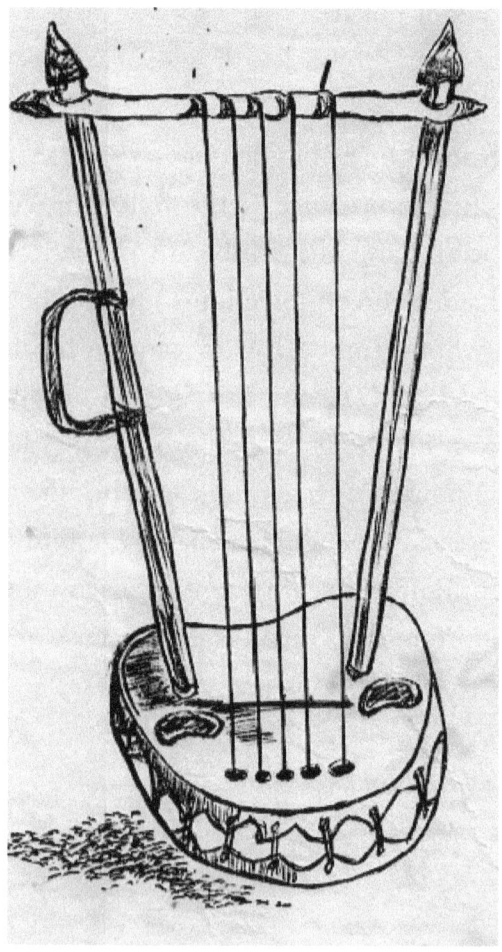

The unknown singer cautions his listeners that they must take care when living among foreigners.

10.4 A Song of the Tedire Clan of Erepi
Nearly all the traditional chiefs of the Ma'di have songs recording their legacies and experiences of this life. One of these songs was

composed by a member of the Tedire clan in Erepi (Kerepi) and was written after an incident involving their conflict with an individual from the Degi clan of Moli. Jangara Modi was his name. The story goes that his cousins from his clan lived amongst the Tedire clan who were related to them through their mother who was a Tedire. One of the cousins happened to inherit a widow from Jangara's immediate family in Moli without his consent and brought the woman to Erepi where he lived. When Jangara who lived in Moli followed the widow with the intention of returning her to Moli, his cousin mobilized members of the Degi section in Erepi supported by members of the Tedire clan, and they ordered Jangara and his small group of followers out of their village. However, before Jangara left the village he threatened that on returning home, he would summon the government soldiers, who were encamped at the headquarters of the Bari chief Gumbiri and take the woman by force after punishing the Tedire elders for keeping her illegally. A few days after Jangara's return to Moli, a rumour began to circulate that a contingent of policemen (*askari*) accompanied by Jangara and his followers were seen heading towards Moli from Gumbiri's land on their way to Erepi. Alarmed by this rumour, the Tedire fled their villages. In those days any village attacked by the police lost their property in the form of grain, goats, and sheep. In addition, elders were beaten and forced to carry their belongings to Gumbiri's home where the policemen were encamped. No Tedire wanted to wait and see whether such serious punishment would eventuate, and they fled to Gulumbe forest towards the Nile to hide. The policemen did not come. It was mere rumour. But the Tedire and members of Degi section who lived with them were disturbed. On returning home, one of the Tedire men captured the spirit of the incident in the following song in Ma'di:

Anyindre ra Mundru engare Gumbiri dri ree
Odro Nyago ni Gulumbe
Ori Bara ba kadri ba ingole ya
Erepi yoo

A literal translation into English follows:

Look the Authorities who have come from Gumbiri
Have chased Nyago to Gulumbe (forest)
Son of Bara where shall we head (for safety)
Erepi (the people) are finished

10.5 Ma'di Headchief Sabazio Okumu abolishes War Songs

During one of his meetings with chiefs (*opii*), subchiefs (*mukungua*), assistant chiefs (*nyamparaa*), notables and elders of the Ma'di tribe, Headchief Sabazio Okumu issued a verbal standing order forbidding all war songs being sung in Ma'di traditional dances. These songs included those sung by Ma'di clans or sections about their wars with sections of the tribe or with sections of Lokoya and Lokoro (Pari). The order also banned the use of spears in the social dance called *mure* because of the high rate of accidents, some of them fatal, occurring in such dances.[5] In the distant chieftainship of Moli and Erepi, spears, and bows and arrows were still being used in funeral dances known as *dra*. This was perhaps because conformity to the ruling of the headchief was insufficiently scrutinized, but not so in the Lokai area where he was based and where his immediate assistants were close by to ensure its full implementation. Dirges or funeral songs related to past tribal or intertribal wars, could be sung in funeral dances which are occasional. An example of a war song is the following sung for the author by an elder from Moli, titled: ***Ori Jiribi***

Ori Jiribi
Ama Bilinya ni luri esura
Madiru ma
Ba Tile oko a tro
Amolu endru dia ko x 2

A literal translation of the song in English could be as follows:

Son of Jiribi
We shall trace the route used by the Bilinya (people)
I killed myself
The killing in which women are killed
We shall not stay here today

10.6 Effects of Abolition of War Songs

The downside of the abolition of war songs by Headchief Sabazio Okumu was that it has made it impossible to know the history of the wars themselves, because these songs are the oral sources of information about these wars. The decision of the headchief to abolish the songs has also made the present generation ignorant of the sources of those songs which have survived due to their previous popularity especially the songs which had spread to all parts of Ma'diland before the local order was issued in 1953. Such facts as the parts of Ma'diland from which the existing songs originated, their composers, the periods in which they were composed and sung, the subjects they covered became obscure. The oral histories of the tribal, intra- and inter-tribal wars were not the only ones affected by the local order, even the situations or circumstances which had given rise to these songs. The Ma'di as a people are conscious of their historical past and regard the tribal, intra- and inter-tribal wars as natural human phenomena which are forever buried under modern civilization and cannot be revived by the songs which are their histories.

In 2000, Sesitilio Andruga Juma, a long serving school teacher in Ma'di area schools told me that when Headchief Sabazio Okumu issued his local orders during one of his first 'B' court sessions to which he invited many elders from all parts of Ma'diland viz. Moli, Erepi, Nyongwa, Pageri, Patibi, Bori-Opari, Loa, Nimule and Mugali besides the permanent members of the court who were the four 'A' court chiefs of Erepi, Opari, Loa and Nimule, Sestilio said he too attended the court and listened to the declaration banning war songs in *mure*, *dra* and other traditional dances and abolition of the use of spears and other weapons in *mure* and *dra* dances.[6] The reasons the chief gave for taking such drastic measures were to reduce any existing ill feeling among the people of the tribe and the likelihood that anyone who might be susceptible to incitement by the song, succumb to the lust for revenge. Sestilio said the headchief was very particular about the songs that had as their theme intra-tribal feuds because he said those events were regrettable and the Ma'di people as one single family could not afford to kill each other. He said the main causes of intra-tribal fighting were the elopement of wives of one clan with men from another clan, the failure of bad debtors to settle their debts and provocative language such as verbal insults or insulting songs. As for the abolition of carrying weapons, especially spears in *mure* or *dra* which is a funeral dance, he said the headchief gave one example of a woman who bled to death after being accidentally cut by the blade of a spear during a funeral dance in Mugali.[7]

Bernardo Mele Alimo from Mugali gave the name of the woman killed as Dudu Nya Laziri of Paloi clan.[8] Sestilio said that from the very beginning when this local order was verbally given to the attendants of the 'B' court session in Loa, he and other educated members of the Ma'di community knew that it was going to affect the songs and their reason for existence very adversely, but they did not advise the headchief against this decision because of the concrete reasons which he gave supporting it.[9] Today the Ma'di people regard the intra-tribal feuds, which historically affected a few clans in some parts of Ma'diland, as permanently buried events of the past. Furthermore, they believe there are no good reasons for reviving them. They also look at their society as one society, one family with the same goals in life. However, they regret the abolition of the war songs, especially those composed and sung after Ma'di feuds with people on the other side of the tribal boundaries, because by abolishing these songs a chapter in the history of these feuds has been closed. Future generations will not come to know the history of their tribe because the songs were the vehicles which kept this history alive.

10.7 Social Songs of the Ma'di
Star Songs from Bori-Opari

Opari is one of the culture mills of the Ma'di people of South Sudan. From this place originated songs which are considered hit songs throughout Ma'diland. One of the songs which took centre stage in the Ma'di *girigiri* dance branch of *gayi* in the 1950's is titled: *Anya Ta Ili Ili Ili Ka Ado Idre?* (Your knife, knife, what can a knife do?) This song reveals the economic importance of Opari-Bori, from where most of the blacksmiths' products like knives, spears, and arrowheads come. Another famous song from Opari, also sung in *girigiri* dance, is titled: *Zangwa Dralice* (The girl Dralice). It was composed and sung by none other than Dralice Daba, the daughter of Chief Dari Kanyara Isara. As a princess and beautiful woman, young men who were captivated by her, shied away from proposing marriage. She waited for a suitor to propose for a long time but all in vain. So, she decided to express her disappointment in a song which became a hit song throughout Ma'diland, at the time making Daba very famous. The song which many people said was composed by Dralice to console herself goes as follows in Ma'di:[10]

> *Zangwa Dralice la,*
> *Abi anyidri Milla pi inji ama vu di ra.*
> *Judea ba ka ili ai ra ya,*
> *Walele anya kabila undzi. X 2*
>
> *Daba Dralice la*
> *Suru anyidri Pandikeri enji vu di ni*
> *Judea ba ka ili ae ra ya,*
> *Walele anya kabila undzi. X 2.*

The literal translation of the song is as follows:

> *The girl Daba Dralice eh!*
> *Your grandfather Milla has spoiled this land of ours*
> *Judea people will not accept the knives*
> *Oh! Oh! Your clan is bad.*

Daba Dralice eh!
Your clan Pandikeri is the one which has spoiled this land of ours
Judea people will not accept the knives
Oh! Oh! Your clan is bad.

Note: *In a certain epoch and at other times, some tribes in Africa especially the Ibo of Nigeria have said they are Jews. Likewise, the Ma'di people of South Sudan think they are Jews and are one of the twelve tribes who left Israel long ago. The educated among them think the Biblical levirate marriage which they follow, the clan grouping and exogamous marriage system that they practice are some of the Jewish traditions that point to their Jewish origin. There are some early names of Jewish kings which are in Ma'di language or identical to it in sound if not in meaning and these names are: Uri in the Book of Kings,(in Ma'di it means to force) Are (in Ma'di means to scatter), Azza (in Ma'di means to spread out or an honorific utterance by female members of Ma'di community), Ari (in Ma'di means to rush to receive on arrival), Ari is also blood in Ma'di, Uziah (in Ma'di it means he is being interrogated), Ozi (in Ma'di it has multiple meanings, either to ask or to get extinguished like a burning flame). The quoted Jewish names could have different meanings in their language but at least they are common to both languages if not in meaning, then in spelling). Hence, in this song the princess Draba Dralice refers to the Ma'di people as coming from Judea.*[11]

Daba Dralice thinks that her marital misfortune can be traced to the legacy of her family and its background. Her great grandfather Chief Akeri Milla was one of the most powerful Ma'di chiefs in history known for the love he bore for his subjects and his protection of them. He led the many clans of Ma'di from Bori-Opari, Moli, Erepi, Pageri and Arapi and some of the Acholi from Panyikwara to Parajok, to safety when they were threatened by the Mahdists in the 1880's. He led them back to Opari when the Mahdists under their commander Emir Arabi Dafallah were engaged in battle and defeated in their last bastion in Bor, north of Gondokoro. When Milla died in about 1910, his son Minai (Mene) Isara succeeded him and ruled Bori-Opari for about two decades. He was succeeded by his son, Dari Kanyara Isara, the father of Daba Dralice. Dari was also greatly respected by his subjects, and this is the reason why, for princess Daba Dralice to get the right suitor as a husband was a difficult thing, for the sons of common men feared to marry daughters of great chiefs especially famous chiefs like Dari Kanyara Isara. The sons of commoners were not prevented from marrying daughters of chiefs, but most of them could not meet the requirements of the bride price, and therefore they avoided such marriages. The sons of chiefs were encouraged by their fathers to marry daughters of other chiefs when they could get them, and the princesses too would prefer to get married into families of other chiefs. During the era of the traditional chiefs, the lucky daughters of chiefs were married by sons of fellow chiefs. For example, Daba Yomsani, the daughter of Chief Geri Ipele of Moli from Logili clan was seen in a marketplace and a string of beads known as *teyi-teyi* only owned by the chiefs' families was thrown round her neck by Clemente Vumudri Mamur, a prince from Chief Akeri Milla's family of Bori-Opari and eventually she was allowed by her father to get married to the young man.⁽¹²⁾ Chief Geri Ipele himself got married to Liociri, the daughter of Loku Kitchere of the Tedire clan in Erepi (Kereppi) and another daughter of Chief Dari Kanyara Isara got married to a chief in Nimule.

10.8 A Social Song in praise of Sayed Siricio Iro

Siricio Iro Wani, the former member of the Supreme Council of State which ruled the Sudan from January 1956 to November 1958 when it was overthrown by General Ibrahim Abboud, the commander of the Army was a great promoter of Ma'di culture and traditions. When he relocated to Opari, his birthplace from Khartoum in 1959 and built his house there, he joined his people in their village life. He participated in the performance of *gayi*, the social dance and was also good at performing the *mure* royal dance. He had learnt performing these dances and composing the songs for them when he was still a village youth and introduced to them by his father Wani. They were from the Mugi clan. During his active life after his return from Khartoum, one of his relatives composed and sang a song in his praise to brush aside the criticism some of the village folk felt about him and expressed in song. Two of these singers, mentioned by writer Severino Fuli in his book, were Nya-Minyori and Juru Nya-Jobile.⁽¹³⁾ But certainly these songs were based on rumours and ignorance about the good work Siricio Iro Wanison was doing for the Ma'di as well as other people of Southern Sudan. Having been at one time a great national figure, most people out of respect for him avoided to be closely linked with him socially at village level but he was fond of them and associated with them. The song about him goes as follows:

> *Yaiyi Khartoum ge ecule rii*
> *Adri joa mani pkwe*
> *Sayed Iro ye*
> *Ira si le jia Pakworo*
> *Nyindre Khartoum ba ecule rii*
> *Adri joa mani pkwe*
> *Sayed Iro ye*
> *Ira sile jia Pakworo*

A literal translation of the song is as follows:

> *The gentlemen of Khartoum who are being praised*
> *Don't tell me yet*
> *Sayed Iro*
> *Because of drink will be taken to Pakworo*
> *Look, the people of Khartoum*
> *Don't tell me yet*
> *Sayed Iro*
> *Because of beer will be taken to Pakworo*

This song was popular and spread to all parts of Ma'diland and was sung for the *girigiri* branch of the youth dance of *gayi*. Sayed Siricio Iro Wani was said to be very happy with the song because it made him popular among his people in Opari and in other parts of Ma'diland and he himself was fond of singing it as the song indicated his love of his culture and his people who loved him.[14] In Ma'di culture, a great guest is entertained with *pkwete*, a white beverage consumed with the hosts amidst jubilation, songs and dance.

While many Ma'di were praising Siricio Iro Wani for being a

successful person in Khartoum as a leader representing them and other Southerners, a singer in the neighbouring Acholi community who did not know the great role which Sayed Siricio was playing in the government for all people, especially Southern Sudanese, composed a critical song about him. The singer was probably unaware of the great proposal for federation of Southern Sudan which MP Father Saturnino Lohure had proposed in the first parliament in Khartoum, and which Sayed Siricio Iro strongly supported. Iro had also played a significant role during the Juba Conference of 1947 in which he argued that the South was still not yet prepared to share power with the North. He continued to urge the Northern politicians to implement the proposed federation for the South during his presence in the government. The Acholi singer claimed that Iro was buying people with money to support the Arabs in his song titled: *Siricio Wilo Dano gi Rubiya (Sayed Siricio sells people for money)*. I heard the song being sung in 1956 in Iyii by some Acholi who had settled beside the Ma'di. Some Ma'di thought the Acholi singer who composed the song against Sayed Siricio Iro was ignorant of the politics which Iro was positively engaged in for Southern Sudan among the Northern politicians in the 1950's, and if he was aware of it, was merely jealous, and so he came up with such a song to discredit a man who was doing good for all Southerners during his time.

Notes and references

1 This song was resung to the author by Lazaro Nyago Dumo in El Haj Yousif, Khartoum North on 10-1-1995.

2 This song was resung to the author by Bernardo Mele Alimo of Mugali during interview with him at Ombada, Omdurman West on 25-8-2008.

3 Interview of author with Karamelo Dagala Balabas Lomeda in El Haj Yousif, Khartoum North, on 10-9-1995.

4 Op. Cit. Dumo.

5 Interview of author with Sestilio Andruga Juma in Jaborona, Omdurman West on 18-5-2000.

6 Ibid.

7 Ibid.

8 Op. Cit. Alimo interview.

9 Op. Cit. Juma.

10 The song was resung to the author by his mother Rita Keji Lodu Bilal in Juba on 20-11-1992.

11 See Old Testament, Book of Kings.

12 Interview of author with Cuofo Oddu eldest daughter of Chief Geri Ipele of Moli in Hai Game, Juba on 14-11-1994.

13 Boki, Severino Fuli. Shaping a Free Southern Sudan, Memoirs of Our Struggle 1934 – 1985, Limuru, 2002, p.178.

14 Op. Cit Dumo.

Chapter Eleven

Ma'di Chieftainships during Turco-Egyptian and British Colonial Eras

11.1 Turco-Egyptian Administration of Ma'diland (1860-1889)

When the first European administrators came to Ma'diland after it was annexed to the Turco-Egyptian rule following the intrusion into the land in March 1860 by a force from Alfred Del Bono's contingent in Gondokoro,[1] they found that the inhabitants were ruled by powerful chiefs who were rainmakers and commanders-in-chief of their tribal armies. Their country was divided into several chieftainships. They were not chiefdoms because within one area there could exist more than one chief and chiefdom, like kingdom, is too unitary a concept while a chieftainship is a decentralized system. Through these traditional leaders the colonial administrators were able to reach the common people who only trusted their chiefs and were loyal to them. That the chiefs were powerful men in their own domains was pointed out by the colonial administrators themselves in their accounts of the situation published in Sudan Notes and Records, launched by the British colonial administration in the first half of the twentieth century. For example, Colonel Charles George Gordon during his maiden journey to Equatoria in 1874 after taking over as Governor of this vast southernmost province from Samuel White Baker, in his account of the first encounter with the people, wrote to his sister Augusta who was in London, that he had to authorize the seizure of grain from a local *shiekh* (meaning a chief) for his soldiers.[2] He further noted that his predecessor Sir Samuel White Baker was responsible for this lack of cooperation from the natives because during his period as governor of Equatoria (1869-72) he allowed the mistreatment of the natives by his unruly soldiers. Naturally this antagonized the natives and made them refractory towards the new administration. An example of Samuel Baker's lack of responsibility in his role as protector of the people, occurred in 1869 when he was on a visit to Acholi chief Kachiba of Obbo. While he and his wife were being entertained by Acholi dancers, a Turkish officer called Ibrahim who accompanied him on the tour, prepared his force and some Acholi collaborators for the purpose of raiding the Ma'di in neigbouring Bori (Opari) and capturing slaves. Despite opposition to this operation from Chief Kachiba who argued that should the visitor and his entourage leave Obbo, the Ma'di would retaliate by attacking his people, the Turk went ahead with the expedition while Baker turned a blind eye to it. What Baker did was later quoted in a report describing the Turks as setting out to raid the Ma'di, who had never hurt them in the slightest degree.[3] Baker did not even react to the expression of fear by his host Chief Kachiba by preventing the slave expedition from proceeding. A few days later the raiders returned to Obbo bringing along thirty Ma'di as slaves and this was reported by Samuel Baker himself later in his book.[4] Such actions by the colonial administrators caused the chiefs and their subjects to adjust their way of life to suit the prevailing circumstances and respond to the emerging challenges.

In 1894, Ma'diland was for the first time divided into two separate entities by the colonial powers, the British and their Belgian counterparts. During the Berlin conference for partition of Africa amongst the European powers, King Leopold II of the Belgians claimed the section of the tribal land which lies on west bank of the Albert Nile as part of his imperial land. It was called the Lado Enclave, as it covered Lado the capital of Equatoria Province. The part of Ma'di country that lies on the east bank was part of Equatoria Province which covered the whole of the present Torit district and part of Juba district beginning from Gondokoro to Wadelei in Alur country. When it reverted to Uganda it was administered from Entebbe.[5]

In 1909, when King Leopold died, the Lado Enclave reverted to the Anglo-Egyptian administration of the Sudan in 1910.[6] The first border adjustment was made in 1913, and the Ma'di people on the east bank of the Albert Nile were given back to the Anglo-Egyptian Sudan administration while those on the west bank of the river were given to the British Protectorate territory of Uganda.[7] This administrative metamorphosis was by no means a practical division of the tribe for they remained as homogenous as they had always been with their cultural characteristics including language. No section of the tribe was unnaturally transferred from their habitat to a new land.

11.2 Ma'di under British Colonial Administration (1899-1956)

The administration of the Ma'di people during the British and Belgian control of southern Nile valley began in about 1893 after the defeat of the Mahdist forces in their last bastion in Bor under the command of Emir Arabi Daffallah.[8] The area which extends from Bor to Nimule from the former Turco-Egyptian Sudan after the Mahdist revolution of 1885 was the only area liberated from the Ansars before the fall of the rule of the rest of the Sudan from their control following their defeat by the British led forces, which included Egyptian soldiers, in the battle of Omdurman (Kereri) in 1898. The long distance from Entebbe precluded the liberated area from being completely incorporated under Uganda Protectorate administration. It was only the stretch of land from Gondokoro to Nimule that was included in the Nile Province of the colonial administration in Entebbe, capital of Uganda Protectorate. The west bank of the Nile from Lado to the border with the Belgian Congo was administered as Lado Enclave for King Leopold II of Belgium in agreement with the British Crown after the Berlin Conference of 1884 for the partition of Africa among the European nations.

Before these changes, the Ma'di were administered as a homogenous community during the Turco-Egyptian era in Southern Sudan (1841-1885), first from Gondokoro after Ma'diland was annexed to the authority of the Khedive in 1860,[9] then from Lado when Governor Charles George Gordon moved the capital there from Gondokoro in 1874.[10] The capital was moved later from Dufile (Odrupele) from 1888.[11] This is where Governor Emin Pasha transferred his headquarters to in the face of the advancing Mahdist forces under the command first of Emir Karamallah and then later of Omar Salih and finally of Emir Arabi Dafallah.

As the British colonial administration deepened its roots in bringing the traditional leaders and their subjects under its total domination, the structures of the chieftainships became even more pronounced. Bigger chieftainships were easily identified and singled out from the smaller ones facilitating the imposition of a policy of divide and rule, a policy pursued by the colonial administration in Africa in general. This was particularly significant during the Anglo-Egyptian Condominium administration of the Sudan (1898-1946).

In Ma'diland, from the beginning the most influential chiefs were recognized and given more important roles to play in establishing the colonial system and enhancing its effectiveness. In northern Ma'diland, at the beginning of the twentieth century, recognition was given to the Logili, Mugi and Ukeyi chieftainships of Moli and to the Tedire clan of Erepi (Kerepi). In the eastern part of Ma'di country, recognition was given to the chieftainship of the Pandikeri clan of Bori while in the southern Ma'diland, the Odupkwe clan enjoyed the upper hand over other clans, the main ones being the Puceri, Koyi and Pamotto, which also had traditional leaderships of their own. In central Ma'diland, the leaderships of Palungwa clan in Arapi, the Pageri and Nyongwa clans were brought into the limelight by the colonial administrators for easy control of the rest of the people. As the native administration became stronger with more power being given to influential chiefs over smaller ones, a situation of rivalry was created among these traditional chiefs. At first the level of education of the chiefs was not seriously considered by the colonial administration as very few chiefs had basic education in missionary schools. But when an education system was instituted and adopted for the whole of South Sudan, it was thought imperative to educate the sons of chiefs, who would eventually inherit the powers of their aging fathers and equip them with the skills needed to administer their subjects on civilized lines. This was reported by writers Sanderson and Neville Passmore quoting Captain E.T.N. Grove, District Commissioner of Opari the advocate of this policy.[12]

11.3 The Colonial Education Policy and Ma'di Native Administration

The colonial adminstration in the Sudan introduced an educational policy for the Southern provinces that was geared towards educating middle class officials who would eventually become clerks, accountants, village schoolteachers, post office clerks, court clerks and para-medical personnel.[13] In 1948, Juba Trade School was opened to meet the challenge of training these cadres. This educational system covered elementary, intermediate, and vocational training institute levels. Individuals who aspired to be chiefs were expected to have achieved at least up to intermediate level in this system of education in order to qualify them for appointment to these positions. As the chiefs were special assistants to the local government administrators, especially the district commissioners in discharging their duties, their education before becoming chiefs was of paramount importance. It was for this reason that E. T. N. Grove, the Commissioner of Opari District, where the Ma'di people are found, wrote and issued a proposal for an educational system for his district and to be adopted for Mongalla Province should it prove effective. In his proposal he said that the sons of chiefs and notables in Opari district should be given priority in education, so that the sons could take over the responsibilities of leadership from their fathers and administer along civilized lines.(14)

The Church Missionary Society (CMS) established an elementary level school at Nyakaningwa in 1918, operated it for one year and closed it down for two main reasons. Firstly, the medium of instruction was Acholi which was not understood by most of the pupils who were Ma'di and secondly, there was a lack of teachers because the Acholi teachers brought from Uganda could not continue due to the poor wages offered. When the school closed due to lack of funds and teachers,(15) very few of its pupils returned upon its re-opening after a year. Those who returned to the school after another successful year of instruction were taken for further education to Malek, south of Bor in Dinkaland where the CMS had a school with higher classes run by Archdeacon Shaw, a Briton. Among these pupils were Eberu Drani, Ruben Surur Iforo, Wani Muku and Icaka Opi.(16) Eberu Drani eventually reigned as chief on the throne of Tedire clan in Erepi, while Ruben Surur Iforo assumed the minor chieftainship of the Odupkwe clan in Lokai. Meanwhile in Moli, Akeri Geri who did not return to school succeeded his father, Chief Geri Ipele of Logili clan following his death in 1933. Although the teaching they received was barely enough to enable them to write their names, it was far better than being completely illiterate. It also somewhat realized the dream of Captain E. T. N. Grove of educating sons of chiefs to take over responsibilities from their illiterate fathers and administer as he said along civilized lines.(17) Education was necessary for the traditional chiefs to enable them to conduct censuses in their immediate domains and ascertain the number of people under their control, the amount of graduated poll tax that they needed to collect annually and to ensure that court proceedings were documented for easy reference. It was also necessary for them to know the number of domestic animals such as cattle, goats and sheep in the possession of their subjects.

The Catholic missionaries who were based in Loa in central Ma'diland were also instructed by the District Commissioner of Opari to follow the government policy of giving priority of enrolment in their school to sons of chiefs and those of Ma'di notables.

11.4 Ma'di Chiefs suspicious of the Colonial Education Policy

Most Ma'di chiefs in the 1920's like Droko Beshir of Pamotto clan in Nimule, Olikwi were still suspicious of colonial officials inviting their sons to venture out of the home. Droko Beshir and other Ma'di chiefs still harboured a fear of the slave trade. They thought their sons might not return like many young people who were in the past allowed by their chiefs and parents to carry the loads of ivory and animal skins on a payment basis after assurances by the white men who owned these items that they would return as soon as the goods were delivered to Gondokoro or Rejaf, but many of them were never seen again.

The Catholic missionaries were adept at learning African languages and Italian priests who worked among the Ma'di learnt to speak and to write the language. This newly acquired skill had made them popular among the people. When they visited one village after another and met the chiefs and notables about the education of their children, the people began to trust them calling them *mundru ko ba*.[18] This signifies that they are not authorities who deceive people in surrendering their sons to them for enslavement, but these are 'people like us.' Due to this approach, some of the chiefs became less fearful and they sent boys to school who were brought by their parents to stay in their households or in the neighbourhoods of the chiefs' residences to live with their relatives. Chief Droko Beshir, according to writer Emmanuel Kitchere Gray, sent to Loa elementary school the following boys: Lulo Tiri, Zozimo Ogo, Valfredo Droko and a few other village boys who eventually acquired education sufficient to serve in the government at certain levels.[19]

Some of the chiefs still remained suspicious of the British colonial administrators by branding them as people bent on destroying the social fabric of their chiefdoms by taking away their sons to prevent them from succeeding them when the appropriate time came or brainwash them into changing the status quo. So, there were several thoughts going through the minds of the chiefs that discouraged them from complying with the educational policy drawn up by the Opari District Commissioner in the early 1920's. But the Catholic missionaries somehow managed to educate a larger number of Ma'di lads like Jelindo Chaka who became court clerk of Chief Eberu Drani of Erepi, Aniceto Amoli who became court clerk of Chief Kerubino Drapaga of Loa 'A' court and Dario Ossuekwi became the court clerk of Chief Akeri Geri in Moli. Even some of the subchiefs *mukungu* were educated at elementary level in the Loa Catholic School. The Ma'di chiefs who had not been to school eventually realized the usefulness of education. In the 1950's, and in the period after independence of Sudan in 1956, many chiefs sent their sons either to the Protestant Church Missionary Society (CMS) school in Nyakaningwa, Opari or to the Catholic school in Loa and the successful ones were sent to Okaru Intermediate School on Lokoya Lowoi Mountain. Chief Akeri Geri sent his sons Dario Loku and Stanley Kute to Opari Nyakaningwa, while Eberu Drani sent Joseph Kebulu the son of his cousin's brother Ame Jiribi to school at Loa.

In Opari, the family of the Pandikeri chieftainship of Akeri

Milla benefitted a great deal from the presence of the (CMS) school in their backyard and sent a goodly number of boys from the big family to it. Clemente Vumudri Mamur, Furunato Modo, both of whom became chiefs in the Pandikeri lineage in Opari at different periods, while Samuel Okomi and Samuel Liyo from the same royal family who attended the CMS School in Opari became a teacher and a government official respectively. Okomi had been to a teachers' training school and eventually was promoted to the post of headmaster of an elementary school. Sending children to school became the duty of every Ma'di chief in subsequent years and this not only concerned their own children but the children of their subjects as well.

In the mid 1950's, Headchief Sabazio Okumu Abdalla of Ma'di made it compulsory for Ma'di parents to send their grownup boys and later girls to schools. The message that this order was to be strictly obeyed was reinforced by him annually at 'B' court sessions held in Loa known as *Opari-angwa* and attended by all the chiefs of the four 'A' courts in Ma'diland, their assistants and representatives of the people in the 'A' courts of Erepi, Loa, Opari and Nimule.

The new approach of modernizing the native administration by educating the sons of chiefs, who were the designated successors of their fathers, met some resistance when the chiefs displayed a lack of cooperation with the district authorities to send their sons to schools. In Ma'diland, the school selected for educating the sons of chiefs and notables was located in Opari and operated by the Church Missionary Society (CMS) opened in 1919 at Nyakaningwa by Rev. Davies.[20] Although the response was poor, at least a dozen sons of chiefs and notables were enrolled in the school.

In 1919, the following sons of chiefs and notables in Ma'diland were enrolled in the Church Missionary Society (CMS) school at Nyakaningwa, Opari operated by Rev. Davies: Akeri Geri, son of Chief Geri Ipele of Logili clan of Moli, Eberu Drani, nephew of Chief Loku Kitcere of Tedire clan of Erepi, Ruben Surur, son of Chief Iforo Loku of Odupkwe clan in Lokai, Wani Muku, son of Chief Muku and Yongo Alimas, son of notable Dumo Betcu Amoni, both of Mugi clan of Moli. Other sons of notables who attended the school with the chiefs' sons included Wani Lou Mbwele, father of the author who was a son of notable Lou Mbwele of Kiloloro clan of Moli, Icaka Opi, son of a notable from Moje clan of Muruli, Moli, and Ernesto Awa, son of a notable of Urugu clan in Eloma, Loa.

However, the school opened in Opari had several drawbacks, the main one being that the language of instruction was Acholi, and the majority of the pupils were Ma'di, most of whom did not speak Acholi. The Acholi language was introduced by Rev. Davies of CMS who spoke Acholi, having learned it in Gulu, the Acholi district headquarters where he was based during the British administration of the Nimule district. It was from Gulu that the teachers for the school were brought originally, to teach the children of the Acholi and Alur officials and workers in Nimule, which was administered from Gulu before the border adjustments between Sudan and Uganda. There were no Ma'di teachers at the time, the Ma'di on the west bank of the Nile being administered as part of Lado Enclave under Congo. Much time and effort were wasted teaching these Ma'di boys to speak and write Acholi before embarking on other subjects such as Arithmetic and English. Yet on leaving Nyakaningwa the beneficiaries of the educational system were to use the Ma'di language in discharging their duties. Had the medium of instruction been Ma'di, within one year more than a dozen boys who attended the school would have learned a great deal. Using Acholi as the medium of instruction had a negative impact on the Ma'di pupils and they learned very little during their one-year presence in Opari. The school under the administration of Rev. Davies had to be closed down after operating for only one year due to the lack of funds. The teachers brought from Uganda had to be paid monthly wages and most resigned. Rev. Davies was quoted as saying that he could not run the school single handed. [21] When the school was reopened about a year after its closure, most of the pupils who had gone home never came back, thus dealing a blow to the government policy of preparing the sons of chiefs for their future roles as educated chiefs. The school was run as a boarding school and the pupils had to supply their own food which was difficult because their homes were far from Opari.

Notes and references

1 Gray, Richard. *A History of Southern Sudan 1838-1889*, London, Oxford University Press, 1961, p.38.

2 Ibid. p.110.

3 Ibid. p.111.

4 Sanderson, Passmore and Neville Passmore. *Politics, Education and Religion in Southern Sudan 1898 – 1964*, p.62. See C. H. Stigand. *Equatoria, The Lado Enclave*, London, 1957 and also L. F. Nalder, *Equatoria Province Handbook Vol. I*, Mongalla, 1936.

5 Ibid. Stigand, p.iv.

6 Ibid.

7 Op. Cit. Sanderson, p.61.

8 Ibid.

9 Op. Cit. Nalder and Gray.

10 Ibid. Gray.

11 Ibid.

12 Op. Cit. Sanderson.

13 Ibid.

14 Ibid. p.62.

15 Ibid.

16 Interview of author with William Alira Yanga quoting information made available to him by his father Yakobo Yanga Lagu, a former student of Opari Primary School in El Haj Yousif, Takamul, Khartoum North on 18-5-1995.

17 Op. Cit. Sanderson.

18 See *Ofo Ma'di Ti Si* (History in Ma'di Language), Loa Catholic Mission, 1945.

19 Gray, Emmanuel Kitchere. The Catholic Church in Loa, 1994.

20 Op. Cit. Sanderson.

21 Ibid.

Chapter Twelve

The End of Ma'di Traditional Powers

12.1 Election of Sabazio Okumu Abdalla as Headchief of Ma'di
The instruction given to the Ma'di by the British District Commissioner of Torit District in 1952 was to seek out a suitable candidate to be headchief who was literate. The Lokai people naturally suggested the younger brother of Cirino Odego, who had been dismissed from the position of headchief by the District Commissioner and left in disgrace. He was Frederiko Bafura, who was then under training in Juba Training Centre (JTC) to become a bookkeeper.[1] But Bafura on learning that the Ma'di people had suggested he succeed his brother Odego, declined the offer. He said he would be out of kilter with the members of his family should he become chief, because his brother did not cease to be chief for the usual reasons such as old age or sickness. Moreover,

his younger brother Debele, who was proposed by Odego to become chief in his stead, died suddenly. His half brother Alimu Dengu, who was interested in the same position was suspected of being the cause of his death, but Alimu denied it.[2] Other people said that Frederiko Bafura was suspicious of his half brother Alimu Dengu. People suspected him of applying witchcraft to keep his brothers and stepbrothers away from the seat of chief which he aspired to occupy. However, Alimu denied applying magic against his stepbrother.

The refusal by Bafura to become chief reformed the Ma'di tradition which stated that chiefs must only come from royal clans, the clans which enjoyed some kind of extraordinary respect in the Ma'di community. For the first time, a member of a subject clan was installed as a headchief for the whole Ma'diland in the person of Kerubino Drapaga, although temporarily until a permanent chief could be found. Kerubino Drapaga came from a small clan called Metu. Although he could write and read Ma'di and a little English, which he had learned in Loa Elementary School, he was not prepared for the heavy responsibility of governing. He was not confident that the deep respect, which was afforded Cirino Odego, his predecessor by the Lokai people, would also be given to him unabated by the same people. There were indications of his reluctance to occupy this important seat longer than anticipated. When the Ma'di people became aware of his attitude, they decided to send a message to educated members of their community in Juba who had formed a strong welfare association called Ma'di Council (MC). The members of this Council proposed that Sabazio Okumu Abdalla, who was a former postal clerk in Torit, be installed headchief. Sabazio Okumu Abdalla also worked as a translator in Torit 'C' Court making him more familiar with court proceedings than any other person. Although the DC in Torit conceded to this suggestion, he felt that the post must be put to a vote. So it was that in April 1952, an election was held in Loa, and the candidates included Frederiko Bafura who declined the post earlier. The name of Bafura was actually put forward by those people in Lokai who wanted him to become their headchief whether he liked it or not. For them the important thing was to be ruled by a member of a royal clan and not another person from a common clan. So, the post was put up for election and the result was that Sabazio Okumu Abdalla was overwhelmingly supported by the educated and the majority of the members of non-royal clans.

12.2 Sabazio replaces traditional Chiefs with ordinary men

When Sabazio Okumu assumed the post of headchief of Ma'di chieftainships in April 1952, his immediate plan was to remove those chiefs who could not write or read in Ma'di or English and were merely chiefs because they came from clans whose powers depended on inherited chieftainships and rainmaking.

Sabazio Okumu Abdalla in the first years of his leadership experienced a lot of opposition from the traditional chiefs he found in power. They overlooked him and considered him an ordinary man from a simple clan. Ruben Surur was one of the figures who disregarded his leadership. Another strong opponent who remained defiant to Sabazio Okumu's chieftainship for over thirty-one years was Chief Akeri Geri Ipele of Logili clan in Moli, whom Sabazio had for unknown reasons avoided to dismiss. Sabazio integrated Moli and Erepi and replaced Chief Eberu Drani with his own court clerk Jelindo Chaka Aperiya of Mugi Palumari branch of Muruli. Jelindo was Sabazio's distant maternal uncle. Jelindo

Fig. No. 7: Ma'di Headchief Sabazio Okumu Abdalla viewing River Nile at Apala Fishing Camp north of Nimule near Fulla Rapids.
(Photo from Regional Ministry of Information, Juba)

Chaka, although from the Mugi clan of Moli was not in the direct lineage of either Wani Muku or Alimas Yongo and therefore did not gain any weight in the contest to be appointed chief. He was from an ordinary Mugi family. Like Sabazio Okumu his mentor, Jelindo Chaka feared Akeri Geri and as a result his chieftainship in Erepi was not strongly felt by those in Moli. He relied heavily on such assistant chiefs as Okumu Alibey Kajamindi, a Mugi man like him and headmen such as Vuni Tusu, of Kiloloro clan. Jelindo also tried to play Kute Musa, the son of Chief Tombe Moli, a cousin of Akeri Geri, against the latter. He even married Buta the daughter of Kute Musa. But all these manoeuvres did not make things good for Jelindo Chaka. He remained a ridiculed chief as long as Akeri Geri was concerned, for Akeri still considered himself the unrivalled chief of the Moli people. The result of this wrangling caused Moli to be maladministered from either Erepi or Loa. The people remained in limbo and regarded neither Jelindo Chaka nor Sabazio Okumu Abdalla as their chiefs but rather the chiefs of clans, as people who did not deserve to be chiefs, although some of the people who so judged them were members of ordinary clans.

In later years after the Sudan attained independence, Sabazio Okumu Abdalla tried to end the tribal or clan-based allegiances among the Ma'di by appointing members of non-royal *bonyi* clans as chiefs. He appointed Aniceto Amoli of Urugu clan in Loa as chief of Nimule and Mugali chieftainships. Aniceto was a court clerk for Sabazio in Loa. The Head Chief also appointed Jinawi Mondi son of Iro Nyengi of Palungwa clan in Arapi as chief in the Opari chieftainship. Jinawi was from a minor chieftainship of Palungwa in Arapi and his forefathers had not exerted much influence on other clans although the chieftainship's tribal war with the Acholi Panyikwara, who killed Nyengwi at the foot of Iwire Hill, was an important moment in the history of the Ma'di. A member of Palungwa, a small royal clan taking over the chieftainship of the powerful Pandikeri clan in Opari was intended by Sabazio Okumu perhaps to impress upon the Ma'di people that he was not totally against the tribal chieftainships, rather it was for their incompetence that he had dismissed them. But Jinawi Nyengwi did not spend much time in the position to which he was appointed, for soon Sabazio had to dismiss him for alleged carelessness and Raphaele Abuni of Padombe clan was appointed in his place as chief of Opari in 1958. Raphaele Abuni was the court clerk for Chief Kanyara Isara of the royal Pandikeri clan. He was murdered by Sudan government soldiers in July 1965 in Opari alongside Atanasio Muru, the teacher of the author in Palotaka Intermediate School in 1963 and 1964. They charged them with collaboration with the Anya-Nya movement following an ambush of an army truck which had gone to bring some water from Kulojobi River for the garrison stationed at Opari. Raphaele Abuni was a tall handsome man who was said to have adopted the smartness of Cirino Odego who liked to wear western suits during court sessions and on other public occasions.

Sabazio was headchief of the Ma'di for almost thirty-one years and he died in 1983. Due to his seniority in chieftainship and his level of education, he was appointed chairman of the council of chiefs of Torit District in the 1960's, a prestigious position he held for several years. Although he belonged to the Gonyapi clan of Opari, which is not a royal clan in the Ma'di system of traditional leadership, his chieftainship was graced with wisdom. During his time, there was justice in Ma'diland, and the people felt the influence of authority.

At the time when Cirino Odego was headchief in Loa, he appointed his cousin Ruben Surur Iforo as assistant chief *mukungu* of Lokai to be in charge of the people's welfare. After Headchief Sabazio's reshuffle, Ruben Surur, the son of Iforo was regarded by his people as equal to the chief at Nimule. He was called Chief Ruben Surur because his clan the Odupkwee was considered nobler than the Urugu clan of Chief Aniceto Amoli and even before the election of Sabazio as headchief, the people regarded the Pameri-Koyi clan of Chief Kara or his son Mohamme or Agala as not being equal in nobility with Surur.[3]

12.3 Abolition of Ma'di Native Administration and Introduction of the Local Government System

The amalgamation of the Ma'di chieftainships by the colonial administration in the southern, central, western, eastern, and northern sectors had given rise to four administrative entities in the whole of Ma'diland. These were named 'A' courts where the judicial proceedings of all cases began. The new administrative set up qualified Ma'diland to have a 'B' court which was higher than each of the four 'A' courts. The chiefs, instead of administering their local affairs such as rainmaking and solving disputes among their subjects by applying their traditional methods, were introduced to a new system of justice. In their old system, court records were mostly kept in memory. But the colonial administration assigned court clerks to the chiefs so that court proceedings could be recorded in black and white. Although the British administrators posted to South Sudan found it difficult to deal with the largely illiterate chiefs, they tolerated them for a long time because these powerful members of society were greatly respected by their people. To dismiss from their roles as traditional leaders those whose positions had been integrated into the administrative system, would have caused chaos.

In Ma'diland, in the 1920's, 1930's, and 1940's, all the illiterate and semi-literate chiefs were left alone to administer their people. In the early 1950's the situation in the chieftainships began to change dramatically. This was the period shortly before the independence of Sudan, which was attained in 1956. As a result of these changes, nearly all the traditional chiefs who combined their resposibilities with rainmaking and land purification rituals as Akeri Geri of Moli, and Ginawi Mondi of Arapi Palungwa, did, lost their posts. New chiefs, mostly former court clerks who did not belong to royal clans but due to their long association with the chiefs and experience, were appointed chiefs in the positions of their former bosses. In northern Ma'diland, the newly created 'A' court of Erepi, had Jelindo Chaka Aperiya, who until his appointment to the post of chief was the court clerk of Chief Eberu Drani of the Tedire royal clan.

12.4 The abolition of Moli Chieftainship led to border problems

Moli chieftainship in the extreme north was abolished despite its large population, extensive area and its special position sharing borders with Kuku across the Nile, Bari, Lulubo and Acholi to its north and north-east respectively. For fifty years disputes arose over the borders between Ma'di, Acholi, Bari and Lolubo, partly because the Ma'di leadership from 1952 up to 2008 did not develop a concrete sense of or recognition of their borders with the tribes concerned. Had Moli been maintained as a chieftainship with 'A' court status, whoever was the chief would have promoted good relations with the chiefs of Southern Bari based in Karpeto, with the Lulubo subchief based in Lokiliri or their headchief with the Lokoya people based in Liria and with the Acholi chief of Panyikwara based at Abara, although the border Moli chieftainship shared with Panyikwara was at the tip of the area near Omeyo along River Ame where it pours into River Iyii. The borders between the three tribes would have been constantly checked and observed. Before the abolition of Moli chieftainship, Chief Akeri Geri had good working relations with the Chief of Bari, Koce Gumbiri at Karpeto, Subchief Tombe Nyudu of Bari, Chief Lado Lolik of Liria, with Subchief Tombe Wani of Lolubo-Aru and occasionally with Paito of Panyikwara who shared a border with Moli chieftainship at the furthest end of their chietainships. Between Moli chieftainship and Abara chieftainship of Acholi lay Opari-Bori chieftainship of Ma'di. The longest border of the Panyikwara chieftainship of Acholi was with the Bori-Opari chieftainship. All these ties were rendered inactive by the abolition of the chieftainship status of Moli.

The new Chief Jelindo Chaka did not strike any good working relations with these chiefs or their successors. The borders with the chieftainships were not visited and the new Chief rarely called to mind such things.

In the amalgamated chieftainships of Mugali and Nimule, Aniceto Amoli from the Urugu clan, who was a former court clerk in Loa 'A' court became chief. Chiefs like Akeri Geri of Logili clan in Moli and subchief Ruben Surur Iforo of Odupkwe clan in Mugali, Lokai grew enormously powerful and commanded great respect among their subjects. Any persons who resented the policy of non-royal elements being appointed chiefs over them were marginalized. Instead of creating the 'A' court of northern Ma'diland in Moli, which lies in a strategic position as a most northerly part of Ma'di country bordering Lulubo, Bari and Acholi lands as stated above, it was unwisely located inland at Erepi. This step was said to have been recommended by Head Chief Sabazio Okumu Abdalla in 1952 upon assuming power and endorsed by the newly Sudanized local government system of administration in Torit. Until the appointment of Jelindo Chaka Aperiya as chief of the amalgamated Moli and Erepi chieftainships, former Chief Akeri Geri claimed chieftainship of Moli and was adamant in his rejection of Sabazio Okumu Abdalla as headchief and Jelindo Chaka as chief of Moli-Erepi amalgamated areas. Jelindo Chaka was from the Mugi clan Palumari section and his family lived in

Muruli and the mother of Sabazio Okumu was also from the Mugi clan. So Jelindo Chaka's appoinment was regarded by some Ma'di people as nepotism. Jelindo did not speak the Acholi language at the time he was appointed chief while his predecessor Akeri Geri was fluent in the language, thus maintaining a good working relationship with Acholi chiefs to his east.

In Mugali, Lokai, Ruben Surur Iforo declared himself chief because he enjoyed the overwhelming support of his people who constituted the majority of the chieftainship. Although this action was tantamount to rebellion, no action was taken against him by Headchief Sabazio Okumu Abdalla who apparently feared a public outcry. Instead, the Headchief tried to appease Chief Ruben Surur Iforo by appointing him subchief *mukungu* for Mugali, a step considered an insult by Ruben Surur and the Mugali people who still regarded him as their chief. Aniceto Amoli found it increasingly difficult to deal with Subchief Iforo and his Mugali subjects and scaled down his visits to the area on official duties. As a consequence, the administration of the chieftainship declined significantly. Mugali chieftainship, before its abolition and amalgamation with Nimule, shared borders with Bori-Opari chieftainship to its north and with Acholiland of Uganda in the south and south-east.

12.5 Loa Local Government Centre No. 1

Before the transfer of Opari District headquarters from Opari to Torit in 1935, following the amalgamation of the administrative entity with Tirangore which had just been transferred to Torit district,[4] the 'C' court sessions were held in Opari and presided over by the District Commissioner. The presence of the DC in Opari had to some extent reduced the influence of the Pandikeri chieftainship of Bori because both its 'A' and 'B' courts were held in the same locations. This gave Chief Cirino Odego of the Odupkwe clan of Lokai the upper hand and he came to be regarded as the headchief of Ma'di. In fact, in the late 1930's and 1940's when Cirino Odego was headchief for the rest of Ma'di excluding Bori, Chief Dari Kanyara Isara who was chief of Bori for over 15 years considered himself to have equal standing with him. It was feared that Kanyara was contemplating a coup to take over the position of headchief of the Ma'di because he spoke Arabic fairly well and the DC in Torit liked him more than Odego who spoke no Arabic. The rivalry between the two chiefs came to public attention and the supporters of Cirino Odego composed a song to that effect. This song clearly spelt out to Chief Dari Kanyara Isara that he should desist from any thoughts of headship over Chief Cirino Odego because the Lokai people would not allow that to happen.

But in the early 1950's after Sudanization of the local government system and the election of Sabazio Okumu Abdalla in April 1952, a clearcut administrative policy was adopted for the whole of Ma'diland. Loa was chosen as the headquarters for Ma'di local government administration having the status of a 'B' court comprising four 'A' courts namely Erepi, in the North, Opari in the East, Loa in the Centre and Nimule in the South. Sabazio Okumu named his headquarters Opari-angwa because in the past Opari used to be the district headquarters where the 'C' court sessions for Ma'di and Kajokeji subdistrict of the Kuku people were held. Kajokeji subdistrict was ceded from Opari district and annexed to Yei district in 1934.[5] Since the importance of Opari had shifted to Torit and Loa became the centre of influence, Sabazio thought it wise to call it Opari-angwa because the past significance of Opari could still be seen in it. Loa itself was made local government centre No.1 at the Torit district level with four other centres and Magwi as centre No. 2, Ikotos centre No. 3, Keyalla centre No. 4 and Bur near Torit as centre No. 5.[6]

From 1952, all the chiefs of the four 'A' courts in Ma'diland used to convene annually in Loa and their assembly was called 'B' court. Chief Jinawi Mondi Sai represented Opari 'A' court, Chief Jelindo Chaka Aperiya attended for Erepi 'A' court, Kerubino Drapaga was for Loa 'A' court and Aniceto Amoli for Nimule 'A' court. However, in 1958, in Opari 'A' court, Chief Jinawi Mondi Sai was replaced by Raphaele Abuni from Padombe clan. The removal of Jinawi from his position as Chief of Opari was considered by Ma'di traditionalists as the final blow which Headchief Sabazio Okumu Abdalla inflicted on native administration. Chief Jinawi was the son of Mondi Sai, a traditional leader of the Palungwa clan of Arapi, and was the last symbol of the Ma'di tribal chieftainships after the replacement of the native administration with the local government system and removal of all the traditional leaders.

Some Ma'di people say that Headchief Sabazio Okumu Abdalla was opposed to the royal clans which exercised great influence over the Ma'di people because he was from the non-royal Gonyapi clan of Bori. They often quote his inaugural speech given in Loa when he assumed power in April 1952 after winning the election to become headchief. They say that he declared that rainmaking and ritual performances to purify the land could not be mixed with the administration of Ma'diland and that these practices were completely separate from the new system as far as local government administration was concerned.[7] He mocked rainmakers, whenever they were brought before him, accused by the people of imposing drought or causing an acute lack of rain in the land. He dealt mercilessly with such in his court by lashing and then imprisoning them till rain fell. Perhaps the confession of one of the rainmakers from Orobe clan of Loa, Arawa Alimo by name, who was lashed and imprisoned several times and once said that he had never been in the sky to know why rains did not fall, convinced Sabazio that rainmakers were actually great pretenders.[8]

It is also thought by some Ma'di political analysts that Headchief Sabazio Okumu marginalized traditional leaders like Chiefs Akeri Geri of Moli and Ruben Surur Iforo of Mugali, Lokai because of their open and sharp disregard and opposition to him. They pointed out that when Cirino Odego was paramount chief of Ma'di he used to have good working relations with Chief Akeri Geri and other lesser chiefs. On the other hand, some people think that Sabazio's serious action against Ruben Surur Iforo of the Odupkwe clan was rooted in his dislike for Odupkwe chieftainship which had championed the opposition to his election in 1952. The traditionalists in Lokai insisted that the name, Federiko Bafura Lubai of Odupkwe clan, be maintained in the list of candidates although he was reluctant to step up for the position from the very beginning. Sabazio maintained Ruben in his position but demoted him to the lesser role of sub-chief *mukungu* for Mugali. Even so, until his death in 2000, Ruben Surur Iforo was known by his supporters as 'chief' and he regarded himself as one. This was the situation with Chief Akeri Geri who regarded himself as 'chief' even after his dismissal and replacement by Jelindo Chaka Aperiya. Akeri Geri Ipele died in July 1985 but at this time he was chief after being confirmed in the post Addis Ababa peace agreement of 1972 which he contributed to as the headchief of Ma'di during the Anya-Nya war 1955-72.

12.6 Opari District Administration (1914-1935)

Opari owes its origin as a district to C. H. Stigand, the first District Commissioner of Kajokeji from 1910, who founded it in 1914. Kajokeji itself on the west bank of the Nile returned to Sudan after the expiration of the Lado Enclave in 1910, while the area on the east bank followed the cession of the area from Nimule to Gondokoro by Uganda to Sudan in 1913.[9] According to Leonard F. Nalder, the former Governor of Mongalla province, the district was divided into two halves by the Nile, the Opari District proper on the east bank and the Kajokeji plateau on the west bank. Before its amalgamation with Latuka District and eventual transfer to Torit in 1935, Opari District was described by L. F. Nalder as tribally very unhomogenous. He gave the number of taxpayers as 5,000 who were mainly split between the Acholi and Ma'di groups but of the 3,400 Acholi he said only some 700 were true Acholi, the remainder being Anuak or Lokoro (from Lafon), Lango, Latuka and Lokoya. The Ma'di contained some elements of Kakwa and Fajulu. As for the leading personalities in the 1930's, they were Chiefs Aburri (Latuka-Acholi) of Obbo, Paito (Acholi) and Dari Kanyara Isara (Ma'di).[10]

Following the border adjustment between Sudan and Uganda Protectorate in 1913 when the Ma'di on the west bank of the Nile and Lugbari were ceded to Uganda and the expanse of territory from Nimule to Gondokoro including Terretenya and Latuho, was handed to Sudan, Opari and Rejaf were made one district administered by Captain H. Castle Smith from Rejaf.[11] When selecting Opari as district heaquarters from which the Ma'di, Acholi and Kuku of Kajokeji could be administered, the Governor of Mongalla Province, Major R. C. R. Owen might have considered its strategic position. Ceded from Rejaf in 1914 and administered from Kajokeji till 1918, Opari owed its ultimate existence as a district to C. H. Stigand who craved it first as part of the district administered from Kajokeji after the administration from Rejaf came to an end in 1914. In 1918, it was made the district headquarters for Ma'di, Acholi and Kuku of Kajokeji because of its strategic position, as the town could only be approached from the south and from the north. In the east, Mount Adala provides a natural barrier while to its west lie Avulogi, Motoyo and Nyakaningwa hills and Nyakiti mountain ranges forming a formidable natural obstacle to approaching the town from that direction.

Although there are a number of rivers in the area such as Iyibi (Eyibi), not the Eyibi east of Pageri village, being the largest then Adura and Giramunda whose sources are in Adala Mountain, they flow southward and are too distant from Opari town to be sources of water supply for its inhabitants. The sole water source for the town is River Kulojobi which lies north of the town. This small river flows from the east to the west before it turns north but it is a seasonal drainage and to make it a permanent water source for the inhabitants of the town it will need to be dammed to create a reservoir to satisfy the water requirements of the town's people.

The development of Opari as district headquarters in place of Nimule after the border adjustment between the Sudan and Uganda in 1914[12] made a great difference. Nimule, which was the district headquarters when part of Southern Sudan from Gondokoro to Wadelai was administered from Entebbe, fell close to the border after the boundary adjustment, thus making it not suitable as a district headquarters. Although it has the natural advantage of a port lying within a game reserve which teems with elephants, rhinos, buffalos and other animals, the Nile and its spectacular Fulla waterfalls, the mountain scenery and valleys, Nimule better serves as a tourist haven than as an administrative capital. Hence the move from it in 1914 to Opari was seen by many people as the appropriate course of action taken by the colonial administration in Mongalla province headquarters. Since its establishment in 1914 before its transfer to Torit in 1935, Opari headquarters had ten district inspectors who from 1927 were called district commissioners. They are as follows:

1- Captain C. H. Stigand, 1910-1915; he administered Kajokeji 1910-1914 and Opari (1914).

2- Captain H. Castle Smith, 1914-1914 administered Opari from Rejaf until towards the end of 1914 when its administration was transferred to Kajokeji district.

3- Captain E. T. N. Grove, 1918-19; the first Opari based District Commissioner. Kajokeji was brought under his administration.

4- Major C. H. Ecles, 1919-20.

5- Major R. H. Walsh, 1920-21.

6- Major R. B. Black, 1921-22, 1924-27.

7- Captain A. H. A. Alban 1926-27.

8- Mr. J. Winder, 1930-31.

9- Captain G. P. Cann, 1931.

10- Mr. J. V. D'A Rowley 1934-35[13]. In 1935, Opari was annexed to Latuko district and transferred to Torit with Rowley continuing as DC. It was thereafter administered from Torit till independence in 1956 and after Kajokeji was ceded to Yei district in 1934.

There has always been a question about the wisdom of including the Kuku people of Kajokeji, and the Kuku in Opari district whose land lies across the Nile and is not easily accessible from the eastern bank except through one opening in the side of the mountain across the Nile from Cukole near Muruli-Ludiri in Moli, northern Ma'di. The inclusion of the Kuku in the Opari district administration in 1914 caused them much hardship. In order to attend a court session in Opari before the Inspector of Opari district, an individual seeking justice or the accused and the Kuku chiefs had to walk up the mountain and then descend the gorge leading to the Nile, cross the river in a wooden canoe and complete the rest of the journey on foot to Opari. Even the senior colonial official based in Kajokeji, the assistant district commissioner, had to journey along the same route to Opari and on arrival at Muruli-Ludiri he had to be carried on a wooden bed (*lengeri*) or on a bamboo bed (*sida*) by Ma'di carriers from Muruli to Opari.[14] The Kuku chiefs, who used to come to Opari to attend court sessions, included Chiefs Kole Yengi (Ingi) of Caragolo area and other Chiefs of Kajokeji. In the early 1930's when the Kuku chiefs and notables raised the genuine grievance of being inappropriately put under the administration of Opari district across the River Nile, where there is no road or bridge to the authorities in Mongalla, a decision was taken in 1934 to cede their subdistrict and annex it to Yei River district.[15] The inhabitants of Yei River District are the Kakwa, and the Pajulu, who speak the Bari language which the Kuku people also speak. The other tribes are: Keliko, Avukaya of Tore, Lugbari of Kimba, Morobo and Kaya and Makaraka of Wandi. Kajokeji town is connected to Yei District Headquarters directly by a road some 65 miles long.

On the other hand, the Acholi, the eastern and north-eastern neighbours of the Ma'di, were included with them in Opari District for administrative purpose. Even the location of the district headquarters, although within Ma'di territory was not far away from Acholiland. In addition to that, many Ma'di people in Opari besides their own language had learned to speak Acholi. The proportion of Ma'di in Opari district who speak Acholi is higher than that of the Acholi who know Ma'di. This explains why some villages like Owinykibul, Winyalonga and Ogwangmeda have Acholi names but are essentially Ma'di villages named by them, being bilingual and not by the Acholi people. A Ma'di scholar, Professor John Mairi Blackings, who is bilingual, and who speaks, and reads and writes the Acholi language very fluently, has authored an English-Acholi, Acholi-English dictionary in Great Britain. The book is acclaimed by Acholi academics not only in South Sudan but in Uganda and elsewere, for its usefulness and the fact that it is the first of its kind.

In other social developments, there was tribal interaction through intertribal marriages. When Opari district headquarters was established, the colonial administrators might have noticed the common usage of the Acholi language by the Ma'di people in the area. It is said that in the household of Chief Akeri Milla in Bori (Opari), who was a Ma'di, it used to be difficult to ascertain whether the residents of the chief's household were Ma'di or Acholi because they used the two languages interchangeably.[16] However, it must be acknowledged that the chief's mother, Nyajele Joloko was from the Acholi tribe of Panyikwara clan of Pajomo[17] and her helpers and dependents could also have been from her tribe and therefore spoke their language, Acholi. In fact, even after the report by the Governor of Mongalla province, the number of Ma'di who were bilingual and spoke their mother tongue plus Acholi were widespread and were found in Mugali through Nimule, Loa, Pageri, Nyongwa, Erepi, Moli to Iyii. The bilingual Ma'di academic Professor Mairi as already mentioned wrote his English-Acholi,

Acholi-English dictionary while in Great Britain where he was a research fellow at Strathclyde University in Glasgow. It is therefore very ironic that very few Acholi speak Ma'di, only a few from those in Panyikwara who share a border with the Ma'di of Opari. The Acholi themselves after the amalgamation of Opari and Torit districts were divided into four 'A' courts namely: Panyikwara headquartered in Abara, Magwi, Parajok and Agoro and the 'B' court, headquartered in Magwi. In the same period, Magwi 'B' court became Local Government No.2 while Loa administrative headquarters renamed Opari-angwa (little Opari) by Headchief Sabazio Okumu Abdalla in 1952 was made Local Government Centre No.1. When Opari was a district and the Acholi of Panyikwara and of Magwi were annexed to it, Parajok and Palwar were still being administered from the Chua County of Eastern Acholi district of Uganda. Parajok and Palwar were handed to Sudan in 1924, ten years after the creation of Opari as a district.

It might have been this linguistic situation that led the Church Missionary Society (CMS) which came from its Gulu base in Uganda where the common native language was Acholi, to use Acholi as the medium of instruction in its elementary school at Nyakaningwa, a Ma'di village, instead of Ma'di, the indigenous language. This, however, proved a disadvantage to the school founders as the majority of the children in the neighbourhood were Ma'di, and because the medium of instruction was not their mother tongue, the output of the school was very poor. Very few Ma'di who attended the elementary school at Opari, Nyakaningwa went to Nugent School Loka and other intermediate schools and most of the distinguished personalities from Opari attended the Catholic elementary school at Loa and Okaru intermediate school. They included Siricio Iro Wani, Severino Fuli Boki, Sabazio

Okumu Abdalla and Melichior Lagu Damiano. The introduction of Acholi as the medium of instruction discouraged a lot of Ma'di lads in Opari, who were the majority, from continuing with their education in the school, in their homeland. Two of these pupils were Kalichino Yanga Abiku and Adislao Loduma Mairi who went to Opari from Muruli-Ludiri west of Opari.[18] The indifference of Ma'di parents towards the elementary school in Opari, Nyakaningwa is one of the reasons which led to the closure of the school briefly in 1920.

12.7 Nimule District Administration (1893-1913)

During the Turco-Egyptian rule of 1821-1885 and at the time of the annexation of Southern Sudan to the entity in 1841, Nimule served as a resting station for imporant visitors and administrators of Equatoria Province, while Ma'diland became part of the foreign administration. Although strategically located, being on the east bank, the colonial administrators did not make it a permanent military post. Nearly all the military stations in Equatoria Province, created during the Turco-Egyptian administration from Bedden in the north to Dufile (Odrupele) in the south, were established on the west bank of the Nile for military reasons.[19] The stations were Bedden, Kirri, Muggi, Labore, Ayu the only one on the east bank, and Dufile (Odrupele). Nimule was famous for its tamarind *aradeb* tree which offered shade for visitors who rested under it. Among the dignitaries who passed through Nimule and rested under the tamarind tree were Samuel White Baker (1872), Colonel Charles George Gordon (1874), Winston Churchill (1877) and Emin Pasha (1878). Presidents Jamal Abdel Nassar of Egypt and General Ibrahim Abboud of Sudan added their names to the list of visitors when they rested under the tamarind tree in 1960.

During the lull in administration caused by the collapse of Turco-Egyptian rule following the Mahdist revolt of 1883 in Northern Sudan and the assassination of General Gordon, the Governor-General of Sudan in 1885, Nimule lost its affluence and influence. This Ma'di fishing village attracted the attention of the colonial administration in Uganda Protectorate when the Mahdist threat to the southern part of Equatoria Province was eliminated by the defeat of the Mahdist dervishes under the command of Emir Arabi Daffalla based in Bor in 1893 by joint British and Belgian forces commanded by Lt. Colonel Martyr, a Briton.[20] The colonial administrators of Uganda annexed part of Equatoria Province stretching from Gondokoro to Wadelei in Alur country in the south. They chose Nimule as an administrative centre because it was midway between Gondokoro and Wadelei. It was then that the colonial administrators came from Entebbe to visit Nimule occasionally on government business. During this period, stone buildings on Gordon Hill overlooking Nimule in the valley from the north were constructed by the Ugandan administration, of which the foundations and ruins can be seen today. A German scholar who visited Nimule in the early twentieth century published the results of a census of the district conducted in 1904. Such records confirm that Nimule had indeed been a small administrative town of importance.

While Nimule flourished as a district town, across the River Nile was New Dufile established by the Belgians of Lado Enclave, an entity claimed by King Leopold II of Belgium. It had been part of South Sudan which was lost by the Mahdists during the revolt to take Sudan from the Turks and rule over it.[21] Belgian soldiers, officials and civilians used to cross to Nimule from their base on the west bank. Though such crossings were illegal, some human interaction still occurred. This was seen in the seepage of Bangala, a variant of Lingala, the semi-official language used in the Lado Enclave besides French. Many Ma'di in Nimule learned and spoke Bangala. For example, the aunt of a medical dresser, Lukada of Koyi clan who was alive until 1960 could still speak Bangala.[22] Another prominent figure among the Ma'di who could speak Bangala was Ito Kafiri of Pageri clan whom J. V. Rowley said had been a sergeant in the Belgian army.[23] Some people thought that he was a watchman hence his name 'kafir'.

Apparently, the British administration in Entebbe, at that time the capital of Uganda Protectorate, had no intention of keeping the land from Nimule to Gondokoro it had been administering from Nimule for Uganda, permanently. This explains why, during their administration, they did not build the infrastructure one would expect to find in a district town. Some of the personnel who worked in Nimule were Alur, a Lwo speaking people who were brought from Wadelei, the western southernmost station of Equatoria Province during the Turco-Egyptian era. Today the Alur are found in north-western Uganda and Pakwach is their main town. Others live in the Democratic Republic of Congo (DRC). When a major border adjustment took place between Sudan and Uganda in 1910 following the death of King Leopold II of Belgium and the return of Lado Enclave to Sudan as agreed upon in Brussels by England and Belgium in 1888, the fate of part of Equatoria Province from Wadelei to Gondokoro also needed to be decided. It was resolved that a point a few miles south of Nimule was to be the international border between Uganda and Anglo-Egyptian Sudan. Sabazio Okumu Abdalla, who was Ma'di Headchief in Sudan from 1952 to 1983, and some elders claimed that the border point was first at Odruto, a few hundred metres south of Nyigeri. Today the borderline is in the middle of the bridge over River Anyama or River Ame as the Ma'di call it, just two miles south of Nimule township. Ma'di elders claim that in the 1950's the present situation was the result of a smallpox epidemic in the area covering Nimule and Attiak.[24] To prevent the spread of the disease, a medical order was issued restricting the movement of people from both directions at the bridge over River Anyama. When the epidemic subsided, it was found that River Anyama offered a natural boundary between Uganda Protectorate and Anglo-Egyptian Sudan and so the two governments in Entebbe and Khartoum, both controlled by the British, recognized this point as the border between the two nations. Ma'di headchief Sabazio Okumu Abdalla was engaged with chiefs of Attiak and Moyo on the Uganda side in discussing the actual borderline and the talks were funded by the two colonial governments in Sudan and Uganda. They were in fruitful discussion in Gulu when the Torit mutiny of August 18, 1955, by No. Two Company of the Equatoria Corps broke out and the border talks were abruptly closed down, never to be resumed again.[25]

After the border adjustment of 1913, the Ugandan colonial officials withdrew to their country leaving Nimule to the Sudanese colonial officials since they were British in both cases. The new position of Nimule relative to the border disqualified it as a district headquarters as it was too close to the international boundary, so the provincial authorities in 1914 in Mongalla decided to transfer the district headquarters to Opari, deep in the interior. From Nimule to Opari is some 32 miles.

As a town at the edge of the River Nile where navigation was possible, the two colonial governments in Sudan and Uganda decided to make use of Nimule as a port for passengers and commercial goods. So, a quay was built at Nimule in the early 1930's for this purpose. At the same time an airstrip was also constructed east of Nimule township to render air services for travelling government officials and tourists from both Sudan and Uganda. Nimule was then connected to Pakwach, a railway terminal in Uganda by steamer service and to Juba by road and air services thus confirming the town's importance as a tourist town. From about 1933, Yakobo Yanga Lagu, a Ma'di from Moli was appointed by the office of the governor in Juba as clerk for the quay in Nimule and worked there for several years recording goods and passengers passing through the port for the Sudan Railways authority.

Notes and References

1 Interview of author with Celestino Vuga Ruben Surur in Juba on 22-11-1994.

2 J.V. Rowley. *Note on Ma'di of Equatoria Province in Sudan.* Sudan Notes and Records No. XXIII, 1940, p.284.

3 Interview of author with Dr. Anthony Lagu Gilo at Takamul, Haj Yousif, Khartoum North on 26-10-1994.

4 Gray, Richard. *A History of Southern Sudan 1838-1889*, London, Oxford University Press, 1961, p.38.

5 Nalder, L. F. *Equatoria Province Handbook, Vol. I*, Mongalla, 1936, p.18.

6 See notes prepared by Marko Aloma Koka, former Local Government Inspector of Magwi Area Council for presentation to Ma'di-Acholi Border discussion in Torit, 2012.

7 Interview of author with Sestilio Andruga Juma in Jaborona, Omdurman West on 15-5-2000.

8 Interview of author with Azaria Gilo in El Haj Yousif,

Khartoum North, 1995.

9 Op. Cit. Nalder.

10 Stigand, C. H. *Equatoria, The Lado Enclave*, London, Frank Cass, 1968.

11 Op. Cit. Nalder.

12 Ibid.

13 Ibid. pp.162-64.

14 Informant on this fact was Koka Lou Mbwele a.k.a Iseni, paternal uncle of author in Juba in 1974.

15 Op. Cit. Nalder, p.50.

16 Interview of author with Khalicino Yanga Abiku in Juba in 1978.

17 Interview of author with Paramount Chief of Pageri Payam, Dario Yona Modomon in Torit on April 17, 2012.

18 Interview of author with Adislao Loduma Mairi in Juba on November 22, 1994.

19 Op. Cit. Sanderson, p.67.

20 Op. Cit Stigand, p.lv.

21 Op. Cit. Gray.

22 Interview of author with Chief Ben Maku Lukada in Al Haj Yousif, Khartoum North, on 20-9-1998.

23 Op. Cit. Rowley, p.291.

24 This statement was made by Ruben Koka Yanga, a senior postal official in Juba in 1976 when politicians, among them Severino Fuli and Joseph Kebulu, were discussing the boundary of the constituency in which Ma'di area fell for the purpose of elections.

25 Mananyo, a Ma'di elder gave this information to the author in El Haj Yousif, Khartoum North in 1999. He said he met Ma'di headchief Sabazio Okumu Abdalla when he returned to Loa from

the Gulu border meeting and told him about its closure following the news of the Torit mutiny of August 18, 1955.

Chapter Thirteen

The History of Iyii (Kit)

13.1 Beginnings of the Border Contests, the Ma'di Case
In South Sudan, the Acholi and Ma'di have been living side by side as neighbours peacefully for decades, without any side claiming the territory of the other. When their areas were invaded and colonized by the Turco-Egyptian forces in the second half of the nineteenth century, and later overtaken and administered by the British colonial power at the beginning of the twentieth century, the lands of the two tribes remained uniquely separate from each other and were essentially the same territories on January 1, 1956, the date Sudan attained its independence from Britain. The borders of the tribes, their chieftainships, the districts, and provinces in which they live today were recognized by the British administrators. They, with the help of the chiefs and elders of the

tribes applying every effort to produce reasonable results, drew the borders in their natural positions. Natural features, landmarks, or bodies such as mountains, rivers, valleys, uninhabitable forests, huge tropical trees, old paths, roads, and rocks helped the British administrators demarcate the boundaries of the tribes so that none was deprived of its natural territories. Today, the Ma'di borders with the Acholi are marked by hills, rivers, rocks, valleys, old paths, roads, huge trees and Kadakada forest, which was recognized by the past chiefs and elders of the two tribes since the British era.

The old boundaries remained while the Europeans, the British and Belgians, reorganized the administrative arrangements of the lands under their control. The lands on the eastern bank of the River Nile from Gondokoro to Nimule were taken by the British Uganda Protectorate in about 1893 and administered from Entebbe. The area on the western bank of the Nile stretching from Lado Mountain north of Juba and running southward to the Congo, including a swathe of land east of Western Equatoria, became Lado Enclave, and was administered by the Belgians under King Leopold II from 1888.[1] The original lands belonging to the Ma'di, and the Acholi remained under their occupation with their traditional leaderships unaffected. What was new after partition of the lands in the southern Nile valley, was the assumption of administration of the eastern bank of the Nile as part of Uganda Protectorate from 1893 to 1913 from Nimule, as a district of Nile Province overseen from Gulu and Entebbe.[2]

In 1913, a border adjustment took place between Uganda and Sudan and the territory from Gondokoro north of the present Juba to Nimule reverted to Sudan[3] and the British colonial administration in Mongalla decided to move the district functions from Nimule, a Ma'di village to Opari, another Ma'di village deeper into the interior in 1914. The distance between Nimule and Opari is some 32 miles.

13.2 Iyii, its History and Inhabitants in Brief

The history of Iyii is the story of the River Kit, the Juba-Nimule Road which crosses it with a bridge and the tribes which have been settled on its southern and northern banks for decades after the construction of the road. Before the building of this important artery road in the period 1928-32,[4] there were no disputes over territorial boundaries between the Ma'di and Bari on the one hand, nor between Ma'di and Acholi or even between Bari and Acholi on the other. Today, however, the situation is different and complex. The Lulubo feel that part of their territory today is being occupied by the Acholi, who are their eastern neighbours, alleging that the Acholi have expanded westwards from their settlements in Agoro and Omeyo reaching as far as the Juba-Nimule Road. These statements were made by a Lulubo chief called Paride Tongun during the Juba meeting convened by the Commissioner of Eastern Equatoria Province, Colonel John Okwahi at the Arapi Teachers' Training Institute in 1988. The chief was called to the meeting as an observer with his Bari counterpart, Chief Clement Koce Gumbiri.

Before the construction of Juba-Nimule Road, the piece of land between Lulubo-Aru and Ma'di was a wilderness having been abandoned by the Moli people who were escaping dangerous raids by Lokoya-Langabu, the Acholi-Agoro clan called Kicari (Koyo) and Lokoro (Pari) warriors. The latter group attacked the people of Moli in 1927 during the youth leadership of Angalure and the kingship of Rwoot Kidi of Pari (Lokoro).[5] Songs of these raids on the Moli people by the Lokoya-Langabu exist today as historical references. The documented history of the Moli reprisals, especially on the Lokoya-Langabu, also attest to this statement.

The majority of the Moli people who had been settled in the territory of Iyii for centuries were from Logili and their allied clans. Their withdrawal from this land created a vacuum and this had encouraged the raiders to continue with their deadly pursuits deep inside the Moli territory unhindered. They went as far as Mejopadrani, the present Borokodongo which lies between Iyii and Moli Tokuro, and penetrated into Pamidi and Palutu villages of Moli. They captured young boys and girls and today their descendants can be seen among the Lokoya-Langabu and Pari (Lokoro) communities. Ukal Kawang Julu, a Pari researcher who had apprised me of these facts in an interview for this book, confirmed their occurence. My other informant on the Lokoya-Langabu version of their raids on Moli villages is Alex Locor Nartisio, himself a Lokoya from Lowoi who knows their history very well. Also, Lokoya men and women whose parents were captives from Moli have traced their families back to the Moli people. If there were people such as Bari and Acholi in this zone at the time of those raids, they would have acted as a buffer to prevent the raiders from reaching Moli on their deadly missions. The construction of the Juba-Nimule Road in the period 1928-32 opened up the area to the Bari and Acholi. When the vehicle carrying the British Governor of Mongalla Province at the time, Mr. Leonard Fiedling Nalder, passed by to formally declare the road open for use, the Ma'di, Bari and Lulubo people, whose lands the road traversed, were jubilant. The Acholi people, whose land was far from the new road were also attracted by the services which the road provided and some of them decided to come and settle along it.[6]

These tribes were aware of the benefits that would accrue from the use of this road, not only by the officials of the colonial government at the time, but also by themselves. The opening of the road has expedited the imposition of law and order, and raids such as were conducted on the Ma'di people of Moli by the Lokoya-Langabu, the Acholi-Agoro clan called Kicari (Koyo) and Pari (Lokoro) and the Moli reprisals, have not only been minimized but completely curtailed. The last combined raid by the Agoro-Acholi Kicari (Koyo) clan and Lokoro on Moli villages, was in 1929 when the Angalure age group of the Lokoro (Pari) were in authority during the reign of Rwoot (king) Kidi.[7] Here also I cite Julu, the Lokoro researcher who has been so kind to history as to let the past experiences of his people with the Moli to be known by present and future generations.

13.2.1 The Ma'di of Iyii

The Ma'di people of Moli were encouraged by the opening of the Juba-Nimule Road in 1932, and decided to revisit their ancestral land from which they had previously been ousted by Lokoya-Langabu, Lokoro (Pari) and Agoro Kicari (Koyo) raiders. It was in the dry season of 1934 that Chief Akeri Geri of Moli decided to send an advanced team from his Logili clan to Iyii to reclaim their ancestral land, since there were no longer any raids or threats from the above-mentioned people. He assigned this task to Awira Rabo, the son of Nyama of Aruju section of Logili clan, and his brothers Jojo and Primo Ayira. Chief Akeri also urged his cousin Kute Musa, son of Tombe Moli, the former chief and other Logili family heads in the persons of Swapere Katika, Mondi Sai, Paco, and Wani Lokili Boronji to move and build their homes in the eastern part of their ancestral land which lay between Iyii River and Mount Barijokwe their border with the Bari of Gumosi and Nyokir.[8] Other members of the Logili clan who moved to Iyii from Moli included Longa Gangiri and his half brothers namely, Agapito Wani, Didako Abiyo and Paitone Opi. Thomas Droko a.k.a Nyamucungu and his brother Andruga Lotwoni and Oliya Tombe a.k.a David and their families, all from the Logili clan, also moved to Iyii. Besides members of the Logili clan, there were members of other clans, such as Mattia Mandu, his cousin Karlo Hindi and Amisi of Nyai clan, Parizio Betcu of Dedi clan, Yanga Itiri of Ijupi clan, Aciko and his son Ulu Cavu of Orolo clan, Guwala and his brother Milla Palacido of Mugi clan, Lodu Leju Bilal of Dongu clan, Sumai Betcu of Monocu-Nyongwa clan, Adibara of Gonyapi clan and Wani Lou Mbwele, father of the author, of Kiloloro clan, who also built their homes in Iyii.

13.2.2 The Bari in Kit
The first Bari elder to come with his family to settle on the southern bank of River Iyii was Babala.[9] He came in about 1936 and built his home east of those of the Ma'di because his fellow tribesmen were not around to keep company with him. He was followed by elder Nyombe and his family in the same year. Tombe Nyudu from Gumosi clan, who eventually became the subchief for the Bari community in Kit, came later, in about 1937 and settled across the river on the northern bank. As more and more people settled in those parts the fear of being alone in the wilderness diminished. The number of Bari people from Gumosi and other villages near the Nile kept increasing and soon the place was filled with people. Where Tombe Nyudu settled, other people like Kasiano, the father of Christopher Legge, the teacher who taught Arabic in Loa Elementary School for boys and girls in Ma'diland in the

1960's, elders Gore, Lokule, Umba and another Gore also moved in with their families. Other Bari heads of families who emigrated to Iyii and settled there included Marcello Loberia, Nikolao Yanga and Lojong Nyori, who said he was from the Nyori-Logili group related to the Logili of Ma'di. The group was joined in the late 1940's by Boyi Sebit, a Bari trader from Juba who built his shop on the north bank of River Kit. Boyi made available essential goods for sale to all the communities of Iyii (Kit); Bari, Ma'di, Acholi and Lulubo-Aru. Boyi was the father of Nagib Boyi, who held a constitutional post in the Central Equatoria government in Juba in the 1990's. As a small boy, the sisters and even parents of the author used to bring him along when they came to buy salt, pieces of soap and other items from Boyi's shop. Boyi was also the friend of my father, Wani Lou Mbwele, with whom he used to converse in Arabic.

Across River Nyolo, there was the small shop of another trader called Mahmoud also from the Bari tribe and he came from Juba. The Bari in Kit were mostly Catholic and the priest of Karpeto parish, Father Gualandi followed them in the 1950's and constructed a chapel which was also used as a village school on the north bank of River Kit. On the southern bank, Father Negrini from Loa Catholic Mission built a chapel south-east of Kute Musa's village for prayer service for the Ma'di because the Ma'di in Iyii were also mainly Catholic.

13.2.3 The Acholi in Iyii
It is said that the first Acholi families to settle in Ombiyo, an area which contained a cluster of villages built some two to three miles south of the Ma'di villages, arrived in the area around 1939.[10] The first to come was a man called Lojukureng, the father of Latana

Omiyati of Oloro clan with his family. Another man from the same clan of Oloro who came with Lojukureng was called Okeny. Okeny was from the Oloro clan and was a relative of Tete Nya Anyira, the great paternal grandmother of the author, and Tete was the mother of Guma, the author's grandfather. Lojukureng is regarded as the founder of Ombiyo and was followed by Okongo, father of Ocira and his family members and they were from the Palabek clan. Then came Timateo Alimu and his family and they too were from the Palabek clan. There were other elders such as Leji Atanga, father of Beshir of Pakala clan, Israel Olebe who built his house near Work Gang Camp No. 12 Jokoki, Felice Kenya and Remijo Aremo of Palabek clan who eventually became headman of the road workers.[11] These people are said to have come from the Palabek area of Panyikwara on Pageri-Torit Road and were mainly from the Palabek, Oloro and Pakala clans. There was a man called Orani who was said to be a member of Logili clan and related to Tombe Urutwe, who used to visit him in his home at Ombiyo. He too emigrated from Panyikwara Palabek where he had settled, having moved there due to some family problems. Orani first lived with Urutwe in Rarengo village in central Kugi forest near Bori-Opari.

For the Ma'di in their Iyii villages to visit Moli, some 13 miles to the south where the bulk of their kith and kin lived, they had to pass through the villages of the Acholi, and this was unusual. The Acholi villages were built mainly on the right-hand side of the road when approaching from Nimule. The Ma'di villages of Iyii were located between milestones 67 and 70 along the Juba-Nimule Road. The Acholi of Ombiyo were connected by a footpath which ran eastward till it joined the Pageri-Torit Road at Palabek, their original home area.

Crossing two borders to Iyii

The Acholi who built their homes south of the Ma'di villages in Iyii came from the Abara chieftainship. They crossed two borders to reach their current location. The first is the border between Abara chieftainship of Acholi Panyikwara and the Ma'di chieftainship of Bori-Opari. Then they walk through the Opari chieftainship and cross the common border between Opari chieftainship and its sister chieftainship of Moli thus crossing two administrative boundaries before reaching their present home area. The Ma'di in Iyii call the villages in which their Acholi neighbours have settled, Bori-angwa because they cross the Bori-Opari chieftainship of Ma'di to come to where they are. *Bori-angwa* means 'small Bori' because where they relocated to in about 1939, the Acholi inhabitants are closer to Bori than to the Moli chieftainship.

13.3 The Moli border with Acholi of Omeyo across River Ame

The border of Moli chieftainship with its sister Opari chieftainship is marked by Afoyi River east of Mejopadrani (Borokodongo). Further north, the border is marked at the confluence of Ame River with River Iyii east of Iyii village of the Ma'di, whose head was Kute Musa, some thirteen miles from Moli Tokuro, the chief's home. Running across River Ame, the border continues in a bent line then it turns northward to Nyolo River.[12] The border between Ma'diland and Acholi territory was marked by natural features and was redrawn by the colonial administrators in Opari in consultation with Chief Mene of the Pandikeri clan, Chief Geri Ipele of Logili clan in Moli and their Acholi-Panyikwara counterpart, Chief Paito. The same boundary was respected by the colonial administrators in Torit when Opari was joined to it and transferred there in 1935. The Acholi people do not share a border with the Moli Tokuro village of the Ma'di except at the northernmost area of the chieftainship where the border was with Lulubo-Aru in the north and a short distance in the east with Omeyo area of Acholi.

13.4 The Lulubo across Nyolo River

The territory of the Lulubo people begins from the north bank of Nyolo River. It stretches towards Juba and ends where they share a border with the Bari and towards the east their neighbours are the Lokoya of Lirya. In the south-east, the Lulubo share a border with the Acholi of Agoro and Omeyo. Across the bridge over River Nyolo on the south bank and just a few meters from the edge of the bridge lies their common boundary with the Ma'di people of Moli. This natural boundary has been there between the two tribes since time immemorial and was officially demarcated by the colonial administrators in 1913, when the area from Wadelei in the present Alur country in modern Uganda to Mongalla in modern Sudan administered by the British from Entebbe, capital of Uganda Protectorate, was ceded to Sudan.[13] Following the fall of the Turco-Egyptian administration of Sudan and the subsequent advent of the Mahdist administration in 1885 and in the absence of administration in Equatoria Province, which was abandoned by its Governor Emin Pasha in 1889, this territory became part of Uganda. Meanwhile the territory on the western bank of the Nile from Lado to Lugbari country had become the Lado Enclave which was claimed by King Leopold II of Belgium in 1888 after the Berlin Conference of 1884 for partition of Africa. The agreement struck between the Belgian King and the British Crown was that the territory was to remain in his possession until his death, upon which it would revert to Sudan.[14] In 1909 the King died and so in the following year there was an exchange of territories. Part of what was Lado Enclave inhabited by the Lugbari and Ma'di peoples on the west bank of the Nile was given to Uganda. Three years later, in 1913, the land from Gondokoro to Nimule, which was administered by Uganda, was ceded to Sudan. Maps drawn in pre- and post-independence periods of the Sudan clearly indicate that the south bank of Nyolo River was their border with the Ma'di. A man called Gembuye was a friend of Wani Lou, father of the author, and they used to exchange visits. The author saw Gembuye several times in his family's village of Moli, and on one of his father's visits to Gembuye in Aru Nyolo, the father of the author took along the author's mother and the author himself.

In setting borders the British did not just draw a line on paper. They did so only after critical observations, checks and counter-checks of the position of each of the tribes affected, and after exhaustive enquiries into the historical possessors of these lands, information gleaned from their inhabitants including chiefs and elders.

On the other hand, the area between Rivers Kit and Nyolo had seen intermittent fighting in the past between the Lokoya-Langabu and the Ma'di of Moli. These accounts are contained in the traditional histories of the two communities given by both Ma'di and Lokoya historians. The warriors from the Moli side collected the abandonded spears of Lokoya-Langabu fighters, who had fled after losing a battle, and buried them under a huge tree among several trees which stand on the left-hand side of the road from Nyolo River. This was reported to the author by Davide Droko, the son of Tombe Urtwe, an elder of Moli who saw the resting place of the weapons.[15] War songs composed by artists from the two tribes point to these conflicts. Lulubo, especially its

Aru section, are also aware of these feuds.(16)

In current border disputes, the Lulubo complaints are mostly directed at the Acholi of Agoro and Omeyo, claiming that they have moved westward from their territory and occupied Lulubo lands along the Juba-Nimule Road. Lulubo Chief Paride Tongun mentioned this during the Juba meeting called by the Commissioner of Eastern Equatoria Province in 1988, at which he and the Bari chief, Clement Koce Gumbiri, were invited as observers to attend to the Acholi-Ma'di border issue. The Lulubo also complained about the Bari, accusing them of moving northward, thus encroaching on Lulubo land around River Nyolo. In the 1950's, the Lulubo area across River Nyolo was frequently visited by Ma'di, Acholi and Bari of Iyii because of Mahmoud's retail outlet where they could buy essential items such as salt, pieces of soap, ready made clothes and other items brought from Juba. Mahmoud's small shop served as an alternative to the store of Boyi Sebit on the other side of the River Kit. The Lolubo also claim that their border with the Ma'di is over Kit River bridge and not across Nyolo River bridge as previously believed, thus challenging the original border line fixed during British rule.

Of the Lulubo leaders who were prominent in the history of the border contests between Ma'di and Bari, and between Acholi and Ma'di and between Lolubo themselves and the two tribes of Bari and Acholi, stands Headman Tombe Wani, who once arbitrated between Chief Akeri Geri of Ma'di, Moli and Sub-chief Tombe Nyudu of Bari section in Kit in 1952. The dispute concerned the land across Iyii River, the possession of which Tombe Nyudu challenged Akeri Geri. The Lulubo were administered with the Lokoya tribe, under Juba District and their chiefs who had experience of the issues in the area were Tongu Luwala and Head Chief

Lolik Lado, who in 1952 reconciled Tombe Nyudu and Akeri Geri and told them that the border between the Ma'di and Lulubo was on the south bank of River Nyolo. Captain Cooke, the DC of Juba District, once brought him in the company of other chiefs to this place to show them.[17]

13.5 The beginnings of a Ma'di-Bari border contest

It is certain that the border dispute in Iyii was created by the local government administrators of both Juba and Torit districts of former Equatoria province, who did not adhere to the clearly marked lines drawn by the British colonial officials. These officers had meticulously consulted the chiefs and elders of the tribes in the area before they fixed the boundaries and made it possible for the administrators who followed them to know where their jurisdictions began and where they ended. But post-independence officials had no policies or development programmes for the Kit area. The border between the Ma'di and Lulubo-Aru was the only one easily identified because it aligned with the southern bank of River Nyolo, a natural landmark. The border between the Bari and Ma'di is also easily established because it follows the Juba-Nimule Road from Karpeto road junction north of Moli Tokuro. It occasionally falls to within a few meters of the water drainage works of the road (*mujura*), wanders one or two kilometers from the road for some distance westward then turning towards the road again, follows it until Iyii River, which it crosses. It ends on the bank of Nyolo River.
[18] But whether the Ma'di are comfortable with this alignment of the boundary between them and the Bari, is yet to be determined because the history of the previous occupation of the lands demarcated does not seem to have been considered. However, both Bari and Ma'di communities adhere to the 1956 border.

Their present location was considered when drawing the borders, however some Ma'di clans such as the Logili had once lived for decades in areas in which their presence today is not noticeable. There were several factors which led to their dislocation from those places. One of those factors was the invasion by the Lokoya-Langabu, Pari (Lokoro) and Acholi-Agoro (Koyo-Kicari) communities. These places can be identified today by the Ma'di names which remain as living proof that these places were once occupied by Ma'di clans. For example, River Lupaingwe and Mount Barijokwe which fall in Bari territory today, are natural features which were once occupied by the Ma'di. *Lupaingwe* in Ma'di means 'white stone.' Meanwhile the maps issued pre-independence, at independence and in the post-independence era in Sudan bear witness to these borders. A visit to these areas will surely convince anyone that it is totally unnecessary for the four tribes to argue with each other about their common borders. These borders were accurately demarcated by British officials during colonial times after meticulous consultation with the tribal chiefs and elders of the areas.

Today the matter has been complicated by competing claims. And the populations of the tribes are more diffuse. The borders between the Lulubo and Bari, Lulubo and Acholi, Ma'di and Bari and Ma'di and Acholi are contested. In 2008, following the Kit intertribal border meeting attended by the representatives of the four tribes, Bari, Lulubo, Acholi and Ma'di, the Lulubo issued a statement in which they acknowledged sharing a border with the Ma'di, but they moved the border post southward from the south bank of Nyolo River to the middle of Kit River bridge giving them a foothold on the north bank of River Kit where they used not to be, thus complicating the issue of reasserting the borders further. As for the Omeyo people of Acholi, they know that the territory west of them used to be the passage through which the Lokoya-Langabu, Lokoro (Pari) and Koyo (Kicari clan) used to reach the Ma'di in Moli to launch their terrible raids. During this period, the area stretching from the point where the bridge on River Kit lies today was controlled by the Logili clan of Ma'di backed by allied clans who lived with them. This land stretches from here up to Mejopadrani (Borokodongo), Ma'di villages most of whose inhabitants were from Logili clan, that is, the territory south of River Kit. As for the land west of the bridge, the area now contested by all four tribes, this was controlled by the Logili clan, and the clans allied to them from Mount Barijokwe near River Lupaingwe. The current borderline between the Acholi Omeyo and the Moli Chieftainship is above the Ame River which has a sharp bend and flows westward pouring into River Kit just a few metres from the confluence of Rivers Afoyi and Kit. Where River Afoyi joins Kit is the point where the Ma'di inhabitants of Luworo village of Iyii fetch their drinking water. The author's father, Wani Lou Mbwele from the Kiloloro clan and his maternal grandfather, Lodu Jote Mori a.k.a Bilal from Dongu clan, built their houses in Luworo, a Logili village, and as a boy the author lived there, and so can vouch for the accuracy of the above information which he is happy to share with his readers.

If Juba-Nimule Road had not been constructed it would be anyone's guess as to which parts of the areas now contested by the four communities would be claimed. In Kit, ever since the place came into existence, subchiefs such as Tombe Nyudu of Bari and Kute Musa Tombe of Ma'di acted as stand-ins for their chiefs in the areas they originated from and took their instructions from those chiefs. They collected graduated poll tax from their fellow tribesmen (and only them) and submitted it to their heads, and organized court sessions in which their chiefs came to officiate. Subchief Tombe Nyudu was answerable to Chief Koce Gumbiri of Karpeto in southern Bari, and Kute Musa, who was the cousin of Chief Akeri Geri of Logili clan in Moli, was answerable to Akeri. After the latter's removal as chief, he was obedient to Jelindo Chaka Aperiya who became chief of Nyongwa, Erepi and Moli. The Acholi too, used to hold court sessions chaired by the chief of Panyikwara in Ombiyo, their village area in Kit. But their position was more complex than that of the other two tribes, Lulubo and Bari, because they cross two borders. These are the borders of the chieftainship of Abara with that of Bori-Opari chieftainship, and the border between Bori-Opari with its sister chieftainship of Moli. There were some Acholi families who emigrated from Agoro and Omeyo and settled in the land between the south bank of River Nyolo and the north bank of River Kit, but because of the presence of the Bari in the north and Ma'di on the south banks of River Kit it was not possible for them to join and have direct tribal administrative links with members of their community who have settled in Ombiyo beyond the Bari and south of Ma'di villages.

13.6 The 1952 minor clash over the River Nyolo border

In 1952, a bitter quarrel erupted between Chief Akeri Geri of Ma'di, Moli section and Subchief Tombe Nyudu of Bari tribe from Gumosi clan of Karpeto chieftainship under Koce Gumbiri. The bitter exchange of words between the two men was over the border separating Ma'di and Lulubo. Tombe Nyudu claimed that there was no boundary between Ma'di and Lulubo and that it was his tribe which had a border with the Lulubo. The area contested was the land between Rivers Iyii and Nyolo stretching for about two miles which was the border between the Ma'di and Lulubo tribes. Akeri took an axe and angrily cut a big gash in a shea butter fruit tree (*lulu*) on the south bank of River Nyolo, to mark the border between Ma'di and Lulubo. This action angered Tombe Nyudu who felt that Chief Akeri Geri was challenging his claim that the Bari had a border with the Lulubo.[19] The heated exchange attracted the attention of the wives of the Bari subchief who got involved in the squabble. Akeri's wife, Aleka daughter of Headman Tombe Wani of Lulubo-Aru, joined in and a scuffle broke out between her and two wives of Tombe Nyudu. Then Anitida the wife of Zakaria Lendi, brother of Chief Akeri Geri and Avelina Meli, the wife of Jentilio Lodu, the youngest brother of the Ma'di chief, Ngayu Kute a woman from Moli, who was in Akeri's entourage also joined in the scuffle against the Bari chief's wives. Headman Tombe Wani, the host of the two chiefs and his Lulubo-Aru people separated the two groups and the subchief particularly appealed to the two chiefs to respect the law, their positions, the dignity, and relations of their people. Tombe Wani, whose chieftainship was under Headchief Lolik Lado of Lokoya, reported the stand-off between the two chiefs to Lolik, who also had control over the Lulubo people.

Chief Akeri Geri composed and sang the following song to assert his authority over this land in 1952;

> *Meliya ni Awire le ebeko*
> *Nyitce nyi agori*
> *Nyeja Nyolo ni ko,*
> *Ori Ipele ka vu rini ase ni.*
> *Meliya ni Awire le ebeko*

Meliya will not be abandoned by Awira
If you think you are a man
Don't cross Nyolo River
The son of Chief Ipele rules over this land
Meliya will not be abandoned by Awira

Meliya is the home of Awira Rabo. It is a few metres east of the complex built by J. J. Okot on the south bank of River Kit after the Comprehensive Peace Agreement (CPA). In the ruins of the old home stands a mango tree and this was the garden of Awira in which he planted one or two mango trees. After the Addis Ababa Agreement of 1972 following the death of Awira, this place was turned into a market by Akeri Geri as chief of Moli under which Iyii falls.

13.6.1 Chief Lolik Lado on a peace mission to Moli

Chief Lolik Lado accompanied by his sergeant Rombe promptly traveled by lorry to Moli in 1952 and spent the night in the house of Subchief Okumu Alibe, son of Kajamindi of the Mugi clan in Baribari village.[20] Next morning, Chief Lolik sent for Chief Akeri Geri in his home at Garamu two miles away to come and join him to travel by lorry to Loa, where the headquarters of the Ma'di native administration was located so that he, Lolik could report his presence in the Ma'di area and the purpose of his visit to Ma'di head Chief Sabazio Okumu. The issue which had brought him to the Ma'di area was to arbitrate in the conflict between Chief Akeri Geri of Ma'di and Subchief Tombe Nyudu of Bari. Sabazio Okumu Abdalla, who had just assumed power as headchief of Ma'di being elected just a few months earlier by Ma'di officials serving in the government in Juba and Torit, joined head Chief Lolik and

Chief Akeri Geri to travel to Nyolo, the site of the conflict. Both headman Tombe Wani and head Chief Lolik Lado confirmed to Tombe Nyudu, Chief Akeri Geri and head Chief Sabazio Okumu that the Ma'di had a border with the Lulubo, and it was located on the south bank of River Nyolo, running for a few meters along the southern bank of the river. The part of River Iyii at this point lies inside Ma'di territory. The two arbitrators said that the Bari came to the area around 1936 to benefit from the services accorded by Juba-Nimule Road whose construction in the period 1928-32 was completed in 1932.[21]

The emigration of the Bari to the areas in the period 1936-39 and of the Acholi in about 1939 from Palabek to Ombiyo, was due to the population decline experienced by the Ma'di of Moli in the 1920's. As recently as 1927, the Pari (Lokoro) warriors under the youth group leadership known as Alangure raided the Ma'di in Mejopadrani[22] which in 1932 was renamed Borokodongo by Andrea Farajalla, a Bari from Juba district, who was then the Juba-Nimule Road foreman under Engineer Mujaranga, who was believed to be a Greek. Borokodongo is camp No. 13[23] when counting the camps from Juba.

13.6.2 The 1982-83 Ma'di-Bari border Contest

Along the border between the Ma'di and Bari there is a stretch of land belonging to Moli near the area of Bari of Nyarabanga. The Moli people said that they had abandoned this land due to constant attacks by man-eating lions.[24] This piece of land was used by the Ma'di people of Moli for cultivation of cassava and other seasonal crops such as sorghum and sesame (*simsim*). The place was named *Orisoko*, which means 'a coward cannot cultivate there' because of the numerous lions. This name was given to this farming village by an elderly man called Jangara Modi from Degi clan of Ma'di.[25] In the early 1940's, Jangara Modi built a hut there and encouraged other people from Moli to join him despite the lions and lionesses which constituted a menace to the Ma'di cultivators and the Bari people in the neighbouring villages of Nyarabanga. As recently as 1956, Ma'di cassava cultivators were planting their crops in the fields at Orisoko during the chieftainship of Koce Gumbiri of Karpeto, southern Bari and Chief Akeri Geri of Moli. Several prominent members of the Ma'di tribe from Moli had lived and cultivated in Orisoko and among them were Avudomoi, Lagu Kolima, Andruga Odosi and Wani Bire all of Ijupi clan, Ogwe of Nyai-Molonyi, Tombe Nyigola of Paluda, Asili of Jeru, Opeto of Monocu-Nyongwa, and Keri Doka of Degi clans respectively. Some of the elders mentioned above died in Orisoko in the 1940's and were buried there. Ambayo is the last village of Moli and between it and Orisoko there is Ee'eli Hill. Near this hill is a small forest known as Luwaluwa where once Abeya of Mugi had a field under cultivation.[26] Orisoko remains the most viable agricultural land of the Ma'di on their border with the Bari.

There is also another agricultural area called Vollo, which was the home of Ruba of Dedi clan of the Ma'di and his family.[27] This area, which falls between Nyarabanga and Mejopadrani (Borokodongo), was requested by the Bari of Nyarabanga from Ruba to be used by them for growing crops because their own areas had become worn out after repeated cultivation. Ruba agreed on condition that the land revert to the Moli people when they need it for cultivation, and he invited two persons each from Ma'di and Bari to witness the temporary handover to the Bari people. On the Ma'di side were Yongo Alimas Dumo and Tombe Nyula, and on the Bari side were Tombe Nyudu and Logiro.[28]

13.7 Chief Akeri's testimony in Juba on the Ma'di-Bari border

When Chief Akeri Geri of Moli was brought to Juba in 1978 by the two members of parliament from his territorial constituency, Joseph Kebulu Ame and Jabulon Jada Yanga so that he could brief them about the extent of the northern border of the Ma'di and Bari of Juba district in Iyii, as it is called by the Ma'di and Kit by the Bari, indeed he narrated to them the truth as he knew it. The Ma'di villages of Iyii lie some 14 miles north of Garamu, the seat of the court of Chief Akeri Geri in Moli Tokuro. In his explanation to the parliamentarians, he confirmed that when the Juba-Nimule Road was constructed in the period 1928-32 and became usable to traffic around 1932, it attracted Bari and Acholi tribesmen who were originally living in areas unconnected by roads, to come and settle along it so as to benefit from the social and economic services such as vehicular transport, trade and commerce. He said the workers' gang camp No. 12 at Iyii was named Jokoki, by Andrea Farajalla, a Bari from Juba district, who was the road foreman at the time of its construction under the supervision of an engineer, thought to be a Greek who was nicknamed *Mujaranga* by the Bari people in the period 1928-32. Akeri said the move of Ma'di families to Iyii and settle there was spearheaded by Awira Rabo and his brother Jojo, who were sons of Nyama of Logili clan, Aruju section. He said he had proposed the idea to these people to move to Iyii in 1934 when he was chief. He defended his decision by saying that the spot where the Iyii villages were situated and the territory in which Lupaingwe River flows to join River Iyii in the north was the land inhabited in the past by his clan of Logili and other Ma'di clans allied to it.[29] The chief said that their dispersion from the area and retreat southward was due to tribal wars, citing the Moli-Lokoya Langabu feud, and

Acholi-Agoro (Koyo-Kicari) and Lokoro raids on Moli villages before the construction of Juba-Nimule Road.

Writer J. V. Rowley, who was District Commissioner of Opari in 1934 and of Torit in the period 1935-38 conducted research on Ma'di people and documented that the Logili had first settled in Gumosi and hypothesized that they were originally Bari but Ma'dinized over time due to interaction with the latter people.[30] That they lived in Gumosi confirms the claim of Chief Akeri Geri who said that their ancestors once lived near Mount Barijokwe, west of the present Iyii villages of the Ma'di, not far from Gumosi and fetched their drinking water from River Lupaingwe.[31] *Lupaingwe* in Ma'di means 'white stone.'

The Logili, the most populous clan in Moli given their wide distribution in both Sudan and Uganda, is purely a Ma'di clan. This clan is divided into three major sections, namely Luworo, the royal section to which Chief Akeri Geri belonged, Aruju of Awira Rabo and Logili Pa-Eyia of which Akile's family belonged in Loa, Ongoro. These sections are distributed in Sudan and Uganda, and on the Sudan side they are found in Moli, Bori-Opari, Erepi, Loa, Iyii, and Mugali. In Uganda they are present in Palorinya, Okolo and Zinyini in the Ma'di district. The Logili are also found in Pacilo and Abolokodi where they had emigrated from Sudan during a famine called Ma'acika Joloro in the early 1930's.[32]

13.8 Mejopadrani (Borokodongo)

The population of Mejopadrani (Borokodongo) area consisted of several Ma'di clans of Mugi-Kolowa headed by Julu Lango, Logili clan headed by Ovu Manya, Gunyia clan headed by Awolo Kute, son of Kidi Aguluru and Ruba of Dedi clan. There was one Bari clan, the Dungo whose members settled in Mejopadrani in

1939 while on their way to southern Bari after their refuge in Bori-Opari ended, during the leadership of Chief Akeri Milla of the Pandikeri clan, when their area was invaded by the Mahdist dervishes in 1888. In 1892 when the last Mahdists stronghold at Bor in Dinkaland under the command of Emir Arabi Daffallah was dislodged by a combined force of British troops and troops of the Congo Free State commanded by Lt. Col Martyr, a British officer from Uganda Protectorate,[33] there was relative calm in Equatoria and all the tribes who sought refuge in Bori (Opari) land and later further to the south-east in the Acholi territory of Parajok came back to Opari. In Opari, the following tribes – Bari, Lulubo and Ma'di clans from Moli, Pageri, Arapi and Erepi, were asked by Chief Akeri Milla to return to their original home areas because there was a shortage of land for cultivation. Most Ma'di clans returned to their original home areas leaving behind the clans who were originally inhabitants of Bori-Opari before the flight to Parajok. As part of this relocation, a large group of the Dongu clan also set off on the return journey to Nyokir, their original home area near Karpeto in southern Bari. But most of them did not make it back to their original homes. Drongwa Musukani settled in Kugi forest, a hunting ground for Ma'di north-east of Moli Tokuro, and named his home – Nyajogi near Ogwariregege.[34] The Ma'di version of the name 'Ogwariregege' is *Oguregerege*, so-called because it was built near a large block of stone whose shape resembled a kind of Ma'di basket called *rege*, which is thatched using sliced bamboo. It is thought that the name was corrupted as a result of the language difference. Drongwa Musukani eventually became a headman for his Dongu people. Meanwhile, Titifano Tombe, Kaconi Paulo, Jakaliya Loro, Yukano Ladu, Ben Lado, Martin Gonda, Yakobo Atala, Daudi Lotara, Apollo Lodu and other Dongu elders settled first in Mede, then moved on to Nyajogi near Ogwariregege (Oguregerege) where they joined Drongwa Musukani their kinsman.[35] But while the Juba-Nimule Road was under construction in the period 1928-32 they moved to Mejopadrani and built their homes near the workers' camp named Borokodongo by Andrea Farajalla, the Bari road foreman brought from Juba. Since then, these Dongu elders have remained there, abandoning the idea of returning to southern Bari. They were attracted at first by the opportunity to work as labourers in work gang camp No. 13 of the Public Works Department (PWD). At this time, the workers in this camp were mostly from Pandikeri and Logopi clans of Bori-Opari.[36] As time went on they found that settlement along the Juba-Nimule Road was economically viable, more so than venturing into the interior where trade, commerce and transport would be difficult. At the time of their settlement at Mejopadrani, there lived members of the Mugi-Koluwa clan led by Lango Sai and his sons, one of whom was called Avelino Rocu. There were other members of Mugi-Koluwa clan such as Odego, Cuma, Fuli and also Avu Manya of Logili clan, Kute Awolo, son of Kidi Aguluru of Gunyia clan and his brothers Lino Wani and Zozimo Koce, who all lived in Mejopadrani. The Acholi people were settled at Palabek area in Panyikwara. Not a single Acholi lived in Mejopadrani. As in the west, the original border of the Ma'di with the Bari was across Lupaingwe River which flows from the mountains west of Mejopadrani northward to join River Iyii (Kit). The name *lupaingwe* in Ma'di means 'white stone' for *lupa* is 'a large piece of stone' while *ingwe* stands for the colour white. This name was given to the river because it flows through white stone.

13.9 The Dongu of Mejopadrani (Borokodongo)

The members of the Dungo clan, many of whom speak Acholi due to their long interaction with the Acholi people during their refuge in Acholi territory after their escape from the Mahdist invaders, were on their way back home to Nyokir, Gumosi, Nyangiri around 1939. Upon arrival in Mejopadrani (Borokodongo) they decided to settle there after they were warmly received by the members of the Ma'di clans of Mugi-Koluwa of elder Lango Sai, son of Nyainga, his brother Odego, cousins Cuma and Fuli, the family of Ovu Manya of Logili clan, Avudumoi of Ijupi clan, Awolo Kute, son of Kidi Aguluru of Gunyia clan and his half brothers Lino Wani and Zozimo Koce. The Dungo elders who came and settled in Mejopadrani (Borokodongo) included Titifano Tombe as head and Kaconi Paulo as senior member alongside Jakaliya Lodu, Yokano and Ben Lado and their families. West of Mejopadrani across the Juba-Nimule Road was Vollo, the village of Ruba of Dedi clan of Ma'di, and the land of the Bari extends westward from there. Vollo was later leased to the Bari of Nyarabanga for agricultural purpose by Ruba in about 1940, an agreement witnessed by Ma'di Chief Yongo Alimas Dumo and elder Tombe Nyula of Moli on the Ma'di side and Chief Koce Gumbiri of Karpeto, Sub-chief Tombe Nyudu and Logiro on the Bari side.[37]

1-Findings on border issues

This study has established the following facts concerning border disputes:

At the root of the Ma'di/Bari territorial dispute is the Ma'di claim that the border between Ma'di and Bari runs from the northern side of the three headed Foki Mountain, placing the eastern head and the smaller middle head called Lafonia on the

Ma'di side leaving the northern head as Bari territory. According to Swapere Katika of Logili clan, the land priest whose home was constructed under the eastern section of the mountain, the border between Ma'di and Bari is between the smaller head called Lafonia and the big head in the north giving the Ma'di two heads of Foki Mountain. This border area has not been visited for familiarization purpose by the chiefs from either tribe, nor by local government administrators for a long time. They have not acquainted themselves with the land features which include the small streams flowing from the Mountain.

What has further complicated and added confusion to the border contests among the four tribes, Bari, Ma'di, Lulubo and Acholi, is the claim made by the Lulubo community that their border with the Ma'di is in the middle of Kit bridge and not on the south bank of River Nyolo as previously believed. They say this border was fixed by Captain Cooke, the DC of Juba District after the construction of Juba-Nimule Road which was opened for traffic in 1932. This development has led the Bari to believe that the Ma'di have practically no land on the northern bank of River Kit. But local government administrators doubt the position taken by the Lulubo people saying that Captain Cooke could not have changed the border arbitrarily without the involvement of his counterpart, the DC of Torit District, at the time a Britisher like himself, because Loa Government Centre No. One fell under the jursidiction of Torit District.

The new Lulubo position (that their border with the Ma'di is in the middle of Kit Bridge) obliges the Acholi to move to the Juba-Nimule Road from the east and butt up against the Bari which was previously not the case thus disturbing the old border between Moli chieftaincy and Agoro-Omeyo. Aforetime the Acholi had no border with the Bari. But today they have moved across the Ma'di territory of Kit, ignoring its legal status, and reach as far as Lupaingwe River (or Whitestone River in Ma'di language). This development has made the point where the border between the Lulubo land and Acholi area of Agoro-Omeyo on the one hand, and that between the Acholi and Ma'di areas are diffused. Around Nyolo River, there is a land dispute between Lulubo and Acholi on the eastern side of Juba-Nimule Road and this was reported by Lulubo Paramount Chief Paride Tongun in 1988, and also stated by Lulubo MP Paul Yugusuk at the Kit conference of September 4, 2008. The same viewpoint is expressed in the Lulubo position document issued in 2009.

There have been several complaints from the communities involved to the local government administrations of Juba and Torit Districts of former Equatoria Province, especially during parliamentary elections, but the offices of the local government inspectors in Juba and Torit have consistently ignored or failed to attend to the problems partly because their administrations lacked data, and partly because they lacked the commitment and seriousness required to address the issues.

No proper approach to solution finding has been applied and as a result the problem has remained unresolved for many years. What could have been done was to involve Bahr El Jebel Province as the Kit border affects not only the Bari and Ma'di territories, and Lulubo and Acholi lands, but in fact lies between the two provinces.

2 Conclusion

All the communities, Ma'di, Acholi, Bari and Lulubo, have agreed that there is a need for the local government authorities to review the borders in the contested areas. Eastern Equatoria and Bahr El Jebel provinces, which are now known as Eastern and Central Equatoria States, should expedite this matter which has strained relations among the four tribes and any delay in tackling the problem will continue to impede progress in the whole area of Kit basin. The administrations of the two states, Eastern and Western Equatoria, need to take swift action to investigate the borders between them at the points of contention. What is needed here is to involve the state mechanisms already established for addressing land issues. The Bari and Lulubo need a clear administrative border between them in the Kit area.

One aspect of the Kit matter, which is important, is the human element. Despite the pertinent complaints against encroachment into others' territories for administrative, economic, and even political purposes, complaints which have strained relations among these communities, social intercourse has been positively noticeable among the Bari, Ma'di, Lulubo and Acholi. Intertribal marriages have become a common feature in Kit, and these should continue. The authorities should solve the border issue to improve the lives of the people in these areas even more. The people of Kit should celebrate their special status as the point of meeting of the four tribes. Nowhere in the rest of South Sudan can one find such human interaction and a cradle of social harmony.

3 Recommendations

Social and economic infrastructure should be established in the area of the Kit banks where deposits of fertile soil for agricultural purposes are found so that the inhabitants there can benefit from development.

The members of Ma'di, Acholi, Bari and Lulubo tribes, who

have lived in the areas peacefully for decades should foster good neigbourliness, respect their tribal boundaries and leaderships, ignore the attempts by politicians to disconcert them for political gain, and continue their peaceful coexistence and interaction, nurture a spirit of cooperation, and make Kit township a centre for growth as it lies strategically halfway between Juba and Nimule.

Politicians in the four communities of Acholi, Bari, Lulubo and Ma'di must avoid exploiting tribal diversity for their own gains, an example being claiming the territories of others in order to expand their constituencies for election purposes. It is only when they respect the rights of other people that the national goals of reconciliation, unity, mutual progress, and peaceful coexistence can be realized.

Notes and references

1 Stigand, C. H. *Equatoria, The Lado Enclave*, London, Frank Cass, 1968, p.90. See also L. F. Nalder. *Equatorial Province Handbook, Vol. I*, Mongalla, 1936, pp.18, 162 and Richard Gray. *A History of Southern Sudan 1838-1889*, London, Oxford University Press, 1961, pp.10-5, 38.

2 Ibid. Nalder and Gray. Also see Passmore Sanderson and Neville Passmore. *Politics, Education and Religion in Southern Sudan, 1898 – 1979*, London, Oxford University Press, 1979, p.62-66,

3 Op. Cit. Nalder and Gray. See also Gabriel Warburg, *The Sudan under Wingate, Administration in the Anglo-Egyptian Sudan, (1899-1916)*, Frank Cass, London, 1971, p.117,

4 Op. Cit. Nalder, p.162-164 and Sanderson.

5 Interview of author with Ukal Kawang Julu, researcher from Pari (Lokoro) community in El Haj Yousif, Takamul, Khartoum

North in 1995.

6 See paper prepared by Victor Keri Wani for Kit Conference of Bari, Ma'di, Acholi and Lulubo tribes held on 6 September 2008.

7 Op. Cit. Julu.

8 Interview of author with Rafaile Miri Amisi and Sabina Jaguru Nyoma, both from Iyii in Juba on 10-9-2008 and 12-9-2008 respectively. Also, statements given by Sabina Jaguru, Rafaile Miri Amisi in Juba when the Ma'di delegation was preparing for Ma'di-Acholi Meeting in Torit scheduled for 16-19 April 2012.

9 Interview of author with Rafaile Miri Amisi and Sabina Jaguru Nyoma both of Iyii in Juba on 10-9-2008 and 12-9-2008 respectively. Also, statements given by Sabina Jaguru, Rafaile Miri Amisi in Juba when the Ma'di delegation was preparing for the Ma'di-Acholi Meeting in Torit on Iyii, Owinykibul and Opari scheduled for 16-19 April 2012.

9 Ibid.

10 Ibid. Op. Cit. Stigand.

11 Op. Cit. Wani paper.

12 Interview of author with Chief Akeri Geri of Moli in Juba in 1982.

13 Op. Cit. Nalder, p.50.

14 Ibid. Op. Cit. Gray.

15 Statement made by David Droko, son of Tombe Urtwe during meeting of Ma'di delegation in Torit prior to Ma'di–Acholi meeting scheduled for 16-19 April 2012.

16 Interview of author with Olympio Tombe Wani of Daba royal clan of Lulubo-Aru in El Haj Yousif, Al Takamul, Khartoum North, 20-12-1995.

17 Interview of author with Chief Odoriko Loku Diego Mude in Torit on 15-5-2005.

18 Op. Cit Wani paper.

19 Ibid.

20 Ibid.

21 Op/ Cit. Nalder.

22 Op. Cit Julu.

23 Interviews of author with his mother Rita Keji Lodu Bilal in Juba on 23-11-1997.

24 Ibid.

25 Ibid.

26 Ibid.

27 Ibid.

28 This information was given by Marcello Wani Silingi during meeting of Moli elders at Moli Tokuro on 20-12-2011.

29 Op. Cit. Rowley, p.279.

30 Ibid.

31 Op. Cit. Geri interview.

32 Op. Cit. Rowley.

34 Op. Cit. Nalder.

35 Op. Cit. Keji interview.

36 Op, Cit. Odoriko interview.

37 Op. Cit. Silingi.

Chapter Fourteen

Supernatural Men among the Ma'di

14.1 The Land of Supernatural Men

Every human community in different epochs has had their supernatural men and women. These were people who had extraordinary physical power to perform acts which other people, in fact the majority of the members of their communities, could not do. Some of these men and women had extraordinary intelligence which other people did not possess.

Among the Ma'di, there were also people who had supernatural powers at different times in their lives. These men and women influenced the lives of their own people and the neighbouring tribes greatly. Most members of the Ma'di community recognized the important roles which were played by these supernatural men such as Geri Akudi and Tombe Bworo and women amongst them, because their actions benefited the whole community and never opposed it.

14.2 Construction of the Mongalla-Rejaf-Opari Pathway (1915-1919)

At the beginning of the twentieth century, the Mongalla-Rejaf-Opari road which ran along the east bank of Bahr El Jebel River was under construction. This road followed the old pathway used in the 1860's, 1870's and 1880's by the former governors of Equatoria province namely, Samuel White Baker (1869-72), Colonel Charles George Gordon (1874-1878) and Emin Pasha (1878-1889), their soldiers and the officials under them. The pathway was also used by the Turkish, Egyptian and Northern Sudanese soldiers, officials, and employees of the government system then in existence. European and Arab merchants who came to the south for trade purpose, European explorers, John Henning Speke and James Augustus Grant, who completed the search for the source of the Nile river, walked along parts of this path before meeting Samuel Baker in Gondokoro on February 23, 1863.[1] The path was also used by European adventurers and hunters. The pathway connected the string of military camps created by the government on the west bank of the Nile from Rejaf through Bedden, Kirri, Muggi, Labore (Moli), Ayu (Kor Aya), Dufile, Wadelei and Foweira.

The pathway was surveyed by an English engineer, while it was being simultaneously constructed as a road from Mongalla through Rejaf east to Opari. This road was probably constructed between 1915 and 1919 because due to the lack of this infrastructure, Opari was temporarily administered first by Major H. Castle Smith from Rejaf and later by Major Black from Kajokeji. Opari was selected as district headquarters in 1914 after the territory extending from Gondokoro to Nimule was ceded by Uganda to Sudan in 1913.[2] If the construction of the road reached

Moli area in about 1918, then Captain E.T.N. Grove, the first resident District Commissioner of Opari, posted in that year, would have been in charge.[3] Opari was designated in 1914 as district headquarters instead of Nimule which was abandoned in 1913. The initiative to move the district headquarters to Opari emanated from C. H. Stigand, who was given the assignment of instituting an administration in the areas reverted to Sudan by the Congo Free State following the death of King Leopold II of Belgium in 1909. This followed the agreement reached with the British Crown in 1888 after the Berlin conference of 1884 for partition of Africa by European nations when this area reverted to Sudan from Uganda in 1913. The District Headquarters was transferred from Nimule to Opari in 1914.

14.3 Geri Akudi

When the British road surveyor reached Malandu in Moli area, he drew the line along which the road was to pass to a point where a huge tropical tree called *muyu* stood. He could have made a bend in the road to avoid the tree, but his plan dictated that the road must be straight at this point, and surprisingly it must pass where the huge *muyu* tree stood. The road engineer had no labourers and depended on the inhabitants of the area through which the new road was being constructed to supply the necessary labour. Their job was to uproot trees, dig and clear the old pathway which was being turned into a road. The Inspector of Opari District came to Malandu to celebrate the entry of the road into his district from Rejaf district, and defended the engineer who had instructed the inhabitants of Malandu to remove the huge *muyu* tree as directed to let the road pass through the spot it was occupying. The people were told to dig round the tree and make it to fall down, cut its trunk and branches into small pieces and carry them away from the site to give room for the road to pass. The trunk of the tree was so big that it could only be encompassed by the stretched arms of two men.

At that time, every large clan in the area had a chief. Ingani Kuyu was the leader of the Ukeyi clan of Mua-Muruli, while Lagu Abala was the leader of the Cokorokwa branch of the Mugi clan and Geri Ipele was the chief of the Logili clan. These chiefs, who were rainmakers in their localities, were instructed by the Inspector of Opari District to ensure that their subjects carry out the task assigned to them within the specified period, which was one week. Then the District Inspector and the Road Engineer left for Opari.

The Ma'di people in Malandu were greatly disturbed by the order of the District Inspector which confirmed the instruction the road engineer had given them. They were concerned about the short time, just a few days, given to them to accomplish the assignment and the threat of serious collective punishment should they fail to have the work done within the specified time.

The people regarded the assignment given to them as an impossible task, called in their language – *lumara*. Considering the age of the tree, which none of them knew because they were born when the tree was almost as old as it was that year, and considering the enormity of its size and height, they concluded that the work given to them was actually a punishment. They compared the assignment with the compulsory grain contribution and declared that it was far more onerous than the impost of a basketful of grain and a goat, which was the usual graduated poll tax extracted from individuals by the authorities. At that time, the people who lived in the south-eastern area of Malandu were referred to as *Moli-ingwe* ('the white Moli') because they had selected this colour as their emblem, and they were comprised of the Logili clan and other smaller clans that associated themselves with it. Those people who lived in the northern and north-western parts consisted of the Mugi clan and other smaller clans, called *Moli-ini* ('the black Moli') according to the colour they likewise had chosen as their emblem. Lagu Abala, the most respected man from the Moli-ini side asked his cousin called Geri Akudi how the great task (called in Ma'di language *lumara*) which the authorities had assigned to the people of Moli could be accomplished within the specified period, which was very short indeed. Geri Akudi was known for his power of effecting great changes just by speaking. Just by speaking out about something it was done as he wished. He remained silent for a long time. Then he replied to the question of his cousin by addressing the many people of Moli who had gathered near the *muyu* tree saying: "Yes, people of Moli, what can we do to rid ourselves of this great task (*lumara*) assigned to us by the authorities?"

One of the elders called Kute Aganasi, father of Loku Maraji of Mugi clan, said that the people of Moli-ini and Moli-ingwe had always appreciated what Geri Akudi did on behalf of the entire community and he believed that they should do the same if he would do the work entrusted to them on their behalf. It should be noted that Geri Akudi was a man of extraordinary power among the Moli people. Whenever he spelt out an incantation for something to happen, it would be as he had called for. In one incident, Geri Akudi and his fellow hunters were said to be returning from a hunt without meat because they did not come across any animal to kill, when suddenly an antelope got up from its hiding place and burst out, running away. Geri Akudi promptly stopped and began to spell some incantations looking down. When he raised his head, he told the people who were with him that they should follow the antelope to skin it and cut its parts for distribution amongst themselves. Before anyone had time to ask how a running antelope could be followed, skinned and its parts cut into pieces so that everybody in the group had a piece of meat to take home, they heard the loud cry of a dying antelope. The animal had hit itself against a dry stump and seriously injured itself. By the time the men reached it with the intention of finishing it off by spearing, it was already dead.

14.4 The Fall of the Muyu Tree

Geri Akudi was delighted with the sentiment expressed by Kute Aganasi that the whole of Moli appreciated his public role and said that the task before them was a simple assignment, like a little fly sitting on the end of a person's nose.

"People of Moli-ini and people of Moli-ingwe." Geri Akudi addressed them. "Do not worry so much because the task before us has been fulfilled already. Tomorrow, you will not see this *muyu* tree standing here."

He raised his face up to stare at the tree. Then he lowered his head slowly till his eyes rested upon the trunk of the tree at the bottom.

Lagu Abala asked him, "Which direction will the tree fall Geri?"

"Huum! Its branch will face the east and the roots will be clearly seen from the west," Geri Akudi replied. "Let us all go home now," he added.

The people of Moli dispersed from the place of the gathering, which was under the shade of the same *muyu* tree which they were tasked to remove and headed home in silence. That evening the sky was very clear and there was no sign of clouds. At night, just before midnight, a strong wind came up and blew from the west to the east. The wind jolted the *muyu* tree once and in one whoosh uprooted it, causing it to fall heavily some distance from where it originally stood, thus making way for the road to pass as planned by the road engineer. The fall of the great tree was heard in distant villages of Malandu. Its branches broke into pieces. The moment the tree fell down, the wind suddenly stopped blowing as if there had never been any wind blowing at all. The first sound heard by the inhabitants of Moli after the heavy fall of the *muyu* tree was of the *turulu* trumpet blown by Lagu Abala to communicate to all the people of Moli that a great event had occurred in their land and that all men must come to the site of the event. He reinforced the message by making a sound by mouth called *sira*, or yodel. Many people identified Lagu Abala by the sound of his trumpet and his *sira*, for the villagers recognized every man by the sound of his traditional instrument such as the trumpet, called *ture* in Ma'di, conch shell, called *bila*, or by the animal horn, called *turulu*. Even a woman is recognized by the shrill, known in Ma'di as *bwilili*, that she makes.

The heavy fall of the tree and the cracking noise associated with it plus the signal from Lagu Abala convinced the people that the promise of Geri Akudi had been fulfilled. The men picked up their sound instruments and light weapons for performing a war dance known as *birabira* and headed towards the place where the tree had fallen.

The people of Geri Akudi's village were the first to attend because the tree was nearest to them and had already started a big fire at the site when the others arrived in small parties singing *birabira* dance songs. A small bundle of grass was lit from time to time to enable the people to have a clear view of the fallen tree.

Where the large roots of the tree once stood, there was a big crater. The number of people swelled, and later drums were brought to the scene and the people of Moli performed *birabira*, a dance which is associated with celebration of victory.

Birabira was followed by *jenyi*, another kind of dance in which the people also sang war songs, for they felt they had won a battle against colonial oppression. They danced till morning and several goats were supplied by Lagu Abala of Mugi clan, Geri Ipele of Logili clan and Ingani Kuyu of Ukeyi clan, and slaughtered on the spot for food for the many people to eat.

Meanwhile a man called Andruga Odosi of Ijupi clan, who was a corporal of Police serving in the office of the Inspector of Opari District, cut short his leave in a village of Moli and returned to Opari to inform the Inspector about the fall of the *muyu* tree. Both the Inspector of Opari District and the road engineer were startled when they heard that the tree has fallen without the people of Moli digging round it and cutting its large roots to weaken it.

"You are sure they did not first dig round the tree before it fell?" the Inspector asked his corporal in pidgin Arabic.

"No sir, they did not dig at all," Andruga Odosi replied in the same language.

"How then did the tree fall?" the Inspector enquired further.

"Someone called Geri Akudi caused the fall of the tree," Odosi added.

"What did he do to make the tree fall down?" the Inspector asked.

"Geri Akudi just called the wind and it uprooted the tree and threw it down."

"Incredible! If he did that then he must be a god of your land," the Inspector concluded mockingly.

Doubting the story reported by Odosi (*Wod al Sid*), the Inspector of Opari District, accompanied by the road engineer and the corporal himself, left Opari for Malandu two days after they received the startling news from the corporal. When they were within sight of the area (*logo*) at a place from which the *muyu* tree used to be seen clearly because of its great height and spreading branches with its green leaves, it was no longer there. The Inspector of Opari District, who was more familiar with the geography of the area than the road engineer, being a regular visitor, recognized the absence of the tree.

"The wood is no longer there," said the Inspector to the road engineer.

When they arrived at the scene, a few men who had returned there after two days of celebration received them. Among those present were Kute Aganasi, Lagu Abala and Geri Akudi, the supernatural man himself.

The first question the Inspector asked was: "Who pushed the tree down?"

"It was the sacred power that pushed it down," replied Aganasi.

"Whose power is it?" the Inspector asked.

"The power of Moli," Kute Aganasi replied, avoiding as a traditional practice to attribute the happening directly to Geri Akudi because what he had done was on behalf of the entire population of Moli.

The two Englishmen looked at each other in total puzzlement. They could have solely attributed the fall of the *muyu* tree to a natural phenomenon, but the fact that the wind spared all the neighbouring trees convinced them that some kind of African magic was at work.

The Inspector arbitrarily ordered that all the people in Malandu villages were to be exempted from further clearing of the bush and removing of trees in the area through which the road was to pass. He said that in future they would not be lashed as before in order to force them to carry out this community work since they had proved cooperative with his administration. The Moli elders thanked the Inspector of Opari district but told him that they would carry out the remaining assignments given to them by the road engineer as it was a national project. After all, they said, the road would link them to Mongalla, the province capital.

14.5 The Story of Tombe Bworo, his life and times

Tombe Bworo was one of the greatest of the famous men of the Ma'di tribe. He was not a chief, but no one could equal his contribution to Ma'di culture during his lifetime. Tombe not only influenced the lives of the Ma'di people but his active role in community affairs also greatly affected the neighbouring tribes and beyond.

The Bari, Kuku, Acholi, Lokoya, Latuko and Lulubo knew Tombe Bworo very well. It is said that when Tombe was spotted from afar approaching a village, word would spread quickly of his coming and mothers would frantically remove their children from the scene for fear that he might later snatch one of them for his food. Tombe for his part, was aware that the people, especially mothers, harboured a fear of him. He invariably assured them of safety and professed that he was just a human being like them and that they had no cause to think otherwise. But nobody listened to or accepted such assurances because Tombe's life was shrouded in mystery and stories of his opponents being attacked and killed by leopards, abounded.

Taban lo Liyong, a distinguished scholar from the Kuku tribe, was the first to write about Tombe Bworo in his internationally acclaimed literary work, "The Eating Chiefs." He devoted several pages of this book to describing the influence exerted by Tombe Bworo on his people, the Kuku. Certainly, Tombe Bworo had much in common with the Kuku people, for one of his sisters, Gune, married a Kuku man from Kajokeji. Gune was married by Paranakole, a brother of chief Rudu of Kajokeji. They lived in a neighbouring chieftainship which lies west of Caragolo, the seat of another Kuku chief called Kole Yengi (Ingi), who was a great friend of Tombe Bworo. Besides his sister being the wife of a Kuku husband, two of Tombe's wives, Caraka and Likia were from the Kuku tribe and Tombe himself, issuing from the Patibi clan, was also related to members of the Patibi clan section who were also found among the Kuku in Kajokeji.

Due to his propensity to resolve outstanding issues between two persons or between two conflicting parties who might be quarrelling over a woman or cattle, wealth or even the ownership of land (which was a common cause of conflict among tribal chiefs) and his practice of engaging leopards to end the stalemates, the Kuku people had their share of admiration mixed with dislike of Tombe Bworo.

The central aspect of the aura surrounding Tombe Bworo was the widely held belief that he could turn himself into a leopard. He used this power to solve his personal problems or the problems of other aggrieved people. But Tombe never used his mysterious power to treat anybody maliciously, to disadvantage or harm them. All his interventions were aimed at solving the dilemmas of people who had been wronged by others, or other matters reported to him for resolution. He reformed society by effecting the return of the property of the weak which had been seized by the powerful, after the failure of those involved to solve their dispute amicably.

If Tombe Bworo was hated, it was by those whose mischief he worked hard to counter so that the community could exist without vice. People who scorned his intervention in advancing the cause of justice, discerned in his name 'Bworo' (which in the Ma'di language means 'throat') the killing of people and the swallowing of their flesh. To this group of people, the name 'Tombe Bworo' stood for fear, terror and even death, while the unjustly treated regarded him as justice personified.

Tombe Bworo was born in the mid-nineteenth century in Opari area in a village north of the present African Inland Church premises at Nyakaningwa. His father was Mori of the Patibi clan (Moyi-ba sub-section) and his mother was Kicu nya Droko of the Paluda clan. Since the Ma'di people are patrilineal or patriarchial, Tombe's descent is traced through his father and so he was a Patibi Moyiba by clan. His ancestors are said to have come from a place at the foot of the two conical headed rocky mountain west of Torit Town. The mountain is called *Moyi-be-dri-lata* by the Ma'di, which means 'the twin-headed mountain of the hyena.'

The area where members of the Patibi clan are believed to have lived in the past is today occupied by the Lofirika people who are probably a section of the Otuho tribe. The eastern inhabitable slope of the mountain was occupied by other Latuko people whose chief in the first half of last century was Lomweka. The Patibi (Moyi-ba) legend states that the tribe had been occupants of the fertile lands at the foot of Moyi-be-dri-lata, which the Lofirika call Mount Irege, and others call either Chubul[4] or Ondiro.[5] It is likely that archeological excavation at the location would be profitable for broadening our understanding of the development of human settlement during the prehistory of the region. The Patibi (Moyiba) in their legends relate that the main cause for abandoning their villages at the foot of Mount Moyi-be-dri-lata was the disappearance of their children while their elders were away in the fertile valley cultivating food crops.

The disappearance of the children was later traced to an old man who was also a member of the clan and who because of his advanced age used to remain at home as protector of those left behind. The old man was suspected of killing and eating the children in the absence of their parents.

Another factor that could explain the disappearance of the children, advanced by people who did not believe in human beings turning into leopards, was that since these people lived under a mountain which had a multitude of caves inhabited by hyenas and leopards, it was likely that these wild animals used to sneak outside during the absence of the elders and snatch the children for food. Whatever the cause of the mysterious disappearance of their offspring, the Patibi (Moyiba) had a bitter quarrel among themselves and decided to abandon their abode for new lands. A group, of whom Tombe Bworo's ancestors were members, moved westwards towards the Nile valley and settled in what today is called Bori (Opari) and many members of this clan are still found there today. A larger number built their home called Patibi on Kadafoyo high ground on the east bank of Eyibi River along the Pageri-Torit Road. Other members of the clan, probably those whose elder was suspected and then accused of eating other people's children, went towards the south-east. Today they may be the assimilated members of the Latuko tribe completely detached from their Ma'di origin. British writer J. V. Rowley observed that some of the Patibi claimed Otuho origin and that the section which came to Ma'di was headed by a man who feared his brother had become a cannibal and was therefore a dangerous person.[6]

In 1984, Melikiore Duku Tilifoni, a Patibi from Deretu near Moli went from Torit to Katire to purchase some groundnut seeds for planting. During his search for the item, he came across an old couple who told him that their ancestors were Patibi and that they were Ma'di and that some of them could be found as far away as Ikotos. The couple told Duku that their foreparents were totally assimilated into the Latuko community and culture, and that very few of them could remember the legend of their Ma'di origin.[7]

Besides this Patibi legend about Moyi-be-dri-lata and Melkiore Duku's discovery of fellow Patibi clan members in Katire, there is hardly any information which can suggest an historical link between the Ma'di, a central Sudanic people and the Latuka from the Nilo-Hamitic group or Sidama people. However, in the past, the two communities might have shared a common border if J. P. Grazzalora's investigation and subsequent documentation of the Luo migration can be taken as the basis for reasoning. He has stated that the Luo people passed southwards in a corridor which separates the Latuko and the Ma'di. This route taken by the Luo linked Wipari in the north and Pajook in the south and lay west of Latuko country and east of Ma'diland.[8]

John Mack and Peter Robertshaw have also studied the question of the relationship between the Latuko and the Ma'di and the theory that before the arrival of the Luo or their passage from north-west to the south along a corridor which separated the Latuko and the Ma'di, there was some minor interaction between the communities who are not linguistically related, and this is indicated in their common use of some words. *Tolu* is the Ma'di word for 'an axe', while the name of the same tool in Latuko is *atolu*, while the Masaai, inhabitants of the western Rift Valley in Kenya and Tanzania also call the axe *entolu*.[9] This coincidence can only be explained if we accept that the Ma'di are an ancient people of the southern Nile valley and probably were the first to settle there and to introduce iron smelting. Seligman in his comprehensive research of the people of Southern Sudan has said that the Ma'di used the iron ore which occurs on Nyeri Mountain slopes for making iron implements,[10] supporting the theory that the Ma'di were early users of the axe, the tool other tribes know by the same name. It may also be no coincidence that the Ma'di expression for "what did he or she say?" is *ojo adu?* while that of the Latuko is, *ojo angayi?* Here the word *ojo*, which in both languages means 'to say,' is the link.

The family of Tombe Bworo moved from Opari area to Erepi. Then they moved again, this time to Nyigo under the foot of Mount Kotopila in Nyori near the Jumiya-Liro confluence. Nyigo was the home of Tombe's maternal uncle, and his mother Kicu was from the Paluda clan, and he probably went there for some reason because according to Ma'di tradition, a man can only live in the same village as his maternal uncle if he is in serious disagreement with his father or paternal uncles or he is an orphan pending a resolution of a dispute through reconciliation. In Tombe Bworo's case one thing is certain. Mori, his father was presumed killed by Lokoya-Langabu raiders who had been carrying out excursions in the Moli area for some time, and this might have led to Tombe's emigration to Nyigo to render protection to his maternal uncles and their families. Another explanation may be his alleged inclination to change into the form of a leopard, for which he was greatly feared by many people including members of his own Patibi clan.

Although Tombe Bworo never admitted publicly that he had ever turned from his human form into a leopard, his engagement of leopards in settling scores with adversaries or in ending disputes between parties remains until this day, a great mystery.

Kire was the name given to the bands of Lokoya-Langabu warriors who used to raid Moli villages in the last quarter of the nineteenth century and during the first decades of the twentieth century. Other names with which they were known by the Moli people were *Orii* and *Koyo*. But the Koyo is a clan of the Agoro people who in the past also used to raid the Moli villages in collaboration with the Lokoro (Pari) people.[11] It was in one of the raids that Mori the father of Tombe Bworo was probably killed but his body was never recovered.

After the evacuation of Emin Pasha, the Governor of Equatoria province from his capital at Lado in 1888, to avoid the imminent attack from the north by the Mahdist forces, there was an administrative vacuum in the region. Tribes whose brutalities were previously controlled by the Turko-Egyptian administration returned to their wild ways of life. It was in this context that Mori, the father of Tombe Bworo was suspected to have been killed by Lokoya-Langabu warriors. When Tombe traced the killers of his father to Langabu villages of Lokoya, it was said that this was to avenge his father's death at their hands. People claimed that Tombe Bworo turned into a leopard then stealthily followed some Lokoya-Langabu warriors to their homeland after they have carried out reconnaissance in the Moli area. Upon his return from Lokoya country, Tombe briefed the Moli leadership on what he had seen there. It was his report that was used for planning the decisive reprisal raid on the Lokoya, a remarkable blow which deterred them from attacking the Moli people again. Tombe Bworo himself led the expeditionary task force of archers and bearers of spears from Moli to Langabu, some forty miles away to the north-east.

Kuku country is another district where the name Tombe Bworo will resonate in the legendary tales for many generations. Tombe became involved with the Kuku people through his wives, Caraka and Likia and his sister Gune who was married to Paranakole, the brother of Chief Rudu of Kajokaji. His sister Kidde (Kiden), who used to visit her sister Gune frequently, was the person who directly engaged Tombe Bworo in conflict with the family of Chief Rudu. In fact, Tombe's nickname *Bworo* which in Ma'di literally means 'throat' is interpreted by the Kuku, who are Bari-speakers, as *Gborong*, which is their common name for wild cats, such as the leopard.[12]

It happened one day that Kidde from Mori's wife, Atongo went from Nyigo Kotopila in Moli to visit her sister Gune. This followed news that Gune was being mistreated by her husband Paranakole. The trouble between Gune and her husband had been intermittent and reached a climax when she was suspected by the husband of turning into a leopard and threatening his younger wife. Despite denying having the ability to turn into a leopard from her human form, she was beaten and additionally she was threatened with death should she turn into a leopard again. When her sister Kidde came to see her, the villagers' fear was magnified thinking that Gune was there to spy on them. They imagined that the whole clan of Patibi (Moyi-ba) would later come en masse across the River Nile from Ma'diland in Chukole and turn into leopards to attack them.

Paranakole, the husband of Gune was particularly annoyed to have Kidde as a visitor in his household. He convinced his brother Chief Rudu and other cousins to ambush and beat Kidde to death on the day of her departure to Moli where she lived with her husband Logolo. They were convinced that Kidde could turn into a leopard and pose a danger to their community and their domestic animals having spied on their surroundings during her short visit.

A group of men led by Paranakole lay in wait for Kidde and attacked her when she came upon them on the way. They beat her till they supposed that she was dead, then carried her and laid her under a tree where they believed vultures and wild animals would later feed on her corpse. But Kidde recovered from the serious beating after lying under the tree for many hours. She waited for nightfall so that her assailants could not see her, thus avoiding a second beating, and this time to death. At night she walked painfully to the home of Chief Kole Yengi (Ingi) of Caragolo who was a great friend of her brother Tombe Bworo. Chief Yengi ordered his wives to bathe Kidde with some warm water and to prepare for her some gruel (*lidi*). Meanwhile the chief sent a message to Tombe Bworo in Nyori Kotopila village so that he could come to take his sister home.

When Tombe arrived at Chief Yengi's home, he was saddened by the suffering inflicted on his sister Kidde by Paranakole and his relatives. He asked chief Yengi to send for Chief Rudu and his brother Paranakole so that they could come to discuss with him in Caragolo their mistreatment of his sister.

Chief Rudu accompanied by several orderlies (*askaris*) - *sirikalis* who were armed with spears and machetes, arrived at Caragolo, Chief Yengi's home ready to face Tombe Bworo if it was for confrontation that he had wanted them to come. Paranakole was among the chief's entourage. When Tombe asked him why the members of his clan had beaten his sister Kidde with the intention of killing her, Rudu retorted that he would not waste his time discussing nonsense. He said that Tombe must know that he,

Rudu, was a great chief and not an ordinary and simple man like himself. Chief Rudu said he was aware of the widespread mistaken belief that Tombe Bworo, a poor human being, and a cheat, could turn into a leopard. Chief Rudu however warned him that should he, Tombe Bworo, try to turn into a leopard (which he said he knew could not happen because he was a mere human being), and attack him, he would shoot him dead using his 'Biaza' gun. The chief loaded his single-shot rifle and fired it into the air to demonstrate his seriousness and readiness to shoot and kill should Tombe Bworo attempt to attack him. He also drew Tombe's attention to his orderlies who were his protectors and who were prepared to use their spears and machetes to slay him.[13]

Tombe was known for his patient and gentle approach to his adversaries. He told chief Rudu that there was no need for boasting since a man's bravery was always recognized after his deeds and not before them. He said Chief Rudu should wait and see what would happen.

Tombe Bworo bade good-bye to his friend Chief Yengi and left for Chukole across the Nile on his way to Nyigo, Moli in the company of his sister Kidde. Meanwhile Chief Rudu, his brother Paranakole, the chief's orderlies and other people who accompanied them also left for Kajokeji after the departure of Tombe and his sister westward.

Not long after their separation with Tombe and his sister, Chief Rudu who walked in the middle of his entourage and was flanked on both sides by two armed orderlies was violently attacked by a leopard and killed instantly. His orderlies dropped their weapons and fled in panic, some towards Kajokeji others, in the confusion which ensued, turned back and ran towards Kole Yengi's home in Caragolo.

Today there are legendary songs sung by the Patibi (Moyi-ba) about this attack on Chief Rudu on the bush path after his verbal confrontation with Tombe Bworo. The people of Chief Rudu too have their version of the incident which they tell their generations. Some people among the Ma'di who heard the story of Chief Rudu's demise said it was a mere coincidence that he was killed by a leopard, and it had no link with Tombe Bworo whatsover. Even some Kuku people who heard about the attack on the chief by a leopard thought it was just a coincidence that he was attacked by a leopard after the wordy exchange with Tombe Bworo and dismissed the idea that Tombe, a human being could turn into an animal, a leopard. This was the interpretation put on Chief Rudu's attack.

14.6 Tombe Bworo thrown into prison

A man of the Kuku tribe who came from Kigwo village near Kakokeji once accused Tombe Bworo of turning into a leopard before the Inspector of Opari District. The accuser embellished his case against Tombe Bworo by claiming that he was responsible for the deaths of several people from his village by employing magic which had caused several leopards in the bush to attack people, their goats, and their chickens. The claimant alleged that before Tombe Bworo set real leopards against the intended victims, he slaughtered a goat, performed a rite, and left the meat for the leopards and other wild cats to feed on it. The accuser of Tombe Bworo said moreover that the latter considered leopards his kin. Taking the accusation seriously, the English Inspector of Opari district, who was also district judge, locked Tombe Bworo in jail for a few days, but he released him in front of a crowded court at Opari attended by chiefs, notables and other adults from Kuku,

Acholi and Ma'di tribes, telling the people that a human being like Tombe Bworo could not turn into a leopard. The Englishman dismissed the belief as a typical African myth to the chagrin of Tombe's accusers who murmured at the justice they sought and did not get, ignored by the white man who set Tombe Bworo free.

Elders throughout Ma'diland related similar stories about Tombe Bworo's activities. They say he would let leopards kill the people who were involved in dispute with him or his relatives. It was not unusual for a man whose wife eloped with another man to seek the support of Tombe Bworo who would use his rare power to get the woman to return to her former husband. It was only in the case of intransigence on the part of the second husband to release the woman, that Tombe Bworo would set a leopard loose upon him. Sometimes the leopard would only scratch the victim. At other times it would tear him to death.

Most of Tombe Bworo's actions were arbitrary, which placed him automatically in the position of power, respect and sometimes envy or even outright hatred. It is said that it never happened that Tombe Bworo accepted the undertaking to voluntarily arbitrate on the side of the complainant unless that person was in the right. Tombe never used his supernatural power to disadvantage anyone who was innocent in any dispute. On the contrary, he always acted on the side of the abused, the victimized, the deprived, the weak and the helpless who sought his relief and never in support of the bully, the powerful and the arrogant. That was the world he knew.

14.7 Tombe Bworo's twenty-five Wives

The main reasons why Tombe Bworo married many wives from his tribe the Ma'di, and other tribes namely, Kuku, Acholi, Lulubo, and Bari, were his fame and his ability to solve the problems of individual subjects which traditional chiefs had failed to work out. Even those traditional chiefs who had been vested with authority by the Anglo-Egyptian administration were not always effective at ending discord among their people, making Tombe Bworo's unsanctioned actions the only alternative in community affairs. Men in the societies of the tribes mentioned, and whose intricate problems he solved successfully, honoured him by giving him girls as wives. In this way Tombe Bworo accumulated the highest number of wives in the Ma'di tribe during his generation. Among his wives from the Ma'di tribe were Kade of Ukeyi clan, Andrua of Mugi clan, Abina of Tedire clan, Mundua of Pageri clan, Eriani of Padombe clan, Pita of Ukeyi clan and Inga of Ijupi clan.[14]

14.7.1 Tombe Bworo's Wives from Bari and other Tribes

Liong of Gondokoro was Tombe Bworo's wife from the Bari tribe, Ile was his wife from the Lulubo tribe, Lawino and Akedi of Ngaya were his wives who spoke both Acholi and Ma'di but said they were from the Acholi tribe. From the Kuku tribe, his wives were Likia and Caraka. There were several other wives who spent short periods with him and were divorced by him or they just left of their own accord. Tombe Bworo had several sons and daughters with a number of these wives. His daughter Atongo with Inga said her father had a total of twenty-five wives.[15]

Of all Tombe's sons, the one who inherited his supernatural power or acquired the magic of turning from human form to leopard as many people believed, or who was believed to associate with leopards and wild cats, was Wani Muganda whose mother was Pita of Ukeyi clan.

14.8 Wani Muganda - Son of Tombe Bworo

Wani Muganda became blind when he was affected by an infection, most likely measles, in infancy. His parents, however, believed that he had been bewitched by a black hearted person. Due to his ability to walk unaided to distant places, despite being blind, most people were convinced that Wani Muganda had the ability, like his father Tombe Bworo, to turn into a leopard. They claimed that whenever he was alone on sections of the road where there were no villages, he would turn into a leopard with eyes, to make up some of the distance. One popular story about Wani Muganda, which is known throughout the Ma'di, Bari, Acholi, Lulubo and Kuku countries was his killing of Juma Zaid's pet dog, after he had made a bet with him.

Juma Zaid was a brother-in-law of Wani Muganda. He married his half sister Fatuma Atongo the daughter of Tombe Bworo with his wife Inga of Ijupi clan. In the 1940's, Juma Zaid, who was a lorry driver, lived temporarily in Nimule and he had two pet dogs, one white and the other brown. One day, Wani Muganda went to his home to visit him and his half sister. During a conversation with Juma, Wani joked that he could differentiate between Juma's pet dogs. Juma Zaid laughed and doubted how a blind person like Wani Muganda could see even if he turned into a leopard.

"If I go with you to Kukuland, where the relatives of Chief Rudu live, whom your father is suspected to have killed after turning into a leopard, I shall escape and you will be trapped there because you will not see your way to escape," said Juma Zaid. "If you are truly a leopard, I offer you my white pet dog to kill and eat but you must spare the brown one."

Wani Muganda laughed heartily and said: "Why do you offer me a pet dog of your household? Why not specify your neighbour's dog?"

"No," replied Juma Zaid. "I have two dogs. If you get the white one and not the brown one, I shall know that you are truly a leopard."

"Let us wait and see," said Wani Muganda.

When night fell, a leopard snatched the brown dog of Juma Zaid. The dog made a frightful loud noise which made Juma and other people sleeping outside run inside for fear.

In the morning, while checking the ground scratched by the leopard during its attack on the dog, Juma Zaid said tearfully, "Wani, I now believe that you can turn into a leopard. But why did you kill my beloved pet dog?"

"The brown dog was fatter than the white dog," Wani Muganda replied. "However, take it easy."

This story was narrated to the author by Faraj Juma Zaid, the grandson of Tombe Bworo from his daughter Atongo in Juba in 1988.

In the 1940's at Nimule, Wani Muganda had a heated argument with Yakobo Yanga who denied that Wani Muganda could turn into a leopard because he was a human being. "No human being can turn into a leopard. All what people say is not based on truth," said Yakobo Yanga.

Wani on his part asked Yakobo to bet so that he could prove to him that he had the ability to turn into a leopard.

Yakobo pointed to his 'kraal' (*goro*) and said, "I have some domestic animals in there. You can prove to me your supernatural power by taking one."

Wani Muganda laughed and said they should wait for nightfall and see what would happen. Both men retired. Then night fell and when everything was quiet, a leopard stealthily found its way into Yakobo Yanga's kraal where it killed his fattest ram (*bilogo*) and left it inside.⁽¹⁶⁾

In the morning when this was discovered, Yakobo and his family became afraid. They believed that Wani Muganda could indeed turn into a leopard and that he possessed the magical power to command the wild cats which obeyed him as pet dogs obey their masters, using them to attack people or animals as he chose. This incident and the similar one which occurred in the home of Juma Zaid sent a strong signal throughout Ma'diland, creating fear, especially among the inhabitants of Nimule and Mugali.

14.9 Wani Muganda and Kujur Okidi

Okidi was an Acholi fortune teller or '*kujur*'. One day Okidi sent for Wani Muganda in Opari where he lived to come to help him resolve a dispute that he had with Farajalla Khamis Lado of Mongalla in Bari country. The dispute was over a cow and two goats.

Kujur Okidi claimed that he could treat different kinds of illnesses using traditional medicines. It happened that Farajalla had a family member whose illness had been persistent despite many attempts to treat her by different medicine men and women. When he heard about Kujur Okidi, that he was a powerful native medicine man who could treat the kind of sickness his sister suffered from, he decided to send for the Kujur who came promptly to Mongalla to treat the woman.

Okidi was given a cow and two goats as his fee for treatment. He took the animals to his home in Acholiland, but before long the condition of the patient deteriorated, and she died. Saddened by her death, Farajalla Khamis Lado decided after the funeral to go to Acholiland to reclaim the cow and two goats he had given to

Kujur Okidi in payment of his treatment of the patient. Farajalla was accompanied by several men of his clan. They recovered the cow and the two goats from Okidi.

When Okidi and Wani Muganda arrived in Mongalla and a discussion between Farajalla and Okidi ensued, the former explained to Wani what had taken place. Like his father before him, Wani Muganda always sided with the person whom he considered to be in the right in any dispute, although this may not necessarily have been the case everytime. After digesting the issue between Farajalla and Okidi he told the latter that since he had failed to save the life of Farajalla's relative, he could not expect to keep the cow and the two goats. No service had been given. Moreover, he said he could not do anything untoward in the home of the friend of his late father. Tombe Bworo, the father of Wani Muganda, had several times visited Farajalla Khamis Lado in his Mongalla home and on some visits, he had brought along his son Wani who was then just a boy. Tombe Bworo became a friend of Farajalla after the successful arbitration of a bitter dispute between him and another Bari chief over ownership of some cattle. After assessing carefully that Farajalla was right in the dispute, Tombe Bworo went to the other chief and warned him that he would face serious consequences if he did not return the cattle which belonged to Farajalla Khamis Lado. The Bari chief, aware of Tombe's ability to use leopards in resolving conflicts complied with this directive. From that time, Tombe and Farajalla became great friends. It was during one of these visits to Mongalla that Tombe Bworo got married to his Bari wife, Liong of Gondokoro.

On taking the side of Farajalla Khamis Lado, Wani Muganda roused Kujur Okidi to utter unpleasant remarks about him. However, he did not react angrily to Okidi's remarks. As his father before him, Wani Muganda was not an emotional man. He simply told him to leave him alone because he could not side with a person who was wrong in a dispute according to the principles of his family. Enraged by the position taken by Wani, the 'kujur' said that he was mistaken to believe that Wani could turn into a leopard. It was not the case at all. He accused him of being a great fraudster in letting people believe otherwise. So Kujur Okidi was happy to leave Wani Muganda, who was blind, alone and unaided on his return journey to Opari and departed by himself for his home in Acholiland.

Now Wani expressed an intention to go to Juba. Seeing Wani's plight, Farajalla Khamis Lado offered to book the enchanter on the steamer which had docked at Mongalla quay to take him to the city. But Wani Muganda turned down the offer to travel by steamer. He preferred to walk overland, and he reached Juba before the steamer. He spent several weeks in Juba with his stepsister, Fatuma Atongo, before deciding to go home. Upon his arrival in Opari, Wani was approached by the relatives of Kujur Okidi. They enquired why he did not return immediately. Wani told them that he did not accompany the kujur to Mongalla and that he had remained behind in Juba, so he knew nothing of his whereabouts. [17] This was in the 1940's.

In the 1950's, Wani Muganda was a centre of concern for people throughout Ma'diland. He was regarded as the last survivor of a generation who could turn into leopards to kill people and their domestic animals. I remember in 1958, when I was in the company of other children going to attend a Sunday service in the Catholic Chapel in Moli, that we came face to face with Wani Muganda in the middle of the road. He was coming in our direction. Although blind, he was walking fast but unaided and the only thing which guided him in his negotiation of the road was his walking stick. We dashed to the side of the road trembling with fear. Wani Muganda stopped suddenly and said, "Children, don't fear". We were puzzled how he knew that we were children since he could not see, and we did not chatter because we were afraid of him. Whenever Wani Muganda was around, mothers who became aware of his presence would frantically hide their children.

Wani Muganda was killed in a road accident at a sharp curve at Bibia in northern Uganda in about 1966. His relatives dropped the court case, which would have amounted to substantial compensation. It was rumoured that, months after Wani's death, the driver of the vehicle which fatally knocked him down, was attacked by a leopard and killed.

The relationship of the Patibi (Moyi-ba) with leopards in the bush was so deep-rooted that it is said when Tombe Bworo died at his home on the bank of River Kulojobi in Opari in about 1935, during the traditional funeral dance called *dra* which was performed around his grave to mourn him, a senior elder from his clan gave an instruction for the dance to stop to give an opportunity for a leopard, which had stealthily entered the ceremony, to mourn his brother. The leopard was said to have gone straight to the wooden frame on which the three drums beaten for the funeral dance were hung and lay there. It is said to have spent some time there and then when it woke up to go, the people parted to leave a path for it to walk through. Most of this sounds like a myth, but this myth has influenced most of the Ma'di people and their neighbours for most of the first half of the twentieth century.

14.10 'Siriba' - the Secret of it all

There are a lot of fascinating stories related about the Patibi

(Moyiba) clan and their position in Ma'di society. These stories as mystical as they are, have Tombe Bworo and his son Wani Muganda as the main characters. What is certain to all Ma'di, and other people is that no one ever saw Tombe Bworo or Wani Muganda change from a human form to a leopard and back to human again. What was certainly witnessed were mysterious attacks by leopards on people who had quarreled, or people who had laid a wager with either of them during their lifetime. Even those people who ridiculed them, Chief Rudu and others come to mind, met their doom by the jaws and claws of bush leopards and not by the agency of a human-turned-leopard creature as most people assumed. For more than half a century, people pondered about the mysterious power of Tombe Bworo and later that of his son Wani Muganda, without gaining an inkling as to its origin. They probably used magic to make bush leopards and other cats attack people who were in conflict with them, and nobody knew the secret.

Fatuma Atongo, the senior daughter of Tombe Bworo by his wife Inga of Ijupi clan of Erepi, maintained that their leopard legacy all began with a girl called Accu. When Accu was born, her chest was said to be full of hair like a leopard, but the rest of her body was human. When a young man called Karacapiong from the Patibi (Moyiba) clan approached Accu's father for permission to marry her, the father accepted but told the youngman to bring a herd of cattle to surround the girl completely, so that no part of her body could be seen when she was led to her new home. When Karacapiong brought the required herd of cattle, Accu was brought out from a cave in the mountain called 'Moyi-be-dri-lata,' now the territory of the Lofrika, a Latuko speaking people. She was placed in the middle of the herd of cattle and led to the home of Karacapiong as his wife. After her arrival in her new home, this herd of cattle was driven back to her father as payment of the bride price.

In due time Accu conceived and gave birth to a son named Ojja. One day Ojja jumped like a leopard from the floor to the ceiling of the family hut, got hold of the bamboo framework with both forelimbs and dangled from there for some minutes before his mother hit him on the back with a gruel stirring club called a *lopire,* prompting him to jump down. Ojja was the great grandfather of Mori, the father of Tombe Bworo. That is the origin of the legacy which was handed down to Tombe Bworo and his son Wani Muganda according to Tombe Bworo's daughter Atongo. She said that her paternal grandfather used to blow a note on a magical wooden instrument which could only be understood by leopards in the bush, calling them to come readily to his home and serve as pet dogs. She said she never saw this instrument, which was not shown to anyone, even to the closest relative, and did not spy her father in the process of blowing it which he seemed to do in the middle of the night when everybody was asleep. But she said it was certain that the device was passed on to her father Tombe Bworo, who passed it on to his son Wani Muganda. What was unique about this special conch was that Accu was said to have brought it to her husband as a gift from her father who made it from a plant which grew on the rock in the cave of the mountain, their home.[18]

Notes and references

1 Nalder, L.F. *Equatoria Province Handbook,* Mongalla, 1938. See also Richard Gray. *A History of Southern Sudan 1838–1889,* London, Oxford University Press, 1963.

2 Ibid. Nalder 1936, pp.162-64.

3 George Lomoro Muras, informant of this to author in Torit on 12 November 2004.

4 Rowley, J. V. *Notes on the Ma'di of Equatoria Province*, Sudan Notes and Records No. XXIII, 1940, p.290.

5 Ibid.

6 Crazzolara, J. P. *The Lwoo Part One*, Verona, 1951.

7 Mack, John and Peter Robertshaw. *Cultural History in the Southern Sudan*, Memo No. 8, Azania Institute Magazine.

8 Op. Cit. Rowley p.291.

9 Interview of author with Fatuma Atongo, daughter of Tombe Bworo with his wife Inga of Ijupi clan of Ma'di in Juba, Malakia in 1988.

10 Seligman, C.G. and Brenda Seligman. *Pagan Tribes of Nilotic Sudan*, 1937, Oxford, Oxford University Press.

11 Interview of author with Ukal Kawang Julu in El Haj Yousif, Khartoum North on 14-6-1995.

12 Martin Sebit Kornelio explained this terminology 'Gborong' in Kuku to the author in 1999 in Khartoum. Sebit is from the Patibi clan of Kereppi (Erepi) and his mother is from the Kuku tribe of Kajokeji.

13 Op. Cit. Atongo.

14 Ibid.

15 Ibid.

16 Interview of author with William Alira Yanga in El Haj Yousif, Khartoum North on 14-6-1995.

17 Op. Cit. Atongo.

18 Ibid.

Chapter Fifteen

Findings, Observations, Conclusions and Recommendations

15.1 Findings on Study of Ma'di Life

1- Very little research on Ma'di life has been conducted and it is sparsely documented. A few scholars, mostly western Europeans, such as C. G. Seligman, Chauncy Stigand, Merrick Posnansky and Richard Gray have included some references about the Ma'di in their general works on South Sudan. Among the indigenous Ma'di scholars are, Emmanuel Kitchere Gray, Mairi John Blackings, Azaria Gilo Emilio and the author, who have undertaken this task for the enlightenment of the members of the tribe and those interested to know about the Ma'di. The study has proved difficult because there are very limited sources, both written and oral, available for this work.

2- A few Ma'di academics such as Dr. John Mairi Blackings have recently shown renewed interest in conducting research on Ma'di culture and in documenting their findings in the form of books. Ma'di grammar, Ma'di-English translation, and an English-Ma'di dictionary are some of the subjects he has tackled to the benefit of the Ma'di and other people. There is still a long way to go in the field of Ma'di study for the edification of the public, and Ma'di academics should initiate and focus their interest on such study.

15.2 Findings on Border Contests

3- The abolition of the status of Moli chieftainships, one of the most powerful traditional leadership entities of the Ma'di since time immemorial, was largely responsible for the breakdown of the border equilibriums between Ma'di-Lulubo, Ma'di-Acholi and Ma'di-Bari. This occurred in the re-organization of the chietainships of the tribe by Headchief Sabazio Okumu Abdalla in 1953 following his election to the post in the previous year. Chief Akeri Geri of Moli was concerned about the border points and was known widely by the chiefs and elders of the border tribes viz. Bari, Acholi and Lulubo. However, Chief Jelindo Chaka Aperiya, who took over the leadership from Akeri Geri, did not monitor and check the encroachments of the tribes into Ma'di territory from Moli in the period 1953 – 1984.

4- Despite his dismissal from the position of chief of Moli, the northern sector chieftainship, Akeri Geri remained adamant that he was still chief and declared that he would not take any directives from neither Jelindo Chaka Aperiya, his successor nor from the Headchief Sabazio Okumu Abdalla. The Headchief dismissed him and dissolved the chieftainship of Moli and annexed it to that of Erepi (Kerepi), which was smaller than that of Moli. The situation created by this change led to Chief Jelindo reducing his inspection trips to Moli, especially its border areas, and thus encroachments of the neighbouring tribes of Acholi, Bari and Lulubo into Ma'di land went unchecked by the chief and his assistants. Former Chief Akeri Geri did not recognize Sabazio as Headchief till the latter's death in 1983. He had always said that Sabazio did not deserve to become headchief of the Ma'di because he came from the Gonyapi clan, which had no previous traditional leadership. The Headchief meted out heavy punishment on Akeri in the form of dismissal due to his negative attitude towards him, but we should not forget the victims of this action were the people of Moli and the loss of parts of their territory to their neighbours.

5- All attempts to solve the Acholi-Ma'di border disputes were conducted by the provincial commissioners remotely from their offices in Torit and Juba, and the solutions they directed were not practically executed on the ground because they lacked truth, credibility, and justification. The border issue was also complicated by political motives by those who brought them forward.

6- There have been no regular meetings among the chiefs and elders of Bari, Ma'di, Acholi and Lulubo to acquaint themselves with new developments at their common borders. Since the 1950's, beginning with Head Chief Lolik Lado of Lokoya tribe, who also administered the Lulubo, the chiefs only met whenever there were crises, and these meetings were initiated in most cases by politicians from the area for their political gains and not as a means to solve the problems at the grass roots level.

7- Since colonial times and throughout the period after independence, the district administrations in Juba and Torit districts of Equatoria Province have not concerned themselves with proper administration of the four tribes in the Kit-Nyolo basin thus letting the border situation deteriorate. As each tribe faces uncertainty as to where the actual border between it and its neighbours lies, the people resort to guessing which creates friction with their neighbours. After independence in 1956, the district commissioners and local government officers (*mamur*) were Arabs, who did not know the tribal border points fixed by the British officials and did not concern themselves with the traditional affairs of the tribes.

8- Politicians from areas other than those of the Ma'di have been the root cause of border disputes because they have wanted to expand their constituencies in order to win seats in parliamentary elections.

9- Concerned government officials at the level of provincial commissioner were biased and never serious about solving the border disputes as clearly indicated by their ever-abortive attempts to effect changes since 1977 until 2008.

10- Ma'di Headchief Sabazio Okumu has given a very concise definition of the Ma'di border with the Acholi. He said it lies a few kilometers north of Mulungeng and the border marks are three tropical trees called *iyu* in Ma'di which stand close to each other. He said from here the line goes eastward enclosing Mount Adala inside Ma'di territory and passing north of Pakworo and Winyalonga to Ayipa and Inzi Hills where the Payoko clan lives. Then in a sharp bend the border runs east of Owinykibul along Atapi River. Owinykibul is a Ma'di village in which the following clans live; Mugi, Logopi, Jeru, Pandikeri, Nyongwa, Pavunde, Lulubo, Kiloloro etc after the Adis Ababa Agreement of 1972.

11- Knowing that chiefs come and go, it is the responsibility of a reigning chief and an important responsibility, to acquaint his assistants or those closely working with him, with important facts about his chieftainship. In the years 1979 and 1980, when Sabazio Okumu Abdalla was appointed Overseer by the Project Management for Refugees Affairs (PMRA) in Juba and was given the assignment to supervise the settlement of the Ma'di who had fled their territory in Uganda after the fall of Idi Amin Dada, he decided to settle them in areas which were Ma'di territory in Sudan. Because these settlements were to take place in Choyi in the Loa area, in open spaces in Moli and Bori chieftainships, he involved Akeri Geri Ipele of Moli and Odoriko Loku Diego of Bori-Opari, the chiefs of the respective places. He was also accompanied by Ben Madhvani Lukada, who was a refugee settlement officer in charge of all the areas of Moli and Bori, where the refugees, the majority of whom were Ma'di, were settled. These areas were Kit One, Kit Two, Kit Three and Kit Four, Afoyi One, Afoyi Two, Ame One and Ame Two. After the deaths of Headchief Sabazio in 1983 and of Chief Akeri Geri in 1985, the two men Odoriko and Ben, who worked with them continued in their posts and knew precisely where the border between the Ma'di and Acholi territories lay. Chief Odoriko Loku Diego concurred with the Ma'di-Acholi border explanation given by Sabazio Okumu

Abdalla and reiterated that Owinykibul falls inside Ma'di territory.

12- The Ma'di-Bari common border starts from east of Mount Foki near the Moli villages of Gori and Cecere and runs north-eastward to River Umo and then turns northward in the area of Iyii (Kit). When border problems have arisen and complaints from the communities involved have reached the ears of the administrators of Eastern Equatoria Province in Torit, some attempts have been made by the office of the Commissioner to solve the problems, but concrete solutions have not been found.

13- A proper approach to the problem has not been employed and as a result the problem has remained unsolved for many years. What could have been done was to involve Bahr El Jebel Province, as the Kit border is in fact not only between the Bari and Ma'di territories, nor between Lulubo and Ma'di, nor Lulubo and Acholi lands, but between the two provinces themselves.

14- Administration of the area of dispute from Juba and Torit under which the Magwi rural council falls has been poor, due to unknown border demarcations, lack of cooperation from the inhabitants of the area because of the administrative territorial uncertainty, and therefore services like health, education, the availability of potable water, veterinary servics etc in the region have been at all times insufficient or absent.

15.3 Observations

1- An important aspect of the culture in Iyii (Kit) however is the informal human element. Despite the pertinent complaints against encroachment into others' territories for administrative and economic purposes, which have strained relations among the communities of Ma'di, Acholi, Bari and Lulubo, social intercourse has been noticeable among these tribes. Inter-tribal marriages have been a common feature in Kit for decades and these should continue. The authorities should solve the border issue to make life even better for the folks in these areas.

2- Iyii (Kit) has all the characteristics of developing into a town. It is a special place in South Sudan, to which each of the four neighbouring tribes has easy access. The authorities, whose responsibility is it to render to all citizens, socio-economic services such as health, education, veterinary and agriculture extension services, could easily establish recognized borders for proper administration. The intellectuals from the four tribes have done nothing at all in terms of establishing economic activities in the Kit-Nyolo Rivers basin, and now it is time for them to pool their resources and act in unison. They should focus more attention on the common problems affecting them, especially community-based development programmes, social services such as those of health, sanitation systems, environmental services, improved agriculture, veterinary services, surveying, improved commercial transportation infrastructure, eradication of poverty and illiteracy. All these matters need their cooperation, and correlated approaches. Sincere individual and community contributions are required from intellectuals, chiefs, notables, women, and youth, devoid of tribal or religious sentiments. It is worth mentioning that in Kit since the 1940's there have been both Catholic and Protestant Christians and Muslims such as Boyi, the father of Nagib Boyi and Professor Sebit Boyi. In the 1940's, basic commercial items were brought to shops in Iyii for sale to the inhabitants, by Boyi Sebit, and in Nyolo by Mahmoud from Juba and the two men were the first Muslims to settle in the area. Cooperation with the officials of government organs assigned to administer Kit and the rendering of public service is imperative. Positive intervention of the authorities in any issue affecting the inhabitants of the area should be at the top of the list of priorities in government development programmes.

3- Another aim of this book is to reverse the prevailing negative attitude to the history of indigenous people. Such history is often treated as of little or no significance. I believe that all history taught in schools today has been fashioned in a way similar to that of the Africans. For that matter the Ma'di people and their traditional chiefs, rainmakers and supernatural men have made and are still making theirs. And this is certainly the situation with their Acholi, Bari and Lulubo neighbours.

Another principal aim of this work is to save what little information is available, after much has been lost due to lack of interest, about important aspects of human development such as traditional chieftainships and rainmaking. Finally, I am not blaming our ancestors, especially those who attended school, because the knowledge that was imparted to them in church schools was not sufficient to enable them to undertake the great task of rehabilitating and recording the histories of their peoples. This challenge has fallen upon us, and if we do not write these histories down in the twenty-first century, we shall be censured more than any other generation by our descendants. Having said that, I would like to seize this opportunity to express my appreciation of the roles the Christian missionaries, from both the Catholic and Protestant denominations, have played in conserving some important facts about the Ma'di people as an activity secondary to their spiritual work among them. Without their contributions, additional facts in this book would not have been able to be presented.

15.4 Conclusions

All the communities, Ma'di, Acholi, Bari and Lulubo agree that border identification is a persistent challenge. The matter initially involved Eastern Equatoria and Bahr El Jebel provinces, and now we see it between Eastern and Central Equatoria States. The problem has impeded development in the entire area for many decades. Poor administration has hampered progress. The administrations of the two states need to take swift action to review the borders and check whether they are in line with those marked at independence in 1956 as points of contention. Meanwhile, the Bari, Lulubo, Ma'di and Acholi need a clear administrative line between them in the Kit area. In Eastern Equatoria State, the Ma'di and Acholi have their border problems in Kit and Owinykibul, and these need to be resolved once and for all. The government in Torit should be guided by a robust legal system, the authorities should apply the law and maintain order, and desist from adopting bad policies.

Although it is a good start, it is too early to celebrate the success of this book as the work in its present state is incomplete. It is incomplete for several reasons. Firstly, despite attempting to verify the information obtained on specific topics from several sources, whether archival, oral, from Ma'di or non-Ma'di informants, in each case I found that there was still a need to uncover more facts. At this juncture, the reader whose avid aim is to get a full history of the Ma'di traditional chieftainships, their rainmakers and supernatural men in South Sudan should take note that this objective is not met in this first attempt satisfactorily, although much effort has been exerted and much energy has been spent in the search for facts about the topics selected for these essays. Secondly, because the selected topics cover a long period, two centuries, it has been cumbersome and difficult for the author to state with confidence the dates of events such as those of the inter- and intra-tribal wars, the names of the places where they were fought, and the main actors and actresses involved in them. However, what is consoling to the author (and hopefully the reader) is that there has been marked unanimity among the sources and willingness by individuals to give information on various aspects of the subject tackled, and these were from a goodly number of members of the Ma'di community, and non-Ma'di individual informants, especially those whose tribes who were the main players in the history through their wars with sections of Ma'di, and other social interaction. Informants like Alex Locor Tartisio of Lokoya tribe, Chief Wod al Faraj and Adelinda Aciro, both of Acholi Panyikwara deserve recognition for their great contributions to this work. Their enthusiasm has been a clear indication that the work has been overdue and despite the difficulty encountered in obtaining the required information for inclusion in the accounts on the various topics, appreciation of the efforts of the author from several quarters has been exhibited, which has been a source of inspiration, and perhaps it will also be to the reader.

In this book, several important issues have been raised and discussed from the perspective of the author and one of them is the border contests between Ma'di and the neighbouring tribes of Acholi, Bari and Lulubo. The Bari and Lulubo have also shown concern for adjustments to their borders with the Ma'di. It is therefore the author's fervent desire that this work will serve as an eye opener for the government authorities and tribal leaders in the area, to encourage them to revisit this problem so that they can find an appropriate solution, acceptable to all parties concerned. Peaceful coexistence, social interaction, and common economic development; these things are all that the Ma'di and their Acholi, Bari and Lulubo neighbours need. Already there are positive signs that some of these things are being realized in the region. We should note that there has been a degree of social intercourse from inter-tribal marriages, barter trade, and local communication among these communities for several centuries, in fact since the time their ancestors settled in the southern Nile valley. For that reason, they should not be misled by current political enticements for as one Acholi commentator, Obale Mateo Pa'Okello says – the Acholi and Ma'di communities will forever exist as neighbours and therefore none of them should be misled by current transitory political developments. The Acholi and Ma'di people will remain neighbours so neither side should spoil their long-lasting neighbourliness for short term political aggrandizement. What the authorities concerned need to do now and in the future are honest appraisals of these and other emerging issues.

The author, who was born of Ma'di parents in about 1951 in Moli Tokuro, partly grew up in Iyii and as a village boy he witnessed the positive human interaction which is integral to the social development of the region. When he was a boy, he covered the distance of thirteen miles between Moli Tokuro and Iyii with both his parents several times on foot. These journeys took him practically through the Acholi villages of Ombiyo, which were built in the period 1939 – 1940, that is about four years after the Ma'di had settled in Iyii. Iyii was reclaimed for the Ma'di by

Chief Akeri Geri of Moli in 1934 saying that this was the ancestral land of his Logili clan and other allied clans abandoned because of Lokoya, Lokoro (Pari) and Acholi-Agoro (Koyo-Kicari clan) raids on northern Moli villages in the first quarter of the twentieth century. In these raids many young men and women were either killed or abducted by the raiders and taken to Agoro, Lokoya-Langabu and Lokoro (Pari) lands. The grandchildren of these Ma'di, who have been assimilated into the tribes whose members forcibly took them to their areas, can today vividly remember their roots. As long as they are alive, they should be promoters of peace between their new tribes and that of the Ma'di, their original tribe.

In the border contest between the Ma'di and their Bari neighbor, the part of the region claimed by Chief Akeri Geri starts from Barijokwe near Gumosi in southern Bari, including River Lupaingwe (which in Ma'di language means 'white stone') to the area east of Iyii. J. V. Rowley, the British researcher and writer in his booklet about the Ma'di stated that the Logili had lived in Gumosi before they moved to the area they occupy today. (Rowley 1940: 275) But since the drawing of the border between Ma'di and Bari by the colonialists in their Mongalla headquarters, the former made reference to this historical fact but they did not demand border re-adjustment. There is the small spot in Vollo west of Mejopadrani (Borokodongo) that they would like to have back if the Bari would honour the verbal pact that they concluded on this piece of land with the Ma'di when Alimas Yongo Dumo of Mugi clan was chief of Moli and Koce Gumbiri was the chief of Karpeto in southern Bari. This verbal agreement was witnessed by the Bari chief himself, Bari elder Logiro and Tombe Nyula of Ma'di and the land was passed over by Ruba of Dedi clan. (Chief Marcello Wani Silingi 2008)

To catch a glimpse of the story in Iyii the author travelled through Mejopadrani (Borokodongo), and areas controlled by the three Ma'di clans of Logili headed by Ovu Manya, Mugi-Koluwa led by Lango Sai, Gunyia headed by Awolo Kute the son of Kidi Aguluru and the Dungo clan of Bari led by Titifano Tombe. He also passed through the Acholi family homes of Ombiyo, south of the Ma'di villages of Iyii. Acholi elders at the time included Lojukureng, father of Latana Omiyati, Leji Atanga, Israel Olebe, Timateo Alimu, Felice Kenya and Remijo Aremo. In work gang No.13 of Jokoki, just a mile before one reaches Luworo village of Kute Musa and his fellow Logili people and members of the clan allied to the Logili, I can still remember seeing workers from other parts of Ma'diland. One of them was a short man called Ani from Loa clan of Pavura. About the age of six, the author could speak a little Acholi and in later years he could understand many Bari and Lulubo words. Such is the positive social benefit that is derived from the meeting point of the four tribes, Ma'di, Acholi, Bari and Lulubo. Here arises the possibilty to renew human relations, spearheaded by their forefathers, and convert their social intercourse into human cohesion rather than collusion over borders. There is more than enough land for everybody in Iyii. This contested area could develop into a commercial town, an outcome from which every tribe stands to gain.

15.5 Recommendations

1- The Governments of Eastern and Central Equatoria should immediately form a joint technical border review committee, the membership of which comprises competent surveyors, administrators, chiefs, legal experts and other desirable personnel. They should carry out the task of reviewing the relevant borders within six months and the committee should render their findings and recommendations to the respective Governors of the two states. Only by so doing can this rancorous problem be solved once and for all. Final executive orders to fix permanent borderlines between Eastern and Central Equatoria States should be made after the residents in the areas have been given an opportunity to dispute or accept the recommendations of the committee. If residents appeal against the findings, these appeals should be addressed first before a final conclusion of the issue is reached. Since there is a Standing Border Issues Committee in the State Council, any issue concerning borders in the Kit-Nyolo Rivers valley should be presented to them for final review. Since it is agreed that the borders of 1956 should be respected, where these lie in the Kit-Nyolo Rivers basin, but have become diffused over time, they should be re-established to solve the existing border problems.

2- Immediate social and economic infrastructure should be established in the area, especially in the Kit banks area, which is fertile for agriculture, so that the local inhabitants can profit from the development there.

3- The members of Ma'di, Acholi, Bari and Lulubo who have lived in peace should foster good neighbourliness, continue their peaceful coexistence, nurture a spirit of cooperation, interact and make Kit a growing town as it lies strategically half-way between Juba and Nimule.

4- This work floats like a rudderless ship in a large expanse of unchartered ocean awaiting guidance from readers like yourself who make observations, critiques and reviews. Whatever the medium of communication, these should be copied to the author so that he can consider the points raised and address them in the next impression of the book.

5- The Ma'di youth should learn about the different aspects of the culture of their tribe and those studying in universities and other higher institutes of learning should pick up topics not yet undertaken for a better understanding of Ma'di life and thought.

6- John Mairi Blackings, a Ma'di with a doctorate in linguistics has shown uncommon interest in documenting different aspects of Ma'di life in a publication from the United Kingdom where he resided. He has called for material of different genres concerning the Ma'di and this should be supported by supplying him with the required material for his proposed book.

7- This work has been overtaken by the latest Kit conference held on 6th September 2008. At this conference a temporary solution was hammered out by the Peace and Reconciliation Committee under the chairmanship of the Honorable Mary Nyaluang Ret with the Hons. Alfred Barakat and Ufondi Fibel as members. They decided that the border between Eastern and Central Equatoria States should be the road between Kit and Nyolo bridges. They recommended that this be adopted by the two governors as the right course of action having heard testimonies from citizens indigenous to the area and as the 1st January 1956 maps also indicate.

8- The borders of 1st January 1956 should be respected as stipulated in the Comprehensive Peace Agreement (CPA), 2005 and should be adhered to by all four tribes in the Kit and Nyolo region.

9- Workshops, seminars and conferences should be organized to discuss the borders adjoining the four tribes,

Bari, Ma'di, Lulubo and Acholi in Torit and Juba, and participants in such forums should include academics, intellectuals, chiefs, representatives of civil society organizations, youth, and governments officials of Central and Eastern Equatoria States, other interested people, and organizations. The Government of Southern Sudan, the Committee of Peace and Reconciliation in the Southern Sudan Legislative Assembly, the governments of Central and Eastern Equatoria States and the United Nations body responsible for peace and reconciliation should contribute funds for organizing such important occasions. It was very encouraging to see in the Kit border meeting of 2008, among the participants were the Speaker of the Transitional Legislative Parliament, Honorable James Wani Igga, the governors of Central and Eastern Equatoria States, Major General Clement Wani Konga and Brigadier General Alosious Ojetuk Emor respectively and some senior officials from the two states. Their presence at the meeting in which representatives from Bari, Lulubo, Acholi and Ma'di recounted their knowledge and experiences of the area leaves a lasting impression.

10- The resolution of the Peace and Development Committee in the Southern Sudan Legislative Assembly that the governors of Eastern and Central Equatoria States establish the necessary developmental infrastructure in the Kit-Nyolo area, should be actioned by the government leaders immediately by sending surveyors to the area to survey it. The survey should then be distributed to government institutions such as departments of public health, survey, agriculture, education, roads maintenance and to the inhabitants, assigning land as residential quarters, as commercial plots, and the areas beyond the centre, as land for agriculture and veterinary activities.

List Of Informants

1- Caesar Mori Loku

Caesar Mori Loku attended the border meeting in 1977 at Iyii (Kit) in which Abel Alier Kwai, then President of the High Executive Council for the Southern Region of the Sudan and Dr. Ignatius Gama Hassan, then Regional Minister of Agriculture, Animal Production and Fisheries participated. He also took part in the meeting convened by the Commissioner of Eastern Equatoria Province, Colonel John Okwahi in 1988 and other meetings organized by the Ma'di Welfare Association (MAWA), in Kator 'B' court building in Juba to discuss the same issue. He narrated to the author about these meetings on the border issues several times on different occasions and in different years. Mori was a senior civil servant who served in the Ministry of Agriculture and Animal Production in Juba. He was a Ma'di from Patibi Moyiba clan and a grandson of Tombe Bworo.

2- Marko Aloma Koka Lou

Marko Aloma Koka Lou was a former local government administrator who attended some of the border meetings, including that held in Juba in 1988. As one time administrator of Magwi area council, which accommodates both Ma'di and Acholi communities, he came face to face with some of these challenges several times and related to the author the proceedings of the meetings and his experiences. Marko also prepared some notes on the status of Magwi Area Council for the Acholi-Ma'di peace conference held in Torit on 16-19 April 2012 under the auspices of the Inter Church Committee, drawing on his long experience and detailing the border between Pageri and Magwi councils.

3- Jabulon Jada Yanga

Jabulon Jada Yanga was an MP representing the workers of Equatoria Trade Unions Federation who elected him to the parliament in 1978. Jada told the author about the meetings organized to discuss the border issue, some of which he participated in. He had also taken part in field visits to the border area at Iyii (Kit) with politician Joseph Kebulu Ame to meet the elders of the Ma'di and Acholi communities in Iyii. Jabulon was the half-brother of Joseph Lagu Yanga, and their father was Yakobo Yanga Lagu. Jabulon's mother was Naka Oro from Oloro-Ukeyi clan.

4- Severino Fuli Boki

Severino Fuli Boki represented the Ma'di and Acholi people who have been put together in the same geographical constituency twice, in the parliament in Khartoum in the late 1970's and early 1980's. He briefed the author about the Juba meeting of 1988, called by the Eastern Equatoria Province Commissioner, Col. John Okwahi in which he categorically refused to sign the memorandum of understanding between the Acholi and Ma'di communities because, in his words, it touched on the assassination of Joseph Kebulu Ame of the Ma'di community whose body, he and others carried from the site of the assassination in Palabek, Panyikwara area for burial in Erepi (Kerepi) in April 1986. Fuli said that those Ma'di who had signed such a memorandum of understanding did so without proper discussion of the issue and without the mandate of the Ma'di people. Severino Fuli is the writer of a book titled, *Shaping a Free Southern Sudan, Memoirs of Our Struggle 1934-1985*, which provides details about political developments in Southern Sudan touching on Acholi-Ma'di relations and misunderstandings in the past, and some of his observations in the book can help in addressing the land issues which confront the two communities in Iyii and Owinykibul.

5- Morris Lodu Wani

Morris Lodu Wani was an election officer and enumerator in the census that was conducted in 1982. He narrated to me his experience during the interference of the Acholi chief Ereneo Ayoto in Iyii in his work of enumerating the people in the area during the national census of 1982 saying that the Acholi people in Kit could not be counted together with the Ma'di. Morris was also prevented by Joseph Tombe from counting the inhabitants of Bari origin in the Ma'di village of Mejopadrani (Borokodongo) for the same census in the Ma'di constituency. He narrated many of these stories to the author in the 1990's.

6- Saulo Obalkare Yuggu Lotikaro

Saulo Obalkare Yuggu Lotikaro was the chief of Molungeng in northern Opari. He briefed the author about the claim of some members of his own clan that they are Acholi, notwithstanding their own clan history which has that they emigrated to Bori from southern Bari and actually belong to the Paibonga clan. They do not belong to the Ngaya, which is a nickname given to them by one of their elders after their fighting with the Acholi Ayom clan in defence of the Pambili clan of the Ma'di, whose number was decimated before their arrival by the Acholi clan of Ayom and Agoro raiders. He said that the border between Ma'di and Acholi was north of his village of Molungeng at the three trees known as *iyu* and that Owinykibul was a Ma'di area because the Acholi moved there after the Addis Ababa agreement of 1972, after the place was opened up by the Anya-Nya led by General Joseph Lagu.

He said that during the rule of Chief Akeri Milla, a lot of places were given Acholi names by the Ma'di (who are bilingual) and this did not mean that the places belonged to the Acholi.

In 2005, Saulo said that he was 65 years old and was the chief of Molungeng 'A' court of Opari 'B' court, Pageri area council. He was born in Molungeng village of Ma'di parents of Paibonga clan. He was elected chief by his people in 1988 in Juba. Saulo narrated to me the development of the leadership of the Paibonga (today referred to as Ngaya) beginning with his grandfather Lotikaro to his father Yuggu. He also has a vast knowledge of the Pandikeri chieftainship of Bori (Opari) and provided me a wealth of information about its development starting from where it began, its zenith and decline. The border issue is a complex matter in the wider context of relations among the Ma'di, Acholi, Bari and Lulubo people who are neighbours, and Saulo is well versed in the origin of the problems and where the old borders lay. He said the border between Bori-Opari and Acholi Panyikwara chieftainships lies at the point where three huge tropical trees called *iyu* in the Ma'di language stand along Opari-Torit Road north of Mede village.

He said his grandfather Iyiali had always told the family that they had come from Bari and are originally Paibonga, but since that time they had adopted Ma'di traditions and culture and had become Ma'di after many years of interaction with the indigenous people. Saulo said however that for personal reasons, some of his brothers say they are Acholi because they speak the language and live in the border area between the two tribes, Ma'di and Acholi. He said he personally disagreed with this position because those relatives of his who advocated it did not refer to their history starting from the time they arrived in Kugi plain, their discovery of the Pambili clan of the Ma'di in the plain, and their conflict with the Acholi clan of Ayom in defence of the Pambili, whose population was severely decimated by the Ayom and Acholi-Agoro raiders. He said that speaking Acholi did not make someone a member of that tribe and gave the example of the family of Akeri Milla. Milla's great grandfather was an emigrant from Loringa, Acholi Parabongo in Uganda, but Milla and his whole family said they were Ma'di by naturalization. The Ma'di of Bori embraced them as their own people and were always ready to defend them against enemies and be their subjects because Milla was also their chief. That is one way to interpret Akeri Milla's family background according to Saulo Obalkare. But the explanation of the origin of the Pandikeri people given by their own intellectuals, men such as Samuel Okomi, the son of Jiribi Lakilonyi and Samuel Liyo, was that their ancestors were a Ma'di group who fled from Bori-Opari long ago hence their name *Loringa Parabongo* which means 'refugees of Parabongo'. This clearly indicates that they were refugees in Parabongo having fled from the Ma'di area, for *loringa* in Acholi is for people who flee from some problem. In the Acholi language *oringa* means 'to run'. When Ma'di from Opari and Erepi fled as refugees during the 1955-72 strife, they were accommodated in Olwal by the Pandikeri, who remained behind at the time of the return of Akeri Milla's ancestors to Bori-Opari. These people said they were Ma'di and had come to this Acholi land in Uganda due to problems of the past. The Acholi said that the Ma'di refugees, who had run away from the Arabs in Sudan to them, should feel at home in Olwal, Parabongo. Among the Ma'di who settled there were Yozefu Legge of Ukeyi clan and Sarafino Kanga of Mugi clan. The Acholi of the place called them *loringa ayela* meaning 'refugees' or 'those who ran away from conflict'.

7- Adislao Loduma Mairi

Adislao Loduma Mairi says he was born in about 1923 at Ludiri-Muruli, Moli. He belongs to the Moje clan. He is one of the few persons from the Ma'di tribe who participated in the Second World War of 1939-45 as a soldier of the British imperial army in East Africa. He was a driver of transport vehicles and drove extensively in the region of the Horn of Africa. Based in Embakasi, the main army depot in Nairobi, capital of the British colony of Kenya, Adislao transported troops and equipment to stations in Mogadishu in Italian Somaliland after it was captured by the British forces. Adislao gave me substantial information about the chieftainships in Moli and was present when in 1935 the district commissioner of Torit gave power to Chief Akeri Geri Ipele and assigned the work of sub-chief *mukungu* to Ingani Kuyu of Ukeyi clan because the D.C. said the Logili chief had more households than those under the control of Ingani. Under Akeri Geri there were 200 families while Ingani was in charge of only 80. This meeting took place in Melikwe in Muruli-Ludiri and was attended by the heads of families in Moli. Adislao himself was present at the meeting.

8- Lazaro Nyago Dumo

Lazaro was born in Bori-Opari of Ma'di parents from Kiloloro clan in about 1935. He received a few years of elementary education in Loa Catholic Mission. In the mid 1960's, he joined the Anya-Nya movement and participated in the establishment of Owinykibul as the military headquarters of Major General Joseph Lagu. In 1969 under the supervision of Captain Peter Mogga Kobaa he took part in the construction of Owinykibul airstrip used by the Israeli friends of the Anya-Nya for air-dropping military supplies for their liberation war against the Arab government army of Sudan. Lazaro narrated to me the story of Chief Akeri Milla of Bori from Pandikeri clan, who in about 1889 led the Ma'di people from Moli, Erepi, Nyongwa, Pageri and Arapi to the Acholi land of Parajok from Bori-Opari to escape the Mahdist forces who were based in Rejaf, and who raided the people for slaves and their domestic animals for food as far away as Moli and Erepi (Kereppi). Lazaro was very conversant with the clans of Opari and told me a lot about them for my research. He was a retired game scout and relocated to Khartoum during the civil war in Southern Sudan fought by the SPLA. It was in El Haj Yousif, Khartoum North that I interviewed him several times to collect data for this book. In the process he gave me information about the transition of power from the Logopi clan to that of Pandikeri. During the same interviews Lazaro provided me with information on the chieftainships in Bori-Opari and the rivalry among the sons and grandsons of Akeri Milla over the succession to the seat of the chieftainship. Nyago had grown up in Bori-Opari and had seen the ditches dug round the villages in Ayipa by the Ma'di people after their relocation from Ayaci near Parajok to prevent Obbo warriors from killing people under cover of darkness.

9- Cuofo Oddu Geri

Cuofo Oddu Geri was the eldest child of Chief Geri Ipele of Moli from Logili clan with his wife Juru Nya Leju of Dongu clan. She said that before his death, her father told his eldest son Akeri Geri to give her much respect, because had she been born a man, the leadership would have been hers. She narrated to the author the history of her royal family whose leadership had a great impact on the inhabitants of northern Ma'di in general and of Moli in particular, in the first half of the 20th century. The interview was conducted in Juba, Hai Game on 14 November 1994.

10- Akeri Geri Ipele

Akeri Geri Ipele was the chief of Moli. He succeeded his father Geri Ipele who in about 1932, was taken to prison to Juba. Chief Geri was tried together with the Kuku Chief, Kole Yengi of Caregoro, Kajokeji, for ordering an ordeal for suspected witches in their respective chieftainships. The ordeal involved the serving of water in which a little ash from fire making sticks was dropped. The suspected witches were required to drink this to prove they were innocent of the accusations leveled against them. The man who carried out this exercise was called Lokudu from Ngaya clan of Bori. (Severino Fuli 2002: 230) Several women drank the water and died. In Moli, two women suffered constipation and died, and their death led to the chief's arrest. Akeri Geri's chieftainship was interrupted two or three times by suspensions from his position by the Torit District Commissioner. He was among the first sons of Ma'di chiefs and notables to be sent to the Church Missionary Society (CMS) School in Opari in 1921 and when that school was closed down that same year, he did not go to school again. Since 1953, he was no longer a chief following his removal by Head Chief Sabazio Okumu Abdalla from the post and the appointing as Chief, Jelindo Chaka Aperia for Erepi and Moli, which were amalgamated into one chieftainship and its headquarters was located in Erepi. During the last nine years of the 17-year Anya-Nya War, Akeri was reappointed chief of Moli till his death in 1985. He was interviewed by the author in Juba, Hai Commercial in August 1982.

11- Rita Keji Lodu Bilal

Rita Keji Lodu Bilal, popularly known as Lokere, is the mother of the author. Born in Aduro near Muruli-Moli in about 1920, she was married to Wani Lou Morjan, father of the author in about 1936 in Moli Tokuro, Baribari. Lodu Bilal Leju was the name of her father, and he was from the Dongu clan of southern Bari whose parents emigrated to Bori-Opari during the Mahdists' invasion of southern Bariland. After the Mahdists' occupation of Equatoria province ended, Lodu and some of his relatives moved to the Moli area where they settled and, since the end of the nineteenth century, they have lived among the Ma'di people. Keji's mother Ossa Eriani was from the Paluda clan of the Ma'di. Lodu Bilal was the stepbrother of Juru Nya Leju, the wife of the great Moli chief, Geri Ipele of the Logili clan. His mother was called Moria Nya Bande from the Pajawu clan of Moli. Rita's mother died when she was very young and she was brought up by her paternal aunt, Juru Nya Leju, in the household of Chief Geri Ipele. This relationship meant she was close to developments in the chieftainship, not only that of the Logili but also of Mugi, Tedire, Ukeyi etc. and the affairs of the Logili leadership with Bari, Lulubo and Acholi chieftainships. Rita witnessed these developments while she was in the household of Chief Geri Ipele and as a very keen observer, she became well informed of these activities. It was this experience that enabled her to narrate to me, her son, these developments for inclusion in this book. My mother also inspired me to undertake this research and prepare its findings for presentation to the public. Despite her lack of education, she was very influential in public life among her fellow villagers in Moli. She died on 29 December 2007 in Juba.

12- Koka Lou Mbwele a.k.a Iseni

Koka Lou Mbwele a.k.a Iseni was the paternal uncle of the author. He was born in about 1897 in Opari, Nyakaningwa where his father Lou Mbwele got married to Idreangwa Nya-Agwele, a step-granddaughter of Pandikeri Chief Akeri Milla by his half brother Koka. Lou's father Golibe Murujalanga and his family had settled briefly at Opari while on their way back to Moli after their escape from the Mahdists in about 1888 to Parajok then to Ayipa towards the end of the nineteenth century. Koka Lou a.k.a Iseni related to me many reliable stories about Ma'di rainmaking and rainmakers, the inter-tribal and intra-tribal wars in which the Ma'di were involved, the histories of these wars and the general history of the Ma'di as it was known to the people of his time. He was a road headman during the construction of Juba-Nimule Road from Mejopadrani, renamed Borokodongo by Andrea Farajalla, in Dereto work gang camp No. 15. Koka Lou died in Juba on 3rd of May 1983 and his body was transported to Moli Tokuro by the author for traditional burial.

13- Idreangwa Nya Agwele

Idreangwa Nya Agwele was the paternal grandmother of the author. As a step-granddaughter of Chief Akeri Milla of the Pandikeri clan of Bori-Opari from the lineage of Koka, the stepbrother of Akeri Milla, most of the stories about the chieftainship were narrated by her to her sons, Koka Lou Mbwele a.k.a Iseni and Wani Lou Mbwele, who was the father of the author and to her daughter-in-law, Rita Keji Lodu Bilal, mother of the author. In return, the trio, especially Koka Lou Mbwele and Rita Keji retold the stories to the author. Idreangwa Nya Agwele was born in Nyakaningwa, Opari several years before her parents could flee to

Acholiland from the Mahdists for safety. Her father was Agwele who was the son of Koka the half brother of Akeri Milla. Her mother Tinya was from the Jeru clan of Idele village located on the bank of Atapi River south of Opari. She might have been born in about 1880 if her first born son, Koka Iseni Lou, it is estimated, was born in 1897 in Nyakaningwa, Opari. Most girls of her time were given away to husbands at the early age of fifteen years or slightly above. She died on 22nd of July 1976 in Moli Tokuro where she was buried.

14- Chief Odoriko Loku Diego Mude
Chief Odoriko Loku Diego Mude came from the Tedire clan of Bori. He was born in about 1920 at Male to the southeast of Opari district headquarters. His father was Diego Mude Muhamme, and his mother was Tinya of Mugi clan. Odoriko went to elementary school at Loa in 1935 and left at the end of second year in 1936. He was baptized as a Catholic in Loa Mission in 1933. In 1937, he traveled to Torit to live with his paternal uncle while searching for employment but did not get a permanent job. During the Anya-Nya Movement (1955-72), he was an influential head of scouts who supplied the Movement with logistics and food. Eventually, he became a chief for Opari and Loa areas. After the Addis Ababa Peace Agreement of 1972, he became the chief of Opari area including Owinykibul. During the SPLA war, in 1989, he left Opari and moved to Juba where he became headchief of the displaced members of the Ma'di tribe. Eager to increase his knowledge, he enrolled as a primary school pupil at the age of about seventy years and studied up to form 8. He enrolled for secondary school classes but could not attend to school and court sessions at the same time, so he suspended his education to manage his duties

as chief. Odoriko contributed substantially to this work because he had a vast knowledge of the Ma'di chieftainships before and after colonial rule. As a native of Opari, he was more instrumental in educating the people about the chieftainships of Bori, who are made up of the forty or so Ma'di clans, than the Acholi who came into the chieftainship during the reign of Akeri Milla. Milla's great grandfathers were Ma'di who sought refuge in the Acholi area of Uganda hence their name *Loringa Parabongo* ('refugees in Parabongo') of Olwal in Uganda. Three clans, namely Pakala, Oloro, and Pajawu who lived in Opari before relocating to the Acholi area (especially Pakala and Pajawu clans) have links with their main bodies among the Ma'di in Jaipi division of Adjumani District in Uganda.

Akeri Milla, whose father was Andruga and whose mother, Nyajele Joloko was an Acholi from Panyikwara of Pajomo clan, is said to have brought members of the Acholi-Panyikwara to Bori during his rule and they lived side by side with his subjects, the Ma'di. That situation gave rise to the Acholi emigrants speaking Ma'di, although not so perfectly, hence their name 'Acholi-Ma'di.' It is said that the Ma'di who learnt to speak Acholi spoke it perfectly, unlike the Acholi who spoke Ma'di imperfectly. To date the estimate of Ma'di who can speak Acholi as a second language, from Mugali in the south to Moli in the north, number in the thousands, while the number of Acholi who can speak Ma'di is insignificant. Some Ma'di places bear Acholi names. Owinykibul, Winyalonga, Ogwangmeda, etc. have been named by the Ma'di who are bilingual and not by the Acholi people as they are in Ma'di territory. Some people including Saulo Obalkare Yuggu, a chief of Opari from Paibonga (Ngaya) clan of Bori-Opari say that Owinykibul was named by General Joseph Lagu who thought it was a good hiding place where the government soldiers could not get him and his soldiers, and their presence could only be heard by the sound of drummming. Lagu is multilingual. Besides his mother tongue, Ma'di, he can speak, read, and write Acholi well, and also speaks and reads the Dinka language perfectly besides English and Arabic. The Ma'di people not only speak Acholi but write and read it as well. The first Acholi-English, English-Acholi dictionary was written by a Ma'di academic, Professor John Mairi Blackings (PhD) and his effort has been praised not only by Acholi academics in South Sudan but even those in Uganda. The parents of the author could speak Acholi fluently and his brothers, who followed him in birth are bilingual and so is his only sister. The author himself can speak Acholi fairly well.

Most of the Ma'di who could speak Acholi learned it while they were refugees in the northern Acholi districts of Gulu and Kitgum in the period 1964-1972, during part of the period of the Anya-Nya liberation war. Many Acholi wondered why so few of them speak Ma'di and those who do know it speak it poorly. The reason they concluded was that the Ma'di language is very difficult compared with their language which they say is easy to learn to speak. They deny the opinion held by some Ma'di people that they are simply not interested in learning to speak Ma'di.

15- Alex Locor Tartisio

Alex Locor Tartisio comes from the Lokoya tribe of Lowoi section. I have known him for a very long time when both of us were employees of the Regional Ministry of Culture and Information in Juba. Alex was in the radio and telegraphic section of the ministry while I worked at Radio Juba, another unit of the same ministry. When I became the director of Radio Juba in 1986, I traveled regularly to Khartoum where the headquarters of the broadcasting corporation to which Radio Juba belonged were located and while there, I used the radio and telegraphic facilities for communicating with my office in Juba. Alex was in charge of this unit in the Southern Region coordination office. Through such working relations we became more aquainted. When I was appointed Minister of Social Affairs (Information, Youth, Sports and Social Welfare) in Eastern Equatoria state capital Torit, in 2004 I again met with Alex. He was in charge of the radio and telegraphic unit attached to the state secretariate. It was in Torit that I introduced to him my book project on Ma'di history, especially the part about Moli whose inhabitants were once engaged in inter-tribal conflict with the Lokoya-Langabu people, and I asked him whether he knew of the history of this conflict and if so whether he could narrate to me the Lokoya version of this story for comparison purposes. He responded positively and said it was, in truth, good to write down the history of the Lokoya-Langabu-Moli conflict for the next generations to learn from and avoid similar hostility in the future. (People have now become civilized and Christians who are meant to love each other.) I was very happy with his response and immediately prepared some interview sessions with him. In fact, we talked about the matter more than twice in the month of May 2005. The data on the conflict between the Lokoya-Langabu and the Ma'di of Moli which I collected from Alex, was more than I expected to discover for the book.

16- Chief Mamur Wadal Faraj
I knew Mamur Wadal Faraj in Juba in the 1970's when he was a storekeeper in the Public Works Department (PWD). The PWD became the Regional Ministry of Works, Construction and Public

Utilities after the Addis Ababa Peace Agreement of 1972. His house was in Kator residential area just a few metres from the Juba Bridge which joins the west and east banks of the Nile. I interviewed Chief Mamur in Takamul, El Haj Yousif, Khartoum North in 1995 where he had moved to from Juba. Chief Mamur explained to me the circumstance which led to the assassination of Ma'di Chief Nyengwi Iro under Iwire Mountain in the Acholi Panyikwara area by an Acholi man from Goloba clan. He said as far as he knew, there had been no conflict between Acholi and Ma'di since the two communities were administered together by the Uganda colonial government from Nimule, a Ma'di village, when the land from Gondokoro to Nimule was part of Uganda Protectorate. They were again put together, this time with the Kuku from across the River Nile and administered by the British of the Sudan from Opari, another Ma'di village. Mamur added that no one who talks about such things could compete with him, because he was the most elderly of the individuals who had gone to school in the old days and knew a lot about the oral history of the two tribes. He said that all the talk about land claims and counterclaims was political and did not involve the Acholi people who knew where their borders were with the Ma'di. He explained that the Ma'di of Opari share borders with Panyikwara, where he came from, and with Obbo and Parajok areas of the Acholi.

"And who among the elders of the Acholi has not heard about Ma'di Chief Akeri Milla and his friendship with the Acholi people?"

Mamur added that in 1988 he attended a meeting with Acholi and Ma'di intellectuals in Juba called by the Commissioner of Eastern Equatoria Province, Colonel John Okwahi, and advised them to guide their people wisely and live in peace because they are neighbours and their ancestors had led good lives together.

I found Chief Mamur Wadal Faraj conversant in Acholi history, just as he knew the histories of the two communities, Acholi and Ma'di, and gained from him a great deal of information. Concerning Owinykibul, he said it used to be a hunting ground which lay at the meeting point between Obbo and Parajok on the one hand and the Ma'di of Opari on the other. He said this place became inhabitable after General Joseph Lagu chose it as his military headquarters during the Anya-Nya war. Because it was very close to Acholi land it was easy for them to claim it. But he said since the spot is within the tribal border between the Acholi and Ma'di it is difficult to say whether it belongs to the Ma'di or the Acholi. Elders, whose parents used to go hunting there, should be the ones to ask to give the most honest explanation about this land, which the two tribes should not quarrel over but share amicably.

17- Adelinda Aciro
At first Adelinda Aciro, an Acholi from Panyikwara, resisted talking to me about the slaying of Ma'di chief Nyengwi Iro of Palungwa clan by an Acholi assassin under Iwire Hill. But eventually a young woman who was her niece succeeded in convincing her that my enquiry into the matter was purely for historical and educational purposes. When she consented and narrated to me the story about the assassination of the chief, I gained an insight into this history from an Acholi from the area for the first time. Adelinda also sang for me the song composed by the Acholi Panyikwara clans on Nyengwi after they killed him. My spoken Acholi is poor but after singing the song repeatedly after Adelinda, I was able to interpret it for documentation purposes. It was in 1995 at Takamul, El Haj Yousif, Khartoum North that I interviewed Adelinda Aciro.

18- Lazarus Yuggu Lotikaro

Lazarus Yuggu Lotikaro was a member of Paibonga clan of Bori-Opari. He was an official in the Regional Ministry of Culture and Information in Juba when I first met him in 1976 to discuss issues related to the ties of his clan of Ngaya with the people of Opari. He first corrected me by saying that the right name for his clan is Paibonga and explained further that the name 'Ngaya' was a nickname given by members of his clan who used to boost to the Acholi clan of Ayom and others that they have defeated them in war because they were bitter like a kind of sorghum when tasted. Actually, the Paibonga inter-tribal war with Ayom and other Acholi clans including the Agoro people was rooted in their defence of Pambili, who were the first Ma'di clan they found in the Kugi plain when they first arrived with their cattle from Bari country. Lazarus said that when his ancestors came to the Ma'diland of Opari, they came upon the Ma'di clan of Pambili whose leader was a man called Bire. He said their ancestor Lojobi who brought them to the Ma'diland became a friend of Bire who, together with his people, welcomed them very warmly. He said the Pambili were very few because they were killed regularly by members of Acholi clans especially the Ayom and the people of Agoro. When the members of his clan, the Paibonga, joined the fight on the side of the Pambili they defeated the spear-bearing Acholi bands of warriors and chased them up to Got Banda. They never returned to fight the Pambili, because the Paibongo settled beside them. He said the fighters of the Pambili clan used ineffective weapons, molded mud with slings, to fight the Ayom and the result was that they were always defeated and killed in large numbers. The reason why the Pambili had settled at the northern end of Kugi plain was to escape from the Ayom marauders but even there they were exposed to the Agoro fighters. At first, marriages between the leaders' families of the two clans, the Pambili and Paibongo, were unthinkable because they considered themselves brothers and sisters. After many years of interaction permission was granted to members of the two clans to marry each other.

19- Erodionne Murulu Jiribi
Erodionne Murulu Jiribi was an elder from Pa-Akori clan. He was born in Arapi Palinyi in the early 1920's and was one of the first Ma'di youth to attend Loa Elementary School in the late 1920's and in 1928-33 he attended Torit Artisan School operated by the missionaries of the Catholic Church. In the artisan school he learned carpentry, building, mechanics and driving. He began work as a driver-mechanic in Torit Catholic Mission and later moved to Layibi Technical School in Gulu, Uganda operated by the Catholic Church. He was later employed by the Department of Survey under Mr. Grey who took him along to Entebbe when he was transferred there. Erodionne supplied me with useful information about the Lokai chieftainship under Cirino Odego, the assassination of Chief Nyengwi Iro of Palunga clan of Arapi by Acholi hunters under Iwire Hill. He also sang for me the Arapi songs composed after their reprisals on the Acholi killers of Nyengwi. When old lions and lionesses followed the newly constructed Juba-Nimule Road from the direction of Juba in the early 1930's and caused havoc in the Ma'di area killing a number of people, Erodionne was a young man and he participated with a group of elders in hunting the beasts. He was present when Chief Ruben Surur of Lokai led his followers from Mua to hunt the lioness called Foni, eventually killing her in Ibbi stream near Mua village. She had mauled a woman and her child. Erodionne was

taken to Khartoum by one of his sons in the late 1980's during the civil war and he passed on there before the Comprehensive Peace Agreement (CPA) of 2005.

20- Ukal Kawang Julu

Ukal Kawang Julu is a researcher from Pari (Lokoro). He has researched the life of his people and their culture for a book. The Lokoro were among those people who raided the Moli area of the Ma'di in late 1927, killed them and abducted their children whom they took to their land. As a researcher, Julu honestly provided me with substantial information about the raids and abductions from my area for inclusion in this book. I met him in Korton Kassala, Khartoum North in 1995 and since then we have become friends. Actually, the Lokoro live far away from Moli, about 65 miles, but they were aided in their trek to the Moli area by a clan among the Acholi of Agoro called Koyo or Kicari. Although they now call themselves *Pari*, the Moli people they raided and whose daughters and sons they abducted and carried away to their land, know them as Lokoro and for historical reasons they are referred to as such in this book.

21- Karamello Dragala Balabas Lomeda

Karamello Dragala was born in the 1930's in Melekwe, Loa. He attended Loa Elementary School briefly then left in the 1950's for Juba where he enrolled as assistant driver in the Department of Veterinary Services. From Juba he was taken to Rumbek and worked in Tonj and later in Wau. From there his unit in the veterinary service was engaged in tsetse fly control and was moved to Nyala in western Sudan where Balabas worked till he was pensioned off in the early 1990's. I interviewed him in 1995 and

1996 while I was in the process of collecting information for this book in El Haj Yousif, Takamul in Khartoum North where both of us were residents. Despite the fact that he left Ma'diland in the 1950's, what he had learned about the cultural, social, and economic developments in the area earlier was so vast that he had a wealth of information to provide when asked. He said that when he was a young man in Melekwe near Loa, he used to participate in *gayi* and *mure* dances with Ma'di Chief Cirino Odego who liked these dances very much and from this common interest they became friends. He was adept at beating the mother drum for the mure dance. It was from Balabas that I learned more about the natural bridge over the Nile, which was first written about by an Englishman called Mr. Wayland, whose article appeared in Uganda Journal No. 1 in 1937. Balabas said he accompanied his father, Konide Lomeda, across the bridge over the Nile several times because the family sacred shrine was in the cave across the river and his father used to go and perform rituals there. He acknowledged that the writer's statement that the bridge used to break off to leave a gap for about two years and to begin forming again with soft vegetable material from upstream lasting for about four years, was true. Furthermore, he agreed that even elephants used to cross over from Nyeri Mountain using the bridge to come and eat food crops like cassava and sorghum in the fields of inhabitants of Melekwe and Ongoro, and they used the same route to return to Nyeri Mountain. Balabas's family belongs to the Pamotto clan, the largest contingent of which are found in Nimule. He also recounted to me the relationship between his family and that of Chief Ogokwi of Padibe, Acholi, who claims Pamotto descent.

22- Paulo Dralile Bigo

Paulo Dralile was born in the 1940's in Olikwi, Nimule and attended Loa Elementary School in the late 1950's up to the third class. In 1959 he ventured to Juba seeking for employment and first worked with a Greek merchant dealing in liquor and spirits. In about 1960 he travelled by steamer on the Nile to Northern Sudan disembarking in Kosti, then proceeded to Khartoum. He spent many years in Khartoum working as a labourer in several institutions including the Indian Embassy. In 1995 and 1996 I interviewed him about life as he had learned of it and seen in Ma'diland before he left the rural setting as an adult to emigrate to urban centres. He was knowledgeable about Ma'di traditional dances, the mure and gayi and their songs, and about the chiefs' roles in administering the tribe. He also explained to me the rivalry for the leaderships among the clans of Nimule, especially the Koyi led by Agala and Pamotto under Droko Beshir.

23- Sestilio Andruga Juma

Sestilio Andruga Juma was a long service elementary school teacher who taught for over forty years in schools in Ma'diland. He wrote a number of papers on educational values but none of these works were published to benefit Ma'di and other children because the works were in Ma'di. They could have been translated into English since they were teaching and reading materials. Songs are represented in the aggregate of materials used by teachers to educate children. They are also a powerful medium for keeping alive the histories of the people, especially at the village level. When Chief Sabazio Okumu Abdalla within a few months after his election to that position in 1952 abolished tribal war songs in Ma'di traditional dances, Sestilio as a teacher at the time, felt that a step backward had been taken, because a lot of teaching material would eventually be lost. He said he was present at the meeting of chiefs, sub-chiefs, assistant chiefs, notables, elders, and teachers from all parts of Ma'diland called by the headchief to announce the new policy, which he witnessed during his tenure. Included in the policy was the abolition of all war songs whether they were about inter- or intra-tribal wars sung during the normal *mure* social dance or funeral dance. Violation of this directive constituted a serious breach with punishment on those who refused to adhere to the new directive. I interviewed Sestilio Andruga Juma in Jaborona, west of Omdurman in 2000.

24- Remijo Lodu

Remijo Lodu belongs to the Dongu clan of Bari and lives in the Ma'di village of Mejopadrani (Borokodongo). The group to which he belongs moved from Nyajogi village of Dongu in the Kugi forest originally founded by Drongwa Musukani. The Dongu group which settled in Mejopadrani was led by Titifano Lado in 1939 on its way to Nyokir, the original homeland of the Dongu clan in southern Bari, but they cut short their journey when they found that it was more advantageous economically and socially to settle among the Ma'di along the newly opened major Juba-Nimule Road. Hence, they decided to settle in Mejopadrani in Moli chieftainship under Chief Akeri Geri whose mother, Juru Nya Leju was a member of the Dongu clan. The Dongu clan settled among the Ma'di in the late nineteenth century. The name Borokodongo was given to the town by Andrea Farajalla the senior road foreman in 1930, when the village happened to be at the point where Road Gang No. 13 was stationed. At the time of their arrival in Mejopadrani, Castello, a Greek mineral explorer and excavator was here mining mica and other minerals, so some of the young men decided to join themselves as labourers to Castello's mining group. Castello also constructed a mansion on the hill overlooking the Juba-Nimule Road, the first stone building with a corrugated roof ever built in this part of the world. Remijo was brought up in Mejopadrani and got married to Antonietta Kako, sister of Milla Effremu of Logili clan in Iyii. Remijo gave me a substantial amount of information about the people who lived in Mejopadrani (Borokodongo) in the period 1939-1972. Besides members of his Dongu clan, he knew the Ma'di who lived there with their clans. He said there was not a single Acholi in Borokodongo. During the SPLA war the entire population was displaced. A few came back after the Comprehensive Peace Agreement (CPA) of 2005. Remijo became the most senior surviving member of the Dongu clan in Borokodongo and the Ma'di who lived with him selected him as their assistant chief under Moli Boma of Pageri County.

Annex One

I- Ma'di Constitutional Post Holders In The Past And Present Years

A) LOKAI CHIEFTAINSHIP (SOUTHERN SECTOR)
1- Nasur Romano (Nimule), Minister, 1990's.
2- Donald Azzo Mona (Mugali), MP, Minister, 2000's.
3- Awad Abbas (Nimule), MP, 1990's.
4- Dominic Inza (Mugali), MP, 1990's and 2000's.
5- Julius Ajeo Moilinga (Mugali), MP, 2005.

B) ARAPI CHIEFTAINSHIP (CENTRAL SECTOR)
1- Melichior Ingi Lumanyi (Loa), MP, 1950's.
2- Dr. Gama Hassan (Arapi), MP, Minister, Advisor, 1970's, 1980's, 2000's.

3- Silvestro Otto Lutaya (Arapi), MP, Speaker, 1990's, 2000's.
4- Mrs. Sarah Bua Zozimo (Pageri), MP, 1990's, 2000's.
5- Dr. Edwin Gira Zozimo (Arapi), Minister, 2000's.
6- Juma Angelo Saki (Loa), MP, Advisor, 2000's.
7- Adelino Wani Michael Opi (Arapi), MP, Speaker, 2005.
8- Agnes Lutaya (Arapi), Minister, 2007-2008.

C) MOLI CHIEFTAINSHIPS (NORTHERN SECTOR)

1- Joseph Lagu Yanga (Moli), Army General, President of High Executive Council, Vice President of the Republic, 1970's, 1980's.
2- Jabulon Jada Yanga (Moli), MP, 1970's.
3- Romeo Wani Inyani (Iyii), MP, 1990's, 2000's.
4- Jacqueline John Logotomoi (Moli), MP, 1990's, 2000's.
5- Anthony Betcu Pitya (Malandu), Minister, 2000's.
6- Victor Keri Wani (Moli), Advisor, Minister, 2000's.
7- Emilio Iga (Malandu), Commissioner, 2005-2008.
8- Angelo Vuga Morjan (Moli), Advisor, 2005.

D) EREPI CHIEFTAINSHIPS (WESTERN SECTOR)

1- Redento Undzi, MP, Deputy Speaker, 1950's.
2- Joseph Kebulu Ame, MP, Minister, 1970s, 1980's.
3- Caesar Mori Loku, MP, 1990's.
4- Dr. Peter Tibi, MP, 2005.
5- Martin Milla, MP, 2007.
6- John Andruga, Ambassador, 2000's.

E) BORI (OPARI) CHIEFTAINSHIP (EASTERN SECTOR)

1- Siricio Iro Wani, MP, Member of Supreme Council of State, 1950's, 1960s. Member of Province Council, Juba 1960's.

2- Sabazio Okumu Abdalla, Member of Province Council, Juba 1960's.
3- Severino Fuli Boki, MP, 1970's, 1980's.
4- Mary Siricio Iro, MP, 1980's.
5- Abednego Kenyi Andrea, Commissioner, 1980's, Advisor, 2000's.
6- Melichior Lagu Damiano, MP, 1990's, 2000's.
7- Nicola Oboya Lazarus, Commissioner, 2000's, MP, 2006-7.
8- Tereza Siricio Iro, State Minister in the Government of National Unity, Khartoum 2006-2008.
9- Clement Otto Kulo MP, 2006-2008.

II- MA'DI ADMINISTRATORS/CHIEFS WHO SERVED BEFORE AND AFTER REMOVAL OF TRADITIONAL CHIEFS

1- Sabazio Okumu Abdalla, Head Chief from 1952-83.
2- Jelindo Chaka Aperia, Chief for Erepi, Moli and Nyongwa from 1952-71.
3- Raphaele Abuni, Chief of Opari 1957-1965.
4- Aniceto Amoli, Chief of Nimule and Mugali 1952-1965.
5- Rombe Baraga, Sub-Chief of Erepi in the 1950's.
6- Koka Arisile, Sub-Chief of Patibi in the 1930's and 1940's.
7- Duku Ariga Obadia, Assistant Sub-Chief in Ukeyi-Moli in the 1950's and 1960's.
8- Ariga Bassa, Assistant Sub-Chief of Loa in the 1950's and 1960's.
9- Sai Mondi, Chief of Arapi in the 1940's.
10- Akeri Milla Chief of Bori-Opari from Pandikeri clan in the 1880's to 1910.
11- Silimani Ito Kafiri, Chief of Pageri, one time appointed for

Erepi, Moli and Nyongwa in the 1940's, 1950's.

12- Muhamme Kara, Chief of Nimule in the 1940's.

13- Kute Musa Tombe Moli, Sub-Chief of Iyii (Kit) in the 1940's, 1950's and 1960's.

14- Osman Zelebu, Sub-Chief of Pageri in the 1950's.

15- Hagiga Ajjo, Sub-Chief of Loa in the 1940's and 1950's.

16- Clemente Mamur Vumudri, Chief from Pandikeri clan in Opari in the 1940's.

17- Mene Milla Akeri, Chief from Pandikeri clan in Opari in the 1920's.

18 - Daru (Dari) Kanyara Isara, Chief from Pandikeri clan in Opari in the 1930's and 1940's.

SOME OF THE TRADITIONAL CHIEFS OF THE MA'DI PEOPLE BEFORE AND DURING THE TURCO-EGYPTIAN AND ANGLO-EGYPTIAN ERAS 1840-1899

Nyori, Chief of Muruli, who was the first Ma'di chief to resist the forces of the Turco-Egyptian administration sent from Gondokoro by Alfred Del Bono, the commander of the garrison when Ismail Ali the Khedive ordered the invasion of the lands south of Gondokoro and claiming them for his dominion.

Urube, chief of Moli from Logili clan, assassinated by a servant of Kajamindi of Mugi clan in the mid-nineteeth century for imposing drought which almost wiped out the entirety of cattle owned by the people of Moli.

Akeri Milla, Chief of Bori-Opari, in the 1880's who in about 1889 led the Ma'di people of different clans and some Acholi people of Panyikwara to Parajok when these people were threatened by Mahdist invaders of their territory in the southern Nile valley.

Geri Ipele, Chief of Moli 1910's to 1930's.

Loku Kitchere, chief of Erepi from Tedire clan in 1910-1930's.

Akeri Geri, Chief of Moli in the 1930's to 1980's.

Kenyi Bada, Chief of Lokai (Mua) lived in the nineteenth century. Known for being beheaded by the Tukutuku, Belgian soldiers of Lado Enclave in late nineteenth century.

Loku, son of Chief Kenyi Bada. He was chief of Lokai at the beginning of the twentieth century. Interested in education and gave his son Lobai to the Catholic missionaries for education in Paloro.

Lobai, son of Chief Loku of Lokai. Lived in the early twentieth century in Mua, Ndindi.

Cirino Odego, first Ma'di chief to be a Catholic Christian and ruled in Lokai in the mid-twentieth century and was affected by the abolition of traditional chieftainships in the 1950's by the British colonial system.

Alimu Dengu, son of Chief Lobai, became chief of Lokai twice but for very short durations in the mid twentieth century.

Eberu Drani, son of Chief Loku Kitchere of Erepi, from Tedire clan was one of the sons of chiefs who were sent to school in Opari and Malek in Dinkaland in the 1920's. He was chief of Erepi after his return from school for about two years.

Ingani Kuyu, chief in Moli, Muruli from Ukeyi clan in the early nineteenth century.

Ito Kafiri, appointed chief by the British who acquired him as a man of influence among the Belgians, the rulers of Lado Enclave, in the nineteenth century. He was from Pageri clan which previously had no traditional chieftainship. Kafiri died in about 1957 and he was mourned with traditional dance performed by Ma'di who came from as far away as Metu in Uganda.

Nyengwi Iro, chief of Arapi from Palungwa clan. He was assassinated by an Acholi man from Panyikwara in about 1893 under Iwire Hill.

Menne (Minai) Isra, son of Chief Akeri Milla of Bori-Opari. Succeeded his father in about 1910 as chief and lived in the early twentieth century in Opari.

Dari (Daru) Kanyara Isra, succeeded his father Menne Isra in the 1930's and ruled till the 1940's. He was known for promotion of Ma'di culture especially its songs and mure dance.

Annex Two

Biographical Notes on Selected Distinguished Personalities Among the Ma'di

1-Sayed Siricio Iro Wani: Member of the First Supreme Council of State

Siricio Iro Wani was one of the earliest Southern Sudanese politicians. He participated in the Juba conference of 1947[1] and was among the first five prominent personalities elected to form the first Supreme Council representing the Presidency in the Sudan, whose chairman was selected by fellow members on a rotating basis. He was a prominent participant in the first government headed by Ismail Al Azhari and was one of those Southerners who called for federation in Southern Sudan. He was a prominent

**Fig.8: Sayed Siricio Iro
(photo from Sudan Government archive with courtesy)**

administrator and politician. In a press interview with a journalist in 1985 when enroute to Khartoum where he was invited by Field Marshal Suar Al Dahab to come and advise fellow Sudanese people on issues of unity and co-existence in the country, he told the journalist that he was born in the early 1920's at Opari village in the former Equatoria Province. Sirisio Iro died in Nyongwa east of Opari in 1986.

Sudan Vision newspaper of Khartoum once interviewed his daughter Bruna Siricio Iro before the signing of the Comprehensive Peace Agreement (CPA) on 9 January 2005[2] and she said of her father, "If the Independence celebrations coincide with the achievement of peace, then they will be as beautiful as those of 1956 and for me they will mark the end of a nightmare. Celebrations will then have a special flavour, exactly like those which took place when we got rid of the colonizers." Bruna said that her father Siricio Iro had refused to participate in all the succeesive governments in Khartoum after the coup of General Ibrahim Abboud including that of Nimeiri before and after the Addis Ababa Agreement of 1972 and the transitional government. Nevertheless, she said he had always offered advice whenever asked. He did that with Joseph Lagu, Dr. Nazir Daffa'lla and Jaafar Nimeiri. Bruna said that her father spent most of his time in Opari, his village in Eastern Equatoria, practicing cultivation and fishing. Bruna said she was proud of her father because he was a man of principles. His closest friends were Dirdiri and Mirghani, and he gave their names to his sons besides their Christian and Ma'di names.

Bruna said that her father used to say that he lost confidence in the Northerners when they failed to keep their promise about federation for the South. The difference between her father and some of the present Southern politicians, Bruna told the newspaper, was that "he was always a man of principles, and he was quite an example as an administrator and politician."

The author had seen Sayed Siricio Iro several times as a boy in elementary school at Opari. In 1962, Mr. Kristino Dridulu Muna, the headmaster of Loa elementary school, then accommodated in the abandoned buildings of Opari elementary school in Nyakaningwa which was transferred to Magwi, invited Sayed Siricio Iro to come and address the school during its celebrations. In his address, Iro advised the pupils to take education very seriously because the next stage of political and economic development in the Sudan would involve people who are properly schooled. He recalled the period in which he was in the government which was overthrown by the military but expressed hope that one day the situation would become normal again, especially in the South, when every citizen would be involved in contributing to the development of the country. Siricio demonstrated to his fellow Ma'di people that when one serves in the civil service of any other public service and retires, he should come back to his village and build a modest house, establish a small farm, and enjoy life with his fellow village people. He built a house with bridge walls and corrugated iron sheet roof in Opari town and ran retail shops in Opari itself, in Pageri and at Abara among the neighbouring Acholi community.

2- Joseph Lagu Yanga

Joseph Lagu Yanga was born in 1931 at Momokwe (some people call it Yomokwe) near Aduro in Moli, Malandu.[3] His father was Yakobo Yanga Lagu Api of Kiloloro clan and his mother was Kaluma Marini from Beka clan of Bori-Opari. Lagu began his education at Nimule and later went to Akot, south-east of Rumbek in Dinkaland to attend a school of the Church Missionary Society – CMS in the 1940's and passed the elementary leaving examination and was admitted to Nugent School Loka, north-east of Yei. He joined Rumbek Secondary School in 1952 and sat the Cambridge School Certificate Examination (GCE) in 1957 in Khartoum where the school was transferred to after the August 18, 1955, Torit mutiny by Southern Sudanese soldiers. He entered the Military College in Omdurman in 1958. He graduated in 1960 as a second lieutenant and was posted to El Obeid military garrison and later to Juba headquarters of Southern command.[4] He defected to the Anya-Nya movement in 1963 while on leave at home in Nimule. He signed and ratified the Addis Ababa Agreement in March 1972, subsequently becoming a Major General in the Sudanese army, the first Southerner to do

Fig.9: Mr. Joseph Lagu Yanga (photo from archive of former Regional Government in Juba with courtesy)

so. In 1974, he was appointed by the Commander-in-Chief of the Sudanese Armed Forces, Marshal Gaafar Mohammed Nimeiri as Inspector General of the Armed Forces. In 1975, he became Commander-in-Chief of the First Division of the Armed Forces in Juba. In February 1978, Lagu was elected President of the High Executive Council (HEC) for the Southern Region. He was deposed from this post in 1980 by a group of Southern politicians opposed to him, and he became Assistant Secretary General of the Sudanese Socialist Union (SSU) for Southern Region in Khartoum. In 1982, Lagu was appointed Vice President of the Republic and held the post till 1985. He served as representative of the Republic of Sudan at the United Nations in New York in the 1980's and as Sudanese ambassador in the UK, London. After the independence of South Sudan on July 9, 2011, General Lagu was appointed advisor to the President.

3- Sabazio Okumu Abdalla

Sabazio Okumu Abdalla was from Gonyapi clan of Bori-Opari and was elected Headchief of Ma'di by working officials from the tribe in April 1952, in Juba and then in Loa. During his first 'B' court session in Opari-angwa (Little Opari) which was located in Loa and to which he called practically all the chiefs (*jago*), sub-chiefs (*mukungu*), assistant sub-chiefs (*nyampara*), notables, elementary school teachers and elders of the tribe, he issued his first administrative order putting a stop to all war songs being sung in Ma'di *mure* dances and on other occasions such as funerals. Before this prohibition, some killings in the areas where intra-tribal wars had been witnessed in the past were still being reported but these were confined to individual actions and took place only in deep forests and were not carried out openly in the villages. In the 1930's and 1940's, the feuds were reduced to war songs only and members of rival clans sang them in mure dances without recourse to bloody fights. In 1953, Headchief Sabazio Okumu restructured Ma'diland administratively and amalgamated the larger Moli chieftainship with the smaller Erepi chieftainship thus committing a blunder whose consequences were felt many years later following his decision. The Moli chieftainship shared a border at the tip of its northern territory with Lulubo on the southern bank of Nyolo River, and at the bend of Ame River with Omeyo area of Acholi. Chief Akeri Geri of Moli used to visit these sites frequently to make sure there were no encroachments into his territories by the neighbouring tribes, and met with the sub-chief of Lulubo–Aru, Tombe Wani. Moli also borders Bariland and Chief Akeri

Fig.10: Ma'di Headchief Sabazio Okumu Abdalla (photo from archive of Regional Ministry of Information, Juba with courtesy)

Geri used to exchange visits with Koce Gumbiri, the Bari chief at the time at Karpeto. After over thirty years of dormancy at these strategic locations, unfavourable situations began to emerge. The Lulubo said their border with the Ma'di of Moli was in the middle of Kit River and not across Nyolo River.[(5)] The Acholi of Omeyo said they did not have a border with Moli chieftainship. The Bari too have moved the border posts closer to Ma'di territories near Foki and at other points. These developments occurred because there have been no checks and visits by the succeessors of Chief Akeri Geri. They did not anticipate such changes to occur. Jelindo Chaka succeeded Akeri Geri as chief in 1953.

4- Redento Ondzi Lomena

Redento Ondzi Lomena was probably born around 1925 at Erepi of the Patibi clan. He received an elementary education in Loa and then for higher classes was sent to Rejaf East where the Catholic missionaries were running a school. His colleague was Zozimo Ogo, another man from the Ma'di community. They were later taken to Okaru intermediate school when the school was transferred from Rejaf. On leaving Okaru, Ondzi enrolled in a clerical course at the Juba Training Centre (JTC). After graduation, he became a clerk, served for several years, and then became a storekeeper. In 1956, Ondzi won the election to enter the constituent assembly in Khartoum and was elected deputy speaker till the assembly was dissolved by General Ibrahim Abboud following his coup d'etat of 17 November 1958. Redento then retired to his home in Erepi where he built a small shop and a house as a residence on the junction of Borongole Road and the main Juba-Nimule Road. When the government officials, formerly in the dissolved parliament, were recalled to civil service, Ondzi went back to his former work in the clerical field.

The Addis Ababa peace agreement of 1972 ushered in a new dawn of political participation in Southern Sudan and elections were planned for a parliament in Juba, the regional capital. In 1973, election campaigns to the southern parliament were launched and Redento Ondzi was one of the older politicians to join the race despite advice from the younger people of his constituency that he should leave politics and retire to his home. His constituency covered Ma'diland as well as Acholiland. He used to say to those who spoke against him contesting the election that the competitors would face each other in the field. (*Ama rundre foroa*) Unfortunately for Ondzi, I remember his election symbol was the bed (*angareb*) which those people who did not support him used to say was not a sign of victory but of doom. The *angereb* besides being used for sleeping is used for carrying a sick person to the hospital or a dead body to its grave. Redento did not succeed in that election and did not attempt the contest again in 1978.

5-Yongo Alimas Dumo
Yongo was the son of Betcu Amoni of the Mugi clan from Moli. He was one of the sons of chiefs and notables taken to Opari Protestant School in conformity with the colonial government policy to educate sons of chiefs to prepare them to take over from their fathers and administer along civilized lines.[6] Yongo Alimas did not spend a long time in school for his father might have been one of those notables who did not like their sons staying away from home for fear based on past experience that they might be taken to unknown places by foreigners, never to be seen again. When he became chief of Moli, he implemented a government policy which directed all the people to transfer their homes from Adrwi and Moli Tokuro where they had moved following a lack of good soil for cultivation since the soils in Malandu and Aduro where they had been living for ages were spent and no longer productive. It was the District Commissioner of Torit who ordered the chief to let the people of Moli move to the old road which ran from Rejaf along the Albert Nile to Opari through Malandu. The move made him unpopular although it was government policy and a decision not taken by him.

6- Dr. Ignatius Gama Hassan
Dr Ignatius Gama Hassan was born in Arapi-Palungwa in the late 1930's. His father was Jalingo Hassan of Palungwa clan and his

Fig.11: Dr. Ignatius Gama Hassan (Photo from archive of former Regional Ministry of Information, Juba with courtesy)

mother, Gilasi, was from Jeru clan. Gama began his education in Loa Elementary School and proceeded to Okaru Intermediate School from where, after five years, he joined Rumbek Secondary School. Ignatius (Inyacio) went to Italy for his university education where he studied agricultural science specializing in crop protection including pest control. He worked for some years with an agricultural service company in Eastern Africa based in Nairobi, Kenya. In April 1972, following the Addis Ababa peace agreement signed between the Sudan Government (SG) and the Southern Sudan Liberation Movement (SSLM) with its armed wing, the Anya-Nya, he was picked for a ministerial post and became the first Minister of Agriculture, Animal Production, Forestry, and Irrigation.[7] He served in that capacity till 1977. Dr. Gama represented the Ma'di, Acholi and western part of Torit district in the parliament in Juba from 1973 to 1978. After relinquishing his ministerial position, he served in other capacities but what distinguished him was his engagement in the private sector in which he, with others, established a service company of which he became an executive. Dr. Gama passed on in 2007 in Khartoum and his remains were brought to his home village Arapi where he was laid to rest beside his father Jalingo.

7-Captain Peter Mogga Kobaa

Peter Mogga was the son of Kobaa of Lulubo clan with his wife Nya Logwiya of Paluda clan. He was probably born in 1934 at Moli and attended the bush school in the village under teacher Ibolo Abiyo in 1946. He spent two years here and his colleague at the school, Marko Aloma Koka Lou, can still vividly remember Peter's active roles at the school.[8] Peter went to Loa Elementary School for a year or two and returned home as there was no prospect for further education at the time because there were no intermediate schools to go to.

In 1954, Peter went to Torit and enrolled with Equatoria Corps in Number Two Company. After military training, he was commissioned as a soldier. In mid-July 1955 he went home to Moli on leave. In Torit on 18 August, the same year, he heard the news that his colleagues in Number Two Company had rebelled. Peter decided to walk to Torit as most journeys at that time were done by foot, arriving in the town two days after the mutiny. He found that the garrison town was largely deserted by both the soldiers and the ordinary residents who feared reprisal action by Northern soldiers following the killing of some army officers, officials, and some traders – all of Northern origin. Peter entered the barracks to discover that his personal property, which he had left in the care

Fig.12: Anya-Nya Captain Peter Mogga Kobaa

of his colleague when taking leave, was missing. He concluded that it had probably been looted as the barracks appeared to have been ransacked before being deserted. He decided to return to Moli when he sensed that after the mutiny the army would be in disarray, leaderless, with no one to put the soldiers under one command and control. Many of the soldiers fled to their villages and the mountains to hide in the caves, fearing that the government was already organizing a force to counter their action.

On arriving home in Moli Tokuro, Peter found that the village was awash with rumours that Arab soldiers from Khartoum loaded in large lorries accompanied by vehicles fixed with cages to hold captured Southern mutineers as prisoners, were already in Juba and were about to cross by ferry to the east bank. Peter was persuaded by his family members to immediately leave Moli for Uganda to avoid capture, although it was common knowledge that he was on leave when the mutiny took place in Torit. So, Peter reluctantly went to Uganda as a refugee. And indeed, a few days after his departure, the village of Lulubo was surrounded by Arab soldiers at night in a surprise raid searching for soldier runaways from Torit, only to find that Peter was not in the village. His brother Betcu Ameda Kobaa was picked up and taken by the soldiers to Loa headquarters of the local government for interrogation, but he told them that Peter was on leave and when he heard about the mutiny he walked to Torit and never returned.[9]

In Uganda, Peter found work in a sugar plantation at Kakira, east of Jinja industrial town. It was in 1962 that he joined the liberation movement when a message was circulated by Joseph Oduho on behalf of Sudan African Closed Districts Union (SACDU) first to the students of Rumbek and Juba Commercial Secondary Schools and then to the intermediate schools throughout Southern Sudan that former soldiers of Equatoria Corps of Torit had regrouped after acquiring sophisticated weapons from abroad and were about to launch armed attacks against the Arab occupation army in the South. They were giving the students and pupils in schools an opportunity to strike and time to flee to the neighbouring countries as refugees.

In 1961, Peter got married to Maria Tete, the half sister of the author. His brother Fausto Opi managed the engagement as Peter was fearful of returning to Moli. He however approved of the engagement because he had seen Maria and spoken to her about the affair which was to continue without him. Maria was transported on bicycle carrier by Fausto to Nimule, then on to Attiak where she boarded a bus for Gulu and from there she traveled by railway to Jinja to join her husband in Kakira. In 1962, Peter was commissioned as a first lieutenant in the secret army announced by Father Saturnino Lohure and Joseph Oduho. He was assigned to organize the Ma'di on the east bank of the Nile in Equatoria province and to coordinate with his Acholi colleagues. Peter benefitted from the involvement of his father-in-law, Wani Lou Mbwele, father of the author, who had no previous military background but despite this shortcoming was able to organize the first Ma'di group of fighters bearing traditional weapons, bows and arrows and some matchetes in early 1963. From this group Peter Mogga was able to collect information about the readiness of the Ma'di people, especially those in Moli, to join the liberation struggle and he delivered this information to Father Saturnino Lohure and Joseph Oduho who were encouraged by the situation. In neighbouring Acholi, a man called Obale was the officer in charge who frequently crossed into the Ma'di zone to coordinate activities with Peter Mogga. After the killing of my father, Wani Lou, by Arab soldiers on October 28, 1964, near Pageri, Peter brought together the suvivors of Wani's group and integrated them with men he recruited from other parts of Ma'diland, especially Loa and Mugali. He had over one hundred men under his command but they had no rifles or training although some of them like Paul Betcu had served in the government army and Silvestro Obudra was a former Equatoria Corps soldier. The group had only a few marker ten rifles. Most of the men were armed with Ma'di traditional weapons, bows and arrows from the era of Wani Lou.

In 1965, Peter decided to shoot some elephants when he heard that some Europeans in the Congo were exchanging weapons for ivory and exotic animal hides such as those of leopards, zebra, giraffes, and serpents. He organized a group of strong young men of his force, about fifty in number, to go with him to Congo to buy some weapons with ivory. The journey took the group through Yei district, and they spent two months on the return trip from their camp near Mugali.(10) After resting for a month or two, Peter set off again with more men than in the first expeditionary group and carried some ivory and leopard skins to trade for weapons. He came back after six weeks. Such resourceful journeys continued two or three times and by December 1966, Peter's company was fairly well armed, and he began to launch ambushes on government army convoys along Juba-Nimule Road. One of the men who was close to Peter Mogga during the Congo errands was Josuwe (Josua) Modi who said he nearly died when he ate cassava roots from a Kaliko garden near Yei but was saved by native medicine given to him by a local medicine man. In 1965, the force was replenished with new arrivals from Khartoum, the survivors of the Khartoum massacre of Southern Sudanese on the so-called Black Sunday of 6 December 1964. These were the Ma'di elements of the survivors. In July 1965, another massacre took place in Juba and those men who survived it joined Peter Mogga's group thus swelling the force. Among those who came from Khartoum was Abiyo, the son of Avudumoi of Ijupi clan of Moli, and among those from the Juba massacre, Khalicino Yanga, a former police corporal and telegraph technician Ezekiel Ondu Aturusi. Although I have not come across the disclosure of this great achievement by Captain Peter Mogga Kobaa in the writings of Severino Fuli and of Joseph Lagu, I can excuse them because their plans for the liberation were hatched in Kampala in Uganda and Aru in the Congo. They were aloof from the actual fighters from the beginning of the Anya-Nya.

In 1969 when General Joseph Lagu contacted and struck up a friendship with the Israelis, who promised to supply his guerilla army with weapons and other military logistics, Peter was assigned by Lagu to supervise the clearing of a bush air strip in Owinykibul. Peter's force was transferred to this place to form part of the headquarters brigade.[11] The late Severino Fuli in his book fails to mention the important role played by Captain Peter in the construction of the airstrip and clearance of the supplies when they were dropped by air. However, Chief Odoriko Loku Diego Mude, who was the civilian leader in Owinykibul, told me that the bulk of the work of airstrip construction and clearance of the supplies dropped by parachute was supervised by Captain Peter Mogga. Lazarus Nyago Dumo, who was at the time a soldier in the movement attached to Peter's Company D, concurred with Odoriko's statement, and said he himself participated in the airstrip clearance under the supervision of Captain Peter Mogga.

Another important national contribution made by Captain Mogga was his putting forward, from his people back home in Moli, the name 'Anya-Nya' for the liberation army. In mid 1963, Joseph Oduho after splintering from Aggrey Jaden and other Southern politicians and forming his own party, the Azania Liberation Front (ALF) and Azania Liberation Army (ALA), was not happy with the name of the armed wing of the movement and thought it should have an African name. He had none in mind and so decided to engage his supporters on the eastern bank of the Nile, the part where Torit, his district lies, to find an African name for the movement. He stipulated that the name should sound like the 'Mau-Mau' of Kenya in the 1950's. He decided to send three ambassadors from his Latuko tribe, from Ma'di and Acholi on a top-secret mission to their people living in refugee camps in the border areas. To the Latuho people, he sent Valeriano Orege to Kitgum area where many Latuko people had settled as refugees. Oduho dispatched Pancrasio Ocheng to Palabek and Lokung areas to get a relevant name for the movement from his Acholi people. Peter Mogga, then a first lieutenant and the only senior member of the Ma'di community was sent to the Ma'di area of Southern Sudan where he was popular. It was in Alali forest that he met the Moli group under the leadership of his father-in-law, Wani Lou Mbwele, and received from them their proposed name *Enya-Nya* for the movement. At first Lieutenant Mogga rejected the name which was proposed by his father-in-law Wani Lou, because of the perception the Ma'di people have of *enya-nya* poison which was believed to be extracted by some dangerous Ma'di women from cobra or other species of snake. But Wani defended the name saying that as long as he was in power in Moli should anyone be caught preparing poison for killing people such a person would be arrested and put to death. Wani said that if the name was selected then it would only be confined to the movement, and in any case, nobody would be allowed to mention it. Wani was supported in his proposal and its justification by one of his followers, Vito Abiyo, the father of Jino Longa, the gospel preacher from Ukeyi clan, who at first supported Lieutenant Mogga in his objection. So, when Vito came to support Wani in his proposal, Mogga was convinced and promised to take the name 'Enya-Nya' to President Joseph Oduho.[12]

On arrival in Kampala Peter announced the name 'Enya-Nya' which he had taken from the Ma'di area to Joseph Oduho in their headquarters at Kawempe Township in the north of Kampala City. Oduho on hearing it, jumped from his chair almost touching the ceiling with his head in the movement's Kawempe office building.

He exclaimed: "Anya-Nya! That is the name of our army!" Before asking First Lieutenant Peter Mogga to explain the meaning of the name, Oduho himself narrated that in about 1937 a Ma'di Chief called Akeri of the Madi brought some women to Torit accusing them to the British District Commissioner at the time of being poisoners using *anya-nya* poison extracted from snakes. So, without any delay Joseph Oduho announced that the name of the liberation army was from that time to be known as 'Anya-Nya'. Father Saturnino Lohure, who was the patron of the movement and was based in Aru, Congo, was sent this name and he blessed it as a worthy name for the armed wing of the movement, although he himself had proposed a name related to Pan-Africanism. Actually, at the beginning of 1963, Peter Mogga was the most senior personality from the Ma'di community dealing with issues concerning formation of the liberation army with Joseph Oduho and Father Saturnino Lohure. Joseph Lagu defected from the Sudan Government army in June 1963 and Severino Fuli joined the movement in late June 1963. Wani Lou, who was imprisoned twice in Torit in late 1962 and early 1963 for his anti-government activities was unkown to Oduho and Father Saturnino in Kampala because there was nobody to inform these leaders about his efforts until the time he was killed by enemy forces near Pageri on 28 October 1964.

What Fuli and Lagu say about the name Anya-Nya
General Joseph Lagu Yanga and Severino Fuli Boki were two senior figures from the Ma'di tribe in the Anya-Nya liberation movement. When it emerged that Anya-Nya was a Ma'di name for poison extracted from cobras, it was automatically assumed that one of the two members of the Ma'di tribe, Joseph Lagu and Severino Fuli

must have proposed the name to President Joseph Oduho who had wanted an African name like *Mau-Mau* of Kenyan origin in 1950. But the name Anya-Nya was neither given by Lagu nor by Fuli. It was proposed by an unknown bush fighter, Wani Lou Mbwele, who was the original organizer of the force of fifty-five consisting of elderly and young men from the Ma'di tribe, mostly from Moli, who were based in Alali Forest in the Moli area in early 1963. The name was taken to President Oduho in his Kawempe office, north of Kampala city of Uganda by Peter Mogga Kobaa, an officer in the liberation movement. The two Ma'di leaders defected from the Sudan government at different times, Lagu crossed the border into Uganda on June 4, 1963 (Lagu 2002: 97) while Fuli crossed the border into Uganda on 19 July 1963 (Fuli 2002: 227). Let us read what the two leaders, Lagu and Fuli say about the origin of the name *Anya-Nya* so that the presumption that one of them might have proposed the name is cleared from our minds. From Fuli's book, he quotes President Joseph Oduho as addressing a meeting of his cabinet on 30 July 1963,

"Today we are to give a suitable name for our 'armed forces' which we were intending to launch on the eighth anniversary of the August 18 1955 Equats uprising. . . Our patron had already suggested two titles. We are free to accept either of his or come up with a new one ourselves. He would respect our choice. The suggested names are (i) Southern Sudan Liberation Army (SSLA) (ii) Azania Liberation Army (ALA). . . There had been according to him a country bearing the name Azania in Central, Eastern and Southern Africa and Southern Sudan could have been part of it. If we spport this title, we would call our country the Azanian Republic."

Fuli continues, "The President declared the discussion open, pointing out that he would like a name with clear African connotations. He said an African country had already successfully done it: the Mau-Mau Revolution in Kenya. 'Gentlemen', Oduho added, 'who can explain to me the meaning of the word *anya-nya*? The word had been used from the mid 1930's in Torit district and seemed to have its origin in Torit town. But the word probably originated among the Ma'dis. Could Mr Fuli throw any light on the issue?' Fuli replied that the word Anya-Nya was a Ma'di word and its root was Inyi-nya or Inya-nya. It is a deadly poison extracted from snakes rarely seen which live near forested rivers on hills or mountain sides. (Fuli 2002, p. 236) After I had finished, Fuli said, President Oduho asked the Council whether anyone had a suggestion for the title and they all responded Anya-nya, Anya-nya, Anya-nya. At that President Oduho declared that Anya-Nya was to be the name of the military wing of the Southern Sudanese movement."[14]

Lagu in his narrative has this version on how the name *Anya-Nya* came about. He writes:

"We started with searching for a suitable name for the military. The father (Saturnino) recalled names that had come previously. He admitted that the names Sudan African Secret Organization (SASO) and Land Freedom Army (LFA) etc. were first used in Upper Nile and had been imposed by William Deng who was working separately. The father wanted a name associated with Pan Africans that would attract the attention of African leaders like Dr. Kwame Nkruma, the President of Ghana whose support we needed. The name he proposed was Sudan Pan African Freedom Fighters (SPAFF). I suggested consideration of a local name from any of our local languages, or Juba Arabic. I wanted a name similar to Mau-Mau in Kenya. I argued that Sudan Pan African Freedom

Fighters, or its abbreviation, (SPAFF) would not be attractive and would mean nothing to Southerners. He defended his suggestion saying it would draw the attention of the Pan Africans. SPAFF was adopted as the name for the military wing of SANU. (Lagu 2006, pp.105) After a final tour of the west bank with the Father, I left for Kampala in the first week of September taking with me copies of the operation orders and the leaflet for Oduho and our colleagues. I found Severino Fuli with Oduho. He too had defected from Sudan government service where he was a staff clerk, so Oduho appointed him Administrative Secretary or Minister at the Presidency. I showed them our work with the Father at Aru (Congo) and asked that they get the other colleagues to distribute the documents in advance. Then I expressed my reservations about the name SPAFF and told them that I preferred a local name typically African and South Sudanese name like Mau-Mau in Kenya. Although they were supportive of the decisions taken, they too wanted a local name. They suggested *Inyenya*, a poison extracted from cobra glands cooked with vegetable leaves and rotten groundnuts. The name would symbolize the determination of the military wing of SANU. I welcomed the idea and suggested a slight modification in spelling. I proposed to spell it ANYA-NYA which would be easier to pronounce than Inyenya and that it reads like Mau-Mau, the name of the movement of fellow black strugglers for freedom in Kenya. Oduho and Fuli welcomed my amendment." (Lagu 2006 p.106).

There are three important points to remember from the two versions written by Fuli and Lagu about their explanations on the origin of the name Anya-Nya. (i) Although the Council meeting called by Oduho on July 30, 1963 (Fuli 2002: 236) was to suggest names and select one for the armed wing of the Southern Sudan liberation movement, by asking in his opening speech of the meeting whether there was any member of the Council to explain to him the meaning of Anya-Nya, it means that he had already discussed the name with some other people prior to the Council meeting. When Lagu met Oduho and Fuli they had already adopted the name Anya-Nya so he himself did not know the persons Oduho had discussed the name with and these persons must have been Ma'di, and this is where Captain Peter Mogga Kobaa fits in.

Captain Mogga was an extraordinarily strict officer who kept secret the affairs of the organization and warned anybody of severe consequences should he leak any information about the movement. In a rare revelation about his role in establishing the name Anya-Nya, he told supporters in Wiliwili, his place of respite in northern Uganda that he had not wanted the name *Enya-Nya* at all because it is the name of something terrible used by some evil Ma'di women to poison people. He had preferred another name. He said it was his father-in- law, Wani Lou who insisted that Anya-Nya was a good name. "I did not propose to the Alali group an alternative name for discussion and approval," Mogga told the small group of followers.[15] "I just took the name Anya-Nya to Kampala and presented it to President Joseph Oduho who was overjoyed to hear it. It seemed he had known the name from a past situation already because when I said my people have proposed the name Enya-Nya he jumped into the space, his head almost touching the roof exclaiming loud the name Anya-Nya. 'We have got the name. It is Anya-Nya the liberation army of Southern Sudan.'"

How Captain Peter Mogga left the Anya-Nya Force

In 1971, when the Anya-Nya headquarters was transferred to Labone (Owinykibul Two) after the original headquarters in Owinykibul proper was captured on 25 January 1971 by Egyptian Commandos and units of Sudan land forces, Captain Peter Mogga Kobaa was moved to the new headquarters. In Labone a misunderstanding arose between Colonel Frederick Brian Maggot and Captain Peter Mogga. The colonel, who was army chief of staff, recommended to Major General Joseph Lagu Yanga that Captain Peter be dismissed from the Anya-Nya force. At first Lagu tried to play down the dispute, aware that the Anya-Nya was an army of volunteers and Peter was a volunteer. But Colonel Maggot threatened to resign if Peter was left to continue with his work in the Anya-Nya force. So General Lagu consented and dismissed Captain Peter despite many pleas from veterans of the Torit revolution of 1955, of which Peter was a member, to pardon him and transfer him to continue in another part of Southern Sudan. Lagu did not take their advice nor listen to their pleas and dismissed Peter. This was close to the time of the Addis Ababa talks with the Sudan Government in February 1972. Peter left and was never reinstated for absorption into the army after the peace agreement. Many Ma'di who owed their presence in the movement to Peter regretted his dismissal. Telesforo Imuro, a Ma'di veteran from Mugali who was close to Peter during recruitment of the Ma'di youth and elders into Anya-Nya force in the late 1960's told me in 1972 at Bibia that the loss of Peter from the force was greatly regretted by all the Ma'di in the force because it was he who had armed them by walking five times to Congo through the bush with groups to buy guns and ammunition for the war against the Arabs.

8- Wani Lou Mbwele

Wani was the third child of Lou Mbwele of Kiloloro clan of Moli with his wife Idreangwa Nya Agwele of Pandikeri clan of Bori-Opari. Wani's brothers were, Koka, Droko Festo, and Boyi and his sisters, Mindraa Yona, Rozana Jua and Anyeza Andrua. (16) He was the first child in the family to be sent to school at Nyakaningwa (which some people call Lakaningwa) in Opari in 1920. The medium of instruction at the school was Acholi because the Church Missionary Society (CMS) administrators of the school headed by Rev. Davies, who established it, came from the church headquarters in Gulu, an Acholi town in Uganda and spoke Acholi. But Wani had to drop out after completing just one year of schooling, the total for his lifetime. After attending for one year he could write his name and record his debts and the dates of birth of his children and those of his brother Koka Lou a.k.a Iseni in the Acholi language fairly well. His school mates were Akeri Geri, Longa Destirato, Eberu Drani, Itcaka Opi and others.

When Nimule, the district headquarters reverted to Sudan under the British administration in 1914 following a border adjustment in 1913 between Uganda and Sudan (*Nalder 1936:161-64*), both under the British, the headquarters was transferred to Opari some 30 miles to the north-east. Here the school originally run in Nimule by the Church Missionary Society (CMS) who came from Gulu, Acholi district of Uganda, was also transferred. Wani was employed by the manager of Cukole Cotton ginning factory in 1927 as a houseboy, but in the same year, the Opari District Commissioner, Captain A. H. A. Alban during a visit to the factory asked the Arab manager to give him Wani whom he had observed to be an energetic young man, to go and work in his kitchen. And so thither to Opari went Wani. His duties in the kitchen in

Torit expanded up to 1939 when he became the head cook of the DC, Mr. J. V. Rowley. Most of the British officials including the last DC of Torit, Mr. R.V. Rowley were recalled home in 1940 due to the breakout of the Second World War in 1939 because the Italians in Abyssinia (Ethiopia) were active against the British forces in the region. In May 1940 Mussolini declared support for Hitler and joined the Axis Pact led by Germany against the Allied Forces. When the DC left Torit, Wani too had to leave, and he went to his home in Moli. But in mid 1940 he found work as a head cook for the senior officers of the South African forces based in the transit camp at Borongole in Erepi (Kerepi) on their way to North Africa to fight the Axis forces. Wani worked there till 1945 when the war ended, and the transit camp was closed down.

Due to his relationships with British government officials and South African army officers, Wani became an enlightened member of the Ma'di community (and of his family) touching the political situation in the country. While in Torit, Wani was in contact with some soldiers and officers of the Southern forces of the Equatoria corps which were transferred from Mongalla to Torit, the District headquarters. When the soldiers and their officers rebelled on 18 August 1955, Wani was at home in Moli, and he recorded this event in his notebook. Thereafter he followed the political developments in the country keenly and as a citizen became concerned about the future of southern Sudan in the independent Sudan. He became what would be called today 'a political activist'. When the southern members of No. Two Company of the Equatoria Corps mutinied and later organized an armed struggle from the bush, Wani became a member of the secret cell soliciting support for the movement. However, his clandestine activity was soon noticed by the Head Chief of Ma'di area, Sabazio Okumu Abdalla. During the same period, in 1961, his daughter Maria Tete married Peter Mogga Kobaa of Moli. These affairs hardened the resolve of the chief to arrest Wani and send him to Torit for investigation and trial by the Arab district commissioner.

Peter Mogga was a former member of No. Two Company of Equatoria Corps. In January 1962, Wani was arrested, taken to Torit, and kept there for three months because Mogga was his son-in-law, but there were no credible reports about his anti-government activities given the fact that he was not a member of the disbanded Equatoria Corps, so he was released and sent home. But in late 1962 when it was rumored that Peter Mogga had become an officer of the movement which was being organized in Uganda where he was a worker in a Kakira sugar plantation, Wani was again put under observation and in January 1963 he was arrested for the second time and taken to Torit for investigation and trial. While in prison he narrowly escaped being taken for a killing spree dubbed *Fotur Al Kaid* (Commander's breakfast). Three prisoners including him were to be shot in a musketry field along the Torit-Lafon Road at dawn. Wani resisted the armed soldiers who were sent to take him, arguing that he had an important message to communicate to the Arab District Commissioner before he could be transferred anywhere. After serious consideration, the sergeant in charge of the firing squad consented, and in his place chose another inmate and took him with two others to be shot that day.

In the morning of that day, Wani, his hands handcuffed, and his feet shackled to a rusty chain, was paraded in front of the District Commissioner who was disappointed that he had not been executed at dawn. The DC was reluctant to listen to his story because he had previously strongly denied that he had any knowledge of the secret recruitment of men into the rebel movement, collection of money or provisions for the movement or that he took instructions from a rebel officer. When Wani spoke, he deceived the DC saying that if he released him, he would work for him, trace his son-in-law, and bring back credible reports on his activities. The DC rebuffed his offer saying that this had all the hallmarks of a cheap scheme to affect his escape. But Wani insisted, telling the DC that the government had a long arm and could catch him even if he fled to Uganda (which is where he intended to go) instead of doing the task he had offered to carry out for the DC. The Arab fell silent for some moments carefully considering the argument. Then with great reluctance he agreed, commenting that the government was truly a formidable entity which had the power to catch and repatriate Wani to Torit from Uganda for execution should he be found playing a trick to escape. So, the DC set him free him instructing him to go to Uganda and bring back a good report about his rebel son-in-law, adding that if he did not fulfill his end of the bargain and was caught, he would not be set free again.

When Wani arrived in Loa Government Centre No. One on a government lorry carrying armed policemen who were guarding the salaries of the police force and their rations in Loa and Nimule on the border with Uganda, the Head Chief Sabazio Okumu, who had sent Wani earlier to Torit for trial because of his connection with his son-in-law, Peter Mogga Kobaa, ordered him to be locked in a cell. He did not believe that Wani had been released by the authorities in Torit but was escaping. The police sergeant who commanded the force which came from Torit explained to the Chief that the man was released by the DC and told to go home. But the Head Chief did not believe this explanation and insisted that this release must be confirmed to him by the DC, and so he sent a message to Torit using the police signal facility, an old piece of equipment using Morse code. The reply came back that he should give the ex-prisoner his freedom.

As soon as Wani was released by the chief, he set off for Moli and on reaching his village he spent a few days with his family, organizing the secret evacuation of his children to Uganda, where they were to be hosted by a man from the Acholi village of Pabbo called Maurezio Loka, who had been his close friend since the 1950's. To avoid being arrested again, Wani entered the bush and began to organize some young and elderly men to form a unit of fighters from amongst the Ma'di people of Moli, Malandu, Ukeyi and Iyii.

Wani had some friends in Nyarabanga and Karpeto, villages of southern Bari. When he visited those areas, he was able to win over several men to join him in the cause. Even some Acholi men, on hearing about the existence of this new drive to organize a force in the area to fight the Arab army of occupation, came from Ame and Agoro to join the group and so did some men from the Lulubo people of Nyolo-Aru. They were ready to fight the Arab soldiers. Under the influence of Wani they set up a camp on the west bank of River Afoyi near Borokodongo (Mejopadrani).

The men whom Wani raised in the Moli bush numbered fifty-five, both young and elderly. Among the elderly were Vito Abiyo of Ukeyi clan, father of Jino Longa, the evangelist, Luka Agama of Nyai clan, Silvestro Obudra, a former member of Equatoria Corps in Torit from Degi clan, Paulo Betcu of Logili clan who was a former member of Sudan Defence Force, Lino Manya also a former member of Company No. Two of Equatoria Corps who had returned from Suakin in Northern Sudan where he was imprisoned for life but released in a general amnesty declared by General

Ibrahim Abboud, the President of the country in 1962 and his cousin Yozepe Yanga, father of broadcaster Tombe Dumo. Among the youth were Yoane Odu a.k.a Wosiwosi of Nyongwa-Monocu clan who became Wani's bodyguard, Keri Nyigola of Paluda clan, Beria of Lulubo clan, Loro of Kiloloro clan, Odiya Jojo of Logili clan from Iyii, Yanga Bworo of Lolubo clan from Moli Tokuro, Androga Konjidriga from Malandu, and Kodurato Yugu, a son of Ovu Manya of Logili clan from Moli Tokuro. There were several other men in the group including Natana Omiyati of Oloro clan of Acholi tribe from Iyii, and Lino Wani from Lulubo-Aru tribe.

Wani acquired an old gun from a certain old man in Malandu, who had been hiding it inside the grass roof of his hut for decades. The gun was called *tasi* and it loaded one bullet at a time. It seemed to be either a First World War rifle or an old Belgian rifle from the Lado Enclave era called by the Ma'di *Tukutuku*. This old gun was rusty and could not fire any bullet available at the time but was conspicuously displayed to give the impression that the group was armed even though they only had one gun. Wani trained his men in arrow shooting before deploying them sometimes on Juba-Nimule Road to shoot at the passing vehicles of the government army, a daring action against men who had working guns, some like the Second World War era Bren gun and Sterling, which were automatic.

The other weapons in the possession of Wani's group were several bottles of Molotov cocktail, the locally made petrol bombs which could set fire to a moving vehicle when thrown at it. Their first attack was on a government lorry coming from Nimule to Juba. It was hit about three miles north of Wani's own village of Ateminga in Moli Tokuro. The attacker threw a Molotov bomb at the moving vehicle because they did not have grenades or guns besides the ancient rifle which could not be used because of its age and ineffectiveness.

Wani, the group leader knew that in the whole of Ma'diland there were government guns used by local *askaris* (warders) for guarding the chiefs and these were in Kerepi, but due to the existence of the rebel group led by Wani in the neighbouring area of Moli, the chief, Jelindo Chaka Aperiya moved his residence to Loa where the head chief Sabazio Okumu Abdalla lived with several policemen and a small unit of the Sudan Defence force. The only civilian who had guns in the area was Silimani Ito, a former chief and his weapons, a Marker Five (*Abu Khamsa*) and a shotgun (*Kartus*) were gifts from his son-in-law, Siricio Iro Wani who was a member of the Supreme Council of State in Khartoum from 1955-1958. Wani knew Siliman personally because he had once been chief of Pageri, Nyongwa, Erepi and Moli villages in the 1940's. He wrote a letter to Silimani asking him to give his guns to the group for the cause of national liberation and strongly suggested that he cross the border into Uganda after doing so to avoid being arrested by the government for aiding the rebels with weapons. On the contrary Siliman was reported to have remarked that Wani was the leader of a gang of thieves and when he caught sight of him or his group, he would use his guns to kill them. Since Silimani Ito had refused to hand over his guns peacefully it was resolved by the group in a meeting at their headquarters in Alali forest chaired by Wani, to seize them from him by force. So, on 27 October 1964, Wani Lou led his group to seize Silimani's Marker 5 and the shotgun for the liberation of South Sudan. The attempt to seize the rifles resulted in one of the liberators called Lino Wani from the Lulubo tribe being shot and killed by their owner. When Lino approached the gun owner's hut with a lighted bundle of grass, the light exposed him, and he was seen from afar as he approached. He was hit in the chest by a single shot and fell down dead. Wani, who was waiting for the outcome of the expedition sent to take Silimani's weapons, heard the shot and guessed that someone was hit. Shortly after the crack of the rifle, his men who came running from the scene of the operation, joined him. After listening to the hurried report of the leader of the expedition Wani knew at once that the plan had to be aborted. As group leader, he ordered the withdrawal of his men and their retreat into the bush where they camped to rest before returning to their original camp in Alali, south-east of Moli village.

First Lieutenant Moheidin Al Faki was the Arab commanding officer of the government army unit camped at Loa where the head chief of the Ma'di people, Sabazio Okumu Abdalla lived. When he received report about the attempt by Wani's group to seize the guns of citizen Siliman Ito, the reaction of Siliman and his shooting dead of one of the rebel soldiers, he moved a force of two plutoons to Pageri to assess the situation before following the rebel soldiers into the bush.

Death in the forest

The officer, on learning that Wani and his group had one old *tasi*, the ancient rifle, as their sole firearm (which did not even have a single bullet), and nothing else besides bows and arrows, decided to hunt them down. The government soldiers discovered Wani and his group resting at Walawala riverside, most of them having naps because on the previous night they had been on active duty attempting to seize the Marker-5 rifle and the shotgun from their owner. (He had categorically refused to hand over these guns for the liberation war and instead reportedly threatened to kill Wani and his men whom he called thieves.) In the absence of men stationed as watchmen to alert the group of enemy approach, the government soldiers attacked the group, taking them by surprise. Two young lads, one of them called Kodorato Yugu assigned to keep watch from a treetop in the direction the enemy were likely to approach had got down from their perches. One version of the story says that the boys were afraid that they would be seen from afar by government snippers and shot dead which was contrary to the reason for their assignment. Another explanation was that they got down to roast some maize for breakfast leaving their group vulnerable to enemy attack. As it happened, First Lt. Moheidin Al Faki and his men attacked the group, most of whom were sleeping. Putting up a small show of resistance, the liberators managed to shoot dead two Arab soldiers with arrows, but twelve of them were killed on the spot including Wani Lou Mbwele their leader. Wani was hit on both thighs as he rose from the ground disabled. Before his life was finally taken, he spoke aloud that the attackers must know that they had not killed the flame of freedom which would remain burning till South Sudan was independent. This statement stunned the government army commanding officer as he narrated the story twenty years after his forces killed Wani. Those who died in the attack besides their leader included two brothers, Lino Manya Alimas and Yozepe Yanga Alimas, father of broadcaster Tombe Dumo, Odiya Jojo from Iyii, Beria, brother of Nyadia of Lulubo clan of Moli, Ceasario Modi, son of Miri of Nyori village, Opoli, brother of Satu of Nyori village and Kondzidriga, Lino Wani from Lulubo tribe and four others. Keri Nyigola of Paluda clan was slightly wounded and he managed to escape but when he reached Liokwe village north of Opari, a man picked up his spear and killed him describing him as one of the Moli men who want to spoil the good life of the Ma'di people by declaring a fake war of liberation from the Arabs. He was killed before the villagers who had sent a messenger to the government security forces based in Opari could come to apprehend him. Keri's death brought the total death toll to thirteen. Those who survived this attack included Paulo Betcu, a former soldier who had deserted the government army to join the liberation war and was thought to know the tactic of escaping from the kind of attack which had befallen them. Vito Abiyo, father of the gospel preacher and singer Jino Longa was wounded in the leg, and Yoani Odru, the commander's bodyguard was hit with Sten gun fire in the left side of his stomach leaving him with multiple wounds. Yugu Kodoratu who was assigned to keep watch from the top of the tree but got down to roast maize when the soldiers attacked and Luka Agama, also survived. This happened north-east of Pageri on 28 October 1964 at about 11.00 a.m.

Who was Wani Lou Mbwele?
Wani was the father of the author, but also in his short life he played an important role in the liberation of South Sudan. Within a short time, he organized a small group of men from his village of Moli and neighbouring tribes, trained them in the use of bows and arrows, the Ma'di traditional weapons, and engaged the soldiers of the Arab army of occupation in his area in skirmishes along the Juba-Nimule Road despite the sophisticated weaponry of the enemy. The most important contribution he made was the naming of the liberation army, Enya-Nya (Anya-Nya) which in his mother tongue, Ma'di is associated with the poison extracted from parts of a cobra snake by fearless and dangerous women. Some of the villagers whose sons were martyred along with Wani

in the bush around Pageri are naturally unhappy about the turn of events. But those who died, like Wani, were volunteers. By his action and death, he left a legacy which in the long run led to the total independence of South Sudan. He died for this objective. He was uneducated like most of those who fought in the two civil wars of liberation of South Sudan. This should serve as an example to people anywhere in the world. Education is simply a process for the enlightenment of a person to effect positive change in his environment. It enables a person to do it better. Men like Wani have changed the world to be a better place for their fellow human beings to live in.

Wani might have been born in 1910 because in 1920 he attended Opari Nyakaningwa primary school opened by the Church Missionary Society with other sons of chiefs and notables. He could write his name and those of his children in the Acholi language, the medium of education in Opari school. In the period 1927-33, he worked first as a houseboy for the Opari District Commissioner and in the period 1933-1940 as head cook for the DC of Torit. In 1941-1945 he served in the mess for the Commander and Officers of the South African forces at Borongole Transit Base for those troops who were heading to North Africa to fight on the side of the Allies during the Second World War.

Wani married four wives but only two of them survived and he had several children with them. His first wife was Kipolo from Urugu clan of Loa who died of a suspected smallpox infection having lived with him for a short time. Then he got married to Rita Keji a.k.a Lokere mother of the author with whom he had the following children – John Sebit, Franceska Foni, Accu, and Victor Keri the author, Arkangelo Tida dec., Salmone Geri and Martin Otce dec. He also married Massimina Tilolu of Nyongwa clan and had the following children with her – Maria Tete, wife of Anya-Nya Captain Peter Mogga Kobaa, Pelista Ossa, Morris Loka a.k.a Lodu, Paskalina Jua, Isaac Omuda dec., Stephen Juma and Elizabeth Foni. Wani also married a wife called Ojwiny from Pari (Lokoro) tribe of Lafon while in Torit and had with her three children – twins Opia and Muya, and Gune. All died at a young age.

Naming the Liberation Army, Enya-Nya (Anya-Nya)
Before his death at the hands of his Arab enemies, Wani proposed that the name of the Azania Liberation Army (ALA) be Enya-Nya (Anya-Nya). Wani responded when the President of Azania Liberation Front (ALF) and commander-in-chief, Joseph Oduho Awuro asked the tribes on the east bank of the Nile in Equatoria Province to find a suitable name for the army of the movement. It was recommended that it sound like the word *mau-mau*, from the Mau-Mau of Kenya in the 1950's. Wani's son-in-law, First Lieutenant Peter Mogga Kobaa of the ALA was one of the three men chosen by President Joseph Oduho of the Azania Liberation Movement/Army to be sent on secret missions to areas near the Sudan-Uganda international border, where their tribesmen were living as refugees, to bring back proposed names for selection as the name for the armed wing of the movement. On the day following the order, Peter boarded a bus in Kampala for Gulu. When he arrived there, he took another bus to Attiak. Upon arrival there he was carried on a bicycle by a scout to Nyigeri. In Nyigeri he entered the bush and several hours of walking brought him to a point where he crossed the international border from Uganda into Sudan. After nearly ten hours of walking, he came to the camp of his father-in-law in Alali forest, south-east of Moli village at

around midnight, and at once held a meeting with the men under arms in the camp. He explained to them the reason for his mission and immediately asked for proposals for names. Several names were given including Foki, Liro, Belekendu, Jumia, Koro – names of a mountain and rivers and a shrine, but they did not impress Peter making him press for more proposals. It was then, at dawn when everyone was tired and feeling sleepy, that Wani Lou, the father-in-law of Lieutenant Mogga and the father of the author, suggested that the name *enya-nya* should be adopted. But Peter and the rest of the camp quickly objected to the name because of the impression the Ma'di people have of *enya-nya*. All rejected the name which means 'poison' saying that it was a horrible name and associated with the compound which was extracted by malicious women from cobra and other poisonous snakes to poison innocent fellow human beings. Many members of Wani's group who were present at the meeting supported Mogga's argument against the name. They also felt *enya-nya* should not be given recognition and nobody would like to associate himself with such a name. Those who supported Mogga's reason for refusing the name Enya-Nya included Silvestro Obudra, the training officer in the camp, Paul Betcu, advisor to camp leader in military affairs, and Vito Abiyo, an elderly fighter. But Wani insisted that, on the contrary, once the name Enya-Nya (Anya-Nya) was selected it would be exclusively applied to the liberation army and anyone who mentioned it in other contexts afterwards would be punished. He said as long as he was in charge of more than fifty-five bow and arrow bearing men, the Alali Group, who were mostly from Moli, he would arrest any woman or man caught preparing poison and punish them by hanging. He said it would be made a crime for any woman or man to kill a snake and extract poison from its parts to kill vulnerable people. After serious consideration of this strong argument and reasoning, First Lieutenant Peter Mogga was convinced and he dropped the other names which were proposed and took to Kampala city the name Enya-Nya (Anya-Nya) to present to President Joseph Oduho.

On arrival in Kampala, Mogga proceeded straight to Kawempe township where the Azania Liberarion Movement and Army offices were located to deliver the name which he was sent to fetch from his tribesmen in the Sudan. When he entered the room, it was reported that everybody on instruction from Joseph Oduho suddenly fell silent to hear what Mogga had in store to announce to the President. About two days previous Pancrasio Ocheng from Acholi community and Valeriano Orege from the Latuko community had brought their proposed names in Acholi and Latuho languages respectively, but Oduho was not impressed and did not comment on them, waiting for that from the Ma'di representative. When Peter Mogga reported that his people had proposed that the name of the liberation army be Enya-Nya, Oduho was reported to have jumped up from his chair, his head almost touching the ceiling in excitement saying out aloud, "Anya-Nya! That is the name! Anya-Nya. We have got it. We have found the right name for our army!" Instead of Lieutenant Mogga explaining the meaning of the name, Oduho himself explained it to the rest of the people in the room saying that in about 1937, when he was a young boy in Torit, a certain Ma'di chief called Akeri brought some women from Moli and presented them before the English District Commissioner (Mr. Rowley) accusing them of using poison (enya-nya) to kill some people and demanded the death sentence for them. One of the women accused was Nya Mujo, who was the wife of a prominent man from Paloi clan in the village of

Leruwa near Deretu. Akeri believed that Nya Mujo had poisoned Enderi, his sister-in-law in Leruwa village. Enderi was the wife of Jentilio Mukaru, a medical dresser in the village. Nya Mujo was never sentenced but died in Torit prison having been remanded for over ten years. Before getting into the vehicle which Chief Akeri brought from Torit district headquarters to transport the accused women in about 1937, Nya composed a song expressing her innocence. The song goes as follows:

> *Ori Ipele no nani mondiri ko ebbi,*
> *Nya Mujo koya Torit aga dina*
> *Owo vule ga keriru idri ko.*

(A literal translation of the song)

> *The son of Ipele (Chief Akeri Geri) is not a governor but a lion.*
> *Nya Mujo (the woman herself)*
> *Is here going to Torit.*
> *Let there be no weeping behind here.*

So Oduho thought Enya-Nya which he pronounced with the Latuho accent 'Anya-Nya' was the most appropriate name for the liberation army and since then it was so called. Even after Oduho relinquished the power of President of Azania Liberation Movement, the name remained the same until the Addis Ababa Peace Agreement of March, 1972 and beyond. Anya-Nya Two was also used by those who formed a new liberation movement in the Upper Nile and Bahr El Ghazal regions in the 1980's.

Fig.13: This family photo of Wani Lou was taken in 1957 at Moli Tokuro, Ateminga village.

In the above picture taken in 1957, Wani Lou Mbwele stands with his two daughters. On his right is Maria Tete, who in 1962 became wife to Anya-Nya Captain Peter Mogga Kobaa, a former soldier of No. 2 Company of Equatoria Corps, and the daughter on the left is Franceska Foni who joined the SPLA in 1989 and served at the rank of corporal in the medical unit for over eight years. She was demobilized in 2008 at Mogiri, east of Juba. The author then in class one village school is wearing a white shirt and is seated on the chicken shelter (*bwolo*) with other children near the father and daughters. Wani named his home *Ateminga*, meaning 'we are waiting for the Arabs'.

9- Bishop Abednego Kenyi Andrea

Popularly known as Reverend Abednego Vuni, the bishop is a member of the Africa Inland Church (AIC) whose foundation was laid by the Church Missionary Society (CMS) from Gulu, Uganda in about 1914. The mission was at first the centre for an elementary school established by Rev. Davies (Sanderson 1979:61-2) of CMS who came from the church's main centre in Gulu, Uganda. Later the mission administration changed hands several times. From CMS it was taken over by the Africa Inland Mission (AIM) and later it became the main centre for the Africa Inland Church. The first indigenous pastor to promote the work of the church was Reverend Andrea Vuni Wale, Abednego's father who became its first bishop. Abednego besides his pastoral work also dabbled in politics and served in various capacities in constitutional positions. From 1989 to 1991, he served as Commissioner of Eastern Equatoria Province in Torit. In 1997, he contested the post of Governor of Eastern Equatoria State in Kapoeta but did not go through with it because the parliamentarians elected Abdallah Kafelo Ameri. In 1998, Abednego served in Kadugli, Southern Kordofan State as advisor to the governor on religious affairs. He was dismissed from the post when he was seen standing shoulder to shoulder with the German evangelist, Reverend Reinhard Bonnke in Khartoum Green Square. The government he served in was led by Muslim fundamentalists who could not tolerate seeing a Christian member of the cabinet associating with Bonnke, a man they considered a sorcerer because he claimed that he could treat disabilities of all types. Abednego was born in Opari in the early 1930's and is from the Beka clan.

10- Bishop Emeritus Paride Taban from Bori-Opari

The Ma'di community of Southern Sudan began to supply indigenous priests to the Catholic Church from 1946 when Avelino Wani was ordained priest in Lacor, Gulu, Uganda. This was followed several years later by the ordination of Father Jekondo Anyugo and other priests, namely Adelino Fuli, the first priest from the Ma'di tribe to be ordained in Rome in 1958 after graduating from Propaganda Fide University, Father Martin Lopidiya and Father Julio Idda. The first priest from the community to be ordained a bishop was Paride Kenyi Taban.

Bishop Paride Taban was born in Opari and partly grew up in Katire where his father was a labourer in the Timber Sawmill. He underwent early elementary education there before joining the junior seminary in Okaru. Bishop Paride Taban is best known worldwide for his contribution to peace in his country of South Sudan. He reached out to the people on the slopes of Boma Mountain who had not experienced peace and development for ages. He created Kuron peace village which acted as the epicenter of interaction for half a dozen tribes who had been living in a state of hostility before Bishop Paride won them over to peaceful coexistence and introduced some development in their area. Paride's singlehanded action improved the lives of these his fellow South Sudanese who had been abandoned and excluded in the past from the overall programme of socio-economic development. Even the British, it seems, who colonized and administered Pibor sub-district of Upper Nile Province where these people lived, whether deliberately or out of ignorance of their existence is yet to be established through research, did little to help them. Bishop Paride is also known for his book *Peace Deserves a Chance* edited by Alberto J. Eisman in 2011. He won a prize from the UN for his

Fig.14: Bishop Emiretus Paride Taban of Torit Diocese, a shepherd of all the people of God whose love and services are directed to all irrespective of their tribes, gender and origins.

work in promoting peace. Bishop Paride retired from the pastoral work of bishop in 2012 and presently leads a quiet life at Kuron and sometimes retires to Juba. His family comes from the Logopi clan of Bori-Opari.

Paride was ordained a priest in 1964, just within the period when foreign missionaries were leaving after being expelled from Southern Sudan by the military junta led by General Ibrahim Abboud. He was made an auxillary bishop on May 4, 1980, in Kinshasa, formerly Zaire by Pope John Paul II. He was installed as Bishop of Torit in August 1983 and was in Torit, the diocesan town, when it fell to the SPLA forces in February 1989. He was detained but calls from the Vatican and other international

Christian organizations secured his release on orders from Dr. John Garang de Mabior. While free, instead of taking refuge in any of the neighbouring countries of Kenya and Uganda, Bishop Paride chose to remain working for the people of God in the liberated areas as a shepherd demonstrating the true love preached by the Prince of Peace, Jesus Christ during his active life on earth. Paride retired as Bishop of Torit Diocese in 2012 becoming Bishop Emeritus. Despite this new position, he has maintained links with his diocesans and other Christians and works tirelessly to help them overcome challenges which hinder the achievement of happiness in this life.

11- Joseph Kebulu Ame
In the late 1950's Joseph Kebulu Ame graduated from Cairo American University with a bachelor's degree and was employed as a secondary school teacher. He taught in Rumbek Secondary School, Juba Commercial Secondary School and Malakal Boys' Secondary School in 1970/71 where he became Headmaster. In 1961-62 while in Rumbek, the late John Garang de Mabior was one of his students of History, while Philip Yona Jambi taught the same class English literature before the students' strike of 1962. In 1972, Joseph Kebulu was appointed by Abel Alier, then President of the High Executive Council, as acting Director of Education in the former Regional Government. In 1978, Kebulu contested the election in the territorial constituency of western Torit and won a seat in the Second People's Regional Assembly in Juba representing Acholi, Ma'di and Latuko of western Torit. He repeated the contest for a seat in the same constituency in the 1982 election and won. In 1983, the Governor of Equatoria Region, Joseph James Tombura appointed Joseph Kebulu to his cabinet

as Minister of Education. He was killed by gunmen in Palabek area of Panyikwara on April 5, 1986, while campaigning for a seat in the election of that year with the ticket of the Sudan African People's Congress (SAPCO). Kebulu was a prince by the standard of traditional chieftainships of the Ma'di in Sudan, belonging to the family of Loku Kitcere, the uncle of Chief Drani Eberu. They belonged to the Tedire clan of Kereppi. In 1981 while on a visit to me in my house with Jabulon Jada Yakobo after my return from a journalism course in West Germany, he encouraged me to take writing seriously when I told them that I was collecting data to write the history of the Ma'di people, their culture and traditions because I did not see the educated Ma'di doing this.

12- Marko Aloma Koka Lou
Marko joined the Sudan local government service in 1972 immediately after the Addis Ababa Peace Agreement. He was among the civil administrators drawn by the Anya-Nya movement for a crash programme of training in Khartoum as local government officials. In 1973, he was posted to Bor in Upper Nile Province as an executive officer. From Upper Nile Province, Marko served in the same capacity in Bahr al-Ghazal province being posted first to province headquarters in Wau then to Gogrial and Raga districts respectively. After several years of service in Bahr al-Ghazal, he was transferred to Equatoria Province, his home base and first served in Yambio district headquarters then he was transferred to Juba province headquarters. He served in Torit and Kapoeta district headquarters as local government inspector following his promotion. It was Marko who laid the foundation of Magwi County when he was assigned from Torit to do a feasibility study and write a report of his findings. Based on his knowledge of the local

Fig.15: Mr. Marko Aloma Koka
(photo from Marko's album 1978 (with courtesy)

government system in Sudan, having attended an advanced course in the Administrative Sciences Institute in Khartoum, and having studied the situation of Magwi County thoroughly, he prepared and presented a comprehensive document detailing the borders between the chieftainships and the land issue. Marko presented his paper during the 16-19 April 2012 Peace Conference between the Acholi and Ma'di organized by the Inter-Church Committee (ICC) in Torit. The author has benefitted a great deal from data on the Ma'di and Acholi borders presented by Marko Aloma Koka Lou.

Fig.16: Mr. Severino Fuli Boki

13- Severino Fuli Boki

Severino Fuli Boki was a politician who had been the longest serving minister of cabinet affairs in the bush governments led variably by Aggrey Jaden and General Emedio Tafeng during the liberation struggle culminating in the Addis Ababa Peace Agreement of 1972. Severino Fuli wrote a book titled: *Shaping a Free Southern Sudan, Memoirs of Our Struggle 1934 -1985.* Although the title of the book gives the impression that what is provided is an exclusive account of the Southern Struggle, the book provides details of the author's personal experience qualifying it to be almost his autobiography. Despite this observation, there are hundreds of pages which give comprehensive descriptions of the parts played by other Southern politicians such as Aggrey Jaden, William Deng Nhial, Joseph Oduho, Father Saturnino Lohure and General Joseph Lagu Yanga in the Southern Sudan liberation struggle. Fuli represented the Ma'di, Acholi and Otuho of western Torit constituency in the

Omdurman Parliament in 1973 and 1981 parliamentary terms. He was a great resource but the government in Eastern Equatoria State never thought of appointing him as an advisor or a Member of State Parliament so that other citizens could benefit from his knowledge. He was born in Opari, raised there and he passed on in 2015 in his birthplace and was buried there.

14- Mr. Angelo Vuga Morjan
Angelo Vuga Morjan was the first Ma'di to enter the University of Khartoum. After studying up to the end of his second year he applied for a British scholarship for a science teaching course and graduated with a high diploma as a secondary school teacher. He taught in Juba commercial secondary school in the early 1960's and defected to Uganda when the Anya-Nya movement intensified its activities in his home area of Moli. He took refuge in Gulu where he taught in Layibi technical secondary school. Later, due to the proximity of Gulu to Sudan, he was suspected by the Uganda government of being involved in secretly supporting the Anya-Nya in Sudan and moved his teaching activity to Saint Mary's Secondary School in Kisubi near Entebbe. In the 1960's and early 1970's he was the representative of the Anya-Nya movement and was a member of the movement's delegation in the Addis Ababa talks between the Southern Sudan Liberation Movementn (SSLM) – Anya-Nya and the Sudan Government in 1972. Vuga was posted as the ambassador of Sudan to Zimbabwe and later defected to the SPLM/SPLA while in Harare. He was prominent in the peace talks between the SPLM/SPLA and the Sudan Government which culminated in the signing of the Comprehensive Peace Agreement (CPA) in 2005 at Naivasha, Kenya. Vuga was appointed Advisor to the Governor of Eastern Equatoria State in Torit, Brigadier

Allysius Ojetuk and spent a few years in the post.

15- Journalist Isaac Vuni Mude

Isaac Vuni Mude first trained as an accountant and worked in Radio Juba in the 1980's in the finance section under the author, who was then the station director. The experience as accountant for a broadcasting institution introduced Isaac Vuni to mass media work and eventually led him to develop an interest in journalism especially photography. In the late 1980's when he moved to Nairobi, Kenya during the second civil war in the country fought by the Sudan People's Liberation Army (SPLA) against the Khartoum Government, he decided to enrol in the Kenya Institute of Mass Communication (KIMC). He graduated with a diploma in Mass Communication and began practicing journalism in Kenya and in the meantime visited the liberated areas of South Sudan for journalistic purposes. When the Comprehensive Peace Agreement (CPA) was signed between the Sudan Government and Sudan People's Liberation Movement, Isaac moved to South Sudan and was briefly based in Juba where he worked in the Ministry of Information and Broadcasting as a journalist. He was later transferred to Torit, capital of Eastern Equatoria State. Practising journalism in emergent nations like South Sudan does not usually bode well for the journalist concerned as those in authority suspect that they are out there to discredit them by highlighting their corrupt practices in their official capacity. Isaac tried his hand at investigative journalism on the factors which led to the failure of the Nile Commercial Bank by filing a report that many people, among them top government officials, borrowed cash from the bank which they never repaid, and this was responsible for the weakening of the bank financially.

He was suspended from his work in the Ministry of Information and Broadcasting without any charge being laid against him and remained under suspension for several years till his tragic death at the hands of unknown gunmen wearing army uniforms in his home area of Kereppi (Erepi). Before his death, he wrote several petitions to the Minister of Information for pardon, but his pleas fell on deaf ears. Isaac had even taken his case to court but an institution like the Ministry of Information cannot be ordered to appear in court in the person of its undersecretary, the top civil servant and the case was thrown out as an administrative issue to be handled at civil service level. Around May 2016, Isaac went to Kereppi in the countryside possibly to cultivate as it was rainy season. He went missing in about June and in September 2016 he was found dead in a cassava plantation believed to have been murdered by the same uniformed gunmen who abducted him with his young cousin. That no alarm was raised immediately after his disappearance in June raises a number of questions. If his abduction had been reported immediately after he was taken from a hut in the village of Borongole as later reported, his release could possibly have been secured by a media institution such as the Committee for Protection of Journalists (CPJ), but the world was alerted to his death three months after his abduction. This remains a sticking point and mystery too. His death was a big blow to the profession of journalism and South Sudan as a nation and to the Ma'di community in particular. As a journalist his death was widely condemned by the journalists' associations worldwide including the CPJ and in Juba by the Union of Journalists of South Sudan (UJOSS), the Association for Media Development in South Sudan (AMDISS) and some Juba based newspapers. Although due to his long suspension by the Ministry of Information he was not able to practice journalism in the country and did not leave a mark in the profession like his colleagues, Isaac, being a hardworking person was able to organize and found Fula Media Research and Development Promotion. He issued a newsletter with well illustrated pages and the photographs were mostly taken by him. He presented a copy of the publication to the author in 2012 at the Citizen Newspaper in Juba. Isaac was a softly spoken person who easily struck up a friendship, an esteemed quality for a journalist in his dealings with contacts. He was from the Degi clan of Ma'di, and his family home was at Dereto on the Moliandro-Juba/Nimule Road junction.

16- Rita Keji Lodu Leju Jote

It is very rare to find an uneducated woman featuring as a distinguished personality within her community, rated high on the scale of her contributions to cultural, social, and economic development. Rita Keji Lodu, the mother of the author, is such a woman. If the reader of this book counts the number of entries of oral answers given by her to research questions asked of a number of individual respondents in this book, he will find that Rita is the leading respondent. Of the 233 oral questions asked of 94 respondents including Rita, she alone supplied 19 answers. This is due to her vast knowledge of the subject explored for this work. Rita gained most of her knowledge about the affairs of the chiefs in Moli from the household of Chief Geri Ipele of Moli who married her paternal aunt, Juru Nya Leju. In addition to that she learned about the affairs of Opari chieftainships, especially those of the Pandikeri chiefs from Idreangwa Nya Agwele, the mother of her husband, Wani Lou Mbwele, father of the author. Agwele was the daughter of Koka, the half brother of Akeri Milla, considered

Fig.17: Mammy Rita Keji Lodu

She was the mentor and main motivator of the author in compiling three books: Ma'di Death, Burial and Funeral Rites in South Sudan (published), Ma'di Traditional Economy in South Sudan (unpublished), Ma'di Customary Marriage in South Sudan (unpublished), Ma'di Traditional Chieftainships in South Sudan 1860-1984 and two other forthcoming titles. The knowledge she possessed despite not going to school, constituted a veritable bank that today enhances our understanding of Ma'di contemporary life.

the greatest chief of Bori-Opari in the late nineteenth and early twentieth centuries. The father of Koka and Akeri was Andruga, the son of Wani. This family relationship allowed Idreangwa Nya Agwele to become familiar with the family history from which

Rita benefitted. Rita was not only very conversant in the affairs of Ma'di chiefs, but she was also knowledgeable about Ma'di traditional economy, Ma'di culture and aspects of Ma'di traditions. She supplied the author orally with much material for various works on these different topics and her name appears several times in the notes and references lists of these books, some of which are still in manuscript form. Rita's marriage to Wani Lou Mbwele, a political activist among his Ma'di community and the discoverer of the name *Anya-Nya* for the liberation army of Southern Sudan under Joseph Oduho in early 1963, bolstered her access to more information about the history of the Ma'di, especially of the chieftainships.

Wani's last journey took him to Pageri in search of guns for the war of liberation. He never returned. He and eleven of his followers were cut down by soldiers of a government army unit commanded by first lieutenant Moheidin al-Faki, an Arab based in Loa, the headchief's headquarters. Before his departure, Wani left a will stating that my mother Keji should only leave Sudan for Uganda when I was safely home from Torit where I was being schooled. My mother waited for me from October 28, 1964, the day my father was killed, until December 20, 1964, when the Commer Lorry which was transporting me and other students from Palotaka Intermediate School and Torit Technical Intermediate School to our homes passed our abandoned village, Ateminga in Moli Tokuro. As we passed the village, we glimpsed a figure running from the abandoned hut of our neighbor, Onorato Mude, towards the road to have a quick look at the lorry. That figure was my mother. She wanted to confirm that the lorry was carrying school children, among whom undoubtedly would be myself. She had been waiting for that moment. Four days later, after my arrival at Nimule, some 40 miles from my village at Moli she came on foot to meet me. The meeting was very emotional as my mother, her face full of tears and her body emancipated due to worry over my safety and improper eating, tried to tell me that my father Wani was dead. She attempted to explain to me the circumstances surrounding his death. Of course, I had already been told about my father by several relatives, one in Torit where the carrier of the news was a little cautious when narrating the story to me. The second person to inform me of my father's death was Thomas Droko Nyamcungu from Iyii who had run from there with his family to Erepi where the lorry carrying us to Ma'diland stopped briefly to let some students from the village disembark as they arrived at their destination. Droko's report was hurried because the lorry in which I was travelling had just stopped briefly to let my fellow students from Erepi disembark. I was among the students heading to Nimule and Mugali villages because I had decided to go and stay with my cousin's sister, Seconda Kidde.

Rita Keji was an extraordinarily brave woman who remained in an abandoned village where she spent over fifty days sleeping alone without fear of wild animals, the leopards, hyenas, and lions, and unperturbed by the government soldiers who used to tour the area believed to be the home of the rebels whom they were hunting. Besides those familial qualities and knowledge of the historical developments in Southern Sudan, an example being the rebellion which she supported by cooking for the Alali group led by her husband, Rita was also a song composer and singer. Many popular songs which are included in this book were sung to the author by her.

17- Dr. Anna Ito Leonardo

Dr. Anna Ito Leonardo holds a PhD in agriculture and served as Minister of Agriculture in the South Sudan government after the country gained independence in July 2011. She also served as acting Secretary General of the Sudan People's Liberation Movement after the position was vacated by Pagan Amum Okich in 2013. Dr. Anna was an appointed Member of Parliament in Juba and when South Sudan joined the East African Community, she became a Member of the East African Parliament in Arusha, Tanzania. Dr. Ito was appointed the head of the advance team which came to Khartoum after the CPA was ratified by President Omer Al Beshir representing the Sudan Government and Dr. John Garang de Mabior of the SPLM/SPLA. After the formation of the Government of National Unity (GNU) in Khartoum, Dr. Ito became the State Minister of Agriculture.

Notes and References

1- Beshir, Mohammed Omer. *The Southern Sudan Background to Conflict*, London, C. Hurst, 1969. Annex on Juba Conference of 1947.

2- Sudan Vision Special Issue 1 January 2005.

3- Yanga, Joseph Lagu. *Odysseus Through State, From Ruins to Hope*, MOB, Omdurman, 2004.

4- Ibid.

5- Verbal statement made by MP Paul Yugusuk, member of Lulubo delegation to Kit 2008 Conference.

6- Sanderson, Passmore and Neville Passmore. *Politics, Education and Religion in Southern Sudan 1898 – 1964*, London, 1979, p.61.

7- Regional Ministry of Culture and Information Publication,

Juba, 1973, p.8.

8- Marko Aloma Koka Lou's story about Peter Mogga Kobaa who attended Moli Bush School under Ibolo Abiyo in 1946 with him. The story was narrated to author in 2019 in Juba.

9- Betcu Ameda Kobaa's story was narrated by Wani Lou to his followers in Moli in 1963.

10- From stories narrated by Joshua Modri a.k.a Nyindreobu, a member of Mogga's Expedition to Congo in 1965 and heard by the author.

11- From stories narrated by William Alira, a member of Anya-Nya movement who was close to Captain Peter Mogga in 1965.

12- Story narrated by former members of Alali group amongst them Silvestro Obudra, in Bibia, northern Uganda in 1965, session attended by author.

13- Boki, Severino Fuli. *Shaping a Free Southern Sudan, Memoirs of Our Struggle 1934-1985*, Loa Catholic Mission Council, Limuru, 2002.

14 Op. Cit. Yanga.

15- Mogga's statement to his followers in Wiliwili northern Uganda in 1965.

About The Author

Profession: *Journalist, author, researcher*

In 2022, the author Victor Keri Wani will hopefully graduate with a bachelor's degree in Mass Communication having enrolled in third year in 2020 to upgrade his qualification in the profession of Journalism in the University of Juba, College of Arts and Humanities. This book is one of five books on Ma'di studies which the author, has written, having pioneered the subject since 1981. The author believes, as any other researcher does, that to do good research work it is always wise to choose a subject which one is familiar with. This is the secret of Mr. Wani's success and it is the reason why he has chosen his community, the Ma'di as a subject to study. On this topic he has written five books. One of them titled; *Ma'di Death Burial and Funeral Rites* introduced by Professor Eluzai Mogga Ladu (PhD) was published by Al Rafiki, Juba in 2019. He has written another book on a subject which he is familiar with and that is titled Mass Media in Sudan Experience of the South 1940-2005. By training, Victor is a journalist with a background in law which he learned in Bukalasa Cooperative College north of Kampala, Uganda in the period 1971-72. He also attended a course on a similar subject in Juba in 1975 from January to March. This civil law is supposed to be applied by the author acting as a judge in arbitration, reconciliation and adjudication in conflicts affecting members of cooperative societies or cooperative unions and not as a judge with the power to send people to prison. But he changed professions and moved to journalism where he has spent over forty years. In this field he has become more active than acting as an arbitrator and the result is that he has authored several books. He left working in the cooperative development sector to pursue journalism in 1975, first as a radio announcer, then as a reporter and finally as a documentary program producer. After years of training and promotion in the broadcasting field, he was assigned the post of director of Radio Juba in 1986 and from there he progressed to the position of deputy director general at grade three super-scale in Radio Omdurman from 1993 to 2002. In August 2004, Victor was appointed advisor on information to the Eastern Equatoria State Government and served under Governor Abdallah Alberto Afoger and in November of the same year, he was named as Minister of Social Affairs (combining information, youth, sports, and social welfare) in Eastern Equatoria State until July 2005.

Born in 1951 at Moli Tokuro, in Torit District, Equatoria Province, a brief resume of his professional training in Journalism follows:

Educational and Professional Background:
- Advanced certificate in Radio Journalism from Kassel University, Witzenhausen and Deutsche Welle Staff Training Institute, Cologne in Germany, Feb-Dec 1980.
- BBC Radio production course in London, Jan-Apr 1977.
- Radio and Television news production in Khartoum, Nov-Dec 1978.
- Radio broadcasting certificate course, Blantyre, Malawi, Nov-Dec 1982.
- Certificate course in Nairobi, Kenya, 1984.
- Diploma in Computer Science with emphasis on information technology, Omdurman, Jan-Oct 2002.
- Certificate on reporting about HIV/AIDS in the Near East, Cairo, Egypt, 2007.
- Certificate in Information course at JICA, Tokyo, Japan, May 2011.
- Successfully attended four years of secondary education 'O' level at Lubiri Senior Secondary School, Kampala, Uganda 1967-1970.

Additional Information about the Author:
- Awarded Advanced Certificate in Cooperative Law and History by Uganda Cooperative College, Bukalasa after a course in the period March 1971, to April 1972.

- Certificate in Cooperative Law and History in Juba, course period January to March 1975.

Knowledge of Languages:
- Has a very good level of written and spoken English
- Writes, reads and speaks good Arabic
- Reads and speaks French fairly well
- Reads and speaks Deutsch (German) poorly
- Speaks the following languages fairly well: Lingala, Kiswahili, Luganda, Acholi
- Very fluent in spoken and written mother tongue, Ma'di

Hobbies:
- Swimming
- Listening to radio
- Viewing news and documentaries on television

Publications by author:

1- Co-author in Professor Taban Lo Liyong's anthology: ***Women in Folktales and Short Stories of Africa***, published in Pietersberg, South Africa, 1994.

2- ***Kenyi's Adventure and Other Stories, a Collection of Ma'di Tales*** introduced by Dr. Larry Soule (PhD.) published in Khartoum, 1998.

3- ***Islam in Southern Sudan, Its Impact: Past Present and Future*** introduced by Prof. Hassan Mekki Mohammed Ahmed (PhD) of Africa International University, Khartoum, 2006.

4- Co-author of ***Narrating Our Future, Customs, Rituals and Practices of Ma'di of South Sudan and Uganda***, ed. Dr. Mairi J. Blackings (PhD), CASAS, Cape Town, 2011.

5- ***Mass Media in Sudan, Experience of the South 1940-2005***, introduced by senior lecturer in Mass Communication, Abubakr Lo from Nigeia, 2014, Juba, South Sudan.

6- ***Ma'di Death Burial and Funeral Rites in South Sudan***, introduced by Professor Dr. Eluzai Mogga Ladu (PhD) and published by Al Rafiki, Atlabara, Juba, 2019.

7- ***A History of Radio Broadcasting in Southern Sudan with Reference to Sudan 1961 – 1992***, Al Rafiki Publishing and Printing Company, Juba. 2020.

8- ***Ma'di Folktales in South Sudan, Jomboloko the Tortoise and 50 other Titles,*** Al Rafiki Publishing and Printing Company, Juba. 2020.

Manuscripts by Author

a) *100 South Sudanese Writers and Their Books: Portrayals, Summaries and Reviews*

b) *Southern Sudan under Nimeiri, 1969 – 1985*

c) *Ma'di Customary Marriage in South Sudan*

d) *Ma'di Traditional Economy in South Sudan*

f) *Sudan Plane Crash of 1971*

g) *An Outline of Ma'di History, Culture, Traditions and Customs*

Works in Progress

- Southern Sudan under Al Beshir 1989-2011
- Interviews, Interviewers and Interviewees in Mass Media
- Sudan Political Divide, Debates on Unity and Secession before Southern Referendum

Bibliography

Year Books

The Guinness Encyclopedia of World History, London, Guinness Publishing Ltd. 1992.

Handbooks

1- Baker, Samuel White. *The Albert Nyanza, Great Basin of the Nile and Explorations of the Nile Sources,* Vol. 2, London, Sidwick and Jackson, 1962.

2- _____ *The Source of the Nile Basin, the White Nile.*

3- Beshir, Mohammed Omer. *The Southern Sudan Background to Conflict,* London, C. Hurst, 1969.

4- Boki, Severino Fuli. *Shaping a Free Southern Sudan, Memoirs of Our Struggle 1934 – 1985,* Loa Catholic Mission Council, Limuru, 2002.

5- Casati, Gaetano. *Ten Years in Equatoria,* 1910, London.

6- C. G. Seligman and Brenda Z. Seligman. *Pagan Tribes of the Nilotic Sudan,* London, Routledge and Kegan Paul, 1965.

7- Crazzolara, J. P. *The Lwoo Emigrations Part I*, Verona, 1951.

8- _____ *Lwoo Part III*, Verona, 1951.

9- Dellagiacoma, V. *History of the Catholic Church in Southern Sudan, 1900-1995*, Khartoum, 1996.

10- Elton, Lord. *General Gordon*, London, Collins, 1954.

11- Gray, Emmanuel Kitchere. *The Catholic Church in Loa*, Khartoum, 1994.

12- Gray, Richard. *A History of Southern Sudan 1838- 1889*, London, Oxford University Press, 1961.

13- Mogga, Dunstan Wai. *The Southern Sudan, The Problem of National Integration ed.*, London, Frank Cass, 1974.

14- Murdock, G. P. *Africa, Its People and their Culture History*, New York, 1959.

15- Nalder, Leonard F. *Equatoria Province Handbook*, Juba, 1940.

16- _____*Equatoria Province Handbook, Vol. 1*, Mongalla, 1936.

17- *Oxford Advanced Learner's Dictionary (OALD) of Current English*, 7th Edition, Oxford University Press.

18- P'Bitek, Okot. *The Religion of Central Luo*, East African Literature Bureau, Nairobi, Kampala, Dar es Salaam, 1969.

19- Bishop Emiritus Paride Taban. *Peace Deserves a Chance* edited by Alberto J. Eisman, 2011.

20- Posnansky, Merrick. *East Africa and the Nile Valley in Early Times* quoted in Sudan in Africa ed.Yusuf Fadl Hasan, Khartoum, Khartoum University Press, 1969.

21- Pritchard, E. Evans. *Witchcraft, Oracles and Magic among the Azande*, Oxford, Claredon Press, 1972.

22- Sanderson, Passmore and Neville Passmore. *Politics, Education and Religion in Southern Sudan 1898 – 1964*, London,

1979.

23- Santandrea, Father Stefano. *The Little Unknown Tribes of Southern Sudan*, 1940.

24- Stigand, C. H. *Equatoria, The Lado Enclave*, London, Frank Cass, 1957 and of 1968.

25- Tibble, Ann. *With Gordon in the Sudan*, London, Frederick Muller, 1960.

26- Toniolo, Elias and Richard Hill. *The Opening of Nile Basin*, London, C. Hurst, 1974.

27- Wani, Keri et. al. *Narrating Our Future, Customs, Rituals and Practices of the Ma'di in South Sudan and Uganda ed.* Mairi, Blackings, CASAS Cape Town, 2011.

28- Yanga, Joseph Lagu. *Oddysees Throuh A Nation from Ruins to Hope,* Mohammed Omer Beshir Centre, Ahlia University, Omdurman, 2006.

Booklets

1- Ladu, Eluzai Mogga. *The Ceremonial Dance of the Lulubo, Kajuwaya*, Juba, New Day Publishers and Printers, w.d. p.3.

2- *Ofo Ma'di Ti Si* (History in Ma'di Language) Loa, Catholic Mission, 1945.

Journals/Newspapers

1- Rowley, J. V. *Notes on the Ma'di of Equatoria Province*, Sudan Notes and Records Vol. XXIII, 1940.

2- *Sudan Notes and Records Volume XIX*, 1936.

Reports/Papers/Drafts

1- Juma, Sestilio Andruga. *Notes on Ma'di Clans,* Juba, 1991.

2- Resolutions of the Second Ma'di National Convention in

Nimule 11th -16th September 2007.

3- A position paper titled: *Olubo Community Stand and Resolution over Border Disputes,* Juba, 10th November 2008. This followed the 6 September 2008 Kit Meeting to discuss the border disputes amongst the Lulubo, Bari, Ma'di and Acholi tribes over Kit and Nyolo Rivers area.

4- Notes prepared by Marko Aloma Koka, former Local Government Inspector of Magwi Area Council for presentation to Acholi – Ma'di Conference on Peace and Reconciliation sponsored by Inter-Church Committee in Torit on April 16-19, 2012. Marko is a former long service local government administrator who prepared Magwi to be a district in 1970s. He comes from Moli chieftainship which shares borders with Bari and northern part of Acholi chieftainship of Panyikwara at Omeyo villages and is well versed in these border affairs.

Unpublished Materials

1- Wani, Victor Keri. *An Outline of Ma'di History, Culture, Traditions and Customs in Sudan,* Juba, 1992, unpublished.

2- Baj, Father Giuseppe. *Linguistic Guide on Ma'di Language: a) Opari dialect; b) Lokai dialect,* MS. n.d.

Maps

1- Maps attached to Equatoria Province Handbook written in 1936 by Governor L. F. Nalder to indicate borderlines of Equatoria.

2- Map presented during 6 September 2008 Kit border conference also clearly shows this border between Ma'di, Lolubo, Acholi and Bari.

3- See the map attached to L. F. Nalder. Equatoria Province

Handbook Vol. 1, Mongalla, 1936, at the back and other maps issued before and after independence in 1956.

Glossary of Ma'di Words Used in This Book Translated into English

Afirindrendre – name of rain shrine of Logili clan member
aiso – seiver of salty water for boiling vegetables
ali – deep
amiya – being shared
avu – to separate
avu – sick
avurukwe – a tree which grows in the river or along it
ayi - summer
ayi – grass
ayi na – three summers
Ayipa – place name
ayila – a type of plant with tiny thorns used in smearing the bodies of rain stones
ati – fireplace
awa pa ga – under shea butter tree
azaka – honorific title

be – mountain
bila – conch made of small animal horn or of slices of bamboo glued together
birabira – a kind of dance performed before *mure* the main Ma'di dance
bo – usually so
bo – forever
bonyi – common people
bwanda – cassava
bwilili – shrill made by a woman while holding her breath during a dance or a cultural occasion
bworo – throat
de – if
De nyidra ra nga tua miya nyini – If you are dead all things are piled upon you.
dra – death or funeral dance
duma – borrowed Bari word which means 'a person'
endre – yam
enya-nya – poison extracted from snake especially cobra
erele – Nile perch
eremu – iron or blacksmith
erepe – another name for Nile perch
eria – listen with
eria-leri-si – can be heard with drum sound
eyi opii – rain makers
goro – kraal.
(tim-Acholi)- hunting zone
igi/eji – a kind of sorghum
ingwe – white
ini – black

iyi – water
iyiali – deep pool
iyu – a kind of tropical tree with bulky whitish trunk which produces thumb size sweety fruits.
jenyi – a kind of dance performed with war song following *mure* the main dance of the Ma'di. It is also performed during funeral dance or after the defeat of an enemy.
Joloko – name of rain of Ukeyi
Kabungo – rain name of Logili clan
kaci – shrine
kaga-aga – crawling
keifo – autumn
kejuwa – exclusively female dance
kerije – calabash.
kiata – sweet potato
kiri – wooden stockade
kitcere – spring
kolonya – squirrel
kolu wa – will stay or can stay
koro – a river shrine for sacrifice
lata – two-headed or two branches
leba – bushbuck
leri – drum
lidi – gruel
lobode – full of baking clay pot
lobwote – mud balls
logi – a large calabash
logo – locality
luceri – a huge tropical tree
lugo – a tropical fruit tree

lumara – great task
lupa – a bloc of stone
Ma'di Opeii – an Acholi village located north of Kitgum town. It is believed that the Ma'di people section of *ope* guineafolk lived here in antiquity
Mejopadrani – a name of a Ma'di village north of Moli and its meaning is an expression of 'I stretch my legs to die or for death'
mejo – I stretch
meli – winter
moyi – hyena
Moyi-be-dri-lata – Two headed mountain of the hyena
meli – winter
moken – a word borrowed from Bari language which refers to mother- in – law
moken na adara – words borrowed from Bari by a Logili clan family as a name of their rain and the name means 'a mother-in-law will be tired' waiting for the rain to stop before starting her journey back home
mugu – a type of yam whose stem grows from the ground upwards onto a tree
mujura – an Arabic word adopted by the Ma'di for water drainage on motorable roadside
mure – Ma'di royal dance
muyu – a tropical fruit tree
na adara – borrowed Bari words which mean 'to get tired'
nana – an African bird with red beak
nga – a thing/things
ni – belonging to or of
ni – for
nya – daughter of

nyaka – a wild beast
nyakiro – war song sung after defeat of an enemy or killing of a wild animal such as a lion or a leopard
nyidra – you die
nyini – for you/ upon you.
nyi mavu yira – you will abandon to pursue me
ogo – deep hole in a tree
okoliro – kite
opa – carved such as wood
ope – guinea folk
opi/opii – chief/chiefs
opigo – servant or slave
owoloro – funeral song
oyaya – land ritual including statements made during its performance
ori – son of
oti – children of or descendants of
oyaa – group cultivation
oyaya di ba – people who prepare food for offering
pa – spread out, extensive
pa – children of or descendants, also another meaning is 'to curve'
pa – leg
pkwete – soft drink made of flour of fermented millet or sorghum.
poyi – special type of wood used in making stockade
ri – encircled completely
ri – two
rudu – sacred grove
si – with
sira – yodel
siriba – a secret action performed on a person without him having

knowledge about it

teyi-teyi – a special strap of beads kept by sons of chiefs for engagement purpose

tore – trumpet

torono – a kind of bird with a long tail

turulu – a sound instrument made of animal horn

uno – a fleshy plant

voi ni ongoli – coarse rope of a hunting net

vu-uvuba – land priest or priestess

Anyi Moli! Ta egori ni di. Anya ndule rii Urube iko? Anya laga dri na si adosi?
"People of Moli, the man is here. Is it not Urube you are looking for? Why do you walk past him?"

www.ingramcontent.com/pod-product-compliance
Lightning Source LLC
Chambersburg PA
CBHW030249010526
44107CB00053B/1645